# Securing the Network from Malicious Code: A Complete Guide to Defending Against Viruses, Worms, and Trojans

# Securing the Network from Malicious Code:

## A Complete Guide to Defending Against

## Viruses, Worms, and Trojans

### Douglas Schweitzer

Wiley Publishing, Inc.

Securing the Network from Malicious Code: A Complete Guide to Defending Against Viruses, Worms, and Trojans

Published by
Wiley Publishing, Inc.
10475 Crosspoint Boulevard
Indianapolis, IN 46256
www.wiley.com

Published simultaneously in Canada

Library of Congress Control No: 2002107899

ISBN: 0-7645-4958-8

Manufactured in the United States of America

10 9 8 7 6 5 4 3 2 1

1B/RT/QZ/QS/IN

# About the Author

**Douglas Schweitzer** is an Internet security specialist with a strong focus on malicious code. Douglas is a Cisco Certified Network Associate and Certified Internet Webmaster Associate, and he holds A+, Network+, and i-Net+ certifications from the Computing Technology Industry Association. He has appeared as an Internet security guest speaker on several radio shows, including KYW Philadelphia, as well as on *Something You Should Know* and *Computer Talk America*, two nationally syndicated radio shows. He is also the author of *Internet Security Made Easy: A Plain-English Guide to Protecting Yourself and Your Company Online*.

# Credits

**ACQUISITIONS EDITOR**
Katie Feltman

**PROJECT EDITOR**
Kevin Kent

**TECHNICAL EDITOR**
Joan Ross

**COPY EDITOR**
Gabrielle Chosney

**EDITORIAL MANAGER**
Ami Frank Sullivan

**VICE PRESIDENT & EXECUTIVE
GROUP PUBLISHER**
Richard Swadley

**VICE PRESIDENT AND EXECUTIVE PUBLISHER**
Bob Ipsen

**EXECUTIVE EDITORIAL DIRECTOR**
Mary Bednarek

**EXECUTIVE EDITOR**
Carol Long

**PROJECT COORDINATOR**
Regina Snyder

**GRAPHICS AND PRODUCTION SPECIALISTS**
Beth Brooks, Melanie DesJardins,
Jeremey Unger

**QUALITY CONTROL SPECIALISTS**
John Bitter, Susan Moritz, Angel Perez

**BOOK DESIGNER**
Kathie Schutte

**PROOFREADING AND INDEXING**
TECHBOOKS Production Services

*This book is dedicated in loving memory of Kurt Schweitzer*

# Acknowledgments

It took the combined efforts of many talented people to bring this book to fruition. I would first like to thank my agent, Carole McClendon of Waterside Productions, for her assistance in finding me a superb publisher. I would also like to thank the brilliant and hard-working individuals at Wiley Technology Publishing who helped to turn this book from an idea into a reality. In particular, I would like to thank Acquisitions Editor Katie Feltman for her confidence in me, and for helping me develop the initial framework of the book. I am also grateful to Project Editor Kevin Kent for making sure my writing stayed on track and for his guidance along the way. I would like to say thank you to my wife/best friend, Monique, for her suggestions, and her revisions were a blessing. Thanks, as well, to my sons Deran and Alex for their enduring patience with me while I was writing this book.

# Contents at a Glance

# Contents

# Introduction

The events of September 11, 2001, literally and figuratively shook the very foundations of our free and open society. One aftereffect has been an increased interest in all aspects of security and its implementation. The FBI announced that the perpetrators of the attacks of September 11 employed the Internet to exchange encrypted messages within their group, illustrating their ability to exploit technology for such purposes. With the use of e-mail continually increasing, the need for protection has never been more evident. All organizations and individuals with computers or networks connected to the Internet are vulnerable to malicious code and viruses. While many individuals and organizations routinely install anti-virus software and dutifully update it on a regular basis, this protection is often ineffective against the "new breed" of malicious code (viruses, worms, and Trojans) that is released into the "wild" each day.

In February 2001, a twenty-year-old Dutchman with the moniker OnTheFly unleashed the AnnaKournicova worm that quickly spread and affected thousands of computers worldwide. Even its creator was shocked at how quickly the worm became so widespread. While causing little physical harm to individual computers, it was most successful due to its use of encryption to avoid detection and because it relied on the use of an innovative psychological ingredient. Anna Kournicova is an attractive tennis star, and OnTheFly knew that most of the male population would be at least intrigued, if not completely tempted, to open the attachment, thereby activating the worm.

While the ability of an Internet worm to spread rapidly did not surprise anti-virus experts, they were concerned about the ease with which this virus was *created*. Using a program called VBS Worm Generator 1.5; OnTheFly was able to create his virus in under two minutes and without the benefit of any programming knowledge. The program, designed to create Internet worms in a commonly used computer language called Visual Basic, was the brainchild of a young South American cracker known as Kalamar and was at one time freely available to anyone on the Internet. Kalamar claims his program was never designed to create destructive viruses and was actually meant to be used as a learning tool to help others better understand viruses. With the exception of being found on some underground hacker Web sites, this program is no longer easily obtainable. Taking its place, unfortunately, are more destructive programs that make ultrasophisticated virus writing techniques available to the Internet masses.

While the AnnaKournicova worm did not carry a destructive payload, more caustic worms quickly followed. In 2001 SirCam, Nimda, and the more recent Goner worm infected hundreds of thousands of computers worldwide and cost companies millions of dollars in damage due to data destruction and lost revenue. Many in charge of IT security were left embarrassed in the wake of these widespread and debilitating viruses. More sophisticated malicious code that exhibited properties of both Internet worms and Trojan horses began to appear and target vulnerable Web servers. Viruses such as Code Red II and BadTrans are examples of two such programs that wreaked havoc by quickly replicating and installing their Trojan horse components on victim computers. Hackers often use Trojan horse programs to steal sensitive information or to seize control of victim computers to use as vectors for their own mischief.

While many of those who were affected by viruses were vigilant about updating their anti-virus software, they still fell victim to the new breed of malicious code. Viruses like the Goner worm actually searched the host victim's computer to quickly disable certain commonly used Internet security software programs, leaving the host computer defenseless. These worms were primarily successful because most companies take a reactive approach to virus defense. The Melissa, I Love You, and the more recent Code Red Worm viruses quickly spread around the globe costing companies millions of dollars in damages and lost time, yet an onslaught of even more potent, deadly, and destructive malicious code is predicted.

While no one can predict when this "Digital Pearl Harbor" will occur, reacting to viruses *after* they have entered your computer is not prudent, nor is it effective. To defend a company from modern-day digital disease, one must now employ a proactive, first-strike approach to defense, and organizations the world over must immediately take a more vigilant stance in protecting their computers and networks from digital disaster. When it comes to virus attacks, ignorance is certainly not bliss. Undeniably, the greatest asset and weapon against preventing a virus attack is knowledge. Knowing how viruses and malicious code infiltrate computer systems, how they affect those systems, and how they ultimately spread and cause more damage exponentially is a necessity, not a luxury.

In order to engage in combat with technologically savvy virus creators in the new millennium, a new, more comprehensive approach to protection must be adopted. Many contemporary e-mail programs now allow scripts to execute automatically and HTML code to be displayed directly in the body of the e-mail without having to open and access any attachment. Taking advantage of these functions, newer "no click" viruses that are surreptitiously embedded directly into the e-mail message body are beginning to appear. These are particularly difficult to combat.

This book aims to explain how viruses work, to explore the different levels of damage they can inflict, and to offer strategies to effectively and proactively combat them *before* they destroy valuable data. Detecting false alarms and hoaxes is also covered. This book also explains how a combination of software programs and social engineering can produce the most effective deterrent to malicious code.

## Who Should Read This Book?

While the title of this book reads *Securing the Network from Malicious Code*, any computer owner who wants to understand the pathology of malicious code will benefit from reading it. Network administrators, security personnel, and even executive officers are finding it increasingly difficult to keep their organizational networks free from the debilitating and costly effects of malicious code. The advent of inexpensive wireless networking and high-speed Internet access has many households and small businesses jumping on the broadband-wagon. Because malicious code can quickly spread throughout a network, understanding how to adequately protect these networks from the threat of malicious code is mandatory. Networks such as those in hospitals, schools, and even government agencies are not immune from the threats posed by viruses, worms, and Trojan horse programs. This book will be a valuable asset to them, as well.

## What Is Covered?

This book is divided into three parts. Each section covers specific topics relating to malicious code. What follows is a brief summary of each of part.

## PART I: THREAT ANALYSIS

The section sets the stage for addressing the topic of malicious code defense by first covering theory and basics. It then explores the "who and why" of malicious code authors. This section concludes with an in-depth explanation of malicious code and other digital threats faced by organizations and their networks.

## PART II: APPLIED TACTICS FOR MALICIOUS CODE DEFENSE

This section begins with an overview of the various computer and network subsystems (instant messaging included) that are the locus of malicious code attacks. It then offers the reader practical, hands-on solutions for defense against viruses, worms, and Trojan horses.

## PART III: LOOKING AHEAD

Due to the increased threats posed by terrorist activities, this section opens with an overview of how malicious code can be used as a weapon by both cyberterrorists and hacktivists. It concludes with the future of malicious code warfare, focusing on the vulnerabilities exposed by the increased use of wireless technology.

# Part I

## Threat Analysis

## IN THIS PART:

The first phase in defending the network from digital threats entails building an understanding of what the threats are, where they are coming from, and who creates them. Malicious code appears in various forms, and its creators are a diverse bunch. In this part, I explore the numerous types of threats derived from malicious code, the mindset of the virus writer, and the damage that viruses, worms, and Trojan horses can exact on vulnerable organizations.

# Chapter 1

# Threats Posed by Viruses, Worms, and Trojan Horses

**In This Chapter**

✓ Data corruption

✓ Data loss

✓ Data theft

✓ Productivity loss

✓ Revenue loss

✓ Corporate humiliation

✓ Damage to reputation

✓ Network downtime

✓ Legal liability

✓ Inappropriate content

✓ Espionage

✓ Sabotage

WHETHER MODERN DAY MALICIOUS code takes the form of a virus, worm, or Trojan horse program, it poses a real threat to organizational networks, causing damage that is often debilitating. The number of people using the Internet has increased dramatically in the last few years, and that number is expected to rise as yet more businesses recognize the importance and necessity of a Web presence. Computer systems are at risk when a threat takes advantage of a vulnerability and causes harm. A threat is any circumstance or event with the potential to cause harm to an organization through the disclosure, modification, or destruction of information, or by the denial of services. The most serious threats at present are the all too familiar viruses and worms that exploit Internet-based services such as e-mail or Internet Relay Chat (IRC). These threats have materialized because both individuals and organizations widely adopt and rely on Internet-based services in their everyday operations. Understanding the different types of threats posed by malicious code is the first step toward defending yourself in the inevitable battle against digital disease.

# Data Corruption and Loss

While an individual computer or server may cost an organization a few thousand dollars, the data stored on that server may be worth the same amount many times over. Every year, the loss of critical and confidential data costs organizations billions of dollars in lost revenue. Nearly any form of code that can be run on a PC can be manipulated toward malevolent action. Viruses, which are designed specifically for the purpose of vandalizing data, are often the cause of file corruption. A virus may inflict damage in different ways:

✓ **By destroying existing data:** For example, one virus may be designed to destroy only document files while another may be formulated to wipe out the entire contents of a hard drive.

✓ **By manipulating existing data:** For example, the WM/Concept macro virus, by interfering with the operation of the "File ⇨ Save As" function in Word, forces documents to be saved only as template files.

✓ **By adding unnecessary data:** For example, a virus can corrupt a file simply by adding or appending superfluous data to it, rendering the file unusable by the operating system.

Files infected by a virus may become inaccessible and/or exhibit strange or unpredictable behavior. Data loss or corruption affects your financial bottom line through missed opportunities and lost revenue. Businesses may find that existing customers or clientele lose faith and no longer do business with an organization that has suffered losses as a result of its failure to safeguard data. When a company's reputation is tarnished publicly with this information, it may also dissuade new customers from engaging in business transactions with the company. When data becomes corrupted, the options are few. One can either attempt to repair the corrupted data with a utility program designed specifically for that task or restore the data from a trusted backup.

Data repair and backup recovery procedures are addressed in Chapter 9.

It is far more expensive to replace data than it is to protect it. It is vital that you take proactive steps to reduce your chance of catastrophic data loss. With the increase in society's reliance on computers, the issue of data security has become even more mission-critical. Whether they are working with an important business proposal, patient medical records, or personal tax information, users today are storing more information electronically than ever before. The loss of critical or sensitive data can have both financial and legal consequences for business and home users alike. Modern computer hard drives can now store enormous amounts of data. Consequently, when viruses or worms succeed in damaging those drives, the amount of lost data can be staggering.

# Data Theft

In today's wired world, confidential information is frequently transmitted and even stored online, sparking privacy concerns and creating new data security challenges. The explosion of Internet use has led to the disappearance of conventional boundaries. The Internet, while creating new and unique business opportunities, has also introduced new data security threats. *Data theft* is a broad term that encompasses not only the actual theft of information (data) but also the unlawful handling or viewing of classified data.

One of the tools used in data theft is the *Trojan horse virus*. Hackers use a Trojan horse program to comb your PC or network for confidential data files. Arriving as an e-mail attachment, this malicious program can compromise a system by opening a "back door" entry into a computer or server. This virus type was demonstrated during the summer of 2000, when besieged AOL employee computers opened the Trojan horse–infected e-mail attachment. During the attack, approximately two hundred member accounts were compromised when the Trojan horse program enabled the intruders to access member passwords and credit card information.

Trojan horse programs are covered in detail in Chapter 4.

# Productivity Loss

It's not surprising that the most widespread and debilitating worms and viruses receive the largest amount of media coverage. Besides their ability to replicate, some computer viruses exhibit another common thread: the ability to deliver a damaging viral payload. Sometimes viruses only display images or messages; other times, they steal or destroy data. However, even if malicious code doesn't contain a destructive payload, it can still become a nuisance by occupying space on your hard drive or memory, resulting in a marked decrease in the overall performance of your computer. When a virus or worm strikes, no matter what its purpose, one aftereffect is lost productivity. The reason is simple: reactive measures require that the virus or worm first be isolated or contained, and then removed from infected computers. However, the cost associated with recuperation from malicious code attacks transcends the simple isolation and removal of malicious code. While virus removal may require numerous man hours and may cost a company hundreds of dollars for just one infected computer, the loss of that computer's productivity can easily cost a company five to ten times that amount. In a company with several hundred (or more) affected computers, productivity loss can have a pronounced and lasting effect on company profits.

When the I Love You computer virus surfaced in May of 2000, U.S. government agencies were affected to varying degrees. According to Jack Brock, the director of government and defense information systems at the General Accounting Office, affected government agencies responded promptly and appropriately, thereby limiting the effect of the virus. According to Brock, federal agencies were primarily affected in terms of their e-mail capabilities. He went on to say, "If an agency's business depends on e-mail for decision-making and service delivery, then the virus/worm probably had a significant impact on day-to-day operations in terms of lost productivity."

The end result is simple: When a virus hits, affected systems are either directly damaged by the virus, or they are shut down to prevent the spread of infection. In either scenario, when an agency or company relies on computers for everyday operations and those computers are inoperable, productivity will suffer.

# Loss of Revenue — Can *You* Afford It?

While the cost associated with preventing malicious code attacks may seem excessive (both in man hours and in actual dollar expenditures), the amount spent on repairs has proved to be staggering. When computers and the networks that contain them are affected by malicious code, they are often shut down or disconnected from all Internet and network access in order to quickly contain the virus and limit its effect.

However, many organizations today have some amount of Web presence. When Web or e-mail servers need to be shut down due to a malicious code attack, revenue losses are inevitable. Those who rely on a Web presence to conduct e-commerce are the hardest hit. Some successful Trojan horse programs have components that enable hackers to usurp a computer and control it from a remote location. Once they control your computer, the hackers can commandeer it (along with a multitude of other Trojan-infected computers) to perform a coordinated distributed denial-of-service attack (DDoS) against a targeted computer or Web site. Denial-of-service (DoS) attacks are distinguished by their perpetrator's blatant attempts to prevent legitimate users of a service from using that service.

Examples of common denial-of-service attacks include the following:

✓ Trying to inundate a network with so many data requests that legitimate network traffic is unable to get through

✓ Attempting to interrupt service to a specific computer or system

✓ Preventing a particular individual (or individuals) from accessing a specific service

✓ Attempting to disrupt connections between two computers, thereby preventing access to a service

In February of 2000, denial-of-service attacks disrupted the Yahoo!, E*Trade, and Amazon Web sites, as well as other e-commerce sites. Analysts estimated that those denial-of-service attacks resulted in millions of dollars in lost revenues for those that were hardest hit among the well known e-commerce sites. In a DDoS attack, the attacks derive from hundreds of computers rather than just one, as in a regular DoS attack. DoS defense mechanisms that are based upon monitoring the volume of data coming from a single computer on the Internet will often fail when the attacks come from many different computers. Rather than receiving, for example, 1,000 attacks per second from just one Web site, the victim might receive one attack per second from 1,000 different Web sites.

The grim fact is that given time, something will eventually go awry with nearly every computer in an organization. Housed within each of those units are millions of bytes of data that will require time to be restored before that computer can return to productivity. Whether planned or unexpected, computer or network downtime ultimately results in lost revenues. In addition, whether it's a virus attack, a hard drive failure, or a stolen laptop, information lost is information compromised.

# Corporate Humiliation — Are *You* at Risk?

Once a virus has been detected, contained, and removed, humiliation may follow. This is particularly true if the media has publicized the attack. Post-viral embarrassment can expose even the most secretive organizations. The American FBI, for example, was victimized in July of 2001. A researcher from the FBI's online security unit accidentally helped spread the infamous SirCam worm across the globe. Before Sircam was detected, more than half a dozen FBI documents (one marked "For Official Use Only") were sent to outside parties. One nasty feature of this worm was that it scoured victim hard drives, randomly selected files and personal documents, and then forwarded a copy of these documents to new victims. Its modus operandi was to search a victim's "My Documents" folder, where a majority of users keep their most sensitive and private documents, and then forward those documents to any names found in the victim's e-mail address book. After sending several of these documents via e-mail to friends, business associates, and strangers, widespread embarrassment was the result.. Embarrassment appears to be the prime objective of the SirCam virus since the time it debuted.

While having your personal documents sent to those you know can be unsettling, viruses also elicit another kind of humiliation, especially to those conducting e-commerce. If an online retailer, for example, is forced to shut down a Web site as a result of a virus or DDoS attack, consumers may feel uncomfortable engaging in future online transactions with that organization. Public perception plays an important role in how effectively organizations conduct e-business. When consumers feel confident that organizations and online merchants use adequate and effective security measures, they are more apt to exchange sensitive data or engage in monetary transactions with those organizations.

The vast majority of PCs around the globe use some form or variation of a Microsoft operating system. Whether one of the many versions of the Windows desktop operating system or the more advanced Internet Information Servers (IISs), these operating systems are often the focus of virus or hacker attacks. Although easier to set up and maintain than UNIX or Linux servers, Windows operating systems are frequently plagued with security holes, making them the target of choice for virus writers and hackers. On the other hand, certain security features have been built directly into the kernel or core of the UNIX and Linux servers' operating systems. For that reason, these operating systems may be preferred for e-commerce and subject to far fewer attacks from malicious code.

To keep yourself safe when engaging in e-business, it may be useful for you to determine the type of operating system being used by a particular Web site or online merchant. You can use a handy freeware utility called ID Serve to accomplish this task (see Figure 1-1). Developed by Internet security analyst Steve Gibson, this utility (available at www.grc.com) enables a computer user to query any online Web server for information about the operating system used by that server. Since not all Web server operating systems are equally secure, utilities such as ID Serve allow computer users to take responsibility for their own personal information.

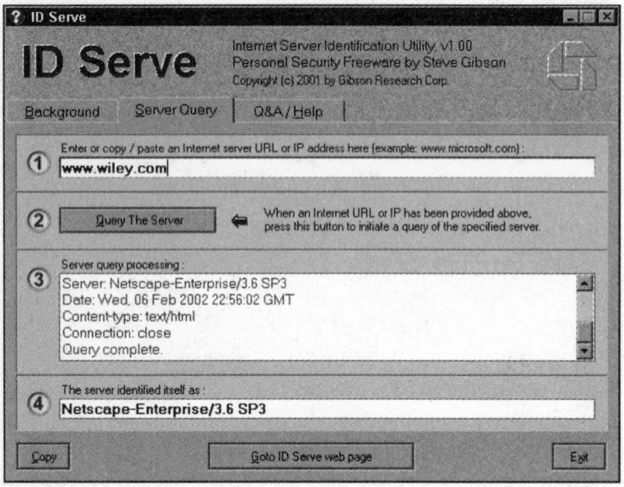

**Figure 1-1:** ID Serve v1.0, Gibson Research Corp

# Damaged Reputation — Will *You* Suffer?

The financial cost associated with virus containment and removal is staggering. However, the price of malicious code attacks often goes beyond the physical, leaving a company's image tarnished after news of an attack spreads. Many of those with an online presence work hard at securing their Web sites against data theft and corruption. As mentioned previously, when potential online customers hear that a particular Web site has been plundered by e-pirates, they hesitate to conduct business with that organization. As a result, consumers may become frustrated if they perceive the attacks to be the result of poor security practices on the part of the organization. Companies sometimes perpetuate the spread of a virus by unintentionally passing it on to customers. Nearly every company that participated in the International Computer Security Association (ICSA) Labs 6th Annual Computer Virus Prevalence Survey 2000 reported at least one virus infection between 1996 and 2000. Furthermore, the number of companies contaminated by at least one virus increased nine-fold during the same period. Once a company's reputation is tarnished, it can take years to fully recover.

# Network Downtime

Like the individuals who use them, computers are more productive when they work together. Computer networks are more popular than ever, and companies of all sizes find them indispensable for efficient business operations. Most organizations — be they manufacturing, insurance, or medical concerns, or even government agencies — rely on network communications as the backbone for operations. The Internet is nothing more than one very large network made up of thousands of smaller networks, technically known as an *Internetwork*. Networks allow for the sharing of information and resources across a small office or a large, geographically diverse area. With society's increased reliance on networked computers, it is safe to say that when computer networks become crippled by a malicious code attack, the effects are devastating.

From airports to local motor vehicle offices, computer networks are in use everywhere in our lives. While the main advantage of networking computers is to allow the sharing of information and resources, it is this same benefit that allows malicious code to spread quickly throughout a network. Most modern day malicious code is designed to spread rapidly throughout a computer network and infect as many hosts as possible, all the while avoiding detection. Since the Internet is nothing more than a very large computer network, it is an ideal environment and breeding ground for the widespread distribution of malicious code. Many companies today use the Internet to network branches of their organization that are geographically separated, making them vulnerable to malicious attack. Again, when networks are incapacitated (or forced to shut down altogether) as the result of a malicious code attack, everyone suffers. What follows is a short list of some of the effects that network downtime can have on an organization:

✓ Loss of revenue or profits

✓ Loss of productivity

✓ Tarnished image

✓ Customer frustration and/or dissatisfaction

✓ Loss of customers or clients

✓ "Paper" losses due to decrease in stock value

To figure what such network downtime can mean to you and your organization, use the following simple formula for determining downtime costs:

Annual Gross Revenue / Annual Business Hours = Per Hour Revenue
Per Hour Revenue × Hours of Downtime = Downtime Cost

The following sample values use this simple formula to illustrate the costs of network downtime for an organization with $10 million in gross revenues and 20 hours of unplanned downtime:

| | |
|---|---|
| Annual Gross Revenue | = $10,000,000 |
| Annual Business Hours | = 2,080 |
| Per Hour Revenue | = $4,807 |
| Unplanned Downtime | = 20 hours |
| Downtime Cost | = $96,153 |

While these "costs" may seem isolated to affect only the incapacitated organization, network downtime can have more dramatic and widespread effects elsewhere. Other companies (or individuals) that rely on the organization for information, services, or goods for their continued operation also suffer downtime (until they find new sources). Imagine if the 9-1-1 network was knocked out by malicious code and emergency calls were unable to get through or if a hospital was unable to access important patient information in a life-or-death situation.

# Legal Liability — Can *You* Afford It?

One inherent feature of most Internet mail worms is the ability to replicate and spread rapidly. Worms commonly infiltrate a host computer's e-mail address book, then e-mail themselves to several (sometimes all) of the contacts found there. The intent of this distribution method is to perpetuate the cycle of causing widespread harm. It is extremely successful because a recipient receives the infected e-mail from one of their regular contacts, thinks it is safe, and opens it.

All companies with Internet-enabled computers share the responsibility of ensuring that their e-mails (whether sent or received by their organization) are free from malicious code. When a company fails to take reasonable, adequate security measures, they expose themselves to the possibility of legal action from someone who receives one of their infected e-mails.

The possibility of legal action was demonstrated recently by the Code Red worm fiasco. This worm affected only computers running certain Microsoft server operating systems, and a security patch was freely available for download from Microsoft in June of 2001 about a month before Code Red's widespread distribution. Even so, few organizations bothered to download and install the patch. Consequently, Code Red infected over 250,000 servers within several hours after being released onto the Internet. Companies that vigilantly updated their software and applied the security patch were spared the effects of this worm.

Hackers and virus writers are directly responsible for malicious code attacks; however, the companies that suffer losses as a result of these attacks will most likely be held liable for any damages they cause. Hackers who break into systems are most often adolescents and cybercriminals; they are not usually the types from whom organizations are likely to recoup large losses.

In terms of legal liability, the malicious coder is bypassed, and the organization that was negligent by allowing the virus to infiltrate its systems is sued by another organization that becomes subsequently infected. Complainants base their case on the ideathat the organization was negligent by not keeping its security measures up-to-date, "allowing" themselves to be attacked (or used by a hacker) and thus imposing losses on subsequent affected systems. While large corporations are protected from such liabilities by legal counsel teams, smaller organizations are often unable to survive this type of lawsuit.

# Inappropriate Content

One of the most disturbing features of malicious computer code is its ability to seize control after it infects a host computer. The possibilities for directed mischief are almost unlimited, as you can see in the following situations:

✓ Once in control, worms or Trojan horse programs can direct an infected computer host to visit adult-oriented or other unsuitable Web sites. The viewing of inappropriate Internet content by employees can cause potential legal problems for any company.

Many Web sites use specific technologies, such as "cookies", that allow Web sites to track and monitor surfing habits. Employees may be held accountable for visiting Web sites that simply appeared on their screens.

✓ Failure to control access to objectionable Web sites (such as those that are pornographic or racist) can expose the organization to lawsuits. More and more people are using the Internet in the workplace. U.S. labor laws dictate that employees have a legal right to security and safety at their place of work, and that includes protection from exposure to objectionable or offensive material. Other protections include freedom from slander, sexual harassment, defamation, criticism, or intimidating behavior. Ensuring that malicious code does not cause an employee to view inappropriate Web content helps minimize the risk that those employees will bring legal action against your organization.

These issues are about controlling information. And just as you don't want employees viewing inappropriate content, you don't want them inappropriately releasing content either. Confidential and proprietary information provides organizations with important tools for remaining competitive and successful in today's demanding business environment. Customer databases, marketing information, and financial and strategic plans are among the most important elements of an organization's current and future business success. A single breakdown in the company's protection of its proprietary information can have serious consequences. When employees have access to critical data, their responsibility for protecting that information must be emphasized emphatically and repeatedly.

# Digital Spies and Espionage

When corporate data is not deliberately safeguarded in order to maintain its secrecy, it is generally regarded as public information. While public information is subject to scrutiny from a variety of sources, "private" information can be scrutinized as well. Organizations gathering data on others in the same line of work have an obvious objective; however, intelligence collecting can originate from sources other than the competition. Espionage can be initiated and bankrolled by industrial competition and even national governments. Spies who work at this level operate under the auspices of large organizations, and they are unencumbered by the limitations facing common, home-based hackers. The Internet not only allows espionage to occur from within an organization's network, but from outside as well. Cyberspies can penetrate networks from remote locations anywhere in the world.

Every year, companies in the U.S. and around the globe lose millions of dollars from industrial espionage attacks. Many of these attacks originate from outside sources, such as competitors, unfriendly countries, and even, in some instances, single individuals. Usually, the general population is not aware of just how uncomplicated it is to breach security at Fortune 500-sized corporations. Even the computer experts employed by these companies find it complicated to combat modern-day cybercriminals. In October of 2000, Microsoft, the world's largest software company, inadvertently allowed cyberthieves to tap into digital software blueprints (containing source code) for some of their products in development. While Microsoft claimed that there was no compromise to the integrity of the source code, spokesman Rick Miller did indicate that this was "a deplorable act of industrial espionage." Using viruses carrying Trojan horse components that have the ability to launch Web sites, steal passwords, or monitor keystrokes, hackers are now plying their trade with malicious code technology. Many security analysts fear the advent of a new era where viruses become the tools by which professionals achieve their goals of corporate theft or extortion.

# Sabotage — The Enemy Within

An often-overlooked area of security risk is a company's own employees. Internal threats pose a real danger to any organization. Disgruntled employees or former employees, those in danger of layoff or those with an ax to grind, can cause considerable damage to an organization's computer network. Many companies enforce policies that prohibit an employee's right to use the company's computer systems either directly or remotely once they have been notified of their pending termination. This also holds true after an employee resigns, particularly if a confrontation occurred.

One of the first well-publicized incidents of the use of malicious code to sabotage corporate computer systems occurred in July 1996, when 37-year-old Tim Lloyd installed a type of malicious "time bomb" program at his place of work, Omega Engineering's manufacturing plant in Bridgeport, New Jersey. The malicious program was triggered by the first employee who "logged on" to the company's computer network. The ill-fated employee soon found that a software time bomb had been unintentionally detonated, methodically and systematically destroying all of the programs critical to running the company's manufacturing operations. To add insult to injury, Lloyd added a line of code to his time bomb so that the employee computer screen displayed a message dialogue that said "Fixing". As a result, no one was alerted to the destructive effects of the malicious code until after the program had been deleted and purged from the system. In the wake of the attack, Omega suffered $12 million in damages and was forced to lay off eighty workers. At Tim Lloyd's trial, jury members deliberated for about ten hours before they found Lloyd guilty of computer sabotage. Omega executives said that prior to his arrest, Tim Lloyd was considered one of their most valued employees during his 11-year tenure with the company.

To further illustrate the security hazards lurking within an organization, the United States Attorney for the Southern District of Florida published this public press release on September 6, 2001:

JURY CONVICTS HERBERT PIERRE-LOUIS OF SENDING COMPUTER VIRUS TO DESTROY PURITY WHOLESALE GROCERS INC'S COMPUTER SYSTEMS
September 6, 2001

Guy A. Lewis, United States Attorney for the Southern District of Florida, announced today that a jury sitting in the Southern District of Florida in Miami found Herbert Pierre-Louis guilty of two counts of knowingly sending a computer virus to cause damage to computers used in interstate commerce. Sentencing is scheduled for Tuesday, November 20, 2001, at 4:30 p.m. before United States District Judge Alan S. Gold. Pierre-Louis faces a maximum sentence of three and a half years in federal prison, a fine of up to $250,000, and mandatory restitution.

This was the first federal computer virus case to go to trial in the Southern District of Florida, and only the second in the nation, brought under 18 U.S.C. Section 1030. This statute makes it a federal crime to send a computer virus which causes at least $5,000 in damage.

The evidence at trial established that Pierre-Louis sent a computer virus from his home in Broward County to four locations of Purity Wholesale Grocers, Inc. of Boca Raton, Florida. The virus was sent to Buffalo, New York, Hopkins, Minnesota, Tacoma, Washington, and Minneapolis, Minnesota. In both Buffalo and Hopkins, the virus put Purity's computer system out of operation for several days and ultimately cost the company over $75,000. Purity is one of the six largest privately held companies in Florida.

At the time Pierre-Louis sent the virus on June 18, 1998, he worked as a computer hardware technician for Purity in Boca Raton. Pierre-Louis used confidential passwords to access and place the virus at critical locations within Purity's computer system. Pierre-Louis had been reprimanded by his supervisor for work-related problems ten days before the virus was transmitted.

"We must vigorously prosecute those individuals who violate federal laws that are intended to protect the South Florida business community," said U.S. Attorney Guy A. Lewis. Lewis noted that sabotage to business assets whether they are real property or computer systems is a serious matter that the federal government must pursue in this time when computers are becoming more and more important to South Florida's businesses.

Mr. Lewis commended the investigative efforts of the Federal Bureau of Investigation. The case was prosecuted by Assistant U.S. Attorneys Richard Boscovich and Kirk Ogrosky.

While these events are disturbing, security analysts estimate that in-house security breaches account for roughly 70 to 90 percent of the attacks on corporate computer networks. Because many organizations focus on preventing attacks from outside their computer networks, the "inside-network" attacks are more frequently becoming the most destructive type of attack.

In-house attacks are a peculiar type of threat. Unlike attacks coming from an external source, these attacks involve intruders who are trusted and authorized to access the network. These attackers actually require network access in order to perform their duties for the organization. Furthermore, they often have a substantial amount of knowledge about the network's architecture, including where critical or sensitive information is located.

Because of their additional knowledge of internal system procedures and configurations, inside attackers have a substantial advantage over attackers who must first break their way in. Organizations are finding it difficult and laborious just keeping external attackers out. Keeping authorized users from abusing their access privileges, while also keeping hackers and viruses from wreaking havoc, makes the job of network administration even more difficult. Because many organizations' network security policy is focused on protecting the perimeter of the network, little attention is paid to what may be occurring within the system. As a result, in-house attacks may not be discovered for months after the attack, long enough for perpetrators to cover their tracks and avoid being detected. A properly configured intrusion detection system or IDS can alert system administrators when an internal or external attack has occurred.

Intrusion detection systems are addressed in Chapter 9.

Traditionally, all computer security efforts have sought to protect the confidentiality, integrity, and availability of information systems:

✓ **Confidentiality** in computer systems prevents the disclosure of information to unauthorized persons. Individuals who trespass into another person's computer system or exceed their own authority in accessing certain information, violate the legitimate owner's right to keep private information secret. Crimes that violate the confidentiality of computer systems include "unauthorized access crimes" as defined by Title 18, U.S.C. Section 1030(a)(2). Because breaking into a computer begins with unauthorized access to an information system, many believe this represents the foundational computer crime offense.

✓ **Integrity** of electronically stored information ensures that no one has tampered with it or modified it without authorization. Thus, any nonsanctioned corruption, impairment, or modification of computer information or equipment constitutes an attack against the integrity of that information. Many of the malicious hacking activities, such as computer viruses, worms, and Trojan horses, fall within this category. The same is true for individuals who purposefully change or manipulate data either for profit or some other motivation, such as revenge, politics, terrorism, or merely for the challenge.

✓ **Availability** of computer data indicates the accessibility of the information and that its associated programs remain functional when needed by the intended user community. A variety of attacks, such as the often-cited denial of service incidents, constitute a set of criminal activities that interferes with the availability of computer information.

These three themes provide the basis for the Organization for Economic Cooperation and Development's (OECD) *Guidelines for the Security of Information Systems* and are included in most textbooks, legislative acts, and media articles on computer crime.

# Summary

The threats posed by malicious code can either originate from outside your organization or from within. Regardless of where they originate, viruses, worms, and Trojan horse programs produce profound and often lasting effects (monetary, reputationtational, and psychological) on organizations of any size. Key points covered in this chapter include:

✓ Data corruption, loss, and theft

✓ Loss of productivity and revenue

✓ Humiliation and damage to corporate reputation

✓ Legal liability and unsolicited viewing of inappropriate content

✓ External espionage and internal sabotage

## Chapter 2

# Virus Writers and Hackers: Architects of Digital Disease

### In This Chapter

- ✓ Profiling those who create malicious code and why they do it
- ✓ Considering copycats
- ✓ Examining the tools of the trade
- ✓ Malicious code using encryption and compression to avoid detection
- ✓ Prosecuting cybercriminals
- ✓ International and domestic cybercrime laws
- ✓ Dealing with juvenile offenders

ON NOVEMBER 2, 1988, Robert Tappan Morris, a 23-year-old doctoral student at Cornell University, unleashed an Internet worm that spread quickly, infecting approximately ten percent (at that time about 6,000) of the computers in the United States. While this worm was not designed to cause any physical harm to infected hosts, it did, according to the U.S. General Accounting Office, cause a loss of millions of dollars due to computer downtime. Many of the affected computers were immediately forced to shut down to stop the spread of the worm and to give computer experts time to decide on a course of action.

Back in 1988, the Internet was only a fraction of the size it is today and the number of hosts merely in the thousands. Today, Internet hosts number over 100 million, a much larger target for malicious attacks. Most companies today have some sort of Web presence; in fact, many companies use the Internet to regularly conduct e-commerce, making it an integral part of the global economy. While the Morris worm was designed only to quickly replicate or spread from one host to another, newer destructive and debilitating worms are continually being developed and launched via the Internet. Why would Morris, or anyone else for that matter, write such code? This chapter examines the architects of malicious code and explains their motivations.

## Virus Writers and Hackers

Viruses and worms that spread quickly and exact a great number of casualties are usually those that garner the most press. For the most part, the perception of the virus writer as a dysfunctional, pimply-faced adolescent with a limited social life typing out malicious code is not very accurate. Robert Tappan Morris, for example, was generally considered a well-adjusted, intelligent young man working on his doctorate at a well-respected university. Many virus writers are stable, teenage males who have normal family relationships and friends and who don't intend to cause great harm with the viruses they develop. Sometimes, the virus writers are married, middle-aged men or women (rarely) with teenage children of their own. The persistent depiction of the virus writer as an angry social misfit bent on destruction is generally incorrect.

When this stereotype is accepted as truth, you open yourself to the danger that trust will be placed in individuals simply because they do not fit into the stereotypical hacker and virus writer profile. Failure to see that anyone might be capable of producing malicious code can lead to misplaced trust in seemingly innocent-looking individuals. On the other hand, it can also lead you to be suspicious of a hapless, expert computer user if he or she happens to exhibit traits that are also those of the stereotypical malicious coder.

Ten years ago, virus writers averaged in their late teens. Today, they average in their mid-twenties. The individuals who create malicious code essentially fall into three categories. These categories (discussed in the next three sections) make up the demography of the virus writer and hacker:

- ✓ The teenager
- ✓ The young adult or college student
- ✓ The mature adult

## The Teenager

Adolescents have a reputation for being rebellious and causing mischief. Thus, it is no coincidence that they represent one of the largest demographic groups of virus writers and hackers.

It's a commonly accepted belief that a mature sense of ethics is something that most every person eventually develops. Parents are supposed to voice authority over their children because children are not expected to know how to make certain decisions on their own. The U.S. court system supports this belief by fostering a juvenile division that is separate from the adult criminal court system. This idea is based on the principle that a young person is not capable of criminal intent in the same sense as an adult.

While many parents feel they have instilled honorable qualities in their children, the impersonal "virtual" nature of the Internet shields adolescents from the moral and ethical constraints of the non-virtual world. Unlike in the world outside where teenagers are usually visible and often noticed and recognized by acquaintances and others, the world of the Internet can easily be used to make one invisible and anonymous. Whereas typical adolescent high jinks are tempered by the possibility of the perpetrator being caught (often red-handed), pranks and even more serious transgressions can be carried out via the Internet in a more leisurely manner and with less likelihood of apprehension. When the hackers are very knowledgeable, they are apt to apply their expertise to successfully cover their tracks. The added fact that the wrongdoers needn't leave their homes to carry out these acts fosters a sense of empowerment and feeling of safety.

## The Young Adult and/or College Student

In the arena of virus writers, young adults and college students are the fastest growing category. This group includes many adolescent malicious coders from ten years ago who have matured physically but have retained the mischief-causing traits of their youth. In my opinion, their added years of knowledge and experience make them particularly dangerous. Additionally, in certain situations young adults may perceive themselves victims whose only avenue for a show of strength is some sort of anonymous virtual retribution.

## The Mature Adult

Representing the smallest group, mature adults are usually highly skilled, with years of experience in one of the computer disciplines (networking, programming, security, and so on). Sometimes, this group includes engineers or programmers that have a statement to make or perhaps an ax to grind. They frequently have access to Internet resources that younger coders and hackers do not. Their knowledge, experience, and tenure make mature adults the most dangerous group.

## Gender

One demographic that has not yet been addressed is that of gender. Hacking and malicious coding are predominantly male activities. While there are several known female hackers and coders, they are few and far between and do not cause a significant threat to Internet security. However, novice or expert, male or female doesn't change the end result; it takes only one well-written Internet worm to wreak havoc and cause widespread data destruction and chaos.

Susan Thunder (an alias), a phone phreaker, was a member of the "Roscoe Gang" along with hacker Kevin Mitnick and others. At times described as a former prostitute or as a "loose" woman, Thunder specialized in hacking military computer systems and allegedly took members of the military to bed in order to steal written passwords out of their pockets while they were asleep. Ostensibly, Thunder elevated her sense of self by carrying out hack attacks. Sometimes called the "queen of social engineering," Thunder was adept at convincing employees of organizations (especially over the telephone) that she had authorization for access into various levels of their systems. It was supposedly Thunder who had the names "Kevin and Ron" (Mitnick) inserted and displayed when the Roscoe Gang allegedly hacked into the computer systems of U.S. Leasing. That incident purportedly led to the first conviction of the notorious Kevin Mitnick (although Thunder had supposedly been holding a grudge after the breakup of a relationship she'd had with another member of the Roscoe Gang). She gained immunity from prosecution for being a witness in the case. Rumor has it that she has given up hacking and has become a successful professional poker player.

## Recreational Hackers

According the FBI, virtually every day sees a report about "recreational hackers" who crack into networks for the thrill of the challenge or for bragging rights in the hacker community. While remote hacking once required a fair amount of skill or computer knowledge, the recreational hacker can now download attack scripts and protocols from the World Wide Web and then launch them against victim sites. Thus, while attack tools have become more sophisticated, they have also become easier to use.

These "recreational" types of hacks are numerous and may initially appear to be benign. Nevertheless, they can have serious consequences. A well-known example of such a hack is the case of the juvenile who hacked into the NYNEX (now Bell Atlantic) telephone system servicing the Worcester, Massachusetts, area. With the use of his personal computer and modem, the hacker shut down telephone service to 600 customers in the local community. The resulting disruption affected all local police and fire 9-1-1 services as well as the ability of incoming aircraft to activate the runway lights at the Worcester airport. Telephone service at the airport tower was out for six hours. The U.S. Secret Service investigation of this case also brought to light a vulnerability in 22,000 telephone switches nationwide that could be taken down with four keystrokes.

Because the perpetrator was a juvenile, however, the hacker was sentenced to only two years probation and 250 hours of community service. He was forced to forfeit the computer equipment that he used to hack into the phone system, and he was obligated to reimburse the phone company for $5,000 in damages. This case demonstrated that an attack against our critical communications hubs can result in cascading effects over several infrastructures. In this instance, transportation, emergency services, and telecommunications were all disrupted. It also proved that widespread disruption could be caused by a single individual from a home computer.

# Why Do They Do It?

The reasons why someone would engineer a computer program with the purpose of harming other people's data are numerous. Most of the time, virus writers are unaware of just how quickly and easily their malicious code can spread. This was precisely the case with the surprised Dutch hacker OnTheFly after he released his rampaging AnnaKournikova worm. OnTheFly used a virus writing kit (freeware available on the Internet) that allowed him to easily generate this infamous worm. Those who would not otherwise contemplate releasing a virus become tempted by the ease with which they can write and release viruses, worms, and Trojan horses with the use of such kits. Only after they see the widespread and damaging effects of their "creations" do most coders start to realize the magnitude of what they have done. The task of the security professional is made that much more difficult since coders are not limited to those conventionally considered a threat. Instead, viruses may originate from individuals of the computer using community who have limited or no programming skills.

## Malicious Code Motives

Sarah Gordon, a respected computer security analyst with over 12 years of experience in the field, has extensive experience interviewing virus writers and hackers and analyses of the virus-writing phenomenon. She has also written numerous research papers on the subject. According to Gordon and other computer virus experts, malicious code writers do what they do:

- ✓ **To feel empowered:** The malicious code writer looking to feel empowered is seeking a sense of superiority over others.

- ✓ **Out of pure curiosity or exploration:** By writing and releasing a virus on to the Internet, malicious code writers sometimes seek to "test the waters" to see just how far their creations will spread and how much damage they will ultimately cause.

- ✓ **As a vector for what they perceive to be freedom of speech:** Virus writers who have a need to be heard may use a virus as a conduit for expressing their views or ideologies.

- ✓ **To make a social or political statement:** The Injustice virus, discovered in March 2001, is an example of a political statement virus, as evidenced by its condemnation of the killing of a 12-year-old Palestinian boy named Mohammad Al-Durra during the ongoing Israeli-Palestinian conflict.

✓ **To illustrate flaws in certain anti-virus software programs or operating systems:** Commercially produced computer programs often contain flaws or bugs that compromise security. Virus writers will exploit these flaws to make them known to the software manufacturer and to bring them to the public's attention.

✓ **As a form of digital graffiti:** Aesthetically, a virus can be likened to piece of art. As with graffiti, malicious coders can use it as a means for sending some sort of message to the world.

✓ **To demonstrate the weakness of contemporary society's reliance on technology:** Malicious coders are aware of society's increased reliance on computers and the Internet. Creating a fast spreading virus or worm that cripples computer systems around the globe demonstrates just how vulnerable contemporary society is to computer attacks.

✓ **Out of boredom:** This may be true of younger virus writers who develop malicious code simply for something to do.

✓ **To gain notoriety:** As was the case with OnTheFly, malicious coders will sometimes include programming code that identifies who authored the virus.

✓ **Because of peer pressure:** Individuals may belong to organized virus-writing groups (usually short-lived), and some of those in the group respond to peer pressure, trying to outdo fellow members.

✓ **To exact revenge:** After being reprimanded or fired an individual may install a virus "time bomb" in an effort to seek revenge against the organization that meted out the reprimand.

✓ **To demonstrate love or admiration:** Viruses are sometimes used as an expression of love toward the object of a malicious coder's affection. This was seen in a 1997 Word macro virus dubbed "Ivana" that would, on the thirteenth day of every month, insert the following declaration of love, *"Na kraju, samo jos da kazem: volim te, Ivana* [by utik]" ("And finally, I would like to say: I love you, Ivana [by utik]") into Word documents.

Knowing the enemy is the best means of defense in any battlefield. Internet security is one of the most challenging tasks in the effort against frauds, hackers, and intruders. Successful security requires more than just knowledge of the areas of danger; it also depends on the ability to identify who the enemies are and what their motives are.

# The Hacking/Virus-Writing Hierarchy

Hackers consider themselves at the top of the hacking and virus-writing hierarchy and regard virus writers at the bottom. Their derision for virus writers mostly stems from the lack of skill required to author viruses and the random and often uncontrolled damage caused when the viruses are released on the Internet. In hacker vernacular, the term *script kiddies* refers to neophytes who run simple, malevolent programs known as *scripts* in the hope of demonstrating a technical proficiency they really don't possess. Virus coders who consider themselves highly skilled sometimes affirm that it is morally wrong to create a virus to specifically cause harm to another's computer, yet they have no qualms about creating viral "source code" and posting it on underground hacker Web sites. Source code is basically the "raw" unrefined computer code that can be used to make up more complex programs. Experienced coders can download source code and utilize it as the foundation for developing complex and lethal viruses.

The creation and circulation of malicious code by some individuals raises issues similar to those raised in connection with the production of handguns. It is argued that it is not the weapons alone that cause harm but that the fault lies with the people who engage them. With viruses, worms, and Trojan horses, it's not the existence of the virus that causes harm, but the activation and circulation of that virus across the Internet that causes widespread damage.

# The Copycats

In May 2000, the I Love You worm was unleashed on the Internet. Spreading far more quickly than earlier worms such as Melissa or ExploreZIP, it crippled government and corporate computers as it infected millions of computers the world over. Since I Love You first appeared, several more dangerous copycat variants have emerged. In August 2000, a password-stealing version of the I Love You worm was discovered. Unlike its predecessor, this more lethal version was not widespread, confined to only a few banks in Europe and the United States.

If a virus is "successful" and receives much press coverage, copycat versions invariably follow. This phenomenon was first observed with the Melissa virus. Melissa was a well-publicized virus with extensive coverage on television and radio, and in newspapers and magazines. Soon after her debut, several copycat variants quickly emerged. The variations included W97M/Melissa.A, W97M/Melissa.B, W97M/Syndicate.A, W97M/Ping.A, X97M/Papa.A, X97M/Papa.B, W97M/Zerg.A, and W97M/MADCOW. Remember, many virus writers are stunned at how quickly and widely their creations spread. In contrast, copycats already know the effects of widespread malicious code and deliberately set their sights on causing digital disaster. The copycat virus writers openly flaunt their ability to release viruses and not get caught.

Found within some viruses is a copy of its own distinct source code. Source codes are subject to "revision". Anti-virus software catches viruses based on keywords in the code, called "signatures". With a change in just a single line of code, the signature of the virus changes and thereby becomes an altered variant of the original. Even slight alterations can sometimes enable the virus to pass undetected through up-to-date anti-virus software. A frightening aspect of viruses is that one needs only rudimentary programming experience to modify virus code enough to create a copycat virus. Viruses have a somewhat collective component in that once a new one is unleashed, hackers may tweak them a little in an effort to keep them spreading. Copycat viruses can sometimes be more lethal to your computer system than their predecessors, as their payloads are modified. Because of copycat viruses, protecting networks from the effects of malicious code requires increased vigilance in an organization's overall anti-virus defense strategies.

For more information on measures that the U.S. federal government is taking to help combat viruses and copycat variants, see Appendix B.

# Tools of the Trade

When a complex job needs to be completed quickly in the non-virtual world, tools are used to make the task easier and faster. The same principle applies to the virtual world of computers. Tools in the form of software programs make the complex task of writing a computer program less demanding. Reputable companies such as Microsoft produce programming kits like FrontPage that provide novices with the ability to create high-quality Web sites without the need for programming knowledge. However, like graffiti artists who use their artistic talents in nonproductive and destructive ways, skilled programmers sometimes create computer programs solely to make the task of writing a virus a simple and virtually foolproof endeavor, one almost anyone can perform.

Virus-writing programs are primarily distributed through underground hacker Web sites. One such program, Senna Spy Internet Worm Generator 2000 Version 1.0 (see Figure 2-1), claims to be the world's first Internet worm-generating software program. Currently in Version 2.0, this program now has several new features and bug fixes that make it a more powerful and dangerous tool than its predecessor. As it seems to be with all software programmers, those who write worm generators are continually working on ways to improve their programs.

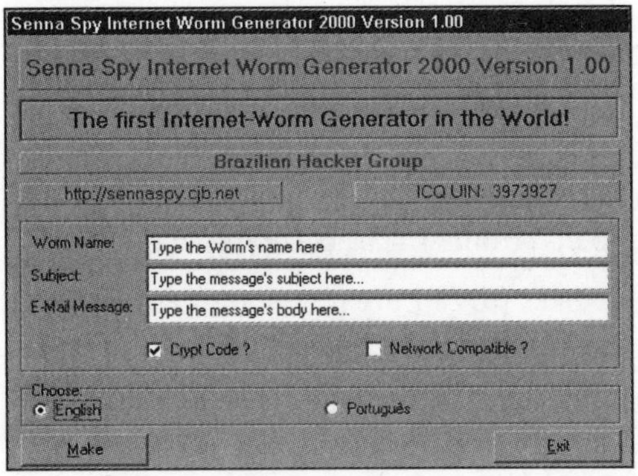

**Figure 2-1:** Senna Spy Internet Worm Generator 2000 Version 1.0

Another program produced by Senna Spy is the Trojan-generating program known as Senna Spy Trojan Generator, now in Version 2001a. Creating a Trojan horse computer virus with this program is chillingly easy. The type of damage caused by Trojan horse viruses created with Version 2001a includes the following:

✓ **Changing monitor resolution:** Making items that appear on the monitor very large forces users to use scroll bars to see their entire screen, and such code can also make it difficult to reset the screen back to its original setting.

✓ **Changing mouse buttons:** Switching the mouse buttons renders the mouse awkward to use and makes the task of resetting it back to its original setting more difficult.

✓ **Changing wallpaper:** Wallpaper is the background that users have selected and are accustomed to seeing on their desktop. It can be replaced with a background that is offensive to the user (or organization) and may be changed to contain inappropriate content.

✓ **Chatting with server:** For example, opening up an unauthorized IRC or ICQ session or instant messaging session.

✓ **Disabling/enabling Ctrl+Alt+Del:** This can force users to access the reset switch in the event of a computer freeze, thereby causing them to lose any unsaved information.

✓ **Executing DOS commands:** DOS commands are executed and run under Windows and can perform destructive tasks such as reformatting a hard disk or deleting critical files.

✓ **Finding files:** Searching a user's hard drive for sensitive information and then marking that information for later access is one example.

✓ **Acting as an FTP server:** FTP or File Transfer Protocol is a common protocol used on the Internet for the sending and receiving of files. In the case of Trojans, the transferring of files can occur without the user's knowledge or consent.

✓ **Hanging up Internet connections:** This effect can prevent a user from accessing the Internet or from maintaining a sustained Internet connection. It may force a user to repeatedly have to reconnect to their ISP, possibly increasing telephone connection costs.

✓ **Hiding/showing task bars:** While more a nuisance than a danger, this effect can cause a loss of productivity while the user attempts to determine the cause of this action.

✓ **Key logging:** Trojans can monitor and log keystrokes (to capture passwords or account numbers) and then send that information back to a predetermined location.

✓ **Opening/closing the CD-ROM drive:** This nuisance can convince users to bring their computer to a service technician, resulting in lost time and productivity.

✓ **Playing AVI or WAV:** Like opening and closing of the CD-ROM drive, this effect is mostly a nuisance, yet it can cause loss of productivity while the system is checked for software and hardware malfunctions.

✓ **Resetting windows:** Such a reset can cause loss of time and productivity while users attempt to reset their windows back to their original configurations.

✓ **Uploading and downloading files:** This possibility is one of the more dangerous aspects of Trojans. Sensitive files stored on users' infected machines may be "stolen" and transmitted back to the virus author without user knowledge or consent.

As amazing and disconcerting as these two programs are, many others are unfortunately available. Remember that 20-year-old OnTheFly created the AnnaKournikova worm in less than two minutes using a program called VBS Worm Generator. Now in Version 2.0 (See Figure 2-2), this program has features that allow users to encrypt their viruses to help avoid detection. Programs like this bring computer virus-writing ability to the masses.

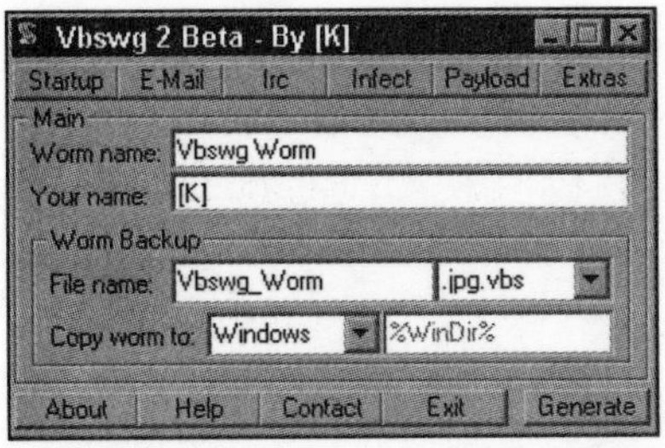

**Figure 2-2:** Visual Basic Worm Generator Version 2.0

# Using Encryption and Compression to Avoid Detection

*Cryptography,* the science of writing in or deciphering secret code, was used during World War II to keep information out of enemy hands. It is often used to convert or store information in a format that allows that information to be seen only by those for which it is intended, while remaining hidden from everyone else. *Encryption* is the ability to turn plain text (the kind you're reading now) into indecipherable text that must then be converted back to its original form before it can be read (understood) by the recipient. As I mentioned earlier in the chapter, those who write viruses often use encryption so that anti-virus software can't detect their creations. Virus detection programs look for programming code that enables programs to replicate or clone. This is one of the methods anti-virus programs use to search for and recognize possible viruses. Using encryption, virus programs can alter replication code and attempt to avoid this type of detection.

Another tactic employed by malicious coders is using a compression utility to alter the binary signature of a computer virus. Virus detection programs use the binary signature of malicious code as a method of detection. Compressing the code can alter viruses such a way that they avoid detection by some anti-virus software. Compression software is legitimately used to decrease the size of computer code. Compression makes programs significantly smaller, thereby reducing the space they occupy on any storage medium. Making a file smaller also allows it to be transferred much more quickly, especially across slower Internet connections or across a company network. Such compression may have the added effect of circulating the virus more quickly. High-quality, free compression utilities such as FileZip 2.0 by Philipp Engel or ZipItFast! 2.0 by MicroSmarts Enterprise (see Figure 2-3) are widely available for download from the Internet.

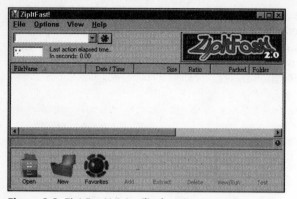

**Figure 2-3:** ZipItFast! V2.0 utility by MicroSmarts Enterprise

# Prosecuting Cybercriminals

In the United States, and in most other countries, it is difficult to find and prosecute individuals who design these types of worm- and malicious code-generating programs. While *writing* a worm-generating program may not be illegal in the U.S., creating and distributing a worm with one certainly is. One of the most publicized cases against a virus-writing cybercriminal occurred in April 1999, following the arrest of New Jersey native David L. Smith, author of the infamous Melissa virus. The following is an actual press release that was issued on December 9, 1999, by the U.S. Department of Justice:

NEWARK — The New Jersey man accused in April of unleashing the "Melissa" computer virus pleaded guilty today to both state and federal charges, admitting that he created and spread the virus that caused millions of dollars in damage, U.S. Attorney Robert J. Cleary and State Attorney General John Farmer Jr. announced.

David L. Smith, 31, of Aberdeen Township in Monmouth County, appeared in state Superior Court and later in U.S. District Court to enter his pleas. Smith admitted spreading the Melissa virus, which infected more than one million personal computers in North America and disrupted computer networks in business and government.

Smith acknowledged in his federal plea agreement that the Melissa virus caused more than $80 million in damage.

Smith, who was arrested by New Jersey authorities on April 1, 1999, pleaded guilty before state Superior Court Judge John A. Ricciardi in Freehold to a one-count accusation charging the second-degree offense of computer-related theft. The state will recommend a sentence of 10 years, which is the maximum sentence provided by law. He also faces fines of up to $150,000. Sentencing date was set for Feb. 18.

Smith pleaded guilty in U.S. District Court in Newark to a one-count Information, charging him with knowingly spreading a computer virus with the intent to cause damage. Smith faces a maximum prison sentence of five years and a $250,000 fine on the federal charge. U.S. District Judge Joseph Greenaway Jr. set sentencing for May 15.

Smith remains free on bail pending sentencing.

The guilty pleas are the result of a joint state and federal investigation, ending in separate but coordinated prosecutions. The state plea agreement provides that the federal sentencing will occur first and that, at the subsequent state sentencing, New Jersey authorities will recommend that the state sentence run coterminously and concurrently to the federal sentence. The coordinated investigations and prosecutions by the state and federal governments represent an unprecedented approach in New Jersey to dealing with computer crime.

"The Melissa virus demonstrated the danger that business, government, and personal computer users everywhere face in our technological society," said Cleary. "Far from being a mere nuisance, Melissa infected computers and disabled computer networks throughout North America."

"There is a segment in society that views the unleashing of computer viruses as a challenge, a game. Far from it; it is a serious crime. The penalties Mr. Smith faces — including potentially five years in a federal prison — are no game, and others should heed his example."

"Computer criminals may think that they operate in a new frontier without boundaries, where they won't be caught. Obviously, that's not true," said Farmer. "We've responded by breaking down traditional borders among federal, state, county and local law enforcement. In this case, it helped us to make an arrest in less than a week."

And said Attorney General Janet Reno: "This plea is a significant marker in the Justice Department's efforts to stop computer crime. In light of society's increasing dependence on computers, the Department will vigorously investigate and prosecute computer crimes that threaten our computer infrastructure."

The guilty pleas were handled today by Supervising Deputy Attorney General Christopher Bubb in Freehold and by Assistant U.S. Attorney Elliot Turrini in Newark.

Smith admitted in state and federal court that he created the Melissa virus and disseminated it from his home computer. He said that he constructed the virus to evade anti-virus software and to infect computers using the Windows 95, Windows 98, and Windows NT operating systems and the Microsoft Word 97 and Word 2000 word processing programs.

According to Paul Zoubek, Director of the state Division of Criminal Justice, the Melissa virus appeared on thousands of e-mail systems on March 26, 1999, disguised as an important message from a colleague or friend. The virus was designed to send an infected e-mail to the first 50 e-mail addresses on the users' mailing lists. Such e-mails would only be sent if the computers used Microsoft Outlook for e-mail.

Because each infected computer could infect 50 additional computers, which in turn could infect another 50 computers, the virus proliferated rapidly and exponentially, resulting in substantial interruption or impairment of public communications or services. According to reports from business and government following the spread of the virus, its rapid distribution disrupted computer networks by overloading e-mail servers, resulting in the shutdown of networks and significant costs to repair or cleanse computer systems.

Smith described in state and federal court how, using a stolen America Online account and his own account with a local Internet service provider, he posted an infected document on the Internet newsgroup "Alt.Sex." The posting contained a message enticing readers to download and open the document with the hope of finding passcodes to adult-content Web sites.

Opening and downloading the message caused the Melissa virus to infect victim computers. The virus altered Microsoft word processing programs such that any document created using the programs would then be infected with the Melissa virus. The virus also lowered macro security settings in the word processing programs. The virus then proliferated via the Microsoft Outlook program, causing computers to send electronic e-mail to the first 50 addresses in the computer user's address book.

Smith acknowledged that each new e-mail greeted new users with an enticing message to open and thus spread the virus further. The message read: "Here is that document you asked for . . . don't show anyone else;-)."

On April 1, members of the New Jersey State Police High Technology Crime Unit, Special Agents of the FBI, and investigators from the Monmouth County Prosecutor's Office arrested Smith at his brother's house in Eatontown. The arrest followed a tip from a representative of America Online to Deputy State Attorney General Christopher Bubb, head of the state's Computer Analysis and Technology Unit.

Following Smith's guilty plea, Superior Court Judge Ricciardi allowed Smith to remain free on $100,000 bail, pending sentencing. District Judge Greenaway allowed Smith to remain free on a $50,000 personal recognizance bond.

For their roles in the investigation and prosecution, Cleary and Farmer credited the State Police High Technology Crime Unit, under the direction of State Police Superintendent Carson Dunbar and the Division of Criminal Justice's Computer Analysis and Technology Unit; the FBI and its New Jersey component of the National Infrastructure Protection Center (INFRAGUARD), under the direction locally of Acting Special Agent in Charge Garey S. Chin in Newark; the Justice Department's Computer Crime and Intellectual Property Section, under the direction of Chief Martha Stansell-Gamm; the Defense Criminal Investigative Service, under the direction of James Murawski, New Jersey resident agent in charge, and the Monmouth County Prosecutor's Office, under the direction of Prosecutor John Kaye.

For its cooperation, Farmer and Cleary thanked America Online. Cleary gave special credit also to ICSA.net, of Reston, Va., for its technical assistance and its virus survey, which included an analysis of damage caused by the Melissa virus.

After reading this article, you can see that it takes an extraordinary amount of resources as well as cooperation between law enforcement and the public sector to bring cybercriminals to justice. In May 2001, David L. Smith was sentenced to 20 months in federal prison for his crime. In addition, Smith was ordered to serve three years of supervised release after completion of his prison sentence and was fined $5,000. U.S. District Judge Joseph A. Greenaway, Jr., further ordered that, upon his release, Smith not be involved with computer networks, the Internet, or Internet bulletin boards unless authorized to do so by the Court. Finally, Judge Greenaway said Smith must serve 100 hours of community service upon his release. Judge Greenaway said the supervised community service would somehow put to use Smith's technology experience. Such sentences are a trend that you are likely to see further evidence of as the legal community becomes tougher on cybercriminals.

# International and Domestic Cybercrime Law

Prosecuting computer virus writers has proved to be an onerous task for at least a couple of major reasons:

✓ Boundaries between countries and nebulous international laws (including extradition laws) have made it difficult for law enforcement agencies to bring charges against computer virus writers. Laws within individual countries themselves are often lacking as well. For example, when Philippine authorities arrested Onel de Guzman in May 2000 for allegedly distributing the infamous LoveLetter virus, he indicated to reporters in a round- about way that, while he wasn't guilty of writing the virus, he might have accidentally released it. In spite of evidence connecting him to the outbreak, authorities were unable to bring any charges against him because at the time of his arrest the Philippine government had not yet passed a law forbidding Internet virus distribution. The absence of such a law prevented U.S. authorities from bringing de Guzman to the U.S. to stand trial. Lawmakers in the Philippines passed such a law in July 2000.

✓ While the U.S. has legislation that punishes those who distribute viruses, the laws seem to overlook those who construct malicious code in the first place. The U.S. government is continually working to develop new standards for prosecuting cybercriminals and has had laws on the books concerning computer crimes for over twenty years. Some legal scholars feel that the U.S. Constitution's First Amendment right to freedom of speech includes the writing of virus source code, as with any other computer program. Under this scenario, writing or creating a computer virus is not considered illegal; however, dissemination of one is. Since many who unleash malicious code onto the Internet get the code from either underground Web sites or use one of the many virus-writing programs available online, having laws that prosecute the coders as well will go a long way in the battle against cybercrime.

## Juvenile Offenders

Making up one of the largest segments of the virus-writing community, juvenile offenders are often difficult to prosecute. Neither domestic nor international laws are prepared to handle these underage offenders. Some virus writers are as young as 13 years old and are usually not charged as adults even for the most serious of cybercrimes. According to the U. S. House Subcommittee on Crime, the number of teenagers in our citizenry is expected to soar to its highest level over the next 10 to 15 years. Some of the most technologically savvy individuals are juveniles who have grown up with computers always at their disposal. Regrettably, some of those juveniles are using their knowledge and years of computer experience to commit some of the most severe computer crimes, seriously compromising critical infrastructures. The need for more stringent laws relating to cybercrime is evident everywhere and extends to juvenile offenders, as well.

The need for stronger cybercrime legislation was demonstrated by the "light" sentence Texas hacker Robert Russell Sanford received in December of 2000, when he pled guilty in the District Court of Dallas County, Texas, to six felony charges of breach of computer security and one felony charge of third degree aggravated theft. According to a December 6, 2000, press release by the U.S. Department of Justice, Sanford, a member of the "HV2K" hacking group, pled guilty to unlawfully obtaining access to computers belonging to the USPS, the State of Texas, the Canadian Department of Defense, and Glinn Publishing Company of Milwaukee, Wisconsin, between November 1999 and January 2000, depriving owners and users from their use of these systems.

Sanford, 18, is a resident of Irving, Texas. Another member of "HV2K," a Canadian juvenile, entered a pre-trial diversion program in Halifax, Nova Scotia, earlier this year for computer activity related to these offenses. Sanford was sentenced to two years in prison on each of the six charges for breach of computer security and ten years on the theft charge. However, despite the strong initial sentencing, the prison sentences were suspended and Sanford was placed on five years supervised probation. Sanford was also ordered to pay $45,856.46 in restitution to the victims of his hacking. As a condition of his probation, Sanford was also required to obtain a high school diploma or graduate equivalency degree, submit to random urinalysis, and participate in community service. Sanford was also restricted in his future use of computers.

For more information and statistics on juveniles and cybercrime, see Appendix C.

# Summary

The architects of digital disease range from adolescents to mature adults and live in all corners of the globe. The following key points are covered in this chapter:

✓ Virus writers are often mislabeled as dysfunctional adolescents with no social life.

✓ The average age of virus writers is shifting from pre-teen to young adult.

✓ Virus writers are predominately male and often initially unaware of how quickly their creations will spread.

✓ Copycat viruses often affect more computers than the original viruses on which they are based; their authors are greater in number and potentially more dangerous.

✓ Virus writing no longer requires programming skills, because programs are now available on the Internet that bring virus writing to the masses.

✓ Virus writers often use encryption and stealth to disguise their viruses, shielding them from detection by even up-to-date anti-virus software.

✓ Current domestic and international laws and regulations are unprepared to handle malicious coders (juvenile or adult) and require overhaul.

# Chapter 3

# Other Digital Threats to Your Organization

**In This Chapter**

✓ Spyware

✓ Badware

✓ Adware

✓ Malware

✓ Human error

MALICIOUS CODE IS A broad term. In fact, the word *malicious* is an adjectival form of the word *malice*, which is defined by the legal community as "the intent, without just cause or reason, to commit a wrongful act that will result in harm to another". In French, the word *mal* translates to *bad* or *badly* in English. In Chapter 1, I review the many threats posed by malicious code. Chapter 2 explores the "who and why" of virus writers. However, malicious code encompasses not only the all-too-familiar viruses, worms, and Trojan horse programs that plague the digital world on a regular basis, but also other, less obvious, more surreptitious computer code. This chapter focuses on the lesser-known and rarely publicized forms of digital threats faced by organizations every day.

## Spyware — Your Hidden Enemy

The practice of using software for the purpose of spying on computer users is not new, nor is it likely to end soon. Put simply, *spyware* is specialized computer code used to monitor, log, and even prevent certain activities on a computer system, generally without the knowledge of the user. After it is placed and activated in someone's computer, spyware secretly gathers information about that user and transmits it back to its creator, usually an advertiser. Other "interested" parties use spyware, as well. Spyware can infiltrate a computer in several ways (all of which are discussed in this and the following sections):

✓ As a simple computer virus or in conjunction with the installation or updating of a computer program

✓ As programs that are automatically installed when you visit Web sites that use them

✓ As an unknown component of download utility

The use of spyware via the public Internet raises both security and privacy issues. Keep in mind that so-called "data collection" programs are not considered spyware if users are warned that their surfing habits are being collected and shared. Since many computer users are not warned, and countless others remain unaware that they are being monitored, individuals and organizations are advised to take responsibility for their own surfing habits — not always an easy task.

To make matters more confusing, malicious programs often masquerade as legitimate computer programs. This was the case recently when a Trojan horse program, disguised as an advertising application, was included with versions of LimeWire, Grokster, and KaZaA, all popular Internet-based peer-to-peer file-sharing programs. The spyware Trojan W32.Dlder.Trojan was contained within an application called "ClickTillUWin," an online lottery program that promised Internet users a chance to win prizes. The common practice of bundling third-party software is a form of advertising that is used often by free software providers. Under normal conditions, users can choose to install some or all of the bundled applications when installing the peer-to-peer file-sharing applications. The ClickTillUWin application, however, was still installed on the user's computer even when the user opted *not* to install it.

## Other "Legitimate" Uses of Spyware

Employee-monitoring software may also be referred to as spyware. Spyware products have become more affordable and easy-to-use, making them attractive to businesses and other organizations that wish to monitor their employees' computer use. Companies justify their use of spyware by asserting that when employees know it is being used, it results in increased security and productivity. They claim that spyware reduces employee misbehavior, leaks of information to the competition, and liability risks. Many employees, however, believe that such monitoring software infringes on their right to privacy. When the implementation of spyware is poorly (or incompletely) communicated to employees, or when the organization is deemed to have gone too far in the monitoring of its personnel, morale may be irreparably damaged and valued employees may be lost.

Spyware is sometimes used by parents to monitor the surfing habits of their children. Parents use spyware to keep an eye on their children's e-mail messages, instant messages, chat room logs, what Web sites they frequent, and even what computer applications they've run and the keystrokes they've typed. Although the legitimacy of the use of spyware in this manner may be debated, it is considered by some to be justified and legitimate.

## Download Utilities That Do More than Help

Computer users in the business and private sectors who download files and programs from the Internet on a regular basis frequently use utilities to help organize and speed up those downloads. Although download "utilities" are generally useful, they can sometimes give users more than they bargained for: in June 2000, a class action lawsuit was filed against AOL/Netscape for electronic eavesdropping on communications between Web site operators and the visitors who downloaded files from those Web sites using AOL/Netscape's popular SmartDownload file utility. This download utility, which was conveniently bundled with the Netscape Navigator browser, gave users the ability to pause and resume downloads and also had several other useful features.

The lawsuit, spearheaded by Christopher Specht, a photographer operating the lawphoto.com Web site, accused SmartDownload of transmitting back to Netscape the location and name of any files transferred using the SmartDownload program (along with a unique identifier) *without* the knowledge or permission of the Webmaster or computer user. Software possessing this characteristic is unlawful, as it violates both the Electronic Communications Privacy Act and the Computer Fraud and Misuse Act. Users seeking a freeware download utility should visit `www.freshdevices.com`. According to the manufacturer, the Fresh Download utility is an easy-to-use download manager software that accelerates the downloading of files from the Internet, such as freeware/shareware, mp3 files, movie files, and picture collections. This software is available free of charge and contains no advertising banners and no spyware components.

## Why Firewalls and Anti-Virus Programs Are Not Enough

Most corporate users operate their Internet-enabled computers under the protection of their company's firewall, while home users usually operate behind one of the many commercially available personal software firewalls (like BlackICE Defender or Zonealarm). Although they protect computers from *outside* attacks, firewalls often leave users vulnerable to betrayal by stealthy spyware programs operating undetected *inside* their computers. Much of the spyware operating in users' computers arrives bundled, or incorporated, in "legitimate" freeware and shareware programs downloaded from the Internet. They may not be "seen" as a threat and would therefore not be detected by anti-virus software programs. Fortunately, certain programs are available that can scan for hidden spyware. These are discussed later in this chapter and detailed further in Chapter 9.

Additionally, firewalls that only monitor and block *incoming* data (such as BlackICE Defender) do not stop spyware from "transmitting" data that it has collected to interested parties. Most software-based firewalls are bidirectional, monitoring data that is both transmitted and received; in spite of that fact, they often fail to stop spyware that was incorporated into, or was masquerading as, a legitimate program because they often use a rule-based protection system. When a user activates what he or she believes to be a legitimate program for which the firewall has no rule, the firewall asks the user for "permission" to allow or deny that program from accessing the Internet. Because the user thinks the program is legitimate, he or she will often instruct the firewall to allow that program Internet access. Allowing the program full Internet access "opens the door", allowing the spyware to operate freely and without detection. The ease with which this can happen can be confirmed by using a freeware program called FireHole, by programmer Robin Keir. This utility demonstrates how easily spyware or malicious code can bypass a personal software firewall and leak information out of a computer. It can be downloaded at `www.keir.net/firehole.html`.

## Detecting and Removing Spyware

As you can see, spyware exists as an executable program on a computer system, with the ability to perform actions like any other computer program:

- ✓ It can monitor user keystrokes and scan files on your hard drive.

- ✓ It can spy on other applications, such as word processors or IRC (Internet Relay Chat) and ICQ (I-Seek-You) chat programs.

- ✓ Spyware can modify your Web browser default home page settings and determine what Web sites you are visiting by monitoring your surfing habits. Then, like Steven Spielberg's E.T, it will "phone home" to report this information to its creator (or other interested parties).

- ✓ It can even notify the spyware company of any attempts to modify or remove it from the system.

Information acquired by spyware can be used by spyware creators for their own internal marketing purposes or sold to other companies for a profit.

Manually trying to locate and remove spyware programs can be an exercise in futility. To sift through any operating system in an effort to find hidden spyware components, an individual must have in-depth knowledge of the operating system's layout and design. Windows-based spyware programs, for example, use certain "keys" located in the operating system registry to launch or control spyware programs. The registry is a hierarchical database within later versions of Windows (that is, 95/98/Me/2000/NT4/NT5) where all system settings are stored. The registry is critical to the functioning of the operating system.

Removing the wrong registry key can be detrimental to the operating system and may even render it unable to boot up. For this reason, it is suggested that only individuals with thorough knowledge of registry layout and function attempt to edit any part of this critical operating system component.

Luckily, a program called Ad-aware can locate hidden spyware and safely remove it from your computer. Ad-aware (see Figure 3-1) by Team Lavasoft (www.lavasoftusa.com) is a free spyware-detection and removal tool that is as easy to use as it is to download. Users may also wish to visit www.spy-software-source.com, home of Spy Software Source. Here, users can find descriptions and links to the various manufacturer Web sites that provide programs for the detection and removal of spyware.

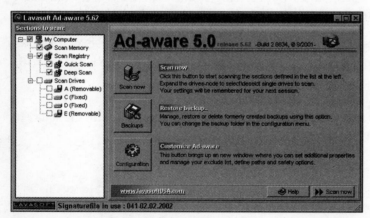

**Figure 3-1:** Ad-aware 5.0 by Team Lavasoft

# Badware — Software That's Bad

The old adage "you get what you pay for" holds true for computer software. Quality computer software from a reputable company undergoes thorough, rigorous testing before being released for sale to the public. Thus, it can be quite expensive. As a cost-saving measure, individuals and companies sometimes search for "free" software on the Internet. Since the Internet spans the globe and is essentially a public network, a plethora of Web sites offer freeware and shareware products.

## Freeware versus Shareware

What's the difference between freeware and shareware? *Freeware* and *shareware* are two different forms of software distribution. Software distributed as freeware may be legally used and copied for noncommercial purposes without the necessity of sending any licensing or registration fees to its authors. Unlike freeware, shareware *does* have licensing and/or registration fees. Shareware distribution enables users to try out the software for a certain grace period prior to purchasing it. In other words, users can determine the usefulness and effectiveness of the software before they buy it. In order to legally use the software after the grace period expires, the user must register and pay for the software as outlined in the licensing agreement. If the user does not want to purchase the software, he or she is directed to remove it from his or her computer. Registering shareware brings important benefits, including increased functionality, future upgrades, better documentation, and tech support.

## The Good and the Bad

However tempting it may be to try freeware, you should remember that there is both good freeware and bad freeware. Good freeware, when installed on your computer, invariably performs its stated function without a hitch. It usually comes with its own uninstall program that allows the user to completely remove the product from his or her system if they so choose.

Bad freeware, also known as *badware*, is computer programming or code that is so poorly written it causes problems (sometimes serious problems) when installed on a user's computer. Bad freeware can lower a computer's overall performance, cause it to freeze or lock up, and in extreme cases, modify the computer operating system in such a way that it no longer boots up. Unfortunately, there is no way to ascertain if freeware is good or bad until it has been installed. Also, keep in mind that malicious code can masquerade as freeware or shareware. The fact that shareware requires licensing and registration does not exempt it from being classified as badware. Because of the risk of serious damage to your computer, freeware or shareware should be monitored carefully during and after installation.

Programs capable of content monitoring are covered in detail in Chapter 9.

One of the best ways to determine whether freeware is badware is to download it from a reputable Web site such as CNET's Download.com (http://download.cnet.com). Here, users rate freeware and shareware software, allowing you to determine if you want to continue with the download or pass it up entirely. Another useful method for testing freeware or shareware, and ascertaining its quality, is to install it on a stand-alone machine isolated from the rest of the network. After installation, the program can be run and carefully monitored for unusual or erratic behavior before it is installed on any other computer.

# Adware — Advertising or Adver-*spying*?

Advertising-supported software, or *adware*, is a software application in which an advertising banner or banners are displayed while the program is running. The developers of these applications incorporate additional software code that delivers the advertisements, which can be viewed through pop-up windows or through a scrolling marquee bar that appears somewhere on your computer screen. Instead of charging a fee for its software, the company generates revenue by selling advertising space that is incorporated directly in the software product.

Adware, like spyware, usually installs additional third-party components on your computer and may exchange demographic data with a remote location via the Internet. Adware has been criticized for occasionally including spyware code that tracks a user's personal information and passes it on to third parties, without the user's authorization or knowledge. Adware containing spyware is seen by many in the legal community as a violation of an Internet user's right to privacy. In fact, online privacy violations via spyware prompted privacy advocate and U.S. Senator John Edwards to issue the following public news statement in January 2001:

WASHINGTON — Senator John Edwards on Monday reintroduced legislation to protect the privacy of people who use computer software programs that secretly track the shopping habits and other interests of Internet surfers.

"Technology makes our lives easier in so many ways, but that convenience can compromise our privacy," Senator Edwards said. "The same technology that puts information at our fingertips also makes our shopping and Web surfing habits, even our medical and financial records, available to the highest bidder."

The Spyware Control and Privacy Protection Act would uncloak so-called spyware programs that use encrypted codes to monitor the activities of unsuspecting computer users and share the personal information with advertisers, telemarketers, or other businesses. Senator Edwards proposed the bill in 2000, but Congress failed to act on it before finishing business late last year.

Under the spyware bill, software providers that use codes to track the activities of Internet users would have to notify consumers in plain language when the users buy or download programs. No information on Internet surfing habits could be collected without first obtaining each consumer's permission. Businesses that gather data would have to let individuals know what information has been assembled, provide a way to correct errors, and safeguard the data against unauthorized access by hackers.

"Spyware is just one of many startling examples of how our privacy is being eroded," Senator Edwards said. "This legislation is a reasonable way to help Americans regain some of their lost privacy. We must find ways to keep confidential personal records confidential."

The measure is one in a series proposed by Senator Edwards to protect the privacy of personal records amassed by Internet businesses, banks, health insurance providers, and telephone companies. He plans to reintroduce the Telephone Call Privacy Act, which he authored last Congress to keep telephone records from being sold without consumers' consent.

Senator Edwards also cosponsored the Consumer Privacy Protection Act, designed to block Internet service providers, Web sites, and advertisers from tracking our Web surfing habits. He plans to back this legislation when it is reintroduced by Senator Hollings.

Note that if a user prefers to have a non-adware product, he or she has the option to purchase a version that does not display advertising banners.

A typical adware development process includes the following steps:

1. An adware company offers a special programming kit that allows shareware or freeware developers to put advertisements directly into the software product.

2. The software developer uses the kit to place the ads into their shareware or freeware product.

3. The software developer distributes their product either on disk or via the Internet.

4. The shareware or freeware products on the end user's computer download advertisements and display them to the end user.

5. The creator of the advertisement pays the adware company a fee for displaying the ad to the end user.

## The Browser Helper Object

A Browser Helper Object (BHO) is simply a small program that automatically runs every time you start your Internet Explorer (IE) Web browser. Typically, BHOs are installed on your computer by another software program. Their integration with the IE Web browser allows them great flexibility with many applications. Though BHOs perform a wide variety of functions, their main purpose is to help you browse the Internet. Most BHOs are legitimate programs and, when working correctly, they add new functions to IE and make your Internet experience more convenient.

While most BHOs are "well-behaved," some do contain adware or spyware that, as described previously in this chapter, surreptitiously monitor the Web sites you visit and report the data to their installer. Even when they do not contain adware or spyware, poorly coded BHOs may cause Web browser or system wide crashes. BHOs have been accused of logging keystrokes while a user is filling out online Web forms at a particular Web site. Some of the more common BHOs are:

✓ Aureate/Radiate

✓ Alexa

✓ Flyswat

✓ Gator

✓ Go!Zilla

✓ RealDownload

✓ Yahoo Companion

## How BHOs Bypass Your Firewall

One concern regarding the use of BHOs is that they are integrated directly into the Web browser. When they access the Internet, it appears as if the access was requested by Internet Explorer. If you are using a bidirectional software-based firewall to protect yourself from spyware or other malicious code, it *will* let any BHO access pass through simply because it assumes that the BHO requests are made by your browser and not as a separate application.

# Detect and Remove — Become a BHO Detective

Several programs are available that assist users in finding and removing poorly written or malicious Browser Helper Objects from computers. Although you can remove BHOs by manually editing the Windows registry, it is recommended that you use software designed for that purpose.

If you want to manually locate and/or remove BHOs from your system registry, you must find and apply the Windows built-in registry editor as follows:

**1.** Click the Start button and go to the Run menu.

**2.** In the Run dialog box, type `regedit` (see Figure 3-2).

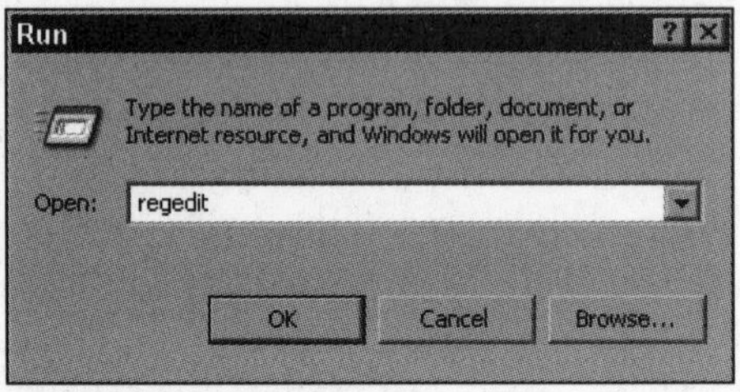

**Figure 3-2:** The Windows Run command dialog box

**3.** Click the OK button or hit the Enter key. The Windows registry editor will be displayed.

**4.** Drill down to the "Browser Helper Objects" registry key (see Figure 3-3) using the following path:
`HKEY_LOCAL_MACHINE\Software\Microsoft\Windows\CurrentVersion\explorer\`
`Browser Helper Objects.`

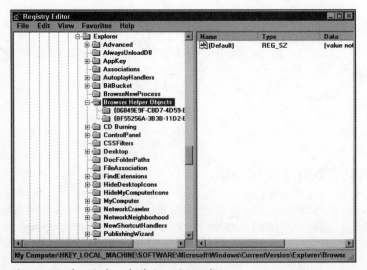

**Figure 3-3:** The Windows built-in registry editor

**5.** Once you have reached the BHO registry keys, you can remove them simply by placing your mouse cursor over the key in question, right-clicking it, then selecting Delete from the drop-down menu.

Keep in mind that deleting the wrong registry key can cause Internet Explorer or other programs to no longer function properly; therefore, this procedure should be attempted only by individuals who are thoroughly familiar with registry editing and function, and even then, only when they are sure that they have correctly identified the offending BHO key.

How does one determine the correct key to remove? Under each key, there are yet more keys — strings of numbers, known as Globally Unique Identifiers (GUIDs), that appear in braces:

```
{004A5780-FF59-11d2-B512-0090271D24F7}
```

Once you have located the GUID, look in the section of the registry called HKEY_CLASSES_ROOT for a matching GUID. The information under that key will tell you which Dynamic Link Library (DLL) is being used, which may in turn help you identify which utility this BHO belongs.

The faster, safer, and recommended way to locate and deactivate BHOs is to use a program designed specifically for that task. BHOCaptor (see Figure 3-4), which can be downloaded for free at www.xcaptor.org, is a user-friendly and useful utility for locating and deactivating BHOs in a Windows-based computer. Deactivation may be preferable to deleting simply because deactivation is reversible in the event you experience a problem with Internet Explorer after deactivation.

The following steps demonstrate how to use BHOCaptor to deactivate a BHO:

**1.** Double-click the program icon.

**2.** The BHO window appears, illustrating all installed Browser Helper Objects.

**3.** The user selects a BHO from the available list and then clicks the Deactivate button to disable the selected BHO.

Users can reactivate a BHO by following the same procedure, only clicking the Activate button instead.

Another excellent BHO locator and removal tool is PC magazine's BHO Cop (see Figure 3-5), which locates and allows you to remove BHO registry keys. Since removing a BHO key can cause operational problems within Internet Explorer, BHO Cop first backs up and saves your old configuration, allowing you to easily "roll back" to your previous settings in the event something goes awry. BHO Cop is a download available at no cost and can be found at www.zdnet.com/downloads.

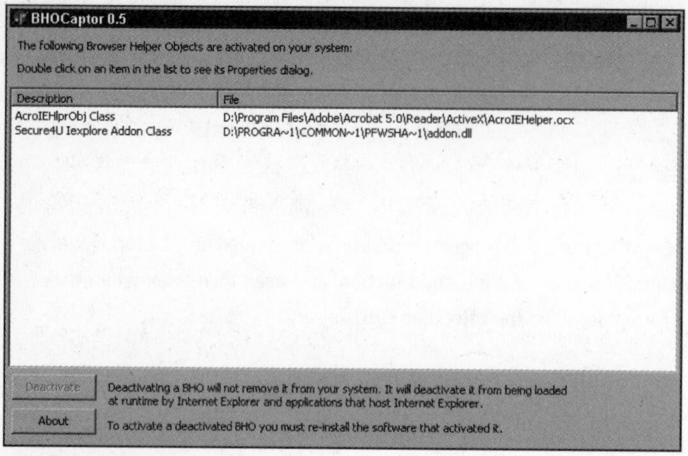

**Figure 3-4:** BHOCaptor 0.5

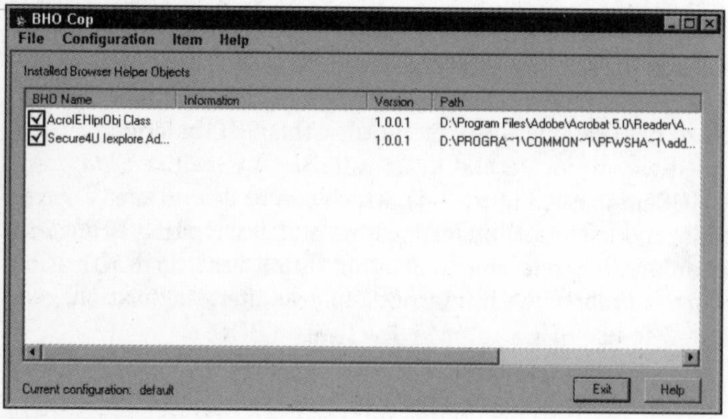

**Figure 3-5:** BHO Cop

The following steps illustrate how to use BHO Cop to back up and then remove a BHO registry key:

1. After installing the program, go to the Start menu ➪ Programs ➪ BHO Cop.

2. A window appears with a list of all correctly installed BHOs.

3. The user selects the BHO they wish to remove by unchecking the appropriate box to the left of the BHO name.

**note**

A check in the box (the default) indicates that the BHO is enabled. To disable a BHO, simply uncheck the box.

Manipulating data in the registry always carries some degree of risk. For this reason, BHO Cop backs up your registry data so you can restore your settings in case something goes wrong. When started, BHO Cop generates or updates a file named `Rescue.reg`. To restore the registry keys and undo the BHO changes you made in the current session of BHO Cop, close down BHO Cop and double-click on `Rescue.reg`. This is equivalent to running the Windows registry editor (`Regedit.exe`) and selecting Registry ➪ Import Registry file. The final step is to delete the `Bhocop.ini` configuration file.

# Malware — Malicious Code *Made*-to-Order

The word *malware (mal*icious soft*ware)* refers to a wide variety of malicious code, scripts, or programs that produce an effect that is uncontrolled and unintended by the user. As shown in the case of adware or spyware, malware often works surreptitiously, hiding its effects from the user. However, as we enter the new millennium, we are faced with an entirely new wave of destructive software that goes beyond the typical computer virus, worm, or Trojan horse program. Until recently, virus writers and computer hackers were basically two distinct breeds, with the virus writer seeking to disrupt and the malicious hacker seeking to infiltrate, control, and steal. However, the distinction between the two may soon end, with far-reaching and serious consequences. We are about to see a new generation of malware that can be delivered like a virus, either through online chat programs or e-mail attachments, but that also goes a step further by manipulating the company network. Early-generation malware such as the infamous Back Orifice Trojan horse created a back door, or "hole," via a common network service, then quietly waited to be contacted by its creator. Early malware wreaked havoc until anti-virus software and firewalls became popular; however, newer, more advanced malware is being used to counteract those defensive measures.

## Next-Generation Malware — Malicious Software Grows Up

Highly sophisticated and refined malware such as the RingZero Trojan horse gained notoriety towards the latter part of 1999. This next-generation Trojan employed a user's network to pass specific information back to a particular Web address. It aimed to find the location of a particular type of server, known as a Web proxy, located somewhere on a company's network. The focus of RingZero was probably to collect information about all proxy servers on the Internet and compile that data into a central database for future use.

On October 22, 1999, the National Infrastructure Protection Center issued the following public announcement about RingZero:

ADVISORY 99-024
"RingZero Trojan Program"
October 22, 1999

RingZero demonstrates a new, aggressive reconnaissance technique that is currently being used to map target systems and could be used to support malicious activities. Large numbers of government and commercial sites have seen an unusual amount of network scans coming from multiple origins in the past two months. This activity involves a Windows-based Trojan program called RingZero that is designed to infect client machines without the users' knowledge.

This Trojan appears to be a remote controlled distributed scanning engine that is configured to scan ports 80 (common port for World Wide Web), 8080 (common port for World Wide Web Proxy Services), and 3128 (common squid proxy services) and send collected IP addresses and open port information to what appears to be a data collection script running on a machine located at www.rusftpsearch.net.

Its origins are currently unknown, but unconfirmed reports indicate that it was distributed initially via e-mail, possibly with another program such as a screensaver or game. Although RingZero appears to contain no malicious code, each infected client machine continues to perform electronic reconnaissance every time it is turned on.

As cited by NSWC's John Green, this activity reflects a significant advance in distributed attack technology because of Ring Zero's transmission rate; dynamic configuration options (may be able to go from scanning to attacking); and automated result consolidation.

NIPC recommends using the System Administration, Networking and Security (SANS) Institute published information to block unneeded services as a defense against the RingZero Trojan. If services on ports 80, 8080, and 3128 are used, system administrator personnel should examine outbound traffic originating from these ports that are directed to unknown or suspicious sites. The NIPC strongly recommends that activity of this nature be reported to the appropriate CERT organizations, information technology security organizations, or the NIPC.

Trojan horse programs such as RingZero often exploit various communication ports to send and receive information. The practice of monitoring and closing ports is crucial to network defense. This process is further explained at various points throughout Chapters 6 through 9.

## Malware Mobility

An important feature found in many types of malware is the ability to pass easily through firewalls. The much-publicized Melissa virus used the Windows e-mail service, while the RingZero Trojan horse used the Microsoft Web service. Since both of these common services are now crucial for day-to-day business operations, they usually traverse firewalls unencumbered. Malware developers are always looking for vulnerable areas to exploit, such as the element of human error.

# Human Error

One of Murphy's "laws of computing" goes something like this: To err is human, but to really foul things up requires a computer. Computers are nothing more than machines that can rapidly manipulate binary code. Contrary to the stance taken by many in the field of Information Technology, computers cannot "think" for themselves. They merely perform functions that they are programmed to. Programmers are human, and humans make mistakes. Even the mighty Microsoft has turned out software that contains bugs in its code. Once bugs or flaws have been discovered (usually by hackers or virus writers), patches become available to "repair" the flaw. Thus, individuals and businesses that use a particular software product must frequently check for product updates. Although it is programmers who create computer software and continuously update programs when flaws are discovered, it is ultimately the responsibility of network or system administrators to regularly seek out and install program updates or revisions, particularly when security vulnerabilities have been discovered. Poor administrative practices, lack of knowledge, appropriate tools, and controls combine to leave the average system vulnerable to attack.

Research promises to alleviate the inadequate supply of tools and applicable controls. These controls, however, tend to be add-on controls. It would be better to deliver a secure system at the onset, rather than building a secure system from parts on a continuing basis. The average administrator has no idea how to perform the required modifications, even when he or she is inclined to do so.

Updating software products and other human-element security factors are covered in detail in Chapter 8.

There are two sides to the human error equation: the programmer who writes the code, and the end user who makes use of the code. Common sense goes a long way in protecting your organization and its networks from malicious code. The National Infrastructure Protection Center (NIPC) slogan "Trust But Verify" succinctly reminds us that safe e-mail procedures must be followed by everyone as we enter the new millennium. Following are the NIPC's seven steps to safe e-mail procedures, as taken from the NIPC Web site (www.nipc.gov) and their online document *Trust but Verify: A Guide to Using E-mail Correspondence:*

1. **Close the preview pane of your e-mail program.** The preview pane is the feature that shows you the contents of an e-mail before you choose to open it. It is often displayed below the pane that displays a list of e-mails, their titles and time of receipt or transmission.

2. **Disable the Java script and Active-X features of your Web browser.** Java and Active-X were designed to run more advanced features and to use services or make changes on the computer you are using. Unless these features are explicitly required, it is safer to deactivate them to prevent malicious scripts from infecting or compromising the computer or the network.

3. **Equip your computer with an anti-virus program,** maintain the most current version, and select the user options that give you the most protection. There are several different types, not just different brands. Some anti-virus programs search for specific file "signatures," others monitor a computer program's activity and prohibit virus-like behavior. There are also cost-free scans from vendors via the Internet that can scan your hard drive and removable disks. Ensure that your anti-virus program will screen attached files.

4. **Save attachments to a disk before opening them.** Do not open the attachment directly from the e-mail program. Save it to a disk, preferably a removable disk, and then scan the disk with an anti-virus program.

5. **Do not open e-mail attachments from strangers,** regardless of how enticing the subject line may be. In addition to e-mails containing damaging computer viruses, there has been malicious spam. The spam plays off human curiosity. It may be an e-mail message or a redirection to another web page. The action is often to solicit donations to organizations claiming to be charities, or barraging computers with pop-up advertising.

6. **Be suspicious of *any* unexpected e-mail attachment, even from someone you *do* know.** It may have been sent without that person's knowledge from an infected machine. The Sircam virus continues to spread by automatically e-mailing itself between users who expect to communicate.

Also, someone might have stolen a trusted person's password and is pretending to be that trusted person.

7.   **Verify suspicious e-mail.** In the event you receive e-mail from someone you know, that has a suspicious title or attachment, contact the sender or the program coordinator by telephone or send them a new e-mail asking them to verify that they did intend to send you that e-mail.

These are *basic* steps that outline malicious code defense.

It has recently been discovered that certain types of malicious code scripts embedded in the body (HTML code) of an e-mail message can automatically execute via the preview pane *even when the user does not actually open and view the e-mail message.*

E-mail procedures are covered in more detail in Chapters 8 and 9. To learn more about the NIPC and the valuable computer security resource they provide, you can visit their Web site at www.nipc.gov.

# Summary

The definition of malicious code encompasses more than just the typical virus worm or Trojan horse program. With anti-virus software and personal firewalls becoming more commonplace, those who write malicious code are finding new methods and vectors to ply their trade. By using freeware and shareware with embedded malicious code, unsuspecting computer users are getting more than just free software. Surreptitiously embedding malicious code in advertisements or downloadable programs without a user's input or knowledge is generally considered an invasion of privacy, but is nevertheless a common occurrence. This chapter includes the following key points:

✓  Spyware programs, which can come from many sources, are often placed on a user's computer without their knowledge or consent. The most common means of distribution is through freeware and shareware programs.

✓  Badware or poorly-written free software can cause more harm than good by crashing your system or rendering it inoperable. It often contains spyware code, as well.

✓  Adware sometimes contains a spyware program that monitors users' online activities and sends the data it collects to its creator or another interested party.

✓  The broad term *malware* encompasses all forms of malicious software. What is considered malware is constantly changing, as computer users become more savvy and aware of its threats.

✓  Human error may allow malicious code to enter your network via poor system administration practices or unsuspecting employees who fail to take simple precautions and follow the rules of safe e-mail messaging.

## Chapter 4

# Types of Viruses, Trojan Horses, and Malicious Code

### In This Chapter

- ✓ UNIX viruses
- ✓ Linux viruses
- ✓ 16-bit viruses (DOS/Windows 3.x)
- ✓ 32-bit viruses (Windows 9x, Me, NT)
- ✓ Boot sector viruses
- ✓ Polymorphic viruses
- ✓ Stealth viruses
- ✓ Multipartite viruses
- ✓ Macro viruses
- ✓ Trojan horse programs
- ✓ Internet worms
- ✓ Network-aware viruses
- ✓ Malicious ActiveX code
- ✓ Malicious Java scripts
- ✓ Malicious VB (Visual Basic) scripts
- ✓ Scrap file viruses
- ✓ Self-activating "no-click" viruses

TEN YEARS AGO, VIRUSES were mostly executable programs (`.exe`, `.com`, `.bat`, and so on) that typically spread via shared infected computer disks. One of the first executable viruses to inflict widespread casualties surfaced in 1991. Upon close inspection, it was discovered that this virus would erase PC hard disks each year on March 6, the birthday of renaissance painter Michelangelo. The "Michelangelo virus," as it was quickly dubbed, spread around the globe, infecting numerous computers running MS-DOS or one of the similar variants of this popular operating system. **43**

Michelangelo retained a low profile until January 1992, when a key U.S. computer manufacturer, Leading Edge, announced publicly that it had accidentally shipped approximately 500 personal computers contaminated with the virus.

About a month later, another major company, DaVinci Systems, admitted that they had accidentally distributed 900 floppy disks infected with the Michelangelo virus during the previous month. Much has happened in the ten years that have since transpired—most importantly, the Internet revolution, which changed the way information is shared. Malicious code that once used a disk to spread now rides on the information superhighway. As computers have become more powerful and are used by more individuals around the world, so too have viruses and other malicious code evolved. In order to understand the threats posed by various malicious codes, it is important to analyze not only why, but how, they have come into being. This understanding enables programmers, administrators and users to better defend their systems against such malicious intent. This chapter focuses on the various types of malicious code and the damage they routinely inflict on computers and networks worldwide.

Protecting yourself and your network from these malicious threats is covered in Chapters 8 and 9.

# UNIX Viruses

Computer viruses have been around for almost as long as computers. The term *computer virus* was formally defined by Fred Cohen in 1983, while he was performing academic experiments on a Digital Equipment Corporation VAX computer system. Fred Cohen is best known as the inventor of computer viruses and virus defense techniques. However, his work on information protection extends far beyond the computer virus realm. In the 1970s, he designed network protocols for secure digital networks carrying voice, video, and data, and he helped develop and prototype the electronic cashwatch for implementing personal digital money systems.

UNIX is an operating system developed by Bell Laboratories in the late 1960s. Despite three decades of use, it is still regarded as one of the most powerful, versatile, and flexible operating systems in the computing world. While initially designed for medium-sized minicomputers, the operating system was soon moved to larger, more powerful mainframe computers. As personal computers grew in popularity, versions of UNIX found their way into those units, and a number of companies produce UNIX-based machines for the scientific and programming communities. One of the most important features of UNIX was that security was built-in during its design, not added as an afterthought. Despite this built-in security, UNIX systems are susceptible to hostile software attacks. However, many of the conventional attack methods applied to other types of operating system environments, such as Windows or Macintosh, are insufficient to cause harm in the more complex environment provided by the UNIX operating system. The popularity and widespread use of the Windows operating system currently makes it the focus for malicious code attacks.

With the exception of a few worms, there has been little malicious code developed to attack UNIX operating systems. While viruses are currently not a major risk on UNIX platforms, file integrity checkers and special audit packages are frequently used by system or network administrators to detect file changes made by other types of attacks. The challenges of malicious code defense faced by users today are good "barometers" of the types of problems users will be experiencing in the future, regardless of which operating system becomes predominant.

# Linux Viruses

Linux is a free UNIX-like operating system originally created by programmer Linus Torvalds with the assistance of developers around the world. Linux is developed under the GNU General Public License, and its source code is freely available to everyone. Linux may be used for a wide variety of purposes, including networking, software development, and as an end-user platform. Linux is often considered an excellent, low-cost alternative to other more expensive operating systems. For many reasons, Linux systems present a difficult environment for viruses. A virus that infects a single system will have only limited access rights, and as such, will have a hard time infecting various files on even that one system. Propagation to another Linux system requires getting over a whole new set of hurdles. Finally, writers producing free software are usually clever enough to avoid creating easy propagation mechanisms for viruses. Even in cases where they do not avoid creating such mechanisms, other programmers will quickly close any holes they discover that were inadvertently left behind. Despite its UNIX-like core, Linux is not completely immune to virus attacks. Between 2000 and 2001, virus experts saw an increase in malicious code written specifically for the Linux operating system. This was mainly due to its increased popularity. New graphical user interfaces (GUIs) and improvements in the ease with which the operating system is set up and configured now make Linux more attractive to less experienced computer users.

Ramen is one example of a recent Linux worm that propagates from one Linux-based server to another. Working in a manner similar to that of the Morris worm of 1989, Ramen affects systems running Red Hat Linux 6.2 and 7.0, two popular types of Linux distributions. Ramen infects these Linux systems by exploiting two known security vulnerabilities. Where successful, the worm replaces the Web server's default page to one that contains the following text:

```
RameN Crew - Hackers loooooooooooooove noodles
```

While this worm does not cause a great deal of harm, it does prove that no operating system is immune to malicious code attack.

# 16-Bit Viruses

Long before operating systems like Windows or the MacOS filled our screens with colorful icons and fancy drop-down menus, DOS ruled the personal computing world. Whenever you wanted a computer to perform a specific function, you were required to type a command at the DOS prompt. The computer's command interpreter would then determine what you requested and carry out the function. DOS was the accepted operating system until the first useable and stable version of Windows became popular. The "DOS era" roughly spanned the years 1980 to 1992 and was witness to rapid advancements as computers quickly became more popular and powerful. DOS itself was subject to revisions and improvements, not unlike the operating systems of today.

The first IBM personal computers used the Intel 8086 microprocessor, which was a 16-bit processor. The bit aspect of a processor refers to the amount of data (data width) that the microchip can process at any given time. Microsoft designed the DOS operating system around the 16-bit microprocessors available at the time. In the DOS era, viruses were simple and spread mostly via infected floppy disks. As mentioned earlier in this chapter, the infamous Michelangelo was one of the earlier widespread destructive viruses, but many others left their mark years before Michelangelo made its digital debut.

Before the personal computer revolution of the 1980s, home computers were essentially toys. Serious computers were primarily utilized by professionals. During the 1980s, personal computers started to reach homes and businesses due to the tremendous popularity of the IBM PC (circa 1982) and the Apple Macintosh (circa 1984).

In the early 1980s, 16-bit DOS viruses were more annoying than destructive. While DOS was a popular target for viruses, Apple computers were not immune. In 1982, the Elk Cloner virus had many Macintosh users scrambling for a cure. The symptoms of this virus included the printing of a poem along with its version number, indicating how many replications had occurred since the original. The virus replicated by placing a copy of itself onto any disk placed in the infected computer.

Towards the latter part of the 1980s, more destructive viruses began to surface. They started to attack a specific area of floppy and hard disks called the *boot sector*. The boot sector is the area on a disk where special computer code resides that allows an operating system like DOS or Windows to load. The new viruses attempted to corrupt a computer's entire hard disk and, if successful, destroy all the data stored on the infected hard drive, virtually transforming the computers into digital paperweights.

## 16-Bit Windows — DOS Gets a Graphical User Interface

In the mid-1980s, Intel Corporation — the world's leading microprocessor manufacturer — developed a new, more powerful and unique chip called the 80286. The Intel 80286 was a much more powerful microprocessor than the 8086. This new "286" chip was still a 16-bit processor like the 8086 but it had special functions that allowed it to perform tasks none of its predecessors could. The 80286 introduced several new features, the most important being its ability to operate in two different modes: real mode and protected mode.

The ability to operate in real mode was retained in the 80286 to permit backward-compatibility with programs written for the older 8086 processors. In real mode, the 80286 operated at 24 bits to utilize up to 16 megabytes (16 million bytes) of memory. In protected mode, however, the 80286 operated at 32 bits, allowing it to address up to one gigabyte (one billion bytes) of memory. Having the ability to use more RAM opened the door to the development of more sophisticated, user-friendly graphical operating systems such as OS2 and Windows.

Around 1993, Microsoft released Windows 3.1, the first stable and practical version of their graphical consumer operating system. It quickly became popular with both business and home consumers alike. The Windows 3.1 operating system gave users the ability to click icons to activate programs rather than enter long strings of typed commands, as was required in MS-DOS. While Windows 3.1 was technically a Graphical User Interface (GUI)–type operating system, it still used 16-bit DOS to provide much of its functionality. Thus, many of the viruses written exclusively for DOS could still wreak their havoc under Windows, since Windows essentially used DOS as its "engine."

## Enter Protected Mode and Virtual Memory

While Windows 3.1 was mainly a 16-bit operating system, one of its features made it more powerful than DOS alone—namely, the ability to use the protected mode functions of the newer processors. By the time Windows 3.1 reached the computing mainstream, the 80286 processor had given way to even more powerful processors, such as the Intel 80386 and 80486. Like their predecessor, these newer processors were also capable of operating in protected mode, allowing them to address up to one gigabyte of memory, far in excess of the one megabyte limitation of the 8086 processor that operated only in real mode.

GUI (graphical-based) operating systems by nature present much higher memory requirements than the less complex, text-only DOS-type operating systems. Since at that time computer memory was expensive, virtual memory working in conjunction with protected mode was designed into Windows 3.1, allowing it to use the physical space on the hard drive as "virtual" memory. When the physical memory was exhausted, Windows 3.1 would "swap out" any idle portions of physical memory to the hard disk, freeing up more physical memory to run programs. When the program was finished and closed, Windows would swap the original data segments back into the physical memory where it originally resided.

Protected mode is a powerful feature that not only allows the addressing of much larger amounts of physical and virtual memory, but also helps "shield" computers from early 1980s real-mode DOS viruses. To date, virus authors have not successfully harnessed protected mode operations. Although some have attempted to master it, their efforts have largely been unsuccessful due to the complexity of its interaction with vital operating system components.

As the next section explores in more detail, in August of 1995, Microsoft released a 32-bit protected mode operating system called Windows 95. This new consumer-oriented operating system incorporated a more powerful 32-bit computer code that fully harnessed protected mode functions. The virtual nature of this 32-bit protected mode operating system helped protect it from many of the real-mode viruses that plagued its predecessor, Windows 3.1. However, while Windows 95 was designed primarily as a 32-bit operating system, it still utilized a substantial amount of 16-bit programming code in order to remain backward-compatible with the well-established base of Windows 3.1 programs.

**note**

Virtual memory is a technique that operating systems use to make up for a lack of actual physical memory. The function of virtual memory is to extend the available memory space (set of addresses) that a computer program can utilize. For example, virtual memory might contain five times as much memory address space as the computer's physical (main) memory. A program using all of virtual memory, therefore, would not be able to fit in main memory all at once. Nevertheless, the computer could execute such a program by copying portions of the program needed directly into main memory at any given point.

# 32-Bit Viruses (Windows 9x/Me/NT)

In August of 1995, amid much fanfare and publicity, Microsoft released its flagship consumer operating system, Windows 95. This new 32-bit operating system was designed to take full advantage of the more powerful 80486 and Pentium processors that began to emerge at that time.

Because it was mostly a 32-bit operating system, Windows 95 did not rely heavily on older 16-bit DOS technology (as did Windows 3.1) for critical system functions. It did, however, retain its ability to run older 16-bit applications to keep it compatible with the large base of DOS and Windows 3.1 applications many computers were still using.

One especially nice feature of Windows 95 was that many of the older viruses that plagued Windows 3.1 were ineffective under the 32-bit Windows 95 operating system. Accordingly, virus writers took on the challenge of investigating the new OS and began developing new Win95-compatible viruses. All of Microsoft's subsequent operating systems, such as Windows 98, Me, NT, 2000, and XP, are 32-bit operating systems. Less popular operating systems, such as Linux and IBM's OS-2, are also 32-bit operating systems, with their own share of viruses; however, they are not major targets due to their limited popularity.

All of these new operating systems proved to be tough malicious code adversaries for quite some time, and by early 1999, there were only a hundred or so "true" 32-bit Windows viruses. Today, 32-bit viruses number in the thousands and are increasing with no sign of letting up. While no operating system is immune to viruses, Windows has always been the main target for malicious coders, simply because it is the most popular and widely adopted consumer operating system.

## 32-Bit Windows Viruses — The Early Years

Not long after the release of the Windows 95 operating system, the first virus specifically written for it was unleashed. The Win95/Boza virus, which surfaced in late 1995, was written by a member of the Australian VLAD (*Virus Laboratory And Distribution*) virus writing group. This prolific virus-authoring group was responsible for around 40 viruses during its existence. The group originated in Australia, but attracted several international members. By the final year of its reign, its membership list had changed several times. Most of the VLAD members retired in 1996, which appeared to be the beginning of the end for this group.

It took some time for malicious coders to understand the new Windows 95 operating system. During the latter part of 1997, viruses specifically aimed at Windows 95 and NT began to appear regularly. Windows NT (New Technology) was a business-oriented full 32-bit robust network operating system that did not rely on any DOS code for operation.

Towards the end of 1997, virus writer Jacky Qwerty/29A, a member of the 29A virus writing group, unleashed Win32/Cabanas.A, the first Win32 *and* Windows NT-compatible virus. Win32s are special programming codes incorporated into the Windows operating systems that allow 16-bit Windows to run 32-bit applications. For example, Win32s allow Win32-based applications to run on Windows 3.1 and Windows NT. Win32 is an extension for 16-bit Windows (3.1$x$) that allows it to use 32-bit programs originally written for 32-bit Windows versions, such as Windows NT 3.$x$, 4.0, and Win9$x$. Because of this, Win32/Cabanas.A was designed to be compatible with Windows 2000, NT, Win9$x$, and even Windows 3.1 when extended with special Win32 patching software.

Because of its ability to affect all Microsoft operating systems, Win32/Cabanas.A turned Microsoft's dream of multi-operating system Win32-compatibility into a nightmare. New Win32 viruses eventually replaced DOS-based viruses, forcing the 16-bit DOS-based viruses to gradually become extinct.

The 29A virus writing group released a great number of 32-bit viruses, some of which were more successful than others. The Win95/Marburg virus drew worldwide attention when several publications unintentionally shipped the virus with CD-ROMs that were included in their magazine covers. This commercial outbreak of the Win95/Marburg virus was mostly NT-compatible, but flaws in its code did not allow it to spread rapidly with Windows NT-compatible machines.

## The Second-Generation Hardware-Destructive 32-Bit Virus

During 1998, newer hardware-destructive viruses began to rear their ugly heads. Taking a quantum leap over other viruses, the Win95/CIH virus became the first virus to take aim at system hardware. This new virus targeted the computer's hard drive and BIOS (Basic Input/Output System). The BIOS is rudimentary computer code (located on a chip inside the computer) that controls hardware functions and is responsible for loading the operating system.

BIOS functions are covered in detail in Chapter 5.

About a year after the Win95/CIH virus first appeared, a "time bomb" in virus code caused a computer disaster. On April 26, 1999 (the same calendar day as the Chernobyl catastrophe), a large number of computers were damaged after being infected with the CIH virus. The virus, which was quickly dubbed "Chernobyl," destroyed data on the infected computer's hard drives and went even further by modifying or corrupting the aforementioned BIOS chip (located on the computer's motherboard). The dissemination of the CIH virus is widely considered the first major virus attack, since there were no globally spanning computer incidents prior to CIH. CIH was so destructive that it spurred Internet security analyst and programmer Steve Gibson to write a freeware program called FIX-CIH to help victims of the attack completely recover.

If you are interested in learning more about the CIH virus, visit www.grc.com, the Gibson Research Corporation's Web site. Here, you can download the freeware program FIX-CIH and learn more about the workings of the CIH virus.

## Next-Generation 32-Bit Viruses Start to Attack the Core

The central computer code of both the UNIX and Linux operating systems is called the *kernel*. The UNIX/Linux kernel acts as the go-between for programs and computer hardware. In other words, it provides a flexible interface for programs to communicate with all the hardware devices on a computer. The kernel has another important function: the handling of memory management functions for all of the computer's running programs, which ensures that these programs do not monopolize the computer's processing power. UNIX and Linux are not the only operating systems to use a central kernel. The ubiquitous Windows operating system actually uses two of them to provide both 16-bit and 32-bit program functions.

Since Microsoft has always endeavored to remain backward-compatible with older software programs, it includes both a 16-bit kernel (kernel16.dll) and a 32-bit kernel (kernel32.dll) to allow older 16-bit and newer 32-bit programs to function. In UNIX and Linux, it is the kernel that provides the user with robust security, and is well protected from hackers and virus writers. Unfortunately, early consumer versions of the Windows operating systems did not afford the robust kernel protection that was provided by UNIX and Linux. This is another reason why Windows-based computers are routinely attacked and infected by viruses. The latter part of the 1990s introduced a new breed of viruses that began to attack the core component (kernel) of the Windows operating system. Once a virus either modifies or controls the Windows kernel, it can affect all programs that require kernel functions.

## New Virus, Same Results

Not long after CIH made headlines the world over, a new 32-bit virus called W32/Kriz.3862 hit the scene. Detected in August of 1999, this virus was set to be triggered on Christmas of that year. When activated, it would erase an infected user's hard disk and attempt to corrupt the BIOS as well, much like the CIH virus did several months earlier. W32/Kriz.3862 attacked the kernel32.dll (32-bit kernel) of Windows 95/98 and NT systems and replaced it with a version of its own. Once it became the kernel, it could attach itself to and affect any part of the computer that used the kernel. Fortunately, it was detected early and widespread catastrophe was thwarted. However, since it replaced the original Windows kernel32.dll with its own version, the kernel could not simply be repaired by anti-virus software. It needed to be replaced. When the kernel is replaced often, the user must reinstall the entire operating system.

# Boot Sector Viruses

Of all the viruses that can affect a computer, the *boot sector virus* — or *system sector virus,* as it is sometimes called — is one of the most feared. Boot sector viruses are so-called because they plant themselves in a system's boot sector. Boot, or system, sectors are unique areas on a computer's hard disk that contain special programs that are initiated to allow a user to boot up a PC. Boot sector viruses infect the master boot record (MBR) of computer hard drives as well as the boot sectors of floppy diskettes. When you turn on your PC, the processor (or CPU) attempts to start the processing of data. However, since the computer's memory is empty, the CPU has no computer code to execute and no reliable way to locate it anywhere else. CPUs can only access computer data that is stored in memory.

To ensure that a PC can always boot, regardless of which chips were used in its production, manufacturers set a standard: Once a computer is turned on, the CPU will always begin the process of executing data from the same location on the hard disk. Engineers developed a single location on the disk where a computer's BIOS can locate and load the boot program that initiates the process of loading the operating system. The location where this information is stored is known as the *master boot record,* or *MBR.*

Some boot sector viruses that have plagued PCs in the past include the following:

- ✓ **AntiEXE:** Also known as Newbug, this virus causes damage to various computer files, specifically executable (.EXE) files.

- ✓ **AntiCMOS:** Also known as LENART, this virus erases information stored in computers' BIOS, rendering the computer completely inoperable.

- ✓ **Monkey:** This virus damages the hard disk upon infection, causing `Invalid drive type` to be displayed whenever the user attempts to boot up the computer.

- ✓ **Michelangelo:** This virus reformats the hard drive on March 6, causing the loss of all stored data.

- ✓ **Stoned:** Most MBR/BS viruses are based on this original Stoned virus. When infected, the PC displays `Your PC is now Stoned!` during the boot process.

Of all the viruses that exist, boot sector viruses are the most successful. They do so well because they are comparatively easy to write, they take control of a computer at a very basic level, and they are easily concealed. The damage they cause ranges from the simple display of a statement to the complete destruction of data on the hard drive or BIOS. When this type of virus destroys the boot sector on a computer's hard drive, the computer can no longer boot up and load the operating system, rendering it inoperable. Through the mid-1990s, boot sector viruses were the most common type of virus, spreading largely in the 16-bit DOS world via floppy disks.

# Polymorphic Viruses — Sometimes, Change Is Not Good

Virus programs (like all programs that run on your PC) are made up of binary code (zeros and ones). The exact order of that code is called the *virus, or binary, signature,* which is different or unique for each virus. Anti-virus software often uses binary signatures as a way to detect known viruses.

Ordinary, legitimate computer programs normally do not replicate, but viral signatures consist of self-replicating computer code. This unique trait gives anti-virus software an additional feature to look for. Anti-virus programs contain databases of all the different replicating viral signatures that are already known to be in the wild. The programs compare the binary signatures of incoming files against a database of already-known signatures, attempting to determine if the code is suspect. To circumvent this type of detection, a more sinister variety of virus was developed. It is known as a *polymorphic virus,* and its binary signature changes continuously.

## Polymorphic Virus Detection

Polymorphic viruses are the most difficult virus type to detect using anti-virus software. Anti-virus software makers spend large amounts of time, sometimes months, developing the detection routines needed to identify just a single polymorphic virus. They are called polymorphic because they are able to generate many different (yet fully functional) versions of themselves with the intent of avoiding detection by virus scanners looking for a particular binary signature. Such viruses might add bogus instructions somewhere in the program's code, attempting to confuse virus scanners looking for binary signatures that match known viruses. More sophisticated polymorphic viruses actually encrypt the virus code and then decrypt the virus each time it is executed.

The concept of using encryption to avoid detection is not new. When a virus is encrypted, its binary signature is changed. Different encryption programs produce different encryption patterns. Some anti-virus software programs try to detect polymorphic viruses through the encryption pattern used. Those who construct polymorphic viruses often use programs that can transform regular viruses into the polymorphic variety. One such program, the Mutation Engine (MtE), can easily be added to existing viruses. Using the MtE, any virus can be transformed into the polymorphic type. The majority of these programs are now recognized by anti-virus software programs.

## Polymorphic Engines — Tools of the Trade

In 1992, a Bulgarian virus writer who went by the moniker "Dark Avenger" created the Mutation Engine (MtE) and distributed it to other virus authors. The program was accompanied by detailed instructions on how to use it. Today, it is not uncommon to find such programs freely available on underground hacker Web sites. The MtE program is not a virus, but simply an "add-on" product that can be used to provide any virus with polymorphic characteristics, making it undetectable by a signature-based virus scanner.

Several polymorphic mutation and encryption engines perform the same basic functions as MtE. The Trident Polymorphic Engine (TPE), for example, is a module that can be included in programs to give them the ability to produce polymorphic programs. The Nuke Encryption Device (NED) is another polymorphic generator that works similarly to both MtE and TPE. While other viruses use encryption to avoid detection, polymorphic viruses go a step further by "mutating," or changing, every time the virus infects a new host.

# Stealth Viruses — The Unseen Enemy

Like its biological counterpart, malicious code needs only to replicate in order to be considered a virus. However, to be successful, malicious code must also have the ability to remain hidden. The general term for the attempt to remain hidden is *stealth*. Some viruses have binary signatures that are highly visible and are easily detected by anti-virus software. Others use various techniques (for example, polymorphism) to remain undetected. Many of the modern day successful viruses are of the stealth variety. Stealth viruses attempt to take over certain areas of your operating system, all while hiding their existence. The virus can take over system functions, such as those used in the reading of files. These functions are commandeered so that when you examine your system, you see what the virus wants you to see: an apparently uncontaminated, virus-free system. When a virus does this, it is considered a full stealth virus.

The infamous Brain virus was the first known virus detected in the wild. It was the first identified stealth virus, as well. The Brain virus was a boot sector virus that utilized the stealth technique of hiding in a computer's memory (memory resident) in its attempt to remain hidden. It could then affect not only the boot sector of the host computer, but also any floppy disk subsequently placed into that computer. The Brain virus evaded detection by intercepting any attempt by an anti-virus or utility program to interrogate the boot sector and redirecting it to the original boot sector (which the virus had relocated to a different location on the disk), a stealth technique.

Programs such as the Norton Utilities cannot detect contamination by such a stealth virus since any request to examine the boot sector would be redirected to the original (moved) boot sector, making it appear to be in its original location. The Brain virus was written by two Pakistani brothers who owned a computer store in Lahore, Pakistan. They wrote and distributed the virus to determine the extent of software piracy of a particular program they were selling to physicians. The program was not destructive in nature; it simply placed a copyright notice on infected disks, allowing the brothers to track bootleg copies. What they had not anticipated was that the virus would spread beyond their borders and affect computers worldwide.

The U.S. Department of Justice, in conjunction with the FBI, maintains a computer crime Web site at www.cybercrime.gov that contains excellent resources concerning cybercrime law. Here users can research current cybercrime legislation and issues, as well as view actual cases involving the prosecution of hackers, virus writers, and other cybercriminals.

# Multipartite Viruses — The Split-Personality Virus

Multipartite viruses have split personalities. As I discussed earlier, the ultimate goal of a computer virus is to spread. In an effort to meet this objective, virus writers have bestowed another disturbing capacity to their viral creations: the ability to perform the function of two separate viruses. These universal viruses can infect boot sectors as well as system files, enabling them to spread further, attack a wider range of potential targets, and inflict additional damages. Multipartite viruses infect both executable files and boot sectors. Sometimes, they begin their destruction by infecting the boot sectors of hard or floppy disks and then "changing," spreading to other files on a computer. At other times, this process may be reversed — the viruses may affect the files first and then the boot sector. Either way, multipartite viruses can be very destructive.

One example of a multipartite virus was the Flip.2153.A, which first appeared around 1993. On the second day of any month between the hours of 4 p.m. and 5 p.m, systems infected with this virus would have their monitor screens displayed horizontally (or "flipped") (provided that the infected computers were using a certain type of display adapter known as an EGA or VGA). In addition, the virus would infect computers with a hard disk partition greater than 32 megabytes in size. If the hard drive contained such a partition (most did), the virus would alter the partition size by making it smaller (less than 32 megabytes). Reducing partition size without the use of special software designed for that purpose results in the loss of all data on that partition.

# Macro Viruses

Macro viruses have the potential to inflict damage to individual documents but can also affect other computer programs. *Macro viruses,* which began appearing in mid-1995, are computer viruses that spread themselves by exploiting an application's own macro programming language. Macro programming language is used to help automate complex or repetitive tasks. Microsoft Word and Excel are popular programs that make extensive use of macros and are, therefore, frequent targets of macro virus attacks. Macro viruses are, in many ways, similar to other types of viruses.

Macro viruses consist of programming code designed to cause replication under certain conditions. As with all forms of malicious code, they can be written to produce a variety of outcomes. Some macro viruses cause the display of a message; others inflict damage to files or documents. Macro viruses can accomplish any task a computer program is able to perform. Macro viruses do not infect individual programs; instead, they infect documents and templates that use macro functions. Opening a document or template that contains a macro virus allows the virus to infect your computer and thus spread to other documents and templates in your computer.

Some macro viruses are more irritating than destructive. Conversely, certain macro viruses are purely destructive. Because macro viruses are written in a universal macro language, they can run on any software platform that understands macro instructions. For example, the macro virus can infect both Macintosh operating system files and files on a Windows-based computer. Largely seen in Microsoft Office documents, macro viruses abounded in the late 1990s.

To help control such viral outbreaks, some users employed the use of an alternate universal file format called *Rich Text Format (RTF)* that does not include the capability to utilize macros. RTF documents include nearly all of the same formatting information as standard Word document files. However, the RTF format does not support the use of embedded hyperlinks like Word files do. Because many documents today include hyperlinks and other information, macro-enabled Word documents are widely used.

In an effort to protect users from macro viruses, all Microsoft office products starting with Word 97 now include "built-in" macro protection. This feature gave users the ability to adjust the level of macro protection they required when using Microsoft Office products. For example, to set macro security levels in Office XP:

1. Go to the Tools menu when working with any office programs. Select Tools ⇨ Macro ⇨ Security (see Figure 4-1).

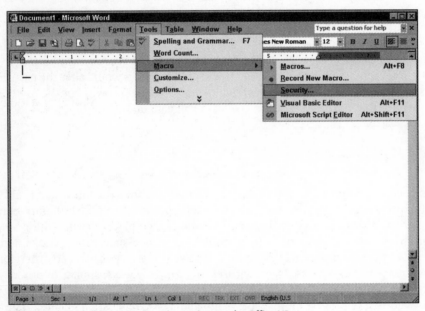

**Figure 4-1:** Accessing macro Security settings under Office XP

2. A dialog box similar to that shown in Figure 4-2 appears. On the Security Level tab, users are encouraged to set their macro security level to High for optimal protection.

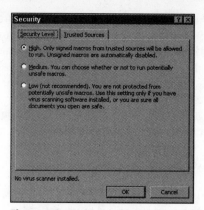

**Figure 4-2:** Setting macro Security settings under Office XP

One of the first macro viruses surfaced in 1995. Called "WordMacro/Concept," it proved that the concept of the macro virus had finally become a reality. Fortunately, this virus did not have a destructive payload and only displayed the text That's enough to prove my point when a user accessed certain infected Word macros. WordMacro/Concept eventually spawned several variants, such as the Concept.FR.B macro virus, which was essentially the same virus as the original "concept" virus but was translated to work with French language versions of Microsoft Word.In summary, two disturbing aspects about macro viruses are apparent:

✓ They are spreading faster than any other virus type.

✓ Due to the ease with which they can be written, their numbers are increasing rapidly.

# Trojan Horse Programs — A Horse of a Different Color

Greek mythology describes an ongoing war between the Trojans and the Achaeans, who realized that they could only win by cunning and not by brute force. After constructing a wooden horse of giant proportions, the Achaeans hid some of their armed forces inside it. Feigning retreat, they abandoned the horse on the plains outside of Troy. Carved into the wooden giant was an inscription that read, "For their return home, the Achaeans dedicate this thank-offering to Athena." The Trojans, fooled into thinking the horse was a "gift," brought it inside the confines of their city walls. That night, while the Trojans were sleeping, the Achaean soldiers sprang from the horse and opened the city's gates, allowing the Achaean army to capture the city of Troy.

A modern-day Trojan horse is a destructive computer program that masquerades as a harmless application. Like its mythological counterpart, a Trojan horse program penetrates a computer disguised as a legitimate program in order to cause harm later. Unlike viruses, Trojan horses do not replicate. Nevertheless, they can be similarly destructive. One of the most sinister Trojan horse programs is the type that masquerades as an *anti*-virus program, but instead helps introduce viruses into your computer.

Trojan horse programs can perform any number of functions, such as destroying your precious data or allowing a malicious hacker to spy on you. Trojan horse programs have been used to siphon data from accounts, search computers for sensitive information, and even spy on the competition in the business arena. One famous Trojan, called Back Orifice, has been credited with numerous attacks worldwide. Developed by the hacker group "Cult of the Dead Cow," this backdoor, remotely administrated Trojan caught worldwide attention. More than 100,000 copies are believed to have been downloaded since its debut in August 1999. Using a scanner designed for the purpose, hackers perform sweeps of the Internet, searching for computers compromised by this insidious Trojan. Once located, the hackers use a special administration tool to connect to the infected computer through a backdoor created by the Trojan, giving the hacker complete control over the victim's machine.

Unlike viruses, Trojans don't usually replicate on their own. Many users have no idea when their computer harbors a Trojan horse program, since those programs often do not hamper computer performance and because they are sometimes missed by anti-virus software.

One solution to removing Trojans from workstations and servers is to routinely reformat and re-install operating systems and applications every three months. While effective, this solution is both impractical and time consuming since any sensitive or critical data must first be backed up. Backing up data also opens the possibility that a Trojan might infect the backup medium as well, thereby re-infecting the host computer once the data is transferred back to its original location. The best solution is to "harden" workstations and servers by taking the necessary proactive steps to *prevent* malicious code from entering the computer's systems in the first place.

## Backdoor Trojans — The Assault Continues

As troubling and disturbing as BackOrifice was, other, more widespread Trojans soon followed. Since its debut in February 1999, the SubSeven Trojan has become the tool "du jour" of hackers targeting Windows machines. Like the infamous Back Orifice, the SubSeven Trojan is divided into two parts: first, the client program that runs on the hacker's own computer, and second, the server component that must be placed into the victim's computer. This placement is usually accomplished through some deceptive means. Trojans often arrive disguised as an electronic greeting card or as a sexually explicit image file. Once the server component is installed, SubSeven's client program allows the hacker to easily monitor a victim's keystrokes, eavesdrop through the computer's microphone, or even peruse the local area network (LAN) to which the victim is attached.

Because Trojans can gain complete control over victim computers, they are sometimes used to commandeer large numbers of computers and then use them to orchestrate a distributed denial-of-service attack (or DDoS). In a DDoS, large numbers of computers are directed to send special "ping" commands to one particular Web address. The intent is to flood that address with so many data requests that its server is overwhelmed, preventing legitimate Web traffic from getting through to any address using that server.

## Hybrid Trojans — The Horse Rides the Worm

As I mentioned earlier, one feature of Trojan horse programs is that they do not replicate on their own. In an effort to change that "shortcoming," hackers began producing self-replicating Trojans. March of 2001 ushered in a new breed of Trojan that used "worm-like" propagation techniques. The Naked Wife Trojan used an e-mail message to send a copy of itself to all the addresses found in a user's Microsoft Outlook address book. Like the AnnaKournikova worm (which promised a glimpse of the attractive tennis star), Naked Wife promised a peek of an unclothed woman in an e-mail message attachment. What it really delivered was a debilitating infection that deleted critical files, thereby making the computer impossible to reboot.

## A Trojan That Fits in the Palm of Your Hand

Malicious code appears to recognize no boundaries. Windows, Apple, UNIX, or Linux — no operating system is immune to its wrath. Even the Palm Pilot personal digital assistant (PDA) has fallen victim to Trojan horseplay. Under the guise of offering a free version of Gambit Studios LLC's Liberty Game Boy emulation software, the Liberty Crack Palm Trojan horse program appeared in August 2000. Liberty is a popular application that emulates Game Boy games on the Palm Pilot PDA. The *Liberty Crack* is a malicious program masquerading as an illegal, but free, version of the Liberty program. When activated, this Trojan could delete all of the applications on a Palm device. As with most Trojan horse programs, temptation through social engineering is used as the tool for initiating the infection.

# Internet Worms — Not Just for the Early Bird

One especially troublesome characteristic of Internet worms is that they can span the globe in a matter of hours. They are also becoming smarter and more dynamic as time passes. Melissa, LoveLetter, BadTrans, PrettyPark, SirCam: Whatever name they bear, they all share the common trait of spreading quickly around the world and leaving serious monetary damages in their wake. In the past several years, dozens of new worms have been introduced and the trend is not likely to end soon. The impersonal nature of the Internet and the increased reliance on e-mail by individuals and businesses both offer virus writers a global playground for unleashing their creations. Internet worms bring Web site traffic to a crawl, disrupt business communications, and cost information technology professionals millions of dollars in man-hours and overtime in their relentless battle to secure their systems.

Because of its universally widespread use, e-mail has been the vector for delivery of the vast majority of Internet worms. While worms have also been written for the Apple and Linux operating systems, worm writers have set their sites predominantly on Microsoft products simply because of the "known" vulnerabilities in several of the Microsoft operating systems and e-mail software programs.

# The Code Red Worm Bypasses Social Engineering

As with the AnnaKournikova and Naked Wife Trojan, social engineering is incorporated in the planning of worm construction. One effective method for ensuring that a worm attached to an e-mail is delivered is to "entice" the recipient into opening the e-mail attachment. A catchy phrase is used, for example, or a glimpse at a provocative picture is promised. While this method proved successful in the past, newer worms such as Code Red had a slightly different modus operandi.

The Code Red worm attacked a known vulnerability in Microsoft's Internet Information Server software (known as IIS). With nearly six million Web servers worldwide running IIS, Code Red posed a serious threat to Internet sites across the globe. A security flaw in IIS gave hackers the prospect of "system level" access to the Web server. System level access is the highest level of access attainable and would effectively give hackers digital carte blanche on that server. The Code Red worm, designed to commandeer the Web servers it infected, used those servers as tools for a distributed denial-of-service (DDoS) attack. For the first 20 days of any month, the worm attempted to spread to as many vulnerable Web servers as possible. From the twentieth day on, it attempted to attack the White House Web site using a DDoS attack. Luckily, Microsoft quickly released a patch to fix this vulnerability before it became too widespread.

# The New Worm in Town

Not long after Code Red made headlines, a spin-off worm called Code Red II was discovered. Code Red II used the same infection mechanism as the original Code Red worm, infecting vulnerable servers by looking for those IIS servers that had not yet been patched. Code Red II uses the attacked computer's Internet Protocol (IP) address to look for nearby systems to infect, operating on the theory that if there is one vulnerable computer, there might be others nearby. The most damaging aspect of Code Red II was that it installed a Trojan-style backdoor on the infected server, leaving the system vulnerable and wide open to any hacker. A hacker, for example, could browse through — even download — files from an infected Web server. Security analysts at the time hypothesized that the worm may have been spread by home computer users who were unaware that Microsoft's IIS Web server software was running on their computers. Not long after the Code Red worms made headlines around the world, the National Infrastructure Protection Center (NIPC) issued the following public press announcement regarding the aftermath of Code Red and Code Red II:

> For Immediate Release August 03, 2001 5:30 p.m. EDT
> Contacts:
>
> Tinabeth Burton, 703-284-5305, tburton@itaa.org — PCIS & ITAA
> Keith Nahigian, 703-622-4494, keithnahigian@yahoo.com — CIAO
> Deborah Weierman, 202-324-8055, dweierman@fbi.gov — NIPC
>
> Code Red — The Aftermath and Behind-the-Scenes Look at the Worm
>     Washington, D.C. — Over the course of the past week, government and industry groups worked together to address the threat of the Code Red Internet worm and to warn the public to take necessary preventative measures to combat its further spread. What is not well-known is the "behind-the-scenes" efforts by technical security experts who did everything from monitor the spread of the worm to personally answer questions from concerned users on how to protect their computers.
>     After a new and stronger version of the Code Red worm appeared in mid-July, industry and government organizations realized the next outbreak could have much more impact on the Internet if

users did not download the software patch to inoculate their system. Going public was not an easy decision, but the impact of not going to the public to ask users for help could have had even worse ramifications, especially if business and home users of the Internet were impacted due to slow response times. There was an unprecedented level of close coordination between government and private sector organizations. Nearly everyone involved in network security or critical infrastructure protection understood the seriousness of this threat. We believe this extraordinary effort significantly blunted the impact of this instance of the worm's infection. We are still not out of the woods — it will be in the "infection" mode until late August 19, 2001, when it switches to "attack" mode. At that time, we will be better prepared to assess how well these efforts paid off.

Because over 1 million individual software patches were applied within the past week, this represents an extraordinary effort for the government/private sector partnership in battling Code Red. Since the patch can be downloaded once and installed on any number of machines, the number of systems actually patched is no doubt higher. Microsoft observed a dramatic increase in the number of downloads during the week of July 30, which suggests that the effort to heighten customer awareness appeared to pay off. Few of the major Web sites were affected by the worm, because many took action after this initial release. The worm would have had a far greater impact if so much effort and cooperation from other industry and government entities had not taken place in the weeks leading up to the Washington, D.C., news conference. Hopefully, public awareness has been raised that a computer needs continual maintenance, especially where security is concerned.

Many countries have processes for handling government security, such as FedCIRC, which is responsible for the security of U.S. government systems. They polled all agencies early in the week to ensure they had secured their internal systems. Getting to small business and home users is much more difficult, as was noted during the response to thousands of inquiries from users around the world. Without the help of volunteers across the security community, it would have been difficult to address, and when these volunteers contacted the owners of infected systems, they got even more cooperation. Comments from Code Red victims included "Thank you. This is one of our partners' systems, housed in our remote data center." "Thank you for the notice. Somehow, this box was missed when we applied the patches." "Thanks in advance. . . . Oh, and thanks for tracking the Code Red scanners on everyone's behalf too. That is a Good Thing you are doing." These are the ones who are now patched. Over the next several days, an attempt to notify the remaining users will be made.

Here are some of the organizations that have been together, day and night, for six days. From the Federal Government: the National Infrastructure Protection Center (NIPC) of the FBI, Critical Infrastructure Assurance Office (CIAO) of the Department of Commerce, and Federal Computer Incident Response Center (FedCIRC) of the General Services Administration. On the private sector side: Computer Emergency Response Team Coordination Center (CERT/CC) of Carnegie Mellon University, Systems Administration and Network Security (SANS) Institute, Microsoft, Internet Security Systems, Inc. (ISS), Cisco Systems, Inc., Partnership for Critical Infrastructure Security (PCIS), Information Technology Association of America (ITAA), Digital Island, Inc., Information Technology Information Sharing and Analysis Center (IT-ISAC), Internet Security Alliance (ISA), UUNet, and America Online.

Self-propagating worms that exploit vulnerabilities in commonly used software platforms will be a vector of choice by hackers as we move forward. These worms require no social engineering and require no action on the part of users, like opening an attachment. As we saw with Code Red, they can hurt us in two ways: they can consume Internet bandwidth during their propagation phase if the numbers are big enough and they can carry harmful payloads, like the instructions to launch against a chosen target. Anyone can be the next target as future worms may result in much more destructive activity.

## The Next-Generation Worm

As you can see from the NIPC press announcement, both the public and private sectors are working hard to combat the new breed of Internet worm. While no operating system can guarantee 100 percent security all the time, computer users will find that a little knowledge goes a long way. Users are now seeing next-generation worms that propagate like ordinary worms but also contain a Trojan component to deliver their payload. The Gokar worm, discovered in December 2001, searched the victim's computer for certain security programs and then disabled them, leaving the computer defenseless. Worms are now starting to incorporate these blended threats and will no doubt use popular file-sharing programs such as Napster and KaZaA as a means for transmission.

# Network-Aware Viruses — Programs *Nobody* Wants to Share

Like people, computers are more productive when they function as part of a team. Networks are all about groups of computers working together and sharing information. Even home users with two or more computers are beginning to see the benefits of sharing information and are jumping on the network bandwagon. A network can be as small as two computers communicating in an office or as large as the entire Internet. As you realize by now, when a virus attacks a computer, the results can be devastating. Malicious code attacks cost companies billions each year in data losses and "clean-up" costs. Virus writers know that organizations are increasingly relying on the Internet to conduct business and share information. As a result, they are developing new "network-aware" viruses.

Malicious code is considered "network-aware" when it has the ability to scan a computer to see if it's connected to another computer for file sharing. Network-aware viruses exploit the file-sharing capability of a network to "share" malicious code with other nodes on that network. Network-aware viruses that use the Internet to spread often outrun the ability of anti-virus companies to quickly find a remedy. In fact, the Melissa worm spread to more than 100,000 computers in its first 24 hours, days before any anti-virus vendor had posted a cure.

One of the earlier network-aware viruses to cause large-scale casualties was the W32/FunLove.4099 worm. First discovered in November 1999, this worm would periodically scan the infected computer for network shares. If other computers were sharing information with the infected computer, the virus would contaminate those computers, as well. In this way, a single computer infected by a virus could spread that virus throughout an entire organization.

More recently, an even deadlier worm, called W32.Magistra.24876.mm, made its way around the globe. This network-aware virus spreads via the Internet through infected e-mails and was able to spread itself over a local area network (LAN). The virus has an extremely dangerous payload and, depending on certain conditions, can erase an infected computer's hard drive data and corrupt the computer's BIOS memory in much the same way that the CIH (Chernobyl) virus did years earlier.

# Malicious ActiveX Code

Years ago, the Internet was only a fraction of the size it is today, and was mostly text-based. Today, the Internet is rich in media content, replete with audio and animation. In order to make a user's Web experience as rewarding as possible, companies like Microsoft developed a special technology called ActiveX that provides the "tools," or components, for connecting ordinary desktop applications to the Web browser. ActiveX allows programmers and developers to create interactive multimedia Web content through the use of programming languages such as Java or Visual Basic. In simple terms, it is ActiveX technology that allows you to open up a Word document or Adobe PDF file directly in your Web browser.

ActiveX is strictly a Microsoft phenomenon, and its components place no restrictions on how it can interact with your operating system. Whenever you download an ActiveX component, you are presented with a "window" that shows the name of the ActiveX code's author and a request for permission to begin installation. This built-in safety mechanism is called *Authenticode* and is used to determine the origin and validity of the ActiveX components.

As wonderful as ActiveX is, it does have one minor shortcoming. Every time you download and run ActiveX components, you convey trust in whoever is asking you to install the components. Consenting to the download (Authenticode) serves only to identify the publisher of the code who is claiming that the integrity of the ActiveX code has been validated. It does not prevent bugs or thwart malicious operation. Since ActiveX controls are actually small programs that are downloaded from Web pages and run directly on your PC, they are capable of performing any action, including stealing and deleting files.

Fortunately, Microsoft has built-in controls that allow a user to adjust their Internet Explorer Web browser's level of security. By opening the Internet Options dialog box located in the Tools menu at the top of Internet Explorer, users can set the security level to medium or higher to prevent any "unsigned" ActiveX controls from being downloaded to their system (see Figure 4-3) Users need to keep in mind that setting this level higher than medium results in a less rich Internet experience. This is due to the loss of some browser functionality due to severe restrictions on the use of ActiveX features and controls. For example, to control the level of security in Windows XP Professional, take the following steps:

1. In Internet Explorer, select Tools ⇨ Internet Properties. The Internet Properties dialog box pops up.

2. In the Internet Properties dialog box, select the Security tab.

3. Click on Custom Level button and set the settings to the desired level via the Reset Custom Settings drop-down menu.

While the previous steps outline the procedure for increasing security in a Windows XP operating system, some older versions of Windows may not allow the user to alter these settings. Users should check their Windows manual or query the built-in Windows Help file for the availability of this option, as well as the specific steps required for their particular version.

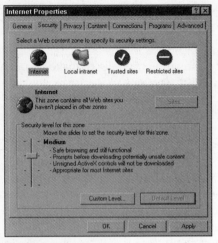

**Figure 4-3:** The Security tab in the Windows XP Pro Internet Properties dialog box

# Malicious Java Scripts — Worse than a Bad Cup of Coffee

Used in Web browsers, JavaScript is a programming language that was co-developed by Netscape Communications and Sun Microsystems for the purpose of "enhancing" the Web browsing experience. JavaScript is sometimes mistaken for the Java programming language, which was also developed by Sun Microsystems. Java is a general-purpose programming language that can be used for developing Web pages and can also be used in non-Internet related programs.

JavaScript is a *scripting language,* meaning that a Web browser simply reads what is written and then interprets the commands. Java, on the other hand, is not directly interpreted by a Web browser because the Java programming code must first be run through a special program, called an *interpreter,* before it can be used by a computer. Java requires more advanced programming knowledge than does JavaScript. JavaScript can be written using an ordinary text editor such as Windows Notepad since it is read and interpreted directly by the Web browser. This means that anyone with a simple text editor possesses all the necessary tools to create a legitimate *or* malicious JavaScript.

Malicious JavaScripts open the door to a number of security and privacy concerns. Running a malicious JavaScript on your browser can allow the capture of passwords or other sensitive information that you believe is protected. Businesses should be concerned because malicious scripts can be used to grant hackers access to restricted or classified parts of the organization's local area network (LAN) via the Internet. Users usually download a malicious JavaScript without their knowledge or consent, as happened in August 2001, when a Japanese auction Web site called Price Loto was hacked and infected with a malicious JavaScript. Users who simply visited the Price Loto Web site using Microsoft's Internet Explorer 4.*x* or 5.*x* automatically downloaded a malicious JavaScript that was programmed to modify the configuration of their computers. PCs affected by the malicious code also experienced other problems, such as difficulty in opening programs and the automatic shutdown of their computers.

# Malicious Visual Basic Scripts — Keep an "Eye" on These

Visual Basic is a powerful programming language used to create programs that can run on a variety of Windows platforms. Visual Basic Scripts (VBSs) are small, easy-to-write Visual Basic programs designed to create fast programs for Windows and the Web. These scripts do not need to be run through a special software interpreter before they can be used by a Windows PC. The scripts are interpreted "on the fly," directly by the operating systems. Unfortunately, VBSs are sometimes created with malicious intent. Many of the recent Internet worms (such as AnnaKournikova, Melissa, and I Love You) were written as VBSs.

Scripts written in Visual Basic always have file names ending with the file extension .vbs, as in LOVE-LETTER-FOR-YOU.txt.vbs, which is the actual full name of the I Love You worm. As you can see with this example, malicious coders often try to "fool" the recipient of the virus by including a double extension such as Example.txt.vbs or Picture.jpg.vbs. They want the victim to open the file thinking it is a "safe" text (.txt) or picture file (.jpg). The last extension is the true extension (.vbs). It reveals that these items are actually VBSs and, like wolves in sheep's clothing, can *potentially* cause great harm.

Malicious VBSs rely on the PC's ability to support the use of VBS files. These files are similar to other executable viruses, with one important difference: They can infect only Microsoft operating systems. VBS viruses have been known to cause a wide variety of damage to the PCs they infect. Visual Basic is an easy programming language, and anyone with minimal coding experience can write just a few lines of code to produce malicious script that will steal valuable data or delete critical system files.

As discussed in Chapter 2, to make the job of creating malicious code as easy as child's play, virus writers have created small programs (or *worm kits*) that can whip up a VBS worm in a matter of seconds. Programs such as the VBS Worm Generator and INDRA Worm Generator are just two examples of the many programs that can be downloaded from underground hacker Web sites, bringing VBS virus writing capability to practically anyone.

# Scrap Files — Malicious Code That Belongs in the Recycle Bin

Imagine a virus that can hide its file type so well that that it can appear to be any kind of file. Since Visual Basic Scripts end with the .vbs extension and many Trojan horse programs are hidden inside executable (.exe) files, their file names can alert you to the possibility that they may contain malicious code *before* you open the files. Any file copied into an open Microsoft Office document (such as a Word, Works, or WordPad document) and then copied and pasted onto the Windows Desktop creates a Windows "Scrap" file. Windows Scrap files end with the extension .shs.

The purpose of Scrap files is to allow text and graphics to be cut and pasted among different Microsoft Office applications. Scrap files can be made malicious when they are used to create and distribute Trojan executable type attacks. Microsoft Office applications can be used to create Scrap files that hide their true executable programs or other content. Since Windows always hides the

Scrap file (.shs) file extension, different file extensions (such as .bmp, .gif, and .txt) may be used to make a program appear to be a harmless file type. This gives anyone with malicious intent the ability to create Trojan executable programs that can "trick" people into opening those programs without suspicion.

To demonstrate how easy it is to create a Scrap file that harbors a hidden executable program, Windows users only may try the following:

1. Click the Start button and select Run. The Run dialog box appears.

2. In the Run dialog box, type **packager.exe** (see Figure 4-4) to activate the Windows built-in Object Packager program (see Figure 4-5).

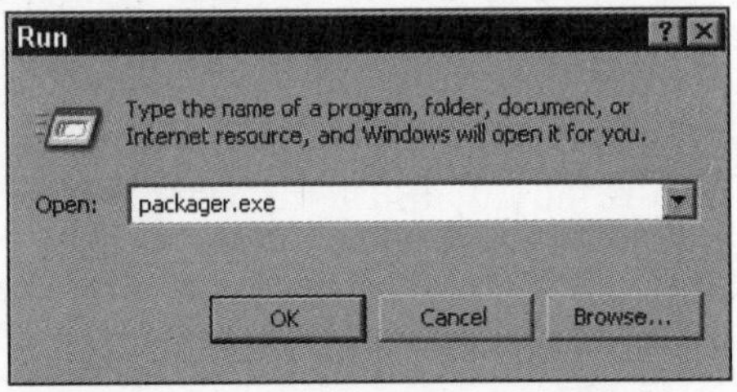

**Figure 4-4:** Running Windows Object Packager from the Run dialog box

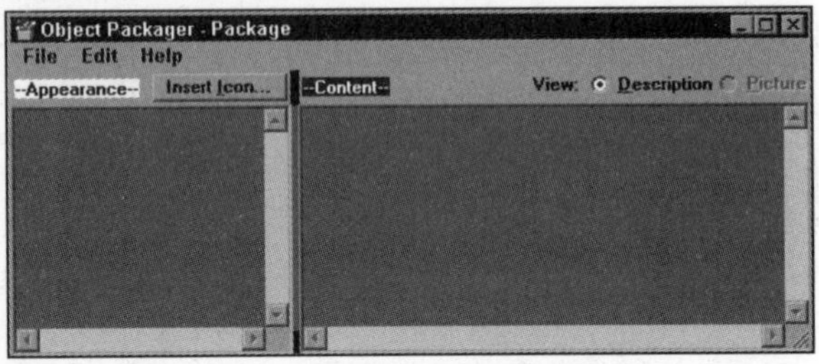

**Figure 4-5:** The Windows Object Packager program

3. In the Object Packager program's drop-down Edit menu, select Command Line.

4. In the Command Line text box, enter **Command.com**.

5. Click the Insert Icon button in the Object Packager program and choose an icon that *looks* like a typical Windows text document. When finished, you should have a picture of the icon in the left pane of the Object Packager program, with the Command.com appearing to the right.

6. Now access the Edit menu from the Object Packager program and select Copy Package.

7. Minimize all open windows and, either on your desktop or in your Windows temp directory, right-click and paste the newly created "packaged" object.

8. A Scrap file appears that you can right-click and rename anything you wish.

9. When you double-click the Scrap object, it launches the Command.com program that simply opens up a "DOS" prompt.

Keep in mind that Command.com is a harmless command by itself; however, it could just as easily be replaced by a simple text command that would destroy the contents of an entire hard drive.

Scrap files are easy to create, yet difficult to detect by anti-virus software programs. Because even small changes can alter the signature of a virus, there is no way for the database of virus definitions used by anti-virus software to keep up with malicious coders. Instead, anti-virus software companies employ heuristic scanning methods to detect Scrap files and other types of malicious code. *Heuristic* virus scanning uses certain intrinsic characteristics to detect unknown viruses. The chief drawback to this type of malicious code scanning is that it sometimes causes false alarms by flagging legitimate programs as potentially harmful.

# The Self-Activating Virus — Sick without the Click

Ten years ago, the idea of the "no-click" virus was just that: an idea. Today, this type of virus is a reality. One of the first of this new breed was the KakWorm, which exploited a known flaw in an ActiveX control. The flaw was actually discovered nine months before the debut of KakWorm, and it made computers running Internet Explorer 5.0 and Microsoft Office 2000 vulnerable to virus attacks even when an e-mail recipient didn't open any attachments. The hole was caused by a programming flaw in an Internet Explorer ActiveX control called `scriptlet.typelib`, and it allowed malicious scripts to run directly within HTML (Web) pages. Consequently, computer users could obtain and spread viruses by viewing malicious e-mail without opening a single attachment. Luckily, the KakWorm did not carry a destructive payload, and Microsoft quickly posted a patch to repair the flawed ActiveX control. The KakWorm was not the first no-click virus to hit Windows computers.

It was shortly before the KakWorm surfaced that the first no-click virus, called "BubbleBoy," popped up. BubbleBoy, which was named after a character from a Seinfeld episode, was relatively harmless. The virus payload was not destructive, but it did alter the infected computer's e-mail settings. The virus simply changed the name of the registered computer owner to "BubbleBoy" and changed the organization name of the computer to "Vandelay Industries," a fabricated company name that Seinfeld character George used in several episodes as a job reference.

Like the KakWorm, BubbleBoy did not require a user to open any e-mail attachment to infect a computer and perpetuate itself. Instead, an *embedded* Visual Basic Script command attached itself to the Outlook address book and sent BubbleBoy-infected e-mail messages to everyone on the address list. Like its predecessor, Bubbleboy took advantage of ActiveX flaws that allowed it to auto-execute in the very popular Outlook e-mail program. While neither of these Internet worms was destructive, they did demonstrate the tenacity of virus writers in their continuing search for program flaws that allow them to create the "new breed" of malicious code that does not require social engineering to be effective and prolific.

# Summary

Over the past several years, viruses, worms, and Trojan horse programs have made headlines around the world because of the damage they cause and the speed at which they spread. Malicious code is the collective term that describes computer viruses, worms, and Trojan horse programs, but it also includes any computer code written to cause harm. Some viruses are simply a nuisance. Some are designed to steal data or otherwise invade privacy. Others inflict a great deal of damage to software programs and hardware devices, with devastating results. The National Infrastructure Protection Center (www.nipc.com) offers numerous resources related to cybersecurity.

See Appendix D for an informative cybersecurity statement by Leslie G. Wiser, Jr., Chief of the Training, Outreach, and Strategy Section of the NIPC.

Key points covered in this chapter include the following:

- ✓ Early 16-bit DOS viruses plagued computers long before Windows made its debut.

- ✓ Windows 32-bit viruses targeted the more sophisticated Windows 95 and NT operating systems.

- ✓ Boot sector viruses were able to alter or destroy a computer's ability to boot up.

- ✓ Polymorphic, stealth, and multipartite viruses can alter their signatures, hide their presence, or take on the characteristics of two or more different types of malicious code.

- ✓ Worms use social engineering in order to spread, and Trojan horse programs can steal data, monitor keystrokes, and otherwise wreak havoc on PCs worldwide.

- ✓ Script viruses use Web page embedded malicious code to cause harm and quickly spread across the Internet.

- ✓ Scrap file viruses hide their file extensions, making them appear harmless (or at least not suspicious) to unwary victims.

# Part II

## Applied Tactics for Malicious Code Defense

**IN THIS PART:**

This part explores the establishment of effective network defense strategies. I start by discussing fundamental networking concepts and the dangers of instant messaging and then delve into the human element in malicious code defense. Although anti-virus software is effective against the threat of malicious code, I discuss the power the organization's human resources have to maintain the overall defense strategy. The design and implementation of an overall anti-virus strategy using a combination of anti-virus software, firewalls, and content monitoring products is reviewed.

# Chapter 5

# Fundamentals Needed for Digital Security

**In This Chapter**

- ✓ Protecting your BIOS
- ✓ Booting and file systems
- ✓ Understanding the File Allocation Table (FAT)
- ✓ Reviewing file system types
- ✓ Considering directories and subdirectories
- ✓ Exploring operating systems
- ✓ The Windows 9x boot sequence
- ✓ Partitioning hard drives
- ✓ Exploring memory (ROM/RAM) issues
- ✓ Protecting the Windows Registry

As THE MAXIM GOES, the best defense is a good offense. This most certainly applies to malicious code. Viruses, worms, and Trojan horses are designed to attack computers and the networks that connect them in any number of ways. Due to the complex interaction of a computer and its operating system, software affects hardware and hardware affects software. Therefore, the inexorable battle to protect computers and networks from malicious code warrants a general understanding of the relationship between computer hardware and operating systems. This chapter reviews the various hardware and software subsystems that are often the locus of malicious attacks. They say if you give a man a fish, he eats for the day, but if you teach a man *how* to fish, he eats for a lifetime. I want to teach you to fish!

## Protecting Your BIOS

As is mentioned briefly in Chapter 4, the *BIOS (Basic Input Output System)* is the rudimentary computer code embedded in chips that are located directly on the motherboard inside the computer. It functions as the intermediary between hardware devices and the operating system.

Whether you are using a Macintosh or IBM-compatible PC, the basic BIOS functions are the same. The BIOS also helps the computer hardware devices locate, load, and utilize the operating system. The first time a computer is turned on, the CPU (processor) retrieves hardware and peripheral information directly from the BIOS. The BIOS is also responsible for booting the computer through instructions that are permanently "burned" directly into the BIOS chip. The BIOS performs all the requisite tasks that are executed at start-up time, including the following:

✓ Running the POST (Power On Self-Test), which tests hardware components for both proper operation and connectivity during start-up

✓ Booting or loading an operating system from either a floppy disk drive, CD-ROM, or hard disk drive

✓ Providing an interface that allows the operating system to find and utilize underlying hardware devices on the computer

Since the BIOS information is permanently encoded into a chip, it cannot easily be altered without the use of a special software program or hardware device designed for that purpose. Information that does need to be changed periodically is stored on a different type of chip (also located on the motherboard) called the *CMOS (Complementary Metal Oxide Semiconductor)*. Working in conjunction with the BIOS, the CMOS's only job is to store user-specific information that needs to be retained and used by your computer during each boot-up. Information stored on the CMOS may include hard disk type and size, display and memory size/type, and even the date and time. Since hardware configurations can vary greatly between computers, the CMOS is responsible for storing specific information about a computer's hardware devices and system settings. A small battery inside the computer allows the CMOS to "hold" this information in memory, even when the computer is turned off.

Most of today's computers have BIOSs, referred to as *"Flash" BIOSs*, that can be updated through the use of a software program provided by the BIOS manufacturer. Flash BIOSs have been the subject of malicious code attacks in recent years. A BIOS that can be updated by software can also be manipulated or damaged by malicious code. This vulnerability was illustrated with the CIH virus, which left many infected machines unable to boot up. The critical nature of the BIOS and its tight integration with the operating system make it a prime target for malicious attack. For this reason, BIOS manufacturers allow for the use of BIOS passwords to help prevent unauthorized users, such as hackers and virus writers, from infiltrating a computer and altering the BIOS settings. When such infiltration and alteration does occur, a computer may exhibit bizarre behavior or may not operate entirely. The exact procedure for setting the BIOS password varies amongst computer systems. In general, users must first access their BIOS settings in order to implement or change a BIOS password. Usually, setup can be entered by pressing a special key combination (Del, Esc, Ctrl+Esc, or Ctrl+Alt+Esc) at boot time. (Some BIOSs allow you to enter setup at any time by pressing Ctrl+Alt+Esc). The AMI BIOS is usually entered by pressing the Del key after resetting (Ctrl+Alt+Del) or by powering up the computer. You can bypass some of the BIOS settings by holding the Ins (Insert) key down during boot-up. This procedure is often helpful where a user has altered the CMOS settings in such a way that the computer no longer boots properly. Users should always check their computer's manual for specific details on how to access their particular BIOS settings.

When malicious code succeeds in *overwriting,* or "flashing," the PC's BIOS, it can render a computer unbootable (even from the floppy drive). In this situation, your only viable solution may be to remove the BIOS chip and re-flash it. Or, if the BIOS cannot be removed or repaired, you may need to replace the entire motherboard. Both of these options are time-consuming and costly. The problem is further compounded if the virus affects more than one computer in an attack on an organization's network.

# Booting and File Systems

On March 6, 1992, individuals and companies around the world turned on their computers to find that a "time bomb" had been ticking inside their IBM-compatible PCs and that this time bomb had gone off. Despite intense media coverage in the months preceding March 6, many companies failed to scan their PCs for the boot sector virus known as Michelangelo. As a result, they suffered one of the worst effects of malicious code: the loss or destruction of data.

Boot sector viruses (covered in Chapter 4) are some of the most troublesome and feared viruses because of their destructive nature and their ability to execute at start-up. The damage capacity of the Michelangelo virus worried many government agencies and prompted the U.S. Department of Energy's Computer Incident Advisory Capability (CIAC) to issue the following bulletin:

The Computer Incident Advisory Capability
Information Bulletin
Michelangelo Virus on MS-DOS Computers
February 6, 1992, 1400 PDT   Number C-15

Name: Michelangelo virus
Platform: MS-DOS computers
Damage: On March 6, will destroy all files on infected disks and diskettes that are accessed.
Symptoms: CHKDSK reports "total bytes memory" 2048 bytes less than expected
Detection: DDI Data Physician Plus! v 3.0C, FPROT 2.01, other anti-viral packages updated since late September 1991

Eradication: DDI Data Physician Plus! v 3.0C, FPROT 2.01, other anti-viral packages updated since late September 1991

Critical Facts about Michelangelo Virus
    The Michelangelo virus, one of the most widespread viruses among MS-DOS systems, infects the Master Boot Record of hard disks and the boot sector of floppy disks. This virus will destroy infected disks on March 6 (Michelangelo's birthday). It infects very rapidly and quietly, usually showing no indication of its presence until a virus detection utility notes its existence.

Infection Mechanism
    This virus is very similar to the Stoned family of viruses (see CIAC Bulletin A-28 for a description of the Stoned virus). When a Michelangelo-infected diskette is placed in the A: drive and the machine is booted, the virus is loaded into memory from the infected floppy disk. It then quickly infects the machine by moving the hard disk's original boot sector to another location on the disk, and installs itself as the boot sector. From then on, any access to another disk spreads the virus to that disk. The disk which infects the hard disk does NOT have to be a bootable system diskette to spread the

infection. Also, all boot infector viruses, such as this one, do NOT affect user files; therefore, a backup prior to eradication will enable full recovery of all user data and programs.

**Potential Damage**

On March 6 of any year, this virus will destroy all data on any disk from which the machine is booted. This occurs by overwriting hard disk sectors 1-17, heads 0-3, tracks 0-255, or the entire diskette with random characters, thus making recovery questionable at best. Note that if your hard disk is partitioned and contains another operating system, such as UNIX, in the area overwritten, that data will be destroyed as well. On all other days of the year this virus lays dormant, merely copying itself to other disks. The infection mechanism of this virus may also cause read errors to occur upon some high density (1.2MB) diskettes.

A problem can occur if a disk is infected by both the Michelangelo and the Stoned viruses AT THE SAME TIME. Both move the 'original' boot sector to the same location on the disk, so when the second infection occurs, the original clean boot sector is destroyed by being overwritten by the first virus. CIAC recommends a low-level format of the disk if this double-infection occurs, although performing the DOS SYS operation may repair a damaged diskette, and performing the undocumented FDISK/MBR operation (in DOS 5.0 only) may repair a damaged hard disk.

**Detection and Eradication**

Because the Michelangelo virus has been discovered relatively recently, only anti-virus products updated since early autumn of 1991 will detect it. If you suspect your PC has this virus and do not have an updated version of a virus scanner, running CHKDSK will report a "total bytes memory" value 2048 bytes less than expected. For example, a PC with 640K of memory will normally return a value of 655,360 bytes; with Michelangelo, that value would be 653,312. Of course, having less "total bytes memory" does not necessarily mean a virus is resident on your machine, as some valid memory resident programs can affect this value as well.

CIAC is aware of at least two publicized cases of this virus being inadvertently distributed by vendors. The vendors involved are Leading Edge and DaVinci Systems; both vendors have made an attempt to contact all recipients of the software involved.

CIAC stresses the importance of checking all incoming diskettes with an anti-viral utility, such as VIRHUNT from DDI's Data Physician Plus! package. CIAC recommends that once a system has had a virus eradicated, it be powered down. The computer should then be observed closely throughout the entire boot-up process. Another virus scan should be performed on the machine to ensure that it is devoid of any virus.

> **note**
>
> While the CIAC announcement you just read was issued to U.S. Department of Energy personnel, it is indicative of the type of announcement that government agencies regularly make to government employees as well as the general public. The CIAC Web site is located at www. ciac.org/ciac and contains a wealth of resources concerning computer security and malicious code threats.

The very first sector on a hard disk, or even a floppy diskette, is called the *boot sector*. The boot sector is a consistent starting point where disk information is stored. It contains special program code necessary to effectuate the starting, or boot up, of the computer. Because this special code is executed each time the PC is booted, it is extremely vulnerable to malicious attack. Damage to the boot sector can make a disk appear to be unreadable by the computer, even if the data stored on the hard drive is not affected. Sectors, on the other hand, are not actual files. They are small "areas" on a data disk that a computer reads as individual units. These sectors are hidden to normal programs, but are essential for a PC's proper operation. They are simply special "reserved" portions located at the beginning of a disk or diskette.

The boot sector also contains another small, but significant, program called the *bootstrap loader*. The bootstrap loader, under direction from the BIOS, physically loads the operating system at start-up. This bootstrap loader program contains information about the physical structure (layout) of the disk, which is known as the *BIOS parameter block*, or *BPB*.

If the disk happens to be a hard disk, a special program called the *partition loader* is included in the boot sector. This program identifies the type of operating system being used (DOS, Windows, or Linux, for example), where the starting and ending sectors are located on the disk, and which partition is bootable. Some hard disks may have several partitions; however, only one of them can be set as bootable. Partitions are covered in more depth later in this chapter. The BPB and partition loader programs are collectively known as the *master boot record*, or *MBR*.

Because the boot sector code is executed every time the computer is started, numerous viruses will "plant" their malicious code here. In so doing, they can load a virus immediately at start-up, even *before* an operating system containing anti-virus software is loaded. This practice accomplishes the virus writer's objectives: to get the malicious code executed frequently and to perpetuate its spread. From a technical standpoint, there is no better location for malicious code than the boot sector. It is automatically executed *every* time the PC is started and *prior* to the loading of any defense programs. To help combat this practice, many BIOS manufacturers have a "built-in" boot sector protection feature.

BIOS boot sector protectors work by safeguarding your hard disk's boot sector and partition sector (MBR) from being overwritten by malicious code. They are mostly effective against boot sector viruses, but they have also been known to cause false alarms when a user attempts to upgrade the computer's operating system. With the rare exception of the multipartite virus, boot sector viruses are spread only via infected disks or CD-ROMs.

One simple boot sector protection measure that users can take is to adjust the BIOS in the computer so that it boots from the hard drive rather than from a floppy disk as some computers are factory-set to do. This circumvents the possibility that a boot sector virus will be transferred to a host computer if the computer tries to boot from an infected floppy unintentionally left in the drive. In general, the steps required to enable BIOS boot sector virus protection or to change the boot drive sequence are as follows:

1. Turn the system on.

2. Press the appropriate key during the POST to access the BIOS Setup.

3. Locate the boot sector virus protection setting in the menus and set it to "Enabled".

4. Select "Save Changes" and exit. The computer restarts.

Since methods of accessing the BIOS settings vary, users may wish to consult their computer's manual or the BIOS manufacturer for instructions on how to change the boot drive sequence.

# File Allocation Table — The Skinny on the FAT

You find far fewer Mac users worldwide than PC users, which may be the reason why thousands of viruses focus their attacks on IBM-compatible PCs and only a handful attack Macintosh computers. Malicious coders usually target the most widely adopted and used computers and operating systems.

Most network PCs and servers run one "flavor" or another of UNIX or Linux. However, these operating systems are still not widely used, due to their complex nature and high learning curve. Windows, also available in a number of "flavors," is subject to far more attacks from malicious coders not only because of its popularity but also because it contains certain inherent vulnerabilities. All the popular consumer versions of Windows (3.1, 95, 98, and Me) continue to use the older DOS-style (FAT) storage system for storing information on the hard disk. With this type of system, data can be more easily lost or destroyed by malicious code. The industrial-strength versions of Windows (NT, 2000, and XP) allow for the use of the faster and more robust file system called *New Technology File System,* or *NTFS*. NTFS supports file system security, whereas the File Allocation Table (FAT) includes no security capabilities.

In layman's terms, the FAT is a "table of contents" used by the operating system to locate files on a disk. Files change in size and may end up being larger or smaller after data has been added or removed. When this happens, the data may not fit back in the same exact site on the hard drive. Data that is too large is broken up into chunks, and pieces are stored in various places around the hard drive in a process called *fragmentation*. The FAT's job is to keep track of all the files on the hard disk, including these fragments.

The 1813 virus, which appeared in 1987, was one of the first viruses to attack the File Allocation Table. This virus, also known as Jerusalem, Jerusalem-B, Friday the 13th, and Black Friday, spreads from machine to machine by way of infected files, via diskettes or over a company's network (LAN). By attacking the FAT, the 1813 virus effectively "erases" files on an affected PC. When the FAT entry has been damaged or deleted, the operating system cannot locate files on the hard disk. The FAT, acting as a "map," is used by the operating system to locate files that have been stored in pieces on different segments of the hard disk.

The Michelangelo boot sector virus also corrupted portions of the FAT, resulting in the "loss" of data on the infected hard drive. On the plus side, when a virus attacks the FAT, it just deletes the FAT entry on the disk; it doesn't delete the actual data. (Remember, the FAT only directs the operating system to the location of the data). Luckily, utility programs such as the ever-popular Norton Utilities by Symantec Corporation are sometimes able to "rebuild" the FAT after this type of virus attack. The less fragmentation a hard drive experiences before the FAT is corrupted, the better the chance that a repair utility can recover the hard drive data. For this reason, regular hard drive defragmentation (at least once a month) is imperative.

With the exception of Windows NT 4.0, all versions of Windows have a built-in defragmentation utility (see Figure 5-1), which is found by accessing the Windows Start menu ➪ Accessories ➪ System Tools. Defragmentation and data recovery utilities are also available by third-party vendors such as Symantec Corporation (www.symantec.com) and McAfee Corporation (www.mcafee.com).

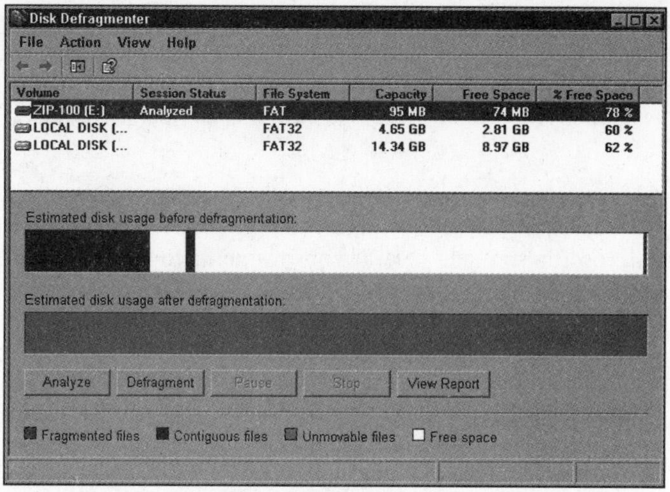

**Figure 5-1:** The Windows XP Pro built-in defragmentation utility

# File System Types

It doesn't matter what type of computer you use or what type of operating system your computer has: it must possess a file system for storing data. Like the legal, letter, or lateral filing systems used in offices to store paper files, computers have digital file systems that come in all shapes and sizes. Many of the earlier file systems were not designed with security in mind and were always vulnerable to attack. As time passed, operating systems became more advanced and computers more powerful. As a result, more secure file systems were developed, as well. As computer hard drives became larger, new file systems were needed to handle the large data overhead that they required. This section reviews the most popular file systems, starting with the oldest and least used.

## FAT12

The oldest type of FAT uses a 12-bit structure to hold data. Because a 12-bit number is relatively small in computer terms, it allows for data storage of only up to 16 megabytes. Since nearly all computers today have hard drives many times larger than that, the FAT12 file system is rarely used except for floppy disks or other removable media holding less than 16 megabytes of data.

## FAT16

Serving both the public and private sectors for the better part of twenty years, the FAT16 file system is still supported by many operating systems. The "16" loosely refers to the amount of data the file system can store on a disk. Used mostly on older systems, and for small partitions on modern systems, FAT16 uses a 16-bit structure to hold data. While the difference between a 12-bit and 16-bit file system structure may not *sound* significant, the latter can store data on hard disks or partitions ranging from 16 megabytes all the way up to two gigabytes (two billion bytes).

Once hard disks began to exceed two gigabytes in size, users of the FAT16 file system were forced to divide their hard drives into partitions. The size of these partitions could not exceed FAT16's two-gigabyte limitation. Windows 3.1 and early versions of Windows 95 used this type of file system. With the advent of Windows 95, a new version of FAT16 called *VFAT* was introduced that included several added features.

## Virtual FAT

With the introduction of Windows 95, Microsoft also made several improvements to the Windows operating system. One significant change was the enhancement of the classic FAT16 file system that had been in use until that point. The new variation of FAT was called Virtual FAT, or VFAT, and it displayed the following enhancements:

✓ Improved performance through faster access to stored data

✓ Long file name support

✓ Better file management capabilities

Keep in mind that VFAT was not a new file system but an enhancement of an old one. It used the same basic directory structure and format as the ordinary FAT. In a nutshell, VFAT was merely a way to store more information under a FAT16 directory. Because Windows 95 allowed the use of long file names, VFAT was needed to overcome the eight-character name and three-character extension limitation (as in `packager.exe`) that plagued DOS and Windows 3.1 users. Given the fact that VFAT is built on ordinary FAT, each file must still have an eight-character name and three-character extension. However, unlike the FAT, the VFAT will allocate additional directory blocks (space) to hold longer file names. Because VFAT relies on the old FAT directory structure (with a few new tricks), VFAT structures can also be damaged by malicious code, leaving data inaccessible by the operating system.

## FAT32 — The "High FAT" File System

Not long after Windows 95 made its debut, Microsoft developed a new 32-bit file system for the Windows 95 platform. Beginning with the second generation of Windows 95, a new file system — FAT32 — was introduced. FAT32 was developed because the size of computer hard drives was increasing at an alarming rate. With FAT16's two-gigabyte partition limitation, users who had, for example, a five-gigabyte hard drive were forced to create three partitions to take full advantage of all the available drive space. Three partitions meant that you had to use additional drive letters like `D:` and `E:` in addition to the standard `C:` that was set up by default.

With FAT32, partition sizes could be as large as two terabytes (one terabyte = one trillion bytes), quite a bit larger than FAT16's two billion byte limitation. Hard drives could have a single large partition, making it easier for users to find files. Besides the ability to support enormous hard drive sizes, FAT32 offered a number of other enhancements:

✓ FAT32 uses hard drive space more efficiently. FAT32 uses smaller clusters (storage spaces) to save data, resulting in a 10 to 15 percent increase in efficiency compared to large FAT or FAT16 drives.

✓ FAT32 is more flexible and provides dynamic "re-sizing" of FAT32 partitions without data loss.

✓ FAT32 is more robust. The boot record on FAT32 drives has been expanded to include a *backup* of critical data structures. This means that FAT32 drives are less susceptible to a single point of failure than standard FAT volumes.

Computers using FAT32 were unaffected by FAT16 boot sector viruses—another important advantage of using FAT32 from a security standpoint. Because FAT32 was very different from FAT16, malicious coders were forced to rewrite their programs to work effectively under this new, more robust file system.

## The High Performance File System

The High Performance File System (HPFS) was originally developed by Microsoft for IBM's OS/2 operating system. The HPFS directory permits file names to be long, to have multiple periods, and to include both upper- and lowercase letters. Unlike Windows NT and Windows 95, however, HPFS does not keep a separate eight-character file name and three-character extension name for each data set as does VFAT. Were a DOS or Windows program running under OS/2 to examine a directory, it would not be able to "recognize" the HPFS data containing long file names.

Considering the fact that HPFS was much more advanced than FAT, one might have expected that HPFS would become quite popular. As fate would have it, HPFS was "tied" to the OS/2 operating system. For numerous reasons (mostly related to technical issues between IBM and Microsoft), OS/2 never became widespread. Thus, as interest in OS/2 faded, so did any chance of support for HPFS. In general, HPFS is not commonly used with today's computers. Key features of the High Performance File System are:

✓ Support for long file names (up to 254 characters) and mixed-case (upper- and lowercase) file names

✓ Better performance due to its efficient design and internal architecture

✓ More available file storage space due to the resourceful way data is stored

✓ Less data fragmentation over time, resulting in less need to regularly defragment the file system

Because OS/2 and its native HPFS never became popular, the number of viruses written to attack the HPFS file system specifically can be counted on one hand. The CIH virus, however, has been known to "hide" on a HPFS partition in computers that have both a Windows FAT partition and an OS/2 HPFS partition on the same hard drive.

## NTFS — The New Technology File System

Many years ago, Microsoft introduced an operating system called Windows NT (New Technology). Unlike the DOS/FAT16 Windows of the time, this operating system used new 32-bit technology and an entirely new file system. Like IBM's OS/2, Windows NT came into existence shortly after technical issues drove Microsoft and IBM to abandon their joint effort to develop a new robust business operating system, forcing each company to undertake such development on their own. Microsoft (having some of the most skilled programmers available) intended Windows NT to be a robust business-oriented operating system. A new file system called New Technology File System (NTFS) accompanied Windows NT. NTFS was a marked improvement in many ways:

✓ NTFS contains many features for improved reliability, including transaction logs to facilitate recovery from disk failures.

✓ Because NT was designed to be a business operating system, data reliability was of paramount importance. NTFS was designed to be able to recover from certain types of data errors on the hard drive.

✓ In anticipation of the high storage capabilities that many businesses require, NTFS was designed to be "nearly" limitless in terms of how large storage partitions on the hard drive could be. While NTFS has a theoretical partition size limit (16 exabytes), it will be many years before hard drives ever reach this size, even at an accelerated expansion rate.

✓ NTFS supports FAT-style eight-character names and three-character extensions, as well as the use of long names (up to 255 characters). File names may also be a mix of upper- and lowercase characters (but are not case-sensitive). They can even contain certain non-letter characters. The main drawback of the NTFS file system is that it is generally not compatible with other operating systems installed on the same computer. Consequently, it is not available when you've booted the computer from a floppy disk.

One of the most important aspects of NTFS (as it relates to the theme of this book) is that it is a more *secure* file system. The NTFS file system improves security by allowing users to encrypt files and folders via the Encrypting File System, or EFS. EFS provides the following benefits:

✓ Users can apply EFS to encrypt offline files and folders. In addition, EFS gives users options for sharing encrypted files or disabling data recovery agents.

✓ EFS technology helps protect sensitive data. If a user encrypts a file with EFS, only that user can open the file and work with it. This is especially useful on laptops, because when a laptop is lost or stolen, the files on the hard drive remain inaccessible to whoever finds it or has stolen it.

The FAT file system is limited because it offers no built-in security capabilities for controlling or limiting user access to folders or files on a hard disk. Without integrated access control, it would be nearly impossible to construct applications and networks that require security. The ability to limit access to sensitive data is made difficult, as well. If you have the choice, use NTFS whenever possible over FAT.

Highly efficient and secure, NTFS is, however, not immune to virus attacks. Within NTFS is a scheme called *Alternate Data Streams (ADS)*. This subsystem allows "additional" data (such as a graphic image) to be directly linked to a file. However, this additional data is not always visible to the end user. The ability to hide executable code in the form of `.cmd`, `.vbs`, `.exe`, or `.bat` files inside alternate data streams that are not visible makes viruses difficult to detect within the NTFS file system. One virus that exploited NTFS's Alternative Data Streams appeared not long after

Windows 2000 was released. Dubbed the Win2K.Stream, this novel virus affects only executable files under Windows 2000. It does not carry a damaging payload; rather, it is considered a *proof-of-concept* virus, since it is the first virus known to exploit NTFS's Alternative Data Streams. When the Win2K.Stream virus is executed or activated, it displays a message on the screen as follows:

```
This cell has been infected by the [Win2k.Stream] virus!
```

When a file has been infected, the virus creates a new name for it. The infected file retains its old name, with the letters :STR appended to the end. (For example, if it infects a file called PROGRAM.EXE, then the name of the new file created by the virus is PROGRAM.EXE:STR. The file PROGRAM.EXE will be hidden.) Each time the infected file is executed, the corresponding program works, but the virus is re-executed as well.

# Directories and Subdirectories — From the Root to the Tree

A file system's top directory is known as the *root* directory. UNIX, Linux, Windows, and Novell NetWare all use a directory hierarchy, or *tree,* to maintain file structure. Unlike a real tree, whose branches extend upwards, a file system's root directory is at the top of the hierarchy, with all other directories (subdirectories) branching down from it. The root directory is the topmost *parent* directory that includes or encompasses all other directories.

In UNIX-based systems, the root directory is represented simply as / (front slash), and in Windows-based systems, the root directory is represented as \ (backslash). Only a select handful of UNIX, Linux, Windows NT, or NetWare network operating system users are given the authority to access all file directories and files under the root directory. Root directory privileges are usually assigned only to system or network administrators because they grant *full* access to *all* files stored on a computer. When you turn on your computer, the root directory is automatically accessed.

In Windows, you observe the root directory when you open up a C:\ (DOS prompt). The root directory contains all other directories and folders, which are called *subdirectories.* It is in the sub-directories that your information is stored and organized on a disk or diskette. In a Windows or Macintosh system for example, subdirectories appear as various folders represented as icons on the desktop or in menus. Nearly all network operating systems protect the root directory by requiring that a password be entered before full access is permitted. In most network-style operating systems (such as UNIX, Linux, and Windows NT) when users log on as system administrators, they are granted *root permissions* that allow them to control *all* of the system settings. Anyone with root permissions can modify the system settings and even delete files. For obvious reasons, having root permissions makes one extremely powerful and potentially dangerous; hence, it is granted only to a select few. It is important that any organizational personnel who have been permitted root privileges follow these three rules:

- ✓ Never modify the system to give their access priority.

- ✓ Never access other users' data or program files for their own purposes without the owners' permission.

✓ Where possible, respect the privacy of all users' files and e-mail, except when they need access for system maintenance or troubleshooting purposes (in cases, for example, of bounced e-mails, running out of disk space, and so on).

It might be worth your organization's time to review who is given root privileges to your system. It may be (as often is the case) that too many people (including contractors sometimes) are given root privileges, unnecessarily creating more risk.

## Getting to the Root with Malicious Code

Because root privileges are so potent, they are a prime target for malicious attack. This was exhibited in 2001 when a flaw was discovered in the Common Desktop Environment (CDE), a graphical interface that runs on UNIX- and Linux-based computer systems. A special network program, called a daemon, ran within the CDE. This daemon accepted client commands for the launching of programs with full root privileges from a remote location. Due to a flaw in the network daemon programming code, a savvy individual could manipulate the amount of data sent, resulting in what is known as a *buffer overflow* and thus causing the daemon to crash. The individual could then gain access to the computer, with full root privileges and the opportunity to execute malicious code.

The buffer is a special area in a computer's memory specifically set aside by programs to hold data. When more data is sent than the buffer can hold, the excess data may "spill" out of the memory area designated by the buffer, giving that data (malicious code included) access to other, non-designated memory areas. Since root privileges allow complete access to all computer resources, malicious code possessing root privileges can inflict a high level of damage. Once this type of vulnerability is discovered, a patch is routinely made available by the software manufacturer to correct the problem.

## Universal Plug and Play — More like "Universal Plug and Pray"

Flaws in programming code are fodder for exploitation by hackers and virus writers. In December 2001, eEye, a leading developer of high-end network security products and an active contributor to network security research and education, discovered three vulnerabilities within Microsoft's Windows XP operating system. The most serious of the three Windows XP vulnerabilities is the remotely exploitable buffer overflow. Someone can write malicious code that would enable him or her to execute commands with SYSTEM level access (similar to full root privileges in UNIX). SYSTEM level is the highest level of access available with Windows XP. According to Internet security analyst and programmer Steve Gibson, the reason the UPnP flaw occurred was as follows:

> The Universal Plug and Play service (UPnP), which is installed and running in all versions of Windows XP — and may be loaded into Windows 98 and ME — essentially turns every one of those systems into a wide-open Internet server. This server listens for TCP connections on port 5000 and for UDP "datagram" packets arriving on port 1900. This allows malicious hackers (or high-speed Internet worms) located anywhere in the world to scan for, and locate, individual Windows UPnP-equipped machines. Any vulnerability — known today or discovered tomorrow — can then be rapidly exploited.

After this vulnerability was discovered and made public, Microsoft quickly made a patch available via Internet download.

Another way to keep hackers and others who write malicious code from exploiting this UPnP vulnerability in Windows operating systems is to download and install the "Unplug n' Pray" utility. This handy freeware program (see Figure 5-2), available at `www.grc.com`, was written by Steve Gibson. An easy-to-use Windows program, it allows users to quickly disable and re-enable the UPnP feature (if needed) with the click of a mouse.

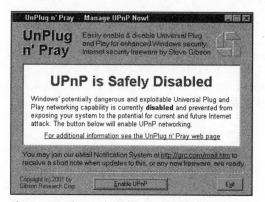

**Figure 5-2:** The Unplug n' Pray utility from Gibson Research Corporation

To install Unplug n' Pray and disable UPnP:

1. Download the program from `www.grc.com`, making sure to note the location of the download.

2. Click the Unplug n' Pray icon. A screen pops up, revealing the status of Plug n' Play.

3. Users can either disable universal unplug or enable it by using the enable/disable toggle button located at the bottom center of the program window.

The potential for exploiting the UPnP is a serious concern that prompted the FBI (through the NIPC) to issue the following bulletin outlining the steps required to manually disable this service in the various Windows operating systems:

ADVISORY 01-030.2
Update: "Universal Plug and Play Vulnerabilities"
December 22, 2001
[Update to NIPC Advisory 01-030 are in bold]

Summary:
This advisory updates NIPC Advisory 01-030 regarding what Microsoft refers to as a critical vulnerability in the universal plug and play (UPnP) service in Windows XP, Millennium Edition (ME) and Windows 98 or Windows 98SE systems. This vulnerability could lead to denial-of-service attacks and system compromise. Microsoft has released a patch (Microsoft Security Bulletin 01-059) for this vulnerability at the following site:

```
http://www.microsoft.com/technet/treeview/default.asp?url=/
technet/security/bulletin/MS01-059.asp
```

Additional information can also be found at the following site:

eEye Digital Security: `http://www.eeye.com/html/Research/Advisories/AD20011220.html`

**Update:**

On Friday, December 21, 2001, the NIPC conducted technical discussions with Microsoft Corporation and other partners in the Internet and Information Security community to identify software and procedure practices to minimize the risk from this vulnerability. The NIPC recommends that users consider taking the following actions.

**Home Users:**

Download and install the patch described in Microsoft Security Bulletin 01-059. For additional security if you are not using the UPnP service, disable it with the following steps:

In Windows XP

1. Click the Start button.
2. Go to the Control Panel tab and press it.
3. Go to the Administrative Tools folder and double-click it.
4. Go to the Services icon and double-click it. It looks like two gears interlocked with each other.
5. Scroll down until you see the "Universal Plug and Play Device Host" service and double-click it.
6. A window will pop up with several tabs; on the General tab there will be a field called "Startup Type:".
7. In the "Startup Type:" field, change the option to "Disabled" and click OK.

In Windows Millennium Edition

1. Click the Start button.
2. Go to the Control Panel under Settings, and select "Add/Remove Programs".
3. Select the Windows Set-up tab.
4. In the Components Field, select "Communications".
5. In the Components Field, scroll down and uncheck the box to the left of "Universal Plug and Play".
6. Click OK.

In Windows 98 and Windows 98 Second Edition

There is no built-in UPnP support for these operating systems except in the case of computers on which the Windows XP Internet Connection Sharing client has been installed.

**System Administrators:**

1. Download and install the patch described in Microsoft Security Bulletin 01-059.

2. Monitor and block ports 1900 and 5000. An increase in traffic on these ports may indicate active scanning for this vulnerability. Also, ensure that a policy is in place that restricts access to your corporate network to those machines that have not yet been patched.

3. Set the UPnP service settings to "Disable." By default, this is set to "Manual."

**Systems Affected:**

Windows XP installs and runs UPnP by default. Windows ME provides native support for UPnP, but it is neither installed nor running by default. Windows 98 and Windows 98SE only use UPnP when specifically installed by the Internet Connection Sharing program.

**Details:**

UPnP is a service that identifies and uses network-based devices. There are two known vulnerabilities in the UPnP service. The first vulnerability involves a buffer overflow in the UPnP service that could give an attacker system or root level access. With this level of access, an attacker could execute any commands and take any actions they choose on the victim's computer.

The second vulnerability is in the Simple Service Discovery Protocol (SSDP) that allows new devices on a network to be recognized by computers running UPnP by sending out a broadcast UDP packet. Attackers can use this feature to send false UDP packets to a broadcast address hosting vulnerable Windows systems. Once a vulnerable system receives this message, it will respond to the spoofed originating IP address. This can be exploited to cause a distributed denial-of-service attack.

Another example of this vulnerability is if an attacker spoofed an address that had the character generator (chargen) service running. If a vulnerable machine were to connect to the chargen service on a system, it could become stuck in a loop that would quickly consume system resources."

# Examining Operating Systems

Operating systems dictate our computing experience. Operating systems are software programs installed on computers that allow the computers to run other programs, called *applications*. The operating system is the most important program installed on the computer. Operating systems perform basic tasks, such as interpreting input from the keyboard and mouse, sending output to the display screen, and keeping track of files and directories on the disk. While they may differ dramatically in the specific features they contain, operating systems all perform the same *basic* function.

Operating systems are the platforms on which applications operate. The type of operating system dictates the types of applications that can be utilized. With the PC platform, for example, the most common operating systems used today are DOS, Windows, and Linux. Some operating systems, such as Linux and Windows NT, exhibit special built-in security features, making them better suited to a business environment. Others are designed to be easy to use and to master, and include multimedia features better suited for the home environment. One hazard faced by all operating systems is the ongoing threat from malicious code attacks. The following section lists the most common PC operating systems and their basic features.

## DOS — In the Beginning . . .

In Chapter 4, I briefly covered the DOS operating system. DOS helped usher in the PC revolution of the early 1980s and was once the most widely used PC operating system. In the past two decades, millions of business and household personal computers have relied on DOS for everyday operations. DOS does not use flashy icons and pop-up menus. Instead, users enter strings of typed text commands at the DOS prompt in order to launch an application or perform a particular function. Microsoft's version of DOS is known as *MS-DOS,* while IBM's version (similar to Microsoft's) is known as *PC-DOS.* Several other companies developed their own proprietary versions of DOS, but these never became as popular or widespread as MS-DOS or PC-DOS. While MS-DOS and PC-DOS are still operating in many computers, modern-day graphical operating systems have largely supplanted them.

To access MS-DOS from within Windows 95, 98, or Me, go to the Start menu ⇨Run and type **command.** Under Windows NT, 2000, or XP, type **CMD.** A DOS prompt "window" (see Figure 5-3) opens, allowing for the input of text-based DOS commands.

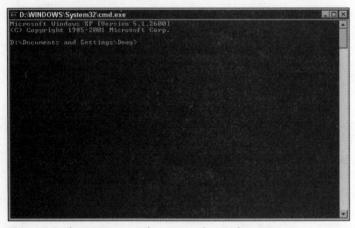

**Figure 5-3:** The DOS/command prompt under Windows XP Pro

It wasn't long after DOS was introduced that it started to become the target of malicious code — mostly simple boot sector or file infector viruses. In the PC revolution's nascent stages, networks were not exceedingly popular. Viruses spread largely via *sneaker nets* through infected floppies. The term *sneaker net* refers to the way users shared information at the time: when a user wanted to share a file with a computer located in a different part of an organization, he would copy the file to a floppy disk and physically run it over. Once DOS viruses began to spread, both IBM and Microsoft began to include anti-virus programs as part of their operating system on later versions of MS-DOS and PC-DOS. Companies such as Symantec and McAfee also developed DOS-based anti-virus products. After the release of Windows 95, many older DOS viruses began to die out simply because they were no longer effective against this more advanced graphical operating system.

# Windows — The "Gooey" Operating System

Back in May of 1990, Microsoft released the Windows 3.0 operating system. It was somewhat of a turning point in the history of personal computers because it allowed users to click an icon to launch a program rather than enter a cryptic command, as was required by DOS. While Windows 3.0 still used DOS as its "engine," it added a colorful Graphical User Interface (GUI) that acted as the interface between the user and DOS. (In fact, when Microsoft was first developing the GUI idea, the original name for Windows was "Interface Manager".) Nicknamed "gooey" (from the pronunciation of GUI), the new interface evolved as color monitors started to replace the aging and boring monochrome monitors that had plagued PCs since their inception.

The use of icons was nothing new to Macintosh users, since Macs had been using them for years before the release of Windows. Nor was Windows 3.0 Microsoft's first attempt at a GUI-based operating system. The "Windows" idea started back in 1981. By late 1985, the new Windows 1.0 operating system was released; however, it never really caught on with the public, and sales were modest. The first practical and stable version of Windows was version 3.0. With this release, third-party vendors began to develop applications at an accelerated rate.

Selling more than 10 million copies, Windows was one of the most successful operating systems in the history of computing. Minor improvements to the operating system in 1992 upgraded Windows 3.0 to Windows 3.1 as the popularity of Windows continued to grow. In October 1992, Microsoft released Windows for Workgroups, which took this very popular operating system to the "networking" level. Businesses the world over could now easily connect and share information between their Windows-based computers in a networked environment. In November 1993, Microsoft made a few minor improvements to Windows for Workgroups and a new version, known as Windows 3.11, was released. In fact, Windows 3.11 was the last upgrade made to this aging operating system.

## August 1995, Do You Know Where Your Operating System Is?

Amid an international media blitz, Windows 95 was released in August 1995. Windows 95 still used MS-DOS to initially boot up, but the operating system would take control of all functions and commands once the Windows 95 GUI interface was started. Using a "mix" of old 16-bit DOS code and 32-bit code, the Windows 95 operating system boasted backward-compatibility with old DOS programs (viruses included), as well as the capability to run new, more advanced and secure 32-bit code. This new operating system was made possible by the tremendous advances made in PC technology in the early 1990s. New operating systems were needed to take advantage of the powerful capabilities afforded by advances made in computer hardware.

Using an entirely new interface, Windows 95 was a multitasking operating system that could run several programs at one time. Multitasking took advantage of the powerful capabilities of newer computers and allowed users to get more work done by permitting the computer to perform several tasks simultaneously. While this concept looked great on paper, computer users who wanted to exploit Windows 95's multitasking capabilities quickly realized that they needed much more than the eight megabytes of memory that Microsoft recommended. Nevertheless, Windows 95 became a huge hit for Microsoft, as millions around the world flocked to purchase the program that allowed users to upgrade their 16-bit Windows 3.1 or 3.11 systems to the new 32-bit operating system.

During the years following its release, Windows 95 saw several changes — some subtle, some dramatic. All the while, the same basic GUI interface remained. Windows 98 enhanced the operating system further by integrating the Web browser with the operating system. This "bundling" of Web browser and operating system prompted the much-publicized anti-trust trial that plagued Microsoft for several years. As the number of Internet users began to grow, operating systems that took advantage of the Internet and programming languages such as HTML and Java were inevitable. The last bastion of the Windows 95–style platform was Windows Me, which was introduced shortly after the turn of the millennium. In 2001, Microsoft introduced Windows XP Home Edition, which used Windows NT's more powerful and more *secure* technology.

# Windows NT — The "Hard Core" Operating System

Back in the 1980s, software giant Microsoft and hardware giant IBM worked jointly to develop a strong, secure operating system for IBM. Called *OS/2,* it was intended to replace the aging DOS. Due to technical issues between the two giants, Microsoft abandoned the OS/2 project in 1990, refocusing its energy on further development of its Windows platform in light of Windows' increasing popularity. Using programming techniques co-developed with IBM, Microsoft determined to develop its own powerful and secure operating system for the new millennium.

By the time 1993 rolled around, Windows NT had blossomed into a serious business-oriented networking operating system. It incorporated several networking and security features not found in the more consumer-oriented Windows 3.1, which made NT an attractive alternative for organizational use. Each new version of Windows NT brought more improvements and security features, making it the most secure and robust version of the Windows platform. This operating system, however, had become very complex. Furthermore, it had a much higher learning curve than Windows 3.1 or 95. Most organizations hired special network administrators to handle the day-to-day needs of the complex NT operating system.

The modern day version of Windows NT is called *Windows XP,* for "eXtreme Performance". Coming in both a business version (Professional) and a consumer version (Home Edition), it is by far the most secure and feature-rich version of the Windows NT operating platform. Unfortunately, flaws in operating system code have plagued Windows NT since its inception. Each new "hole" was followed by another patch to "plug" the hole and restore consumer confidence in Microsoft products. Despite all the advances made over the years, the Windows NT platform (XP included) is still very much the target of malicious code attacks because it is such a widely used platform.

# Linux — The UNIX-like OS with a Finnish Flair

In 1991, Linus Benedict Torvalds, a Finnish student at the University of Helsinki, created an operating system that would become known as *Linux.* With MS-DOS too limited and UNIX too expensive, Torvalds sought to create a powerful, *free* operating system. UNIX was primarily used on larger corporate computer systems and was never made affordable enough to be widely used on the IBM PC platform. After learning computer programming and studying another UNIX-like operating system called *Minix,* Torvalds set forth to create the first version of his operating system. Minix, incidentally, was created by a Dutch professor named Andrew S. Tanenbaum and was also designed to run on ubiquitous IBM-compatible computers.

Linux was designed to run on the PC platform simply because PCs (and their clones) were less expensive than Apple computers and more widely used. Instead of writing the entire operating system himself, Torvalds put the source code on the Web, allowing input from programmers throughout the world for improvements and modifications. This innovative approach proved successful; utilizing the skills of thousands of brilliant programmers produced a powerful operating system. Because hackers were also contributors to the source code on the Web, they certainly added to the resultant high security features of the operating system.

Linux saw many changes in the years after Torvalds wrote his first operating system kernel. Today, numerous versions of the operating system exist. Linux is a free and powerful multitasking network operating system with features that make it stable and secure. Like its industrial-strength brother UNIX, Linux requires that users have password-protected *root* privileges before any system modifications can be made. As a result, core operating system components are well-protected from malicious attacks. Linux is often used on Internet servers because of its stability and hardened security. Linux servers have been known to run for months, sometimes even years, without a glitch.

Recently, several companies have developed graphical "Windows-like" interfaces specifically for Linux (which is a text-based operating system), making it more attractive to a broader range of computer users. Despite these advancements, Linux still remains very much a "hands-on" operating system and requires a much steeper learning curve than Windows or Apple operating systems.

## The Mac Operating System — Consumers Take a "Byte" of the Apple

Long before computer users ever clicked the Windows Start button, Apple Computer Corporation had introduced the Apple Lisa. This model, which made its debut in 1983, used a GUI-based operating system that pioneered the concept of the mouse to mainstream computing. The fact that the Apple Lisa was very expensive and thus never became popular did not stop Apple from introducing the Macintosh series, with an improved graphical operating system, in 1984. Clever advertising, coupled with brisk computer sales, made Apple the fastest growing company in U.S. history. Apple steadfastly refused to license their hardware or operating systems, and therefore, no inexpensive clones were developed. This may be what kept Apple from dominating the small computer market, since PCs were much cheaper and, as such, more attractive to consumers. Over the years, Apple computers have seen steady improvements in both hardware and operating system functions. The ability to manipulate complex graphics is one of the features inherent in the Mac's design, and has produced a large following among graphic designers and engineers.

Despite their unique hardware and software features, Apple computers are not immune to malicious code. Macs have never been subject to the same attack intensity as PCs, simply because they are not the dominant operating system. Some malicious code written for Windows-based computers may, however, also cause harm in the Mac. Because modern-day Macs also use popular applications such as Word and Excel, they too can be affected by the plethora of macro viruses originally targeting PCs.

## The Windows 9x Boot Sequence

Windows 9x is one of the most commonly used desktop operating systems, and its widespread popularity makes it a frequent target of malicious code attacks. Therefore, a basic knowledge of the boot process can help users identify the most vulnerable areas of Windows. Understanding the boot process can help users recover their systems more quickly in the unfortunate event that a malicious code attack renders their operating system unstable or inoperable.

No matter which operating system is used, the computer's BIOS will always run a Power On Self-Test (POST) routine each time the computer is powered up. The purpose of the POST routine is to test the computer's hardware devices to determine what types of hardware are present in the system and if all of the hardware devices detected are functioning properly. After the POST is complete, the operating system is loaded by the bootstrap loader. Because Windows 9x was built using DOS underpinnings, it uses some of the same initial procedures as 16-bit DOS would in order to boot up. However, once 32-bit Windows begins to load, it assumes control from DOS and begins a series of steps to bring the familiar Windows desktop to the user's screen.

## IO.SYS

Because Win 9x requires DOS to initially start the boot process, the first file that is loaded is the DOS file IO.SYS. IO.SYS is a system file in the root directory of the bootable partition that starts DOS in Real mode. It sets up the addressing of conventional memory and loads the real mode (16-bit) device drivers into memory. After all the Real mode drivers have been loaded, IO.SYS reads a file called MSDOS.SYS file in an attempt to process specific devices attached to the computer that might be listed in that file. The IO.SYS file of Windows 9x first uses the preliminary hardware profile from the POST's hardware detection phase in an attempt to initialize the computer's hardware devices. After processing specific devices found in MSDOS.SYS, IO.SYS then reads the Windows Registry file (SYSTEM.DAT) for the settings of any of the devices it found in MSDOS.SYS. If there are other older (legacy) DOS files such as CONFIG.SYS or AUTOEXEC.BAT, IO.SYS loads COMMAND.COM (Command Interpreter) to process both of these files. In a strange sequence of events, IO.SYS first runs to determine whether a CONFIG.SYS needs to be loaded, then drops out to allow the CONFIG.SYS file to load any 16-bit Real mode device drivers, provided they are present. Once the loading of CONFIG.SYS is complete, IO.SYS returns to read MSDOS.SYS again in order to complete the remainder of the startup process.

## MSDOS.SYS

Whether or not CONFIG.SYS or AUTOEXEC.BAT are present in the system, IO.SYS always reads the MSDOS.SYS file first to determine if CONFIG.SYS needs to be read, and then reads it a second time, looking for any 32-bit virtual device drivers (VxDs) and other Windows configuration settings. MSDOS.SYS is a plain ASCII text file that can be read or edited using EDIT.COM, a built-in DOS file editor. Even if a computer was unable to load Windows as a result of a malicious code attack, users could view or edit the contents of the MS-DOS system using the EDIT.COM utility.

## WIN.COM

If MSDOS.SYS is configured to start Windows 9x, it runs a file called WIN.COM that starts the physical loading of the Windows 9x operating system. If WIN.COM becomes corrupted by a virus, Windows will no longer load and users are left with a DOS prompt on their screen. In summary, WIN.COM controls the initial environment and checks and loads the core Windows components.

## AUTOEXEC.BAT

In order to keep Windows 9x backward-compatible with older Real mode devices, AUTOEXEC.BAT may also be used by Windows to launch Real mode devices or to set device parameters. AUTOEXEC.BAT is used to run commands that are required to run each time the computer is started. Viruses have been known to "install" themselves in this file to ensure that they are launched each time the computer is booted.

## LOG FILES

Windows 9x uses a number of log files located in the root directory (C:\) for tracking the state of application and the way those applications load. If the operating system becomes unstable or refuses to load as a result of a malicious code attack, log files can sometimes help determine what part of the boot process is failing or which applications have been affected by the malicious code. The following log files are in a plain text format (.txt) and can be viewed through a command prompt even when the operating system fails to load:

✓ `SETUPLOG.TXT`—Records setup sequence and pass/fail during the initial installation

✓ `DETLOG.TXT`—Hardware detection log file

✓ `NETLOG.TXT`—Networking setup log file

✓ `DETCRASH.LOG`—Hardware detection failure/crash log

✓ `BOOTLOG.TXT`—Success/fail of the boot sequence

# The Partition—How Many Slices Do You Want?

Over the past few years, a dramatic increase has been seen in the amount of information that hard drives can hold. Information stored in computers must be organized in such a way that it can be located by the operating system. With technology constantly improving, hard disk capacity continues to increase and the price of the massive storage devices continues to fall. A hard drive must be partitioned if an operating system intends to store data on it. Like a pizza, a hard drive can be left whole (single partition) or "cut up" into slices, which creates several partitions. The size and type of partition is decision made by the customer when the disk is prepared for data storage (formatted) by the operating system. Once a hard drive has been partitioned and data has been stored on that partition, the size of the partition cannot be changed without the use of a third-party program specifically designed for the task.

All operating systems have special programs that allow a user to partition a hard drive. Once a partition is made, the operating system formats the partition to allow the installation of the file system. These built-in partition programs do not, however, allow you to change the size of the partition after the operating system has been installed. As discussed earlier in this chapter, file systems come in a wide variety of flavors, from the 16-bit FAT file system of DOS to the NTFS of Windows NT.

## Logical Formatting

*Logical formatting* refers to the amount of space (partition) set aside as an area for the sole purpose of storing data. Remember, the physical hard disk can contain a number of partitions (also called *logical drives*). All PCs have at least one physical drive (the disk itself) and one logical drive (the partition). Sometimes, a computer has several different operating systems on one hard disk. In that case, each operating system using a unique file system (Linux or OS/2, for example) possesses its own partition for storing data for that operating system. When the computer is turned on, a menu appears, allowing users to choose which operating system they want to load.

In some situations, two operating systems can "share" a partition if they use the exact same file system. Windows Me and Windows XP are examples of operating systems that could take advantage of this capability. If each was set up during installation to use the FAT32 file system, they could both be installed on the same logical drive (partition) and even share data. Malicious code can attack a partition in a number of ways. By simply altering the partition size, all data on that partition can be destroyed. Fortunately, most modern-day anti-virus software programs offer a defense against this type of attack.

Operating systems such as UNIX and Linux, for example, help protect the partition table by requiring password-protected root privileges before any modifications can be made. Many third-party partitioning programs (for example, Partition Magic by Power Quest) that allow for the use of several operating systems on the same hard disk will also allow password protection to be applied to any partition. They can also hide primary FAT partitions, protecting them from each other and from cross-contamination by malicious code.

# RAID

*RAID (Redundant Array of Independent Disks)* is an acronym that was coined in a 1988 paper by Berkeley researchers Patterson, Gibson, and Katz. It describes an array configuration of multiple inexpensive hard disks, providing fault tolerance (redundancy) and improved access rates. In simple terms, RAID is a method of combining the storage space provided by several hard drives into one unit. RAID is much more than that, however. RAID provides a method of accessing multiple individual disks as if the array were one larger disk. By spreading data access over these multiple disks, the risk of losing all data if one drive fails is reduced. At the same time, data access time is improved. Data loss can occur for a number of reasons:

✓ Hardware failure

✓ Hacker attacks

✓ Malicious code

Fault tolerance is the ability of a computer system to seamlessly respond to any unexpected hardware or software failure. There are many levels of fault tolerance, the lowest being the ability to continue operation in the event of a power failure. Many fault-tolerant computer systems *mirror* all operations — that is, every operation is performed on two or more duplicate systems so that when one fails, the other can take over.

There are a number of different RAID levels. The four most common levels are:

✓ Level 0 — Provides data striping (spreading out blocks of each file across multiple disks) but no redundancy. It improves performance but does not deliver fault tolerance.

✓ Level 1 — Provides disk mirroring.

✓ Level 3 — Same as Level 0, but also reserves one dedicated disk for error correction data. It provides good performance and some level of fault tolerance.

✓ Level 5 — Provides data striping at the byte level and also stripe error correction information. This results in excellent data transfer performance and good fault tolerance. Typically the RAID is used in large file servers, application servers, or anyplace where data accessibility is critical, and the integrity and protection of data is required. Presently, RAID is also being used in desktop systems for CAD, multimedia editing, and playback due to the improved data transfer rates it provides.

# ROM and RAM Memory—What's the Difference?

*Read-only memory (ROM)* is a type of memory that is written once (as with BIOS chips) and cannot be overwritten. Chip manufacturers can store programming code in an area where it can neither be erased nor lose its contents when the computer is turned off. A prime example of this type of code is found in a computer's BIOS. Many of today's ROM chips can be electronically erased and reprogrammed. End users are often required to upgrade programming code on the BIOS chip, but not replace the chip entirely. These chips are commonly referred to as *Flash ROM chips*.

ROM chips that are "read-only" cannot be overwritten or destroyed by malicious code. Some ROM chips are write-enabled, which means that they will readily accept software commands to write data to them. Viruses such as CIH have been known to exploit this feature by overwriting or erasing the ROM chip, leaving the computer inoperable. Some motherboards have a special built-in security feature that can prevent such an attack. In order to flash or overwrite a ROM chip, a special switch (jumper) on the computer's motherboard must first be physically altered. This serves to prevent either accidental or malicious changes to the Flash BIOS.

The computer or motherboard vendor can be contacted for assistance with a specific product. However, if a virus succeeds in erasing or corrupting the Flash BIOS ROM, no software remedy is available. Your PC will no longer be able to boot up, and the Flash BIOS ROM will need to be replaced or removed and reprogrammed in a special programming device. In instances where the Flash BIOS ROM is permanently attached to the motherboard, the entire motherboard will have to be replaced.

*RAM* is an acronym for *random access memory*, a type of computer memory that can be accessed arbitrarily. Unlike ROM, no special switches are needed to read and write to RAM. RAM is sometimes referred to as *main memory*, or *system memory*, because the computer's processor uses it to store data. Applications use RAM to store data or programming instructions. All computers must have some sort of RAM to store the results of data that has been created or modified. RAM memory is referred to as *volatile* because information stored there is immediately lost when power to the computer is turned off. Alternatively, ROM is referred to as *non-volatile memory* because data is permanently "burned into" the memory chip and is not lost when power is removed. Because operating systems and software applications use RAM to store and manipulate data, RAM is a prime target for malicious attack.

A *memory-resident program*, also known as a *TSR (Terminate and Stay Resident)*, is a program that leaves at least a portion of itself in memory after it terminates, then waits for a particular event to take place before reactivating. With DOS or Windows, this generally means that the program "hooks" into the BIOS and waits for a specific keystroke, command, time, and so on. Such code is useful with many types of applications, but it is particularly useful to writers of malicious code. After a computer is contaminated (by launching an infected program, for example), TSR viruses "conceal" themselves inside the computer's memory (RAM), allowing them to easily spread to other files or otherwise gain control over the computer. TSR viruses are no longer a frequent nuisance, since all contemporary virus-scanning programs can easily detect this method of malicious code transmission.

# The Windows Registry — Malicious Code Registers Here!

The Windows Registry was a major innovation with the introduction of Windows 95. The Windows Registry, which is included in all current versions of Windows, is a complex database where nearly *all* the information about your computer is stored — from settings made at the control panel to details about applications. In Windows 95, 98, and Me, the Registry consists of two files in your Windows directory, called USER.DAT and SYSTEM.DAT. In Windows 2000 and Windows XP, the Registry is situated in special reserved locations, called *hives,* found in the \windows\system32\config and \Documents and Settings\ folders.

Before Windows 95, the SYSTEM.INI and WIN.INI files controlled all features of and access to the operating system. This approach, unfortunately, meant that each new installed application brought a new entry into one of these files. This caused the files to become very large over time. The problem was compounded by the fact that many programs failed to remove entries placed in the files when they were later uninstalled. This left many erroneous entries and dramatically slowed down operating system performance. The Registry changed all of this with its single large central database of complete system information.

The Registry is designed to be protected while it is in use, and it should therefore not be possible to copy, delete, or alter the Registry's contents except by certain programs (such as installation programs) or by special Registry editing tools. In Windows NT or XP, you can make security changes to the Registry with User Manager. While the Registry is quite secure, it is certainly not impenetrable. Once malicious code succeeds in infiltrating or manipulating the Registry, it can take control of nearly any operating system function.

Sometimes, malicious code scans the Registry looking for commonly installed security programs in order to disable them. At other times, malicious code may add its own Registry entry that enables the code to execute automatically or each time Windows starts. Trojan horse programs often "use" the Registry to install backdoor programs, allowing hackers to infiltrate infected computers. Whatever the method used by malicious code, the Registry remains one of the most important files on a Windows-based PC.

Procedures for backing up and protecting the Registry are covered in Chapter 9.

# Summary

Every year, thousands of computers worldwide suffer the consequences of malicious code attacks. These attacks cost businesses and consumers millions in both revenue and data losses. In order to defend computers and the networks that connect them, you must understand the various subsystems that are the targets of malicious code.

This chapter covers the following key topics:

✓ The BIOS (Basic Input Output System) and its indispensable role in computer operations

✓ Booting and file system functions, including the boot sector and master boot record (MBR), both targets for malicious code

✓ The role and function of the File Allocation Table (FAT) in DOS/Windows-based PCs

✓ Various file systems used by different operating systems, including their strengths and weaknesses

✓ Directories and subdirectories, including the power of root and administrative privileges

✓ Operating systems and their associated strengths and weaknesses against malicious code

✓ Partitions and their role in every operating system

✓ Memory functions and the critical function of the Windows Registry

# Chapter 6

# Networking and Internet Essentials

## In This Chapter

- ✓ Examining peer-to-peer and client-server networking
- ✓ File-sharing issues and inherent dangers
- ✓ Exploring Java Virtual Machine (JVM)
- ✓ Discussing Internet browsers and their vulnerabilities
- ✓ Considering e-mail issues
- ✓ Commonly attacked TCP/IP ports and their functions

COMPUTER NETWORKS HAVE BECOME an indispensable part of the corporate landscape. With the proliferation of the Internet, individuals and businesses are realizing more and more the importance of being able to access all the Web has to offer. Users from remote locations can connect to their company networks using the Internet as a cost-effective conduit for communication. After linking their local area networks to the Internet, companies often find that their profits and productivity increase. While the Internet has become ubiquitous as a business tool, it is important to remember that the Internet is a *two-way* street. Individuals and businesses connect to the Internet, and the Internet also connects to them. Whenever a company's internal network (LAN) is connected to the Web, malicious code may be able to infiltrate the internal network and quickly spread throughout the organization. The onerous task of detecting and removing the malicious code becomes compounded and costly.

Network-aware viruses are one of the fastest growing types of malicious code. We are living in a progressively connected world that presents a higher risk of malicious code outbreaks than ever before. This risk is exacerbated by increased spreading speed via networks. The rate of malicious code infection becomes greater as network infrastructure improves, giving viruses, worms, and Trojans better transport mechanisms. Understanding how networks work, where common network vulnerabilities exist, and how network-aware viruses exploit these vulnerabilities is vital in the defense against malicious code.

# Peer-to-Peer or Client-Server — Network Computers Like to Share

Computer networks can be as small as two computers linked together to share information or they can be as elaborate and vast as the Internet. Whether large or small, computer networks come in several varieties. The most commonly used network types are:

✓ **Local area networks (LANs)** — Computers in this type of network are located in close proximity to one another (in the same office or building, for example).

✓ **Wide area networks (WANs)** — Computers in this type of network are situated far apart geographically (for example, in different towns or states) and are connected by telephone lines, special high-speed data lines, or radio waves.

✓ **Campus area networks (CANs)** — Computers in this type of network are located within a restricted geographic area, such as a college campus.

✓ **Metropolitan area networks (MANs)** — Similar to a CAN, this type of data network is designed for a larger geographic area than a campus, but is not larger than the confines of a town or city.

One area that has seen a large increase in malicious code attacks is the LAN, or local area network. Network-aware malicious code can seek out other computers on a LAN and then propagate across that network at an alarming speed. Instead of seeing just one infected computer, network administrators or those in charge of security may be faced with dozens, perhaps hundreds, of infected machines. LANs usually use one of two schemes to share data: peer-to-peer or client-server.

## The Peer-to-Peer Network

There are no dedicated servers in a *peer-to-peer network,* nor does this type of network exhibit a hierarchy among its computers. While each computer is capable of sharing its data with others, network security and administration policies must be handled by each computer individually. Within a peer-to-peer network, each computer must be set up independently to determine who may access files and which files can be shared. In this type of network, each computer acts as both a server and a client. In small peer-to-peer networks, users are frequently on a first-name basis; in fact, users often allow other users unrestricted access to all files and system resources. Although it is easy to establish trust in very small computer networks, where one individual knows every other individual, security should still remain an issue. When malicious code infiltrates this type of network (as a result of a lax attitude and the fact that unrestricted access is allowed to data files), the code easily gains full access to the files and resources of all the other computers on that network. This type of setup is inherently insecure and is best suited for very small networks — those, for example, that consist of less than ten computers.

## Peer-to-Peer File-Sharing Web Sites Share Malicious Code

One way virus writers circulate their malicious code is through file-sharing Web sites like Napster, Gnutella, and KaZaA. While file sharing of music on Napster and KaZaA has been quite limited due to recent copyright issues, many Internet users still use the Web sites to "share" files. These types of peer-to-peer file-sharing sites have always been a breeding ground for malicious code. In February of 1991, a chameleon-like worm that assumed the name of the file the user requested was discovered. The Gnutella worm drew attention because it could "grab" an Internet connection and change its name to match the name of the file requested by the user. Futhermore, it offers the user a positive match confirmation. While not destructive, this proof-of-concept virus demonstrated the tenacity of virus writers in exploring every avenue for spreading mobile malicious code.

## The Client-Server Network

Unlike the peer-to-peer network, the *client-server network* offers much greater control over resources and file access. In the client-server network, data, data backup, security, shared files, and print queues are all stored on a central computer called the *server*. The workstations (or *client* computers) connect to the server and receive a security logon request or prompt. The username and/or password determine the level of access that the client is granted to data stored on the server. The chief advantage of this type of setup is centralized control and ease of management. Security is the principal factor in determining whether to use this type of setup or a peer-to-peer network.

Client-server networks are sometimes referred to as *two-tier networks*. In this scenario, a user interface runs on the client computer (workstation), with the database residing on the server. The actual programs (applications) that the user runs can operate on either the server or the client computer. Organizations that use a client-server network will employ network operating systems such as Windows NT, Novell NetWare, or Linux. These network operating systems have all the built-in security features needed to make this type of network environment extremely secure. Unfortunately, client-server networks are still not immune to malicious attack. If the central server is rendered inoperable by malicious code, some or all of the client computers will not be able to login and will, therefore, not have access to information stored on the server.

## Client-Server Malicious Code

Today, networks aren't the only ones to benefit from the use of a client-server relationship. Malicious programs like BackOrifice 2000 also use the client-server relationship to gain access to already-infected computers on the Internet. The BackOrifice client program is typically sent as an attachment to an e-mail message with an innocent-looking file name. However, like the proverbial wolf in sheep's clothing, this insidious Trojan horse program installs a "backdoor" component on the unsuspecting victim's computer. The backdoor gives a remote computer (located anywhere on the Internet) full access to the files and folders on the victim's computer while that computer is connected to the Internet. To complete the client-server relationship, a server program is installed on the attacker's computer, allowing that computer to access the victim's computer via the client program. Some of the actions that can be accomplished through the use of this Trojan are:

✓ Acquiring system information

✓ Stealing password information

✓ Keystroke logging

✓ Registry editing

✓ Access to Microsoft Networking file sharing

✓ Remote restart/shutdown

✓ File/directory browsing, transfer, and management

Unfortunately, all of these actions can be accomplished without the knowledge and/or consent of the end user.

# File-Sharing Issues — Malware to Spare

Computer networks and the network operating systems that run them were born out of the need to share data across distances quickly and easily. Many organizations had networks in place long before former Vice President Al Gore "gave" us the Internet. The advent of the information super-highway transformed the way files and data were shared. As organizations began to realize how much they stood to benefit from using the Internet, many quickly explored ways to connect their internal networks to the public Internet. However, connecting their "safe" internal networks to the "unsafe" public Internet proved to be a dangerous endeavor.

The guiding tenet of computer security is that overall security will only be as strong as the weakest component. In the case of companies connecting their LANs to the Internet, the weakest point is the junction between the LAN and the Internet. Anyone from anywhere around the globe can potentially access files on that LAN. Many organizations use Windows operating systems on their workstations. These Windows computers have file and print sharing enabled, allowing them to share resources on the LAN. Users install the file-sharing feature of Window9x in order to make all or part of their hard disk (or any other disk drive) shareable. Computers with file and print sharing enabled are then visible in other networked computers' Network Neighborhood window, allowing all users to access the shared drive. This is known as "peer-to-peer" file sharing. Windows allows a user to make the disk shareable without a password, but this should never be permitted. The use of a password should always be required.

Always restrict sharing ability to only those parts of the disk that a user needs to share. Users sometimes believe that there is nothing confidential on their hard disk. Therefore, they make it all shareable. They don't consider that they may store confidential data on that shared drive at a later time. Consequently, only individual folders should be made shareable. In addition, unless a user's coworkers need to write directly to the user's disk, the shared folder should be made read-only. Finally, users must be careful to restrict knowledge of the password, and to make sure that their coworkers also remain security-conscious. If a user makes a folder shareable so that a coworker can read it, it will be only as secure as their coworker's computer.

Even when firewalls are employed to help separate and protect the LAN from the Internet, malicious code often gains access to these networks by masquerading as an innocuous file. Using stealth methods like those described in Chapter 4, malicious code can bypass anti-virus software and find residence on a workstation computer or network server.

**caution**

Many organizations are aware that peer-to-peer networking is easy and convenient and helps increase worker productivity. However, in their zeal to network their organization workstations and servers, many fail to make appropriate security assessments, leaving their networks vulnerable to threats posed by hackers and malicious code.

# Mapped Drives — Malicious Code Finds Its Way

To facilitate the sharing of files in a Windows networked environment, users often "map" network drives *into* their workstation PCs. Mapped drives are simply data drives (for example, hard disk, CD-ROM, or removable media disk) from a distant networked PC that appear as a local drive on a user's computer. These mapped drives will appear as "additional" drive icons (E:, F:, or H:, for example), along with any local drives (those physically attached), in the My Computer window.

While mapped drives are designed to allow a user access to data located on another user's computer, they also help malicious code propagate. In fact, using Windows network shares via mapped drives to disseminate malicious code has become quite common. Network-aware malicious code simply searches My Computer, looking for mapped network drives, and then infects those as well. To prevent malicious code from using mapped drives as a convenient way to propagate, some network administrators advise users to forgo the mapping of drives in their entirety and instead just use individual file shares to access data. Individual file shares provide a shortcut (icon) directly to the files you need on another user's computer or server instead of mapping their disk into your computer.

**security alert**

While this "good" security practice obviates the need to map drives, a new breed of worms, such as ExplorerZIP, Funlove.4099, and the more recent Nimda, can search for open file shares (typically not needing these drives to be mapped, only shared) and infect or delete certain files on the shared drives.

# The Java Virtual Machine — The Machine Is Virtual, the Malicious Code Is Real

*Virtual machines* are computer platforms that are implemented in software on top of the "real" hardware platform and operating system. Java is a powerful programming language that is used in many Internet applications and is designed to run on almost any computer platform (Windows, Mac, Linux, and so on). This versatility is made possible by a software program called *Java Virtual*

*Machine (JVM).* Instead of writing several different versions of Java for the various computer platforms, Java programmers need only compile code to operate with the Java Virtual Machine.

Individual JVM programs do vary, however, since each JVM is written to operate uniquely on a specific computer platform. The means that the JVM for a Mac, for example, will not work on a Windows-based PC, and the Windows version will not work on a Linux operating system. Use of the JVM makes Java programming code *very* portable. The same Java code that works on a Windows-based PC will also work on a Mac, provided that both have a Java Virtual Machine running on their operating system. The JVM plays an essential role in making Java portable. It provides an abstract "layer" between the actual Java program and the hardware platform or operating system.

Sun Microsystems (the developer of Java) designed the JVM with security in mind from its inception. As the Internet began to gain momentum, Web browsers such as Netscape Navigator and Internet Explorer included JVMs, allowing users to take full advantage of Java-based Web content. It wasn't long before malicious code found its way to the JVM. In August of 1998, a proof-of-concept virus called Strange Brew appeared. While it did not carry a damaging payload, it did prove the concept that cross-platform Java viruses *could be* written. Strange Brew, however, affects only Java applications, not Java applets (the small Java scripts) that typically run inside a Web browser. Because the Java Virtual Machine has built-in security measures, it does not allow Java applets direct access to the hard disk nor the ability to modify applications. This prevented Strange Brew from reaching other Java code and causing harm.

In January of 1999, the second known Java virus, called Java.BeanHive, was discovered. This virus was designed to infect both Java applets as well as Java applications. Remember, Java applets are small Java programs (written in Java Script) that are often used on Web sites that are downloaded and run by Web browsers while users surf the Internet. Java applets are substantially different from actual Java applications (written in Java) that are used in the stand-alone programs (applications) of desktop PCs and servers.

When a user encounters a Web site that contains one or more Java applets, the applets are downloaded to the user's computer and then executed in the Java Virtual Machine. The virtual machine allows the Java applet to run while ensuring that the user's computer is protected from any *malicious* activity by the Java applet. An inherent part of JVM's design is the fact that it prevents Java applets from accessing the Registry and other critical operating system components of the user's computer. These security features have made Java one of the safest ways to enjoy interactive content over the Internet.

While the JVM made the use of Java applets secure, it also prevented applets from performing some functional and convenient tasks. For example, if somebody wanted to develop a Java applet that could search a database of files on a user's hard drive, it would be precluded from doing so by the JVM's built-in security features. Because Java was designed to be both practical *and* portable, this ubiquitous code was later modified to lessen the restrictive nature of the JVM. The end result of these modifications was that if a Java applet made a request to access certain files it would normally not be permitted to access, a dialog box would pop-up asking the user to grant or deny such permission.

The Java.BeanHive virus was the first to exploit this feature by asking the user to grant the virus permission for full file access. Because the virus was a seemingly innocuous Java applet, some users inadvertently granted it full permission, not knowing it was malicious code. In contrast, Strange Brew did not "properly" request access, and was therefore automatically denied admission to restricted areas by the JVM. In instances where users denied access, the Java.BeanHive virus failed to execute and was immediately terminated.

**caution**

When a user grants a Java applet permission to access restricted areas, they also grant permission to any future Java applets written by the same author.

The best protection against hostile Java applets is to secure your network's access points. Many organizational networks employ firewalls to guard against unauthorized access from the Internet. Nevertheless, a firewall alone cannot protect computers from requesting hostile Java applets. With the addition of content inspection software at the firewall, it is possible to inspect Java content as it enters your network.

**x-ref**

Hardware and software protective measures are discussed in more detail in Chapter 9.

# Internet Browsers and Their Vulnerabilities

Web browsers are the "windows" to the Internet. Internet programming languages such as Hypertext Markup Language (HTML) and JavaScript (JS) were designed to give users quick and easy transport across the Internet. Furthermore, they make up much of the visual information that users see displayed in a Web browser. The first Web browser, called NCSA Mosaic, was developed in the early 1990s at the National Center for Supercomputing Applications (NCSA). All contemporary browsers are based on the original NCSA Mosaic design.

The two most popular Web browsers in use today are Microsoft's Internet Explorer (IE) and Netscape's Navigator. In the mid 1990s, Netscape Navigator was the most popular Web browser available. Feature-rich and easy-to-use, it helped usher in the Internet revolution. In an attempt to "jump" on the Internet bandwagon, software giant Microsoft put a team of engineers to the task of creating its own Web browser. Internet Explorer, as this browser came to be known, was designed to exceed Navigator's capabilities. More importantly, Microsoft decided to give it away free. At the time, Netscape charged a nominal fee for the privilege of downloading their browser.

Free was hard to beat, and as a result, Microsoft quickly took the lead in browser popularity. Then, in an interesting twist, Microsoft bundled its Web browser as part of the operating system with Windows 98. Users thus had little choice but to accept the browser as another operating system component. Netscape, however, filed a lawsuit against Microsoft, accusing them of anti-trust t follows is a partial transcript of the court's conclusion from the much-publicized

No. 98-1232 (TPJ)

CONCLUSIONS OF LAW

The United States, nineteen individual states, and the District of Columbia ("the plaintiffs") bring these consolidated civil enforcement actions against defendant Microsoft Corporation ("Microsoft") under the Sherman Antitrust Act, 15 U.S.C. §§ 1 and 2. The plaintiffs charge, in essence, that Microsoft has waged an unlawful campaign in defense of its monopoly position in the market for operating systems designed to run on Intel-compatible personal computers ("PCs"). Specifically, the plaintiffs contend that Microsoft violated §2 of the Sherman Act by engaging in a series of exclusionary, anticompetitive, and predatory acts to maintain its monopoly power. They also assert that Microsoft attempted, albeit unsuccessfully to date, to monopolize the Web browser market, likewise in violation of §2. Finally, they contend that certain steps taken by Microsoft as part of its campaign to protect its monopoly power, namely tying its browser to its operating system and entering into exclusive dealing arrangements, violated § 1 of the Act.

Upon consideration of the Court's Findings of Fact ("Findings"), filed herein on November 5, 1999, as amended on December 21, 1999, the proposed conclusions of law submitted by the parties, the briefs of amici curiae, and the argument of counsel thereon, the Court concludes that Microsoft maintained its monopoly power by anticompetitive means and attempted to monopolize the Web browser market, both in violation of § 2. Microsoft also violated § 1 of the Sherman Act by unlawfully tying its Web browser to its operating system. The facts found do not support the conclusion, however, that the effect of Microsoft's marketing arrangements with other companies constituted unlawful exclusive dealing under criteria established by leading decisions under § 1.

The nineteen states and the District of Columbia ("the plaintiff states") seek to ground liability additionally under their respective antitrust laws. The Court is persuaded that the evidence in the record proving violations of the Sherman Act also satisfies the elements of analogous causes of action arising under the laws of each plaintiff state. For this reason, and for others stated below, the Court holds Microsoft liable under those particular state laws as well.

Despite being accused of browser "foul play," Microsoft continues to bundle IE with their operating systems. Users can now, however, uninstall IE if they want to install a Web browser from a third-party vendor.

Computer systems are at risk when a threat takes advantage of a vulnerability and causes harm. A threat is any circumstance or event with the potential to cause harm to an organization through the disclosure, modification, or destruction of information, or by the denial of services. Organizations exhibit different vulnerability levels, and they should develop and adopt security policies that reflect their particular sensitivities. Security policies provide the foundation for implementing security controls to reduce vulnerabilities and reduce risks. The cost of security controls that are adopted should be appropriate for the risks involved. For Web users, organizational security policies should clearly state the terms and conditions for the use of the Web, and should assign roles and responsibilities for carrying out those policies.

Managers should assign specific responsibilities for the creation, management, and maintenance of their organization's external Web site. Assigning roles helps implement organizational policies. In smaller organizations, there may only be a need for one individual (a Web site engineer or Webmaster, for instance) to report to the senior manager.

In larger organizations, Web site responsibilities may be spread across several different groups and managers. The Web site manager oversees the overall strategy of the Web site, including coordinating content preparation, distribution, and budget monitoring. The technical staff or the Webmaster is responsible for Web site development, connection, intranet, e-mail, and firewall security. Programmers and graphic artists are responsible for the installation, design, coding, debugging, and documentation of the Web site.

Security policies are covered in Chapter 8.

Vulnerabilities stemming from the use of the World Wide Web are associated with browser software and server software. While browser software can introduce vulnerabilities to an organization, these sensitivities are generally less severe than the threats posed by servers. A number of risks related to the use of WWW browsers to search for and retrieve information over the Internet exist. Web browsing programs are very complicated and are becoming more so. The more intricate a program, the less secure it generally is. As a result, flaws may be exploited by network-based attacks.

Web pages often include forms. As with e-mail messaging, data sent from a Web browser to a Web server may pass through many interconnecting computers and networks before reaching its final destination. Users should be aware that the privacy of personal or valuable information sent using a Web page entry cannot be assured.

Web servers are vulnerable to threats, especially to malicious threats. Web servers can be attacked directly, or they can be used as launching points to attack an organization's internal networks. Organizations should examine the underlying operating system of their Web server, the Web server software, and server scripts for vulnerabilities.

Updating and patching browsers is covered in Chapter 9.

# Establishing Policies to Protect Your Web Site

One way to protect your Web site and to protect yourself from browser vulnerabilities is to establish policies (patterns of behavior) that different types of users of your network must adhere to when engaging in their Web activities. The National Institute of Standards and Technology offers guidelines that may be useful for organizations establishing policies to protect their Web sites. These policies are divided into situations involving low, medium, and high sensitivities to risks that could result from the use of the Web. User, manager, and technical staff member responsibilities are identified where appropriate.

## EXAMPLE POLICY STATEMENTS FOR BROWSING

In low-risk situations:

✓ **User policies:**

- Software for browsing the Internet is provided to employees primarily for business use.

- Any personal use must not interfere with normal business activities, must not involve solicitation, must not be associated with any for-profit outside business activity, and must not embarrass the company.

- Internet users are prohibited from transmitting or downloading material that is obscene, pornographic, threatening, or racially or sexually harassing.

- Users of the WWW are reminded that Web browsers leave "footprints" providing a trail of all site visits.

✓ **Manager policies:**

- Approved sources for licensed WWW software will be made available to users.

✓ **Technical staff policies:**

- A local repository of useful WWW browsers, helper applications, and plug-ins will be maintained and made available for internal use.

In medium-risk situations:

✓ **User policies:**

- Software for browsing the World Wide Web is provided to employees for business use only.

- Only technical staff may download files over the WWW.

✓ **Manager policies:**

- All software used to access the WWW must be approved by the Network Manager and must incorporate all vendor-provided security patches.

✓ **Technical staff policies:**

- Any files downloaded over the WWW must be scanned for viruses, using approved virus detection software.

- Due to the nonsecure state of the technology, all WWW browsers shall disable the use of Java, JavaScript, and ActiveX.

- Only company-approved versions of browser software may be used or downloaded.

- Nonapproved versions may contain viruses or other bugs.

- All Web browsers must be configured to use the firewall HTTP proxy.

- When using a form, ensure that the SSL or Secure Sockets layer or other such mechanism is configured to encrypt the message as it is sent from the user's browser to the Web server.

In high-risk situations:

✓ **User policies:**

- Users may browse the Internet using approved software for the sole purpose of their research or job function.

- No sites known to contain offensive material may be visited.

- Any user suspected of misuse may have all transactions and material logged for further action.

- URLs of offensive sites must be forwarded to the organization's Web security contact.

✓ **Manager policies:**

- An organization-wide list of forbidden sites will be maintained. WWW software will be configured so that those sites cannot be accessed.

- Internet sites containing offensive material will be immediately blocked by network administrators.

- Contractors must follow this policy after explicit written authorization is given for access to the Internet.

✓ **Technical staff policies:**

- All sites visited are logged.

- Web browsers shall be configured with the following rules: They will only access the Internet through the firewall HTTP proxy, and they will scan every file downloaded for viruses or other malignant content.

- Only ActiveX controls signed by the organization may be downloaded.

- Only Java signed by the organization may be downloaded.

- Only JavaScript signed by the organization may be downloaded.

## EXAMPLE POLICY STATEMENTS FOR WEB SERVERS

In low-risk situations:

✓ **User policies:**

- No offensive or harassing material may be made available via the organization's Web sites.

- No personal commercial advertising may be made available via the organization's Web sites.

✓ **Manager policies:**

- Managers and users are permitted to have a Web site.

- The personal material on or accessible from the Web site should be minimal.

- No offensive or harassing material may be made available via the organization's Web sites.

- No organization's confidential material will be made available.

✓ **Technical staff policies:**

- A local archive of Web server software and authoring tools will be maintained and made available for internal use.

In medium-risk situations

✓ **User policies:**

- Users are not permitted to install or run Web servers.

- Web pages must follow existing approval procedures regarding company documents, reports, memos, marketing information, and so on.

✓ **Manager policies:**

- Managers and users are permitted to have Web pages for a business-related project or function.

✓ **Technical staff policies:**

- The Web server and any data to be accessed by the general public must be located external to the organization's firewall.

- Web servers must be configured so that users cannot install CGI scripts.

- All network applications other than HTTP should be disabled (for example, SMTP, ftp).

- Information servers shall be located on a screened subnet to isolate itself from other systems on the site. This reduces the chance that an information server could be compromised and then used to attack these systems.

- If using a Web administrative tool, access is restricted to only authorized systems (via IP address, rather than hostname).

- Default passwords must always be changed.

In high-risk situations

✓ **User policies:**

- Users are forbidden to download, install, or run Web server software.

- Network traffic will be monitored for unapproved Web servers, and operators of those servers will be subject to disciplinary action.

✓ **Manager policies:**

- The Chief Information Officer (CIO) must approve the operation of any other Web server to be connected to the Internet in writing.

- All content on the organization's WWW servers connected to the Internet must be approved by and installed by the Webmaster.

- No confidential material may be made available on the Web site.

- Information placed on the Web site is subject to the same Privacy Act restrictions as when nonelectronic information is released. Accordingly, before information is placed on the Internet, it must be reviewed and approved for release in the same manner as other official memos, reports, or other official nonelectronic information. Copyrights must be protected and permission obtained before placing copyrighted information on the Web site. Public affairs offices or legal authorities should be contacted for advice and assistance.

- All publicly accessible Web sites must be thoroughly tested to ensure that all links work as designed and are not "under construction" when the site is opened to the public. Under-construction areas are not to appear on publicly accessible Web sites.

✓ **Technical staff policies:**

- Remote control of the Web server (that is, from other than the console) is not allowed.

- All administrator operations (such as security changes) shall be performed from the console.

- Supervisor-level logon will not be done at any device other than the console.

- The Web server software, and the software of the underlying operating system, will contain all manufacturer-recommended patches for the version in use.

- Incoming HTTP traffic will be scanned, and connections to unapproved Web sites will be reported.

- Restricting user access to Web addresses provides a minimal level of protection for information not cleared for release to the public. A separate server or partition may be used to separate restricted use information (internal information or internal Web site) from information released to the public.

- All Web sites may be monitored as part of the organization's network administration function. Any user suspected of misuse may have all their transactions logged for possible disciplinary action.

- On UNIX systems, Web servers will not be run as root.

- The implementation and use of CGI scripts will be monitored and controlled.

- CGI scripts will not accept unchecked input. Any programs that run externally with arguments should not contain meta characters. The developer is responsible for devising the proper regular expression to scan for shell meta characters and will strip out special characters before passing external input to the server software or the underlying operating system.

- All WWW servers connected to the Internet will have a firewall between the Web server and internal company networks. Any internal WWW servers supporting critical company applications must be protected by internal firewalls.

- Sensitive, confidential, and private information should never be stored on an external WWW server.

## Patching and Updating Browser Software

In the early days of Internet popularity, as the number of Internet users continued to grow, one fact quickly became evident. With the rush for dominance in the Web browser arena, it appeared that browser security still left something to be desired. In July 1998, Microsoft issued a "special alert" concerning vulnerabilities found in Internet Explorer. The special alert was issued, in particular, to users of Internet Explorer 4.0 or later.

The July 1998 security concern affected certain IE e-mail programs, including Microsoft Outlook 98 and Microsoft Outlook Express versions 4.0 and later. The security issue centered on the way e-mail software handles file attachments with extremely long file names. When users attempt to download, open, or launch a file attachment with a name containing more than a certain number of characters, the program may shut down unexpectedly or malicious code may be executed.

A month later, Netscape Communications issued their own security alert regarding the very same issue. The long file name vulnerability affected mail and news components of Netscape Communicator 4.0 through 4.05 when used on Windows 3.1, 95, 98, or NT platforms. The vulnerability could allow an e-mail or newsgroup message with an attachment having a very long file name to execute malicious code on affected computers.

Over the years, other alerts followed and patches were provided to fix problems in the difficult and perpetual battle for security. Keep in mind that both Microsoft and Netscape have always been forthcoming in describing the vulnerabilites. They have been committed to making their products safe, responding quickly to potential problems by issuing alerts and software patches for their products. For this reason, it is important that Web browsers, e-mail, and operating system software always be kept up-to-date.

# E-mail — Can the Postal Services Compete?

E-mail has revolutionized how information is exchanged. It has become so ubiquitous, it's a wonder that postal services around the globe are still able to compete. E-mail is loaded with features that make it an ideal replacement for traditional mail. The use of digital signatures ensures that incoming e-mail has not been tampered with or altered in transit. Digital signatures, like their handwritten counterparts, are used to validate the identity of the sender.

Modern-day e-mail programs allow users to attach files and documents directly to an e-mail message, allowing them to be "zapped" around the globe in a matter of seconds. Documents that would have taken days to arrive at their destination can now be forwarded to recipients in the time it takes you to read this sentence. Doctors, lawyers, accountants — nearly every industry benefits from the use of e-mail. Notwithstanding all that e-mail has to offer, the fact remains that it poses a serious security threat to its users. As a result of its speed and widespread use, e-mail is one of the fastest and most efficient ways to circulate viruses, worms, and Trojan horse programs. In fact, e-mail viruses remain the single largest threat to Internet users.

As mentioned in the introduction of this book, the AnnaKournikova worm was extremely successful: it spread around the globe and affected so many users so rapidly, it surprised even its author. E-mail programs like Microsoft's Outlook or Outlook Express sometimes act as a catalyst for these malicious code outbreaks. Holes in Outlook's security allowed malicious code to access the e-mail address books of infected computers, thereby providing the malevolent code with the e-mail addresses of its next victims. When the recipients received the viral tainted e-mail, they believed it was sent by someone known to them. They readily opened the e-mail, thereby continuing the circulation of the virus.

Over the past few years, numerous viruses have taken advantage of holes and flaws in Outlook, prompting several security patches. Because Outlook was implicated in the vast majority of viral outbreaks, some security experts claimed that Microsoft was sacrificing security for functionality. They point to the plethora of patches and updates to support their theory.

## The Human Element of E-mail

While programming flaws in e-mail programs are something over which end users do not have much control, their own behavior is. One of the reasons e-mail viruses are so successful is that users are tricked into opening or executing attachments. Modern day viruses, worms, and Trojan horse programs are written and circulated so quickly that many anti-virus scanners cannot detect them. Virus writers are aware of this, counting on the human element of temptation to help perpetuate the spread of their malicious code. This was evidenced with both the AnnaKournikova worm and the "hybrid" Naked Wife Trojan-worm.

While AnnaKournikova did not carry a destructive payload, the Naked Wife Trojan-worm did. Luckily, this virus was quickly publicized, helping to diminish its effect. In the defense against malicious code, the use of social engineering and education is critical.

The use of social engineering and education to defend against malicious code is covered in detail in Chapter 8.

## E-mail Hoaxes — The "Joke" Is on You

E-mail hoaxes were born from the worldwide publicity given to malicious code. Hysteria over contracting a debilitating computer virus has many computer users panicking every time another viral outbreak is publicized. Exploiting these fears, virus writers can sometimes get users to damage their own computers simply by sending false malicious code alerts.

Many gullible Internet users have been duped into altering their own computer systems by removing system files (sometimes critical ones) when they receive what appears to be an authentic and genuine virus warning. Such was the case in April 1991, when countless computer users were told of a bogus new virus called Sulfnbk.exe that threatened to damage their systems. An e-mail message instructed users to perform a file search of their hard drives for this "dangerous" virus. When users of Windows 95/98 or Me performed the search, they invariably found that they were "infected," since their search returned a match for the file in their C:\windows\command directory. This file, however, was not a virus but a utility included by Microsoft as part of the operating system. Its purpose was to restore long file names in case they became corrupted. Although that file is not critical to the proper operation of Windows, this hoax exemplifies how a user can be duped.

Convinced by an e-mail ruse that a critical, legitimate operating system component is a virus, unsuspecting users might delete that "discovered" component and leave their system inoperable. The best defense against such deceptions is awareness. Web sites such as http://hoaxbusters. ciac.org/ and http://vmyths.com/ allow users to verify whether or not the e-mail warnings they receive are genuine.

# TCP/IP Ports and Their Functions

Back in the early 1970s, under contract by the Defense Advanced Research Project Agency (DARPA), Stanford University was asked to create a communications protocol that could exploit the advantages of the wide area network they were developing.

> **note**
>
> A protocol is a set of rules or principles that governs how a computer communicates across a network.

In developing these new protocols, DARPA's request to Stanford was three-fold. The new protocol had to be very reliable. It also had to allow the many different types of computer networks in operation at the time to connect and communicate with each other. Finally, the new protocol needed to possess the ability to select an alternate communications path to its final destination in the event that the original path was severed. Bear in mind that the original purpose of the Internet was to maintain communications links in a wide area network, even if part of that network was destroyed in a nuclear attack. The end result of Stanford University's dedicated efforts was the development of a protocol called *Transmission Control Protocol/Internet Protocol — TCP/IP* for short.

TCP/IP is the fundamental protocol that is relied upon by the Internet for communications. TCP/IP is actually not a single protocol; it is a suite of protocols (called a *stack*) that allows Internet communications to take place. Engineered into TCP/IP was the ability to track and transfer different types of data. Through the use of communications ports, TCP/IP allowed a program on one computer to communicate with a program on another computer across a network. In the case of the Internet, the TCP/IP network stretches across the globe.

More than 65,000 ports are available in the TCP/IP stack; however, only the first 1,023 are commonly used. Each individual port is an "opening," or portal, through which a specific type of information flows. Different applications (for example, WWW, news, chat, or e-mail) use different port numbers. Suppose a user visits a Web site. He or she is connected to port 80 (HTTP port) on the remote computer that "serves" those Web pages. When that same user needs to download his or her e-mail, special e-mail software in his or her computer will connect to his or her Internet service provider using port 110 (Post Office Protocol port) to retrieve messages from an Internet mail server. Hackers and virus writers use port scanners (see Figure 6-1) to locate open ports on computers across the Internet for the purpose of gaining entry. The following is a partial list of commonly used ports and their names:

- ✓ #21 — File Transfer Protocol (FTP)
- ✓ #23 — Telnet
- ✓ #25 — Simple Mail Transfer Protocol (SMTP)
- ✓ #80 — The World Wide Web (HTTP)
- ✓ #110 — Post Office Protocol (POP)

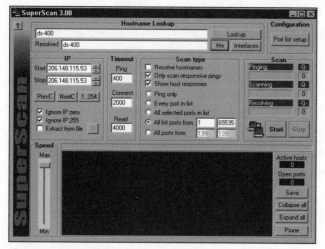

**Figure 6-1:** SuperScan 3.0 by Foundstone, Inc.

TCP/IP ports can play an important role when it comes to malicious code. Trojans like BackOrifice, NetBus, and SubSeven have been known to exploit seldom-used ports by using them as "backdoors," allowing outside (Internet) access to an infected computer. As is mentioned in Chapter 4, Trojan horses are capable of controlling, monitoring, and damaging PCs. Some Trojan viruses, like SubSeven, can also be configured to notify someone when the virus's host connects to the Internet and then relay to that notified person all the information they want about the user. This notification can be made over an Internet Relay Chat (IRC), I-Seek-You (ICQ), or by e-mail.

Firewalls (covered in Chapter 9) are often used to block certain TCP/IP ports to help prevent Trojan horse programs from sending unauthorized communications into or out of a computer.

# Summary

Networks have become an indispensable part of the corporate landscape. Because many house-holds and businesses of all sizes now rely on Internet connectivity, those who write malicious code view them as prime new targets. Network-aware viruses are one of the fastest growing segments of malicious code. The first step in protecting Internet-enabled networks is to understand how networks operate and where the most common vulnerabilities lie. This chapter covers the following key points:

✓ Peer-to-peer networks offer little security and are best suited for small networks.

✓ Client-server networks use a central server and offer more security than peer-to-peer networks.

✓ Network-aware malicious code can spread quickly throughout a company network through mapped drives and shared files.

✓ File-sharing Web sites such as Napster, Gnutella, and KaZaA are a breeding ground for malicious code and hackers.

✓ E-mail is the fastest and easiest way to circulate viruses, worms, and Trojan horse programs.

✓ E-mail hoaxes can have computer users turn on themselves by tricking them into modifying or deleting critical operating system files.

✓ TCP/IP is the language of the Internet and uses ports to send and receive information. Left unprotected, these ports leave computers vulnerable to attack.

# Chapter 7

# Internet Relay Chat (IRC), I-Seek-You (ICQ), Web Page Chat, and Instant Messaging

## In This Chapter

✓ Exploring IRC, ICQ, and their vulnerabilities

✓ Using employee education and social engineering as tools for defense

✓ Using port-blocking firewalls with instant messaging

✓ Using Web-based chat and the risks involved

✓ Reviewing popular instant messaging programs and their weaknesses

✓ Minimizing risk by identifying and eliminating malicious code threats

✓ Protecting instant messaging services with anti-virus software

HUMANS ARE SOCIAL BEINGS, and as such, they enjoy conversing and sharing ideas, discussing problems, and seeking the advice of others. Before the invention of the telegraph and telephone, hand-written messages took days — sometimes weeks — to reach distant destinations. However, when the telegraph was invented in 1844 by Samuel Morse, people could quickly communicate with each other across great distances. Still, its use of dots and dashes (known as Morse code) made the exchanges relatively slow and lacked the finesse of verbal communication.

Alexander Graham Bell's invention of the telephone in March 1876 promised to make the telegraph obsolete. The telephone enabled humans to communicate with each other, not with dots or dashes, but with the actual human voice. It wasn't long before the telephone took the world by storm. In the early 1960s, at the request of the U.S. Department of Defense (DOD), engineers began the task of building a wide area network that could maintain communication links in the event of a nuclear war. The engineers attempted to build this network using the widely available dial-up telephone lines. They quickly found, however, that the circuit-switched telephone system was inadequate for the task and that a new type of network was required. Hence, the birth of the packet-switched Internet. The Internet was initially intended for military communications. However, it was "turned over" to the public in the early 1980s. Individuals and companies then started seeking ways to use it for both public communication and social interaction.

Since the Internet spans all continents, people across the globe can communicate with each other easily and cheaply—at a lower cost, in fact, than if they used long-distance telephone communication. The Internet also affords an anonymous and neutral theater for correspondence. As the Internet increases in popularity, different communication programs have emerged. For example, Internet Relay Chat (IRC), I-Seek-You (ICQ), and instant messaging allow family, friends, and even total strangers to write to each other instantly across the global Internet. Needless to say, malicious code has found its way into all of these communication programs. This chapter covers how the programs operate, assesses their vulnerabilities, and explores the means available to protect users from the plethora of viruses, worms, and Trojans that regularly plague them.

# Internet Relay Chat—IRC the Place to Be?

Originated by Jarkko Oikarinen of Finland in 1988, IRC has become a popular means for Internet communications. IRC first gained popularity during the Persian Gulf War, when Internet users around the world employed IRC to keep informed about news events. Despite the proliferation of subsequent communication programs, IRC remains one of the most popular ways to "chat" on the Internet.

*IRC,* short for *Internet Relay Chat,* is a multi-user, text-based chat system that is run over a network. It gives individuals around the world the ability to "chat" with each other in real-time via typed text. Each user has a moniker (handle) and converses with other users either in a public chat forum or in a private chat room.

Numerous IRC programs, called *IRC clients,* are available to Internet users. They are used to connect to an IRC network. The most popular IRC client for Windows users is mIRC, and the most popular for the Macintosh platform is Ircle. With UNIX or Linux platforms, XChat is very popular. IRC is based on a client-server model, with the client program located on the user's computer and the server located somewhere on the Internet.

Users must first download an IRC client program and then install it on their computer. While connected to the Internet, they launch the IRC client program, which connects them to a server located on the IRC network. Once connected to the IRC server, the users can communicate with other similarly connected users throughout the world.

The amount of chatting is so great that a single server cannot handle the volume, and more than one server (networked together) must be used to meet the demand. Some popular IRC networks are NewNET (www.newnet.net), DALnet (www.dal.net), and Undernet (www.undernet.org). Each network has hundreds of "channels" where people can chat with each other. For ease of use, these channels are generally named according to the predominant topic discussed by the "chatters" on that particular channel.

## The Risks of IRC

While IRC may sound inviting, it also presents some serious security risks. The IRC network has been exploited by malicious code on numerous occasions. Due to the increased risk that networked computers will be infected by IRC-controlled malicious code, the NIPC (National Infrastructure Protection Agency) issued the follow advisory in October 2000:

ADVISORY 00-055
Trinity v3/ Stacheldraht 1.666" Distributed Denial-of-Service Tool
October 13, 2000

New variants of the Trinity and Stacheldraht Distributed Denial-of-Service (DDoS) tools have been found in the wild. As was demonstrated in February of this year, DDoS attacks can bring down networks by flooding target machines with more traffic than the machines can process. This advisory provides an update to previous NIPC DDoS advisories (issued since December 1999) on similar tools such as "mstream," "Tribal Flood Network," and "trinoo." The NIPC has recently determined that masters tied to zombies have been placed on many users' systems, heightening the possibility of a DDoS attack in the future. In addition to large corporate and university systems, affected users also include those with home computers having broadband access such as DSL and cable modem. The NIPC recommends that all computer network owners and organizations examine their systems for evidence of DDoS tools, including Trinity and Stacheldraht.

The "Trinity v3" Distributed Denial-of-Service (DDoS) exploit represents a potentially serious and continuing threat to networked computers running certain versions of the Linux operating system. Trinity v3 is a DDoS tool that is controlled via IRC or ICQ. When a system has been compromised and the Trinity v3 tool installed, each compromised machine joins a specified IRC channel and waits for commands. The Trinity v3 tool enables intruders to use multiple, Internet-connected systems to launch packet-flooding denial-of-service attacks against one or more target systems. At least eight variations of Trinity have been found on the Undernet Internet Relay Chat network, each reporting to a different IRC channel. Trinity v3 responds to commands in IRC channels on lines beginning with "(trinity)," and the "Entitee" version of Trinity responds to lines beginning with "(entitee)."

System administrators should ensure their TCP Port Scanners are configured to scan port 33270, as machines found listening at this port may have the Trinity portshell installed. Trinity v3 is difficult to detect because the agent does not listen to specific ports to receive commands, but receives them over IRC. Watching for suspicious IRC traffic is useful in detecting Trinity v3. It is important to note that if Trinity v3 is found on a system, the system may have experienced root level compromise.

Stacheldraht consists of three parts—a master server, a client, and an agent program—and runs on Linux and Solaris machines. Stacheldraht performs several types of flooding attacks, and has IRC flooding options. The latest stacheldraht variants, "Stacheldraht 1.666+antigl+yps" and "Stacheldraht 1.666+smurf+yps" prompt the user for a password when building the binaries.

The NIPC DDoS detection tool has been modified to detect Trinity v3 and some new variants of Stacheldraht. While the tool is designed to detect mutations of these DDoS tools, it may not detect all variants of the tools. NIPC will continue to update the detection tool as we receive new DDoS variants. Currently, the NIPC tool (`find_ddos`) detects the DDoS exploit in the following operating systems: Solaris on Sparc or Intel platforms, and Linux on Intel platforms. The tool currently detects mstream, tfn2k client, tfn2k daemon, trinoo daemon, trinoo master, tfn daemon, tfn client, stacheldraht master, stacheldraht client, stachelddraht daemon, and trn-rush client. Please refer to `http://www.nipc.gov/warnings/alerts/1999/trinoo.htm` for more information.

In the case of Trinity, the IRC was used mainly as a covert channel for communication. This was not the first time malicious code had been applied in this way. In 1999, the PrettyPark worm also tried to connect to certain IRC servers in order to join a specific channel. The PrettyPark worm sends information to the IRC every 30 seconds to keep itself connected, as well as to retrieve commands from the IRC. Using IRC as the conduit, the distributor of the worm can acquire information about users' systems, including computer name, system root path, version registered owner, registered organization, ICQ identification code, ICQ handle, victim e-mail address, and Dial-Up Networking password. In addition, while a user is connected to the IRC, a backdoor security hole is "opened" through which the infected computer can potentially be used to receive and execute files.

While these Trinity and PrettyPark worms have been largely eradicated, new types of malicious code are always looming on the horizon. Because IRC uses text to communicate, it is difficult to distinguish the "good guys" from the "bad guys." The best way to defend against malicious code obtained via IRC is to use the following three-step process:

1. Install and regularly update a reputable anti-virus software program (discussed later in this chapter).

2. Install a port-blocking software-based firewall (such as BlackICE Defender).

3. Use social engineering (educate users on the potential threats of using IRC), which is covered in the next section of this chapter.

While the need for using anti-virus software seems obvious, the use of firewalls and social engineering for additional protection should not be overlooked. Firewalls can be used to monitor and/or block the TCP/IP ports that malicious code commonly uses to communicate. Some firewalls, like BlackICE Defender by Internet Security Systems, Inc. (www.iss.net), have both intrusion detection and port-blocking features that allow them to detect unwanted intrusions *and* block malicious code communications via IRC channels. Following are other important steps that organizations should take to help control their sensitivity to malicious code threats:

✓ Make regular backups of important work and data, and check that the backups were successful.

✓ Sign up for e-mail alert services that warn about new viruses. Seeing that your users have access to information about the latest computer viruses by presenting them with live virus information, perhaps through an intranet or Web site, is also a good idea.

✓ Watch for Microsoft's security bulletins, many of which can be found at www.microsoft.com/security. These warn of new security loopholes and issues with Microsoft's software.

✓ Produce a set of guidelines and policies for safe computing and distribute them amongst your personnel. Make sure that every employee has read and understood the guidelines and that if they have any questions, they know to whom to speak.

The use of both software and hardware firewalls for malicious code defense are covered in detail in Chapter 9.

# Social Engineering — A Little Knowledge Goes a Long Way

Knowledge is one of the most cost-effective defense measures against the threat of malicious code. When users understand the risks of using a particular service like IRC and follow these simple steps, the threat of malicious attack is greatly diminished:

✓ Never accept a file when you are not completely sure of its content, even when the file appears to come from a trusted source. The reason is simple: viruses, worms, and Trojans that have already infected another IRC user's computer often attempt to send a copy of themselves to other unsuspecting recipients via the IRC channel. The recipient accepts the file because it appears to come from someone they know (and trust). However, once the malicious code is on their computer, it perpetuates the process to spread to other IRC users.

✓ Turn off the DCC (Direct Client Connections) auto-accept feature, found on the mIRC client program. Leaving auto-accept *on* allows unsolicited and automatic acceptance of files (malicious code included) via the IRC network. It is also advisable to have the following file extensions ignored in the DCC settings, `.com`, `.bat`, `.vbs`, `.exe`, `.dll`, `.shs`, and `.js`, as they are the most commonly used extensions for malicious code.

✓ Another well-known method of sending viruses is with the use of multiple file extensions. Because Windows is usually set up by default to "hide" known file extensions (for example, `.com`, `.exe`, `.dll`, `.vbs`, and so on), a file such as `innocentfile.txt.vbs` would appear simply as `innocentfile.txt` to the end user. The `.vbs` (Visual Basic Script) extension is hidden, making the file look like a harmless text file. While many legitimate applications are written in Visual Basic, malicious programs are also written using this and other powerful scripting languages. As a result, *all* IRC file downloads should be carefully monitored. By configuring Windows to display all file extensions, users can avoid the double extension deception. In general, the procedure to display all file extensions is as follows (this example uses Windows XP Professional):

**1.** Open My Computer and select the Tools menu at the top.

**2.** Under the Tools menu, select Folder Options (see Figure 7-1). The Folders Option dialog box appears.

**3.** In the Folder Options dialog box, select the View tab and make sure that the "Hide extensions for known file types" option is cleared (see Figure 7-2).

The exact procedure for configuring Windows to display all file extensions varies slightly for the different Windows versions. Users should consult their Windows instruction manual or the built-in Windows help file for assistance.

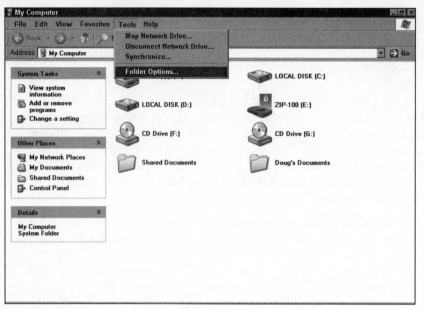

**Figure 7-1:** Accessing Folder Options in Windows XP Professional

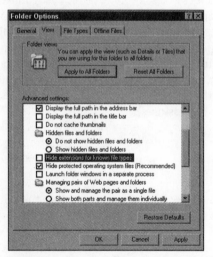

**Figure 7-2:** Revealing file extensions in the Folder Options dialog box

# ICQ — I-Seek-You, Not Malicious Code

Like IRC, *ICQ (I-Seek-You)* is a method of communicating across a network using text. Launched in 1996, ICQ connects friends, colleagues, and people with similar interests across the globe. Instead of communicating by conventional mail, e-mail, pager, or telephone, ICQ makes contacting friends as simple as (or even easier than) calling across a room and initiating a friendly conversation. ICQ is available for all versions of Windows, Macintosh, and Linux operating systems.

*Instant messaging* is the most popular method of communication on ICQ. It enables an ICQ user to send a message that immediately pops up on another online user's screen. ICQ also has other components that allow users to chat, send wireless-pager messages and e-mails, and *transfer* files. A more recent feature, ICQphone, enables users to engage in both "PC-to-PC" and "PC-to-telephone" calling using the Internet.

ICQ's multi-user mode allows individuals and/or businesses to conduct group conferences over the ICQ network. In fact, ICQ supports a variety of popular Internet applications and serves as a "universal platform" from which users can initiate peer-to-peer communications. In summary, ICQ brings together the most commonly used methods of communication using a simple and straightforward approach.

## ICQ — Easy to Use, Easy to Attack

Although ICQ is simple to use, its design makes it susceptible to attacks from malicious code and hackers on the Internet. The very features that attract users to ICQ in the first place are also the ones that make it so vulnerable. Due to its ease of use and overall simplicity, ICQ is used by Internet marauders as a conduit for spreading viruses, stealing files, attacking computers, and in general, wreaking havoc.

From a privacy standpoint, ICQ can leave users' personal information unprotected. Users must register when they initially engage the ICQ program. During the registration process, ICQ collects specific personal information about users, such as name, e-mail address, and location, in addition to other types of optional information. This personal information is stored on the ICQ servers and is available to anyone on the Internet who wants to view it.

A quick search through an ICQ database — accomplished using the ICQ client software or via the Web at `http://web.icq.com/whitepages/search/` — can reveal more information about a user than he or she intended to share, especially with strangers. This surfeit of information can lead to cyberstalking, on-line harassment, and unsolicited messages from Internet outlaws. While these types of problems are also seen in other forms of Internet communications, it is the abundance of information and the ease with which it can be obtained through ICQ that makes these abuses more common in that venue.

## With ICQ and IRC, You Could Be a Goner . . .

Individuals who construct malicious code are always on the lookout for new vectors for distribution. This was evidenced in the latter part of 2001, when a new and innovative mass-mailing Internet worm called "Goner" made its rounds. Goner is distinguishable by its subject line (Hi) and the body of its message, which promises a screensaver. The attachment is called `Goner.scr`. Written in Visual Basic, Goner spreads by e-mailing itself to any contacts found in an infected user's MS Outlook address book. It also goes a step further by propagating itself through online chat programs such as ICQ and IRC.

By using ICQ and IRC, Goner became one of the fastest spreading worms ever seen. It carries a seriously damaging payload: It deletes certain critical program files and also disables some anti-virus and personal firewall programs as it encounters them in infected users' PCs. So serious was Goner's threat that the NIPC issued the following public alert:

ALERT 01-029.1
VBS/Mass-Mailing Worm, W32/Goner.A
December 05, 2001

National Infrastructure Protection Center (NIPC) continues to monitor a mass-mailing worm called W32/Goner.A. This is a very fast-spreading mass-mailing worm that appears to take advantage of Visual Basic Scripting built into Microsoft Outlook and Outlook Express (Windows-based), then propagates using e-mail and an online instant messenger (ICQ). Developing information continues to indicate that this worm mails itself to all addresses within the infected computer's Outlook or Outlook Express address book, sets itself as a server process so it does not show up in the task manager, and deletes the anti-virus definitions from many common anti-virus products. It also searches out and terminates many commercial anti-virus software and firewall product processes.

The e-mail sent, to date, is always the same:

Subject: Hi
Attachment: gone.scr
Message text: "How are you? When I saw this screen saver, I immediately thought about you I am in a harry [sic], I promise you will love it!"

Goner spreads itself via ICQ's online instant messaging program client using the library file `ICQMAPI.DLL`. Goner copies that DLL from the directory `C:\PROGRAM FILES\ICQ\` to the Windows system directory. Goner then sends itself to all on-line users (regardless of mode) from an internal list of online users, via ICQ file transfer. Goner also answers to requests from other users requesting file transfers.

In order to hide its presence and actions, Goner does several things within the system. First, Goner sets itself up as a server process so it does not show up in the task manager as a running program. It then writes itself to the Windows registry so the worm is restarted upon reboot. Goner then searches out and terminates processes from many commercial anti-virus software packages and many commercial firewall products, including those for personal use. This renders the anti-virus software and firewall software temporarily useless. However, infected users may still believe they are protected.

Recommended Actions:

Update virus definitions and scan for presence of the worm. Ensure virus definitions include the signature for Goner or request definition updates from your technical support personnel. Most major anti-virus companies have provided new definition files for this virus. If your definition file pre-dates December 04, 2001, it is not current. Older definitions do not alert on this worm.

For individual users:

Consider deleting unexpected e-mails that contain file attachments without opening them.

Exercise particular caution with respect to e-mails that contain attachments that end in `.exe`, `.vbs`, `.bat`, `.scr`, and `.pif`.

Consider turning off all script and scripting within the e-mail client security settings.

Consider upgrading your e-mail client. Outlook 2002 has many security features enabled by default that would block propagation of Goner and certain other mass-mailing e-mail worms.

These actions may help protect you against this worm and many other mass-mailing malware products in the wild today.

For corporate users and system administrators:

Consider blocking ICQ traffic during an infection to block further propagation. ICQ client-to-server communication is conducted over TCP port 5190.

Consider blocking all messages that have attachments with extensions mentioned above. NIPC recommends having a virus checker at the mail server point that scans all incoming and outgoing messages for malicious code, as well as blocking executable file extensions.

The NIPC suggests blocking TCP port 5190 to help stop the propagation of the Goner worm because instant messaging services like ICQ and AOL's Instant Messenger use port 5190 to conduct communications. Personal or corporate firewalls require that this port be left open to ensure the proper functioning of the software. By quickly configuring the firewall to close this port once a worm is detected, propagation of ICQ worms can be limited substantially.

Since AOL and ICQ software connect to their respective servers at port 5190, a network administrator can easily configure the company firewall to allow communications at port 5190. This way, the AOL or ICQ client program (the one on your computer) can communicate with the server. However, to ensure the safety and integrity of data in transit, the AOL client software establishes a special encrypted two-way communication, called a *tunnel,* with the AOL server. This tunnel creates a *VPN (virtual private network)* between the AOL user and the AOL network.

VPNs are used to send secure encrypted communications between two points across IP networks such as the Internet.

In the case of AOL, this VPN essentially allows complete and open communications between the client and the remote server. Because the AOL client receives its *own* individual IP address on the virtual network, a firewall cannot limit this particular communication. This means that the client is now exposed to all kinds of IP-based attacks—hackers anywhere on the Internet may even have access to any personal Web or ftp servers running on the client machine. The firewall is helpless against these types of attacks because port 5190 must remain open to allow AOL communications to operate.

To see how AOL Instant Messenger communicates through a firewall, refer to Figure 7-3. In this scenario, the AOL client (listed as the second, third, and fourth entries from the top) uses three separate IP addresses to communicate with the AOL server across port 5190. In this illustration, the firewall has been configured to allow AOL to have *full* and unobstructed communications.

# Malicious Code "Seeks" ICQ

Every avenue of Internet communication is vulnerable to malicious code attack, and ICQ is no exception. As with any Internet tool, precautions must be implemented with ICQ to reduce the likelihood that it will be affected by malicious code attacks. Virtually all Internet programs are subject to improvements and enhancements over time.

When security flaws are discovered, small programs called patches are quickly made available to modify the program and close any detected holes (flaws). For this reason, users of ICQ (and in fact, any communications program) should always update their products with the latest versions available. Many programs will automatically check for updates at regular intervals and then alert their users by requesting permission to download and install updated programs. This is a must-do practice, as these updates often offer increased product security in addition to other product enhancements.

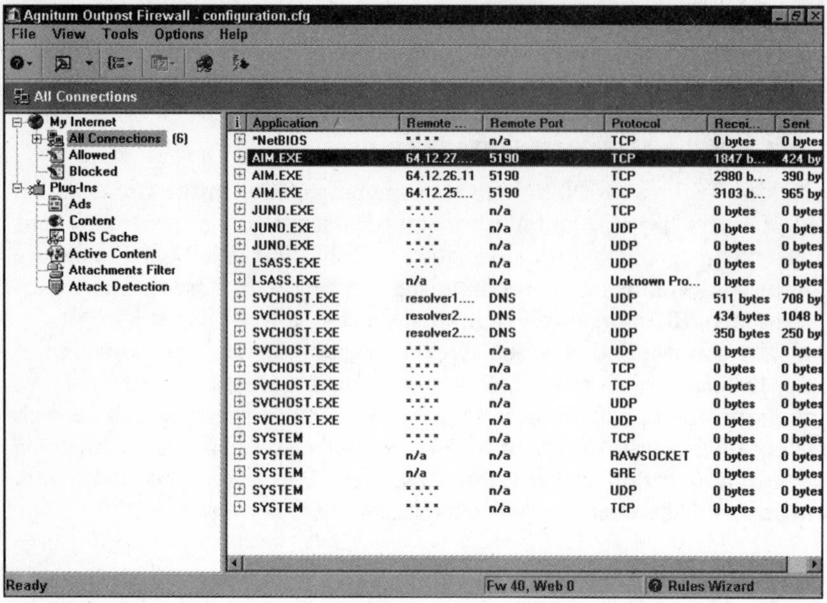

**Figure 7-3:** Agnitum Outpost Firewall Version 1.0 allowing full and unobstructed instant messaging access

As with IRC, users of ICQ should follow three basic rules to protect themselves from the threat of malicious code:

✓ Use updated anti-virus software to scan all downloaded files.

✓ Never accept files via e-mail attachment or file transfer from people you do not know. It is good practice when using the Internet to verify that the person sending you a file is indeed the person they claim to be by asking them to provide information known only to the both of you.

✓ Watch for executable files that have been disguised (as in Coolpic.jpg.exe). Remember, the Windows operating system hides certain final extensions, such as .exe, .vbs, and so on. Files "disguised" by double extensions often contain malicious code: They should be scanned with *updated* anti-virus software before they are executed. As was the case with IRC, configuring Windows to display *all* file extensions helps users avoid the double extension deception.

## Other ICQ Hazards

Besides being aware of threats posed by malicious code, ICQ users should know about some of the other hazards encountered when using this popular service. While the following two hazards are not directly related to malicious code, there are so many users of this popular service that an overview of these threats is warranted.

## THE "CRACKS" IN ICQ

A *crack* is a small piece of executable code that modifies something within a certain program. A crack can be used to modify a time-limited shareware program into a fully functioning registered version. Cracks were even developed to "bypass" Microsoft's powerful new Windows XP Internet activation (anti-piracy) process.

With regard to ICQ, cracks can allow someone to do the following:

✓ View someone's IP address, even if they have activated the "don't show my IP" option on their ICQ Preferences menu.

✓ Add someone to your contact list without his or her consent.

## ICQ FLOODING — DROWNING IN A SEA OF MESSAGES

The term *ICQ flooding* refers to the inundation of an ICQ user with dozens, perhaps even hundreds, of bogus messages. By using a program like ICQMachineGun (see Figure 7-4), a malicious individual can flood another person's ICQ program with so many messages that it causes him or her to be knocked off the ICQ network. Fortunately, ICQ has some built-in features that can prevent this type of attack. To learn how to configure your ICQ client software for maximum-security benefits and for any other ICQ security-related issues, users are encouraged to visit the ICQ help Web site at http://web.icq.com/help.

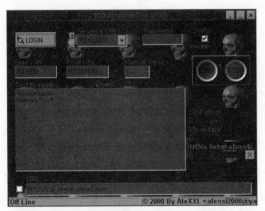

**Figure 7-4:** ICQ flooding with ICQMachineGun

# Web-Based Chat — The "Built-In" Chat Program

Rather than require users to first download and then install a particular chat program, Web-based chat programs allow Internet users with Java-enabled Web browsers (such as IE or Netscape) to run the chat program directly within their Web browser. These "lite" versions do not usually offer many of the security features found in the versions of the program installed separately. These Web-based chat programs are handy when users are not at their own computers, yet want to access their favorite chat programs without having to install them. Like any Web-based application that uses active content, such as JavaScript or Visual Basic Script, any Web-based chat program can pose a security threat to its user.

Executable content embedded in Web pages poses a unique problem for Internet users who are interested in protecting themselves against malicious code attacks. Because executable code is downloaded and executed on a user's computer when they visit certain Web pages, users visiting the "wrong" Web page (one with malicious code) may find their computer (and all valuable information stored on it) compromised. While most anti-virus programs are designed to detect and prevent attacks from malicious code, they are sometimes ineffective against the new generation of active-content malicious code.

A new breed of content-monitoring software, such as Finjan Software Inc.'s SurfinGuard Pro (www.finjan.com) and Tiny Software's Trojan Trap (www.tinysoftware.com), actively monitors all downloaded active content, including executables, ActiveX, and Java scripts. By monitoring how these active-content programs *behave*, both SurfinGuard Pro and Trojan Trap can block malicious activity automatically, before it causes damage to PCs.

# Instant Messaging — The "Instant" Way to Spread Viruses

Many anti-virus experts predict that instant messaging will become an increasingly popular way to spread computer viruses. With more and more organizations around the globe considering including instant messaging capabilities in their company PCs, the threat of malicious code attacks continues to rise.

Instant messaging software can sometimes bypass corporate firewalls, providing another "open door" through which hackers may access the Windows client. This type of security hole becomes the "weak link" in an organization's security chain. As hackers become more sophisticated, they increasingly attempt to enter company networks through the client (workstation) side via any holes they can locate in the system.

Individuals in charge of network security should be aware that the level of protection currently offered against viruses using instant messaging is not as sophisticated or advanced as it is for e-mail. In light of the current lack of security software for instant messaging, the role of social engineering becomes more important. Users must be continually reminded that they should *never* open any unexpected or unsolicited attachments that arrive via instant messaging. Network administrators may want to consider disabling altogether any file transfers via instant messaging.

## MSN Messenger — The Worm Wiggles Its Way In

When Microsoft released its new flagship operating system, Windows XP, in 2001, it included a built-in version of its MSN Messenger program as part of its new .NET campaign. Similar to AOL's Instant Messenger, the new more powerful .NET MSN Messenger allows users to exchange instant messages, share files and photos, collaborate with other users using whiteboards (diagrams and sketches), and make computer-to-telephone calls. While MSN Messenger was indubitably versatile, it wasn't long before malicious code had found another new victim.

A worm that used Microsoft's MSN Messenger application to exploit a browser glitch emerged on February 13, 2002, and spread rapidly despite the existence of a patch covering the security hole. The worm replicated itself by sending messages to other MSN Messenger users, but fortunately, it did not contain a destructive payload. The JS/Exploit-Messenger worm (also known as JS.Coolnow), exploited a hole in the Internet Explorer browser that Microsoft had made public, along with a patch, just two days before the worm surfaced.

## The W32.Choke Worm Strangles MSN Messenger

While the JS/Exploit-Messenger worm put the spotlight on flaws in MSN Messenger, it wasn't the first time MSN Messenger had been targeted by malicious code. In June 2001, a worm dubbed W32.Choke "strangled" users of the MSN Messenger service. Choke is one of the few worms to spread via instant messaging services—in this case, MSN Messenger. W32.Choke requires users to be running MSN Messenger and spreads to additional users who chat with the infected user. While the Choke worm appeared to have a grudge against U.S. President George Bush (the file name was ShootPresidentBUSH.exe), it was not considered a *major* threat by anti-virus companies because it did not spread via e-mail or carry a damaging payload.

One of the primary difficulties with malicious code defense is getting users of flawed programs to apply available security patches. Worms that infect instant messaging services tend to spread more quickly than those sent via e-mail. This is a boon to the worm authors, who wish to contaminate as many computers as possible before any anti-virus updates can be released. Because users cannot always rely on their traditional anti-virus software to detect malicious code received via instant messaging, the use of content blocking software products such as Finjan's SurfinGuard Pro should also be considered.

## AOL Instant Messenger — AIM and the Back Door Man

With more than 100 million users (and climbing), America Online's Instant Messenger (AIM) is the most widely used instant messaging service on the Internet. Packaged as part of their AOL Internet software, AIM is also available as a free download for non-AOL subscribers who wish to use this popular service. AIM supports chat, file transfers, and Internet-to-telephone communications. One drawback to AIM is that it is not compatible with many of the other online instant messaging services; however, this fact doesn't seem to have hurt its popularity. AIM is so easy to use that it has found its way into the corporate landscape. Like certain other instant messaging programs, however, AIM can also be subject to the "slings and arrows" of malicious code.

Flaws in the AIM program have left its users vulnerable to attack from both hackers and viruses. In December 2001, the world's largest non-profit security team (which goes by the name "w00w00") discovered a serious flaw in AIM's software—one that could give a potential attacker control over an AIM user's computer. This was not the first time a security flaw was discovered in this popular service. In fact, AIM has been described by some security experts as a "notoriously insecure application."

Shortly after w00w00 found the flaw, they announced that a program called AIMFilter, written by 16-year-old student Robbie Saunders, would protect AIM users from this type of exploitation. They even offered their Web site visitors a link to the site where AIMFilter could be downloaded. Unbeknownst to w00w00, the program was actually malicious code. When Saunders made his code available for download on December 30, he described the flaws found in AIM that compromised a user's security and then boasted that his AIMFilter would prevent hackers from exploiting these flaws. Saunders, however, didn't report that the AIMFilter forwarded an AIM user's Internet address *to him,* which he then used to generate income at two pay-for-click sites when users opened the filter. The program opened up a backdoor that permitted hackers to take control and redirect the AIM user's Web browser to visit pornographic Web sites. Unfortunately, w00w00 didn't report their mistake until they physically examined the code in detail, which left many users open to this backdoor attack. AOL quickly fixed the problem at the server side (their end) of the IM connection, obviating the need for AIM users to download and install any third-party filters or utilities.

## AIM's Built-In Security Features

Because of the security risks inherent in using instant messaging services, America Online has incorporated two important security features into the AIM program. Since malicious code can propagate easily through AIM's file sharing/transfer feature, everyone using this popular messaging service should be aware of these features. First, AIM allows for the automatic scanning for malicious code on any files that are transferred using this service. To employ automatic scanning, users must have a reputable (and up-to-date) anti-virus program operating on their PC. Because AIM is subject to continuous updates and revisions, the steps necessary for configuring may change slightly from one version to the next. In general, the steps to configure AIM to automatically scan transferred files for viruses are as follows:

1. With the AIM program up and running, select My AIM from the drop-down menu; then select Edit Options ⇨ Edit Preferences (see Figure 7-5).

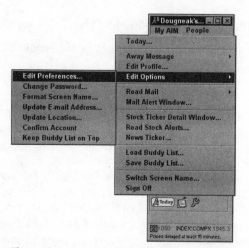

**Figure 7-5:** Accessing AIM preferences via the My AIM drop-down menu (AIM Version 4.7)

2. In the AIM Preferences screen, several options appear in the Category list located on the left. Select File Transfer and then click the Virus Checker button at the bottom right (see Figure 7-6).

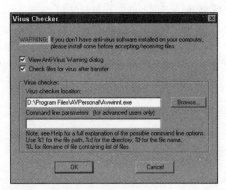

**Figure 7-6:** The AIM Preferences screen (AIM Version 4.7)

**3.** In the Virus Checker configuration box, make sure that both the "View Anti-Virus Warning dialog" and "Check files for virus after transfer" radio boxes are checked (see Figure 7-7) and that the path (location) of your anti-virus software has been indicated in the Virus Checker Location text box. Click OK.

**Figure 7-7:** The AIM Virus Checker configuration screen (AIM Version 4.7)

The exact path to an anti-virus program varies greatly from program to program. AIM attempts to locate the path to some anti-virus products found during its installation. In the event the path to your anti-virus program is not already illustrated, you need to manually locate it using the browse feature. If you don't know the location of your anti-virus program in your computer, contact the manufacturer of your particular product for specific details.

AIM's second important security feature is the File Sharing preferences, located by selecting File Sharing under the Category list in the Preferences screen. Within the File Sharing Preferences screen, users can configure how AIM handles all aspects of file transfers (see Figure 7-8).

Provisions for limiting which AIM users have access to files (for example, those on your "buddy list") and which directories are accessible are found here. For maximum security, users should never check "Allow" for those that are not on the "buddy list."

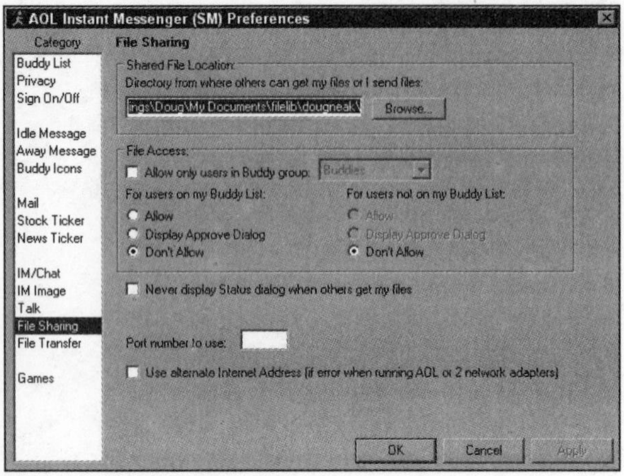

**Figure 7-8:** File Sharing preferences in AIM Version 4.7

## Yahoo! Messenger — Does Malicious Code Yahoo?

The instant messaging market is a rapidly growing target for software developers and Internet Service Providers. In an attempt to grab some of the instant messaging (IM) market from corporate giants such as AOL or Microsoft, companies like Yahoo!, Inc., have developed their own proprietary IM software and services. Few viruses and worms have been specifically targeted at Yahoo! Messenger (probably due to its low market share), but that doesn't mean that users of this service should be complacent. Its users should follow three basic principles applicable to security for *all* IM services (as stated earlier in this chapter):

1. Install and regularly update a reputable anti-virus software program

2. Install a port-blocking software-based firewall

3. Use social engineering (educate all users regarding the potential threats of using IM services)

Bear in mind that malicious code programs such as the infamous SubSeven Trojan (first detected in May 1999) exploit IM programs. The following is a partial list of common instant messaging exploits that are found in this powerful Trojan:

✓  ICQ takeover

✓  Acts as an IRC bot

✓  IRC bot configuration

✓ Microsoft Messenger spy

✓ AOL Instant Messenger spy

✓ Yahoo Messenger spy

✓ Retrieves a list of AIM users and passwords

✓ Retrieves a list of ICQ passwords and usernames

✓ Gets victim's personal information

✓ ICQ pager connection notification

✓ IRC connection notification

✓ Acts as an ICQ spy

✓ Presets connection notification of ICQ number

✓ Presets connection notification of IRC channel or handle (moniker)

This list contains many entries that directly affect and relate to IRC, ICQ, and instant messaging systems. Trojan horses often exploit these popular communication channels in particular. The presence of a Trojan horse can often be detected by using a simple port scanning program. By scanning your network ports (especially those commonly used by Trojan horse applications), you may detect open ports, which could indicate the presence of one of these insidious viruses. Table 7-1 lists a few Trojan horse programs and the ports they use.

**TABLE 7-1 Ports Commonly Used by Trojan Horse Programs**

| Trojan Horse | Port |
| --- | --- |
| Attack FTP | 666 |
| BackDoor | 1999 |
| BackOrifice | 31337, 31338 |
| Big Gluck | 34324 |
| Blade Runner | 5400 |
| Blade Runner 1.x | 5401 |
| Blade Runner 2.x | 5402 |
| BO JammerKillahV | 121 |
| BOWhack | 31666 |
| Bugs | 2115 |

*Continued*

**TABLE 7-1 Ports Commonly Used by Trojan Horse Programs** *(Continued)*

| Trojan Horse | Port |
| --- | --- |
| Deep BO | 31338 |
| Deep Throat | 2140, 6670, 6771 |
| Delta | 26274 |
| Devil 1.03 | 65000 |
| Doly Trojan | 1011,1012 |
| Evil FTP | 23456 |
| Firehotcker | 5321 |
| Fore | 50766 |
| FTP99CMP | 1492 |
| GabanBus | 1245 |
| Gate Crasher | 6969 |
| GirlFriend | 21544 |
| Gjamer | 12076 |
| Hack99 Keylogger | 12223 |
| Hackers Paradise | 456 |
| ICKiller | 7789 |
| ICQ Trojan | 4590 |
| ini-Killer | 9989 |
| Indoctrination | 6939 |
| Kuang | 30999 |
| Masters Paradise | 30129, 40421, 40423 |
| Masters Paradise 1.x | 40422 |
| Masters Paradise 2.x | 40423 |
| Masters Paradise 3.x | 40426 |
| Millenium | 20000, 20001 |
| NetBus | 1245 |
| NetBus 1.x | 12346 |

| Trojan Horse | Port |
|---|---|
| NetBus 1.x | 12346 |
| NetBus Pro | 20034 |
| NutBus 2 Pro | 20034 |
| NetMonitor | 7300 |
| NetMonitor 1.x | 7301 |
| NetMonitor 2.x | 7306 |
| NetMonitor 3.x | 7307 |
| NetMonitor 4.x | 7308 |
| NetSphere | 30100 |
| NetSpy | 1033 |
| NetSpy DK | 31339 |
| Pass Ripper | 2023 |
| Phase0 | 555 |
| Phineas | 2801 |
| Phineas Phucker | 2801 |
| Portal of Doom | 3700, 9872 |
| Portal of Doom 1.x | 9873 |
| Portal of Doom 2.x | 9874 |
| Portal of Doom 3.x | 9875 |
| Portal of Doom 4.x | 10067 |
| Portal of Doom 5.x | 10167 |
| Priority | 6969, 16969 |
| Progenic Security | 11223 |
| Prosiak | 22222, 33333 |
| Prosiak 0.47 | 22222 |
| Psyber Stream Server | 1170, 1509 |
| Remote Grab | 7000 |
| Remote Windows Shutdown | 53001 |

*Continued*

**TABLE 7-1 Ports Commonly Used by Trojan Horse Programs** *(Continued)*

| Trojan Horse | Port |
|---|---|
| Ripper | 2023 |
| RoboHack | 5569 |
| Satanz Backdoor | 666 |
| Schwindler | 50766 |
| Senna Spy | 11000 |
| Silencer | 1001 |
| Shiva Burka | 1600 |
| ShockRave | 1981 |
| Socket23 | 30303 |
| Sockets de Troie | 5000, 50505 |
| Sockets de Troie 1.x | 5001 |
| SpySender | 1807 |
| Stealth Spy | 555 |
| Streaming Audio Trojan | 1170 |
| Striker | 2565 |
| SubSeven | 1243 |
| TeleCommando | 61466 |
| The Invasor | 2140 |
| The Thing | 6400 |
| TheSpy | 40412 |
| Tiny Telnet Server | 34424 |
| Trojan Cow | 2001 |
| Ugly FTP | 23456 |
| Ultors Trojan | 1234 |
| VooDoo | 1245 |
| VooDoo Doll | 1245 |
| WebEx | 1001 |

| Trojan Horse | Port |
|---|---|
| Whack-A-Mole | 12361 |
| Whack-A-Mole 1.x | 12362 |
| WhackJob | 23456 |
| WinCrash | 5742, 4092 |
| WinCrash2 | 2583 |

Free port scanners can be found at www.webattack.com, a freeware and shareware Internet tool provider.

# Minimizing the Risk with Education

According to the Massachusetts-based International Data Corporation (IDC), the number of corporate instant messaging users will increase dramatically over the next few years. For companies aspiring to jump on the IM bandwagon, security concerns become paramount. The easiest and most cost-effective way to mitigate the risks posed by the use of instant messaging is to both communicate *and* implement a security strategy with employees. Remember that instant messaging programs are a very efficient and effective tool for transacting business and need not be avoided altogether. Instant messaging users simply need to remain aware of common tricks used by Internet intruders.

According to an incident report released by the CERT Coordination Center at Carnegie Mellon University in March 2002, misleading messages on IRC or instant messaging services often warn IM users that their computers have been infected with a virus. The phony warning instructs them to go to a specified Web address and download a program to "rid" their computer of the virus or face being barred from the IRC or IM system they're using. This is entirely a social engineering attack, in view of the fact that the user's decision to download and run the malicious code is the deciding factor in whether or not the attack becomes successful. To help combat this type of social attack, IM users are urged to use common sense and *skepticism* when chatting with others on the Web. When a hoax warning is issued, a quick visit to one of the following sites can help users confirm their suspicions:

✓ www.vmyths.com—The Vmyths Web site is operated by Rhode Island Soft Systems, Inc. and traces its roots to a "Computer Virus Myths treatise" first published in 1988. It evolved into the critically acclaimed "Computer Virus Myths home page" in 1995, then moved to Vmyths.com in 2000. While its name has changed over the years, Vmyths remains true to its original goal: the eradication of computer virus hysteria.

✓ http://hoaxbusters.ciac.org — This Web site is jointly maintained by the CIAC and the U.S Department of Energy. The site gives information about chain letters and hoaxes that are found on the Internet; further, the site gives historical information about Internet hoaxes, helps you identify hoaxes when you encounter them, and gives you instructions on what to do when faced with them.

The number one weapon for remaining on the defensive when using instant messaging is *knowledge*.

# Protecting IM with Anti-Virus Software

In contrast to e-mail, messages exchanged using MSN, AOL IM, or Yahoo! services are not usually scanned by individuals or organizations for viruses or malicious programs. Unfortunately, hackers tend to exploit this security lapse by sending attachments containing viruses, worms, or Trojan horses. Because IM often passes without restriction through corporate firewalls, malicious code may well enter a corporate network undetected. One company has recognized this growing problem and has responded by developing IM-specific anti-virus software. BitDefender by SOFTWIN is a powerful, full-featured, IM-specific anti-virus software program. It comes in a variety of versions; the one you choose depends on which IM service you are using. The following versions are currently available at no cost:

✓ BitDefender for Instant Messaging

✓ BitDefender for ICQ

✓ BitDefender for Yahoo!

✓ BitDefender for NetMeeting

✓ BitDefender for MSN Messenger

✓ BitDefender for mIRC

The above-mentioned BitDefender products are currently listed as freeware and do not require any licensing to be used. As stated on their Web site, these products represent the first *proactive* solution available for blocking all viruses threatening the system as a result of file transfers through IM services. According to SOFTWIN, the technology included in BitDefender enables filtering and, if necessary, the disinfecting or deleting of all infected files transferred on a computer. Without affecting the file transfer rate, the moment a transferred file is found to be infected, a window is opened and the user receives an interactive message with the option to delete, disinfect, or block the infected file. If you wish to try this product or need more information regarding BitDefender and other WINSOFT anti-virus products, visit BitDefender on the Web at www.bitdefender.com.

# Keeping Software Up-to-Date

Anti-virus programs aren't the only applications that must be kept current. Nearly all software is subject to revisions and improvements over time. Whenever holes or flaws that compromise the security of a program or product are discovered, a software patch to update the program usually follows. By making sure that instant messaging software is up-to-date, users can avoid being affected by the malicious code exploitation of known vulnerabilities.

# Cyberstalking and Instant Messaging

Although there is no universally accepted definition of cyberstalking, the term generally refers to the use of the Internet, e-mail messaging, or other electronic communications devices such as IRC, ICQ, and Instant messaging, to stalk someone. Stalking generally involves harassing or threatening behavior that an individual engages in repeatedly, such as following a person, appearing at a person's home or place of employment, making harassing phone calls, leaving written messages or objects, or vandalizing a person's property. Most stalking laws require that the perpetrator make a credible threat of violence against the victim; others also include threats made against the victim's immediate family; and still others require only that the alleged stalker's course of conduct constitutes an implied threat. While some conduct involving annoying or menacing behavior might fall short of illegal stalking, such behavior may be a prelude to such stalking and violence and should be treated seriously.

Although online harassment and threats can take many forms, cyberstalking shares important characteristics with offline stalking. Many stalkers — online or off — are motivated by a desire to exert control over their victims and engage in similar types of behavior to accomplish this end. As with offline stalking, the available evidence (which is largely anecdotal) suggests that the majority of cyberstalkers are men and that the majority of their victims are women, although there have also been reported cases of women cyberstalking men and of same-sex cyberstalking, as well. In many cases, the cyberstalker and the victim have had a prior (usually intimate) relationship, and the cyberstalking begins when the victim attempts to change the relationship or entirely put an end to it. However, there also have been many instances of cyberstalking by strangers. Given the enormous amount of personal information available through the Internet, a determined cyberstalker can usually locate private information about a potential victim with a few mouse clicks or keystrokes.

The fact that cyberstalking does not involve physical contact may create the misperception that it is more benign than physical stalking. This is not necessarily the case. As the Internet becomes an ever more integral part of our personal and professional lives, stalkers can take advantage of the ease of communications as well as the increased access to personal information. Additionally, the ease of use and non-confrontational, impersonal, and sometimes anonymous nature of Internet communications may remove some of the disincentives of cyberstalking. Whereas a potential stalker may be unwilling or unable to confront a victim in person or even over the telephone, he or she may not hesitate to send harassing or threatening electronic communications to a victim. As with physical stalking, online harassment and threats may be a prelude to more serious actions, including physical violence.

In general, the primary similarities between offline stalking and online stalking include the following:

✓ The majority of cases involve stalking by former intimates, although stranger stalking occurs in the real world and in cyberspace.

✓ Most victims are women; most stalkers are men.

✓ Stalkers are generally motivated by the desire to control their victim.

In general, the major differences can be summarized as follows:

✓ Offline stalking generally requires the perpetrator and the victim to be located in the same geographic area; cyberstalkers may be located across the street or across the country.

✓ Electronic communication technologies make it much easier for a cyberstalker to encourage third parties to harass and/or threaten a victim (by impersonating the victim in order to post inflammatory messages to bulletin boards and in chat rooms, causing viewers of that message to send threatening messages back to the victim "author").

✓ Electronic communication technologies lower the barriers to harassment and threats; cyberstalkers do not need to physically confront their victims.

The anonymity of the Internet also provides new opportunities for would-be cyberstalkers. A cyberstalker's true identity can be concealed by using different ISPs and/or by adopting different screen names. More experienced stalkers can use anonymous remailers that make it all but impossible to determine the true source of an e-mail message or other electronic communication. A number of law enforcement agencies report that they are currently confronting cyberstalking cases involving the use of anonymous remailers.

Anonymity places the cyberstalker in an advantageous position. Unbeknownst to the target, the perpetrator can be in the next cubicle at work, around the corner, or in another state. The stalker can be a former friend or lover, a total stranger met in a chat room, or simply a teenager playing a practical joke. The inability to identify the source of the harassment or threats can be particularly ominous to a cyberstalking victim, and the veil of anonymity might encourage a perpetrator to prolong these acts. Armed with the knowledge that their identity is unknown, perpetrators may be encouraged to broaden the range of their stalking by pursuing their victims at the victim's workplace or home. The Internet can provide substantial information to this end. Numerous Web sites offer personal information, including unlisted telephone numbers and detailed directions to a home or office. For a fee, other Web sites promise to provide social security numbers, financial data, and other personal information that cyberstalkers might find useful in the pursuit of their victims.

Take the following preventative measures to ensure that you do not become a victim of cyberstalking:

✓ Do not share personal information in public spaces anywhere online, nor give it to strangers, either in e-mail or chat rooms. Do not use your real name or nickname as your screen name or user ID. Pick a name that is gender- and age-neutral. Do not post personal information as part of any user profiles.

✓ Be extremely cautious about meeting online acquaintances in person. If you choose to meet, do so in a public place and bring a friend if possible.

✓ Make sure that your ISP and IRC network have an acceptable use policy that prohibits cyberstalking. If your network fails to respond to your complaints, consider switching to a provider that is more responsive to user grievances.

✓ If an online situation becomes hostile, log off or surf elsewhere. If a situation arouses your fear, contact a local law enforcement agency.

If you are being cyberstalked, take the following measures:

✓ If you are receiving unwanted contact from an individual, make clear that you do not want to be contacted by him or her again.

✓ Save all communications for evidence. Do not edit or alter it in any way. Keep a record of your contacts with Internet system administrators or law enforcement officials.

✓ Consider blocking or filtering messages from the harasser. Many e-mail programs, such as Eudora and Microsoft Outlook, have a filter feature and software can be easily obtained that will automatically delete e-mail messages that originate from a particular e-mail address or that contain offensive words. Chat room contact can be blocked, as well. Although formats differ, a common chat room command to block someone would look like this: /ignore [person's screen name] (without the brackets). In some circumstances (such as threats of violence), however, it may be more appropriate to save the information and contact law enforcement authorities.

✓ If the harassment continues after you have asked the person to stop, contact the harasser's Internet Service Provider. Most ISPs have clear policies prohibiting the use of their services to abuse another person. An ISP may attempt to stop the conduct by direct contact with the stalker or by closing the stalker's account. If you receive abusive e-mail messages, identify the domain (after the "@" sign) and contact that ISP. Most ISPs have an e-mail address — such as abuse@(domain name) or postmaster@(domain name) — that can be used for complaints. If the ISP has a Web site, visit it for information on how to file a complaint.

✓ Contact your local police department and inform them of the situation, giving them as many details as possible. In appropriate cases, they may refer the matter to state or federal authorities. If you are afraid of taking action, other resources are available. Contact either the National Domestic Violence Hotline (1-800-799-SAFE) or a local women's shelter for advice and support.

# Summary

Instant messaging, while convenient and cost-effective, poses security threats to both the individuals and businesses that regularly use it. With the number of organizations using IM services on the rise, the risk of malicious code contamination increases as well. Corporate networks, at an alarming rate, can propagate viruses, worms, and Trojan horse programs contracted via IM services. Through the use of social engineering, product updates, and up-to-date anti-virus software, the risk of harm is dramatically reduced. Key points covered in this chapter include:

✓ Why security holes in IRC and ICQ leave computers and networks open to malicious code attacks

✓ How employee education and social engineering become anti-virus tools

✓ Why some Web-based chat programs leave computers open to attack

✓ Why firewalls can be both a blessing and a curse with instant messaging services

✓ Why flaws in MSN and AOL allowed malicious code to quickly circulate

✓ How one can use IM-specific anti-virus software as part of an overall security strategy

# Chapter 8

# Defending Your Company's Network Using Human Resources

## In This Chapter

✓ Creating network security policies

✓ Applying anti-virus policies

✓ Enacting password policies

✓ Responding to security incidents

✓ Raising security awareness

✓ Choosing proactive versus reactive defense

✓ Identifying Internet hoaxes and false alarms

THE BEST WEAPON AGAINST the threat of malicious code is human resources. Organizations that want to keep their Internet-enabled networks free of malicious code must first understand that security is not a product but a *process*. The most powerful firewall or the most up-to-date anti-virus software is not always enough to detect a fast-spreading worm or prevent a surreptitious Trojan horse application from causing widespread damage. *Social engineering* is hacker-talk for the ability to influence people to the extent that they will perform actions they would not otherwise carry out. Since people are commonly the weakest link in an organization's security chain, social engineering remains the most effective method of circumventing security barriers. Hackers, for example, often try to exploit human weakness before they spend their time and effort on other password-cracking methods. The premise is as follows: Why bother trying to "hack" your way through someone's defense system when you can "coax" a legitimate user to open the door for you?

Social engineering is the hardest form of attack to prevent because it cannot be defended against solely with the use of software or hardware. The best and most successful defense involves implementing sound security policies and educating employees to adhere to those policies. Worms like AnnaKournikova and Melissa were among the first to illustrate the dilemma between trust and e-mail attachments. Malicious code often attempts to exploit the trust that exists between friends, family, and co-workers.

A worm usually owes its success to the fact that a user *accepts* an e-mail attachment from a family member, friend, or colleague when prompted to open it. This strategy has been used on several occasions, as with the NakedWife Trojan and SirCam worm. Upon execution, worms characteristically proceed to send themselves to all contacts found in the victim's address book. Because a great deal of emphasis is placed on encouraging potential victims to open and execute e-mail attachments, educating users as to the correct handling of attachments and the potential threats they pose is paramount to proper defense. This chapter focuses on the human element in virus proliferation and the use of social engineering as a tool for defense against malicious code.

# Creating a Network Security Policy

Before you physically secure a computer network, you must establish a network security policy. Such policies form the core of sound network security. Policies help define which organizational assets are critical and what types of events can threaten these assets. A sound network security policy outlines an organization's expectations for proper computer and network use and the various procedures required to prevent and respond to security incidents. The need for a coherent security policy was detailed clearly in May 1996, when Jack L. Brock, Jr., Director, Defense Information and Financial Management Systems of the U.S. Government Accounting Office issued a statement on the status of security at that time. In his report, he stated the following:

> Attacks on Defense computer systems are a serious and growing threat. The exact number of attacks cannot be readily determined because only a small portion are actually detected and reported. However, Defense Information Systems Agency (DISA) data implies that Defense may have experienced as many as 250,000 attacks last year. DISA information also shows that attacks are successful 65 percent of the time, and that the number of attacks is doubling each year, as Internet use increases along with the sophistication of "hackers" and their tools.
>
> At a minimum, these attacks are a multimillion-dollar nuisance to Defense. At worst, they are a serious threat to national security. Attackers have seized control of entire Defense systems, many of which support critical functions, such as weapons systems research and development, logistics, and finance. Attackers have also stolen, modified, and destroyed data and software. In a well-publicized attack on Rome Laboratory, the Air Force's premier command and control research facility, two hackers took control of laboratory support systems, established links to foreign Internet sites, and stole tactical and artificial intelligence research data.
>
> The potential for catastrophic damage is great. Organized foreign nationals or terrorists could use "information warfare" techniques to disrupt military operations by harming command and control systems, the public switch network, and other systems or networks Defense relies on.

Brock's report further explained the need for assessing attack risks, protecting systems, responding to incidents, and assessing damage, as well as the need for training users and system and network administrators on a consistent basis. According to Brock, solutions such as firewalls, smart cards, and network monitoring systems "will improve protection of Defense information. However, the success of these measures depends on whether Defense implements them in tandem with better policy and personnel solutions."

Brock's report underscores the fact that even the U.S. government must continually fine-tune policies to accommodate its specific needs. All organizations connected to the Internet must likewise develop and enforce individualized security policies.

Without a network security policy, the framework needed for sound network security cannot be in place. Network security policies must be communicated to everyone who uses the organization's computer network.

While specific security needs vary between organizations, certain elements are common to all network security policies. The following steps are essential for establishing a network security policy:

✓ **Identify and locate your personal (or your company's) assets.** This pertains to assets both intangible (data) and physical (hardware). Determine both the value and importance of each asset.

Example: An entire computer system might cost $7,000 to replace, yet the information contained therein might have a replacement value of $107,000. Indeed, if the information were lost, the cost could be even greater if those were corporate assets falling into the hands of your competition.

✓ **Adopt a "Need-to-Know" approach.** An employee's rank in the organization's hierarchy should have no bearing on his or her network privileges.

Example: The manager of the marketing department does not need to know the password that accesses all systems company-wide when her position only requires access to the sales system. A system-wide password could be abused if obtained by the wrong person.

✓ **Sort all information.** Rank how sensitive specific data is and then categorize it according to its status as private, public, unclassified, or confidential. Employees are granted access to the information based upon their classification in a predetermined hierarchy.

Example: A "potential client" list could be restricted to the sales department. The pension plan statements of employees might be accessed only by the accounting department. For highly classified information, individual files and even single documents may have to be tracked at every change of hands. A company policy could be put in place that would require authorization before certain documents could be photocopied or reprinted.

✓ **Determine how likely you are to be victimized.** Assess the likelihood that your assets would be commandeered and the effect that this would have on your organization.

Example: If your organization markets your products via your Web site and that site crashes as a result of malicious code, you must calculate the cost of returning the system to a fully functioning state. Your assessment should include technicians' man-hours, as well as the sales lost during your downtime.

✓ **Regularly verify that your security policy is adhered to.** Perform periodic security audits to determine if your policy is being carried out and if it is remaining effective. If it is found to be lacking, alterations must be made.

Example: The company security policy is evaluated a few months after it is implemented. Several major flaws and some other defects are detected in the system. The major flaws can be corrected immediately, while the other shortcomings may be attended to in a less urgent manner.

✓ **Examine your organization's physical layout.** Relocating certain assets may make them more secure. Sensitive data may have to be kept under lock and key. Remote sectors of your company should not contain valuable assets. In some cases, it is wise to hire additional security officers or alter their work shifts. Dependable locks and employee smart cards are used by many organizations to increase security. Wires and cables must remain inaccessible to all but approved technicians. Windows and drop ceilings (from which access may be gained via an adjoining room) must be adequately secured, as well. Everyone who is physically on the premises must have a reason for his or her presence, and everyone must have a legitimate reason for using company computers.

Example: One highly secure area can be used to house the most sensitive assets. In this way, leaking of passwords and eavesdropping can be prevented, since access to this area is highly restricted.

✓ **Be ready for a crisis.** Performing system-wide backups on a regular basis is an integral part of crisis preparation. A detached (physically removed) site should be maintained outside the company for storing backup information. Being prepared includes having a plan in place in the event assets are lost.

Example: Your corporate headquarters are ravaged by fire. Be prepared by devising a plan that enables you to continue serving your clients' needs. Ascertain the minimum requirements that are necessary to keep your organization functional. Such an assessment will give you an idea how long you can stay in business either in full or partial capacity.

✓ **Decide which employees can access outside data.** What information can be accessed and by whom should be limited for productivity purposes as well as for security reasons. Internal company users need access to external data. When working from remote locations, company employees must be able to access internal company information. Customers and the public require a certain amount of access, as well. If employees are allowed to download software or visit non-work-related sites, the organization should maintain appropriate anti-virus software.

Example: A firewall that is set up to allow access only to specified sites and during specified hours prevents employees from visiting recreational (chat rooms, sports, news, entertainment, pornography) sites that interfere with employee productivity.

✓ **Determine how employees will be impacted by policy changes.** Employees are not always able to adjust to frequently changing passwords, using password-activated screen savers, or activating and deactivating alarm systems.

Example: Your organization may offer employees in-house training or outside courses for instruction in how to adapt to security policy changes. Such education reminds each individual that his or her adherence to security policies positively impacts the entire organization.

✓ **Name a security officer.** A security officer is responsible for enforcing your organization's security policies. One (or several) groups of people may be assigned this task in order to provide "checks and balances" among the groups.

Example: To be effective, the security officer must have rather sweeping powers, possibly including the authority to lock down the building, sever Internet connections, and otherwise disrupt normal business operations. The need for these powers becomes apparent in a time of crisis, when it's too late to start arguing about who calls the shots. One thing that must be determined with certainty, before you hand over the keys to the kingdom: the security officer must be absolutely trustworthy. When you hire or appoint someone to manage security, the background check you perform must be extremely thorough. (Placing the security officer in a position to cross divisional boundaries and within a dual-reporting structure so he or she can feel free to report his or her supervisor without fear of reprisal are also solid ideas.)

# Applying Anti-Virus Policies

In 2001, several malicious code outbreaks targeted organizational computers, exploiting the networks that connect them. Badtrans, Code Red, and Nimda, to name a few, made headlines as they caused mayhem across assorted networks, costing businesses millions of dollars to remove and repair their damage. Because viruses, worms, and Trojans habitually target company networks, organizations (especially those that have their networks connected to the Internet) must implement well-planned anti-virus policies. Installing anti-virus software and then expecting that users or network administrators will ensure that it is kept up-to-date is not a prudent (or sufficient) means of protection. Organizations the world over are discovering that a more holistic approach to virus protection helps them keep the threat of malicious code attack under control.

A sound anti-virus policy addresses the following:

✓ Organizational requirements for anti-virus protection, which include any proactive measures that the organization will take to protect itself against malicious code

✓ Appropriate responses to viral incidents

✓ The consequences to employees for any blatant violation of the policies

Because each organization's security needs are unique, individual requirements vary and need to be tailored based upon the specific demands of the business, as well as the type of environment in which its networked computers operate. Some general concepts, however, can provide a framework upon which to build a solid anti-virus security policy:

✓ Anti-virus protection should be required for every Windows-based computer that is connected to the company's network. No deviation from or exception to this policy should be tolerated.

✓ It should be a violation of the policy to disable or remove anti-virus protection under any circumstances.

✓ The use of anti-virus protection for less popular operating systems, such as Linux or Macintosh, should also be included. Although these operating systems are currently not as prone to virus attacks, each *has* had dangerous viruses written for it.

✓ Some organizations have remote users; the policy must apply to those users, as well.

✓ Policies requiring virus protection for *every* guest user, such as consultants or outside vendors, should be considered, as well.

✓ Carefully consider including a provision that addresses the routine updating or patching of programs. Nearly every software program contains flaws that are routinely discovered and exploited over time. A sound anti-virus policy must include a provision to address how and when patching will be carried out and what actions will be taken when a failure to comply occurs. In the case of serious incidents, such as Code Red, Nimda, or the Adore worm, it may be necessary to take the computer offline until the user or network administrator has removed the virus and restored the system to a sound operating condition. This includes the installation of the patches that might have prevented the incident in the first place. The recurrence of malicious code infection should result in an escalation of the disciplinary process up to and including termination of employment in severe cases of transgression. Patching of software is covered in greater detail later in this chapter.

✓ A well-rounded anti-virus policy must also address the organization's use of e-mail messaging, including how any deviation from or violation of the policy will result in disciplinary action. Although e-mail has become an indispensable part of the corporate landscape, it remains one of the largest threats to IT security. By incorporating the rules of safe e-mail messaging into their anti-virus policies, organizations can significantly lower the possibility that malicious code will infiltrate their networks by careless employees.

The rules for thwarting viruses delivered via e-mail are as follows:

- Do not download any files from unknown people or organizations. Remember: e-mail sometimes appears as if it came from a relative, friend, or acquaintance. If you have reason to doubt the origin of an e-mailed message, a quick confirmation that the sender is someone you trust adds an extra margin of safety.

- Do not open any file attached to an e-mail message unless you know what it is, since some viruses duplicate themselves and multiply through the attachments in e-mail messages.

- Do not open any files attached to an e-mail message originating from an unknown or suspicious source.

- Do not open any file attached to an e-mail communication if it contains an uncertain subject line.

- Delete junk e-mail and chain letter–type e-mail messages. It is suggested that you do not respond to them in any manner. These types of messages are regarded as spam — unsolicited, invasive e-mail that congests your e-mail message box.

- Exercise caution when downloading files from the Internet. Ensure that the source is legitimate and reputable. Verify that an anti-virus program checks the files at the download site. If you are still uncertain, do not download the file at all, or download the file to a floppy disk and test it with your own anti-virus software.

- Update your anti-virus software on a regular basis. Hundreds of new viruses are discovered every month. Periodically check with your software vendors for updates.

- Back up your files on a regular basis. If a virus should destroy your data files, you can then replace them with a backup copy. You should store your backup data files in a separate location from your other work files, at a site preferably not on your computer.

- When attachments are dubious, it is best to exercise caution. Do not open, download, or execute any files or e-mail attachments under questionable circumstances. Not executing is the most important of these caveats.

Please refer to Chapter 3 for a review of the NIPC's safe e-mail suggestions.

# Enacting Effective Password Policies

Passwords are one of the easiest and most commonly used forms of authentication. Composed of a succession of characters, a password is used to identify a user before that user is permitted access to a system or its resources. With proper password usage, you can also prevent unauthorized personnel, hackers, and malicious code from accessing critical areas of a computer. Although asking users to select secure passwords will help improve security, password use alone is not enough. It is also important to form a set of password *policies* that all users must obey, in order to keep the passwords secure.

First and foremost, it is important to impress upon users the need to memorize their passwords. Users should refrain from writing down passwords anywhere, but certainly not on desk blotters, calendars, and the like. Furthermore, storing passwords in files on the computer must be prohibited. In either case, by writing the password down on a piece of paper or storing it in a file, the security of the user's account is totally dependent on the security of that piece of paper or file (usually less than the security offered by the password encryption software).

The BIOS is an area where the use of passwords can be quite helpful. By using a BIOS password, an authorized user ensures that no else one has access to this key component. Refer to Chapter 5 for a more detailed discussion of this topic.

Consider several important factors wherever passwords are used:

✓ **Never** use a word that can be found in any dictionary, English or otherwise.

✓ **Do not** use patterns such as ABCDEF, A1B2C3D4, or 123456.

✓ **Do** use a mix of both upper-case and lower-case letters.

✓ **Do** use a mix of numbers, letters, and punctuation characters.

✓ **Do** make passwords that are formed as an easy-to-remember pattern on the keyboard (adding alphabetic, numeric, punctuation, and other characters). For example, the phrase "every day is a very fine day" could be abbreviated to "ediavfd," and then, by adding two nonalphabetic characters, it could become "ediav44fd." Or you can make a pattern using the numeric keyboard. By pressing "74123," you've formed the letter "L". You might add the letters "ana" to "spell" the easy-to-remember alphabetic-numeric password "74123ana" (or "Lana").

✓ **Do** use a minimum of eight characters.

✓ **Do not** use specific personal words or dates, such as birthdays, names, and anniversaries, or other facts known about you.

✓ **Do** change your passwords *often,* and never reuse an old password.

✓ **Do not** store your password in (or on) your desk or computer; in fact, your password should not be written down at all.

✓ **Never** grant requests for passwords over the telephone. Even junior hackers use this technique to obtain a password, claiming to be the network administrator or another authorized person (a technician, for instance) who will be performing routine system or network maintenance. Telephone requests for passwords should be reported immediately.

✓ **Never** share your password with anyone. This includes *not* allowing another person to type your password for you (technician, co-worker, and so on).

Although properly used passwords provide a secure means of identification, they too can eventually be cracked by even inexperienced hackers. Software tools are available that allow anyone with an ordinary desktop computer to crack password codes. These password cracker programs (see Figure 8-1) are frequently used by corporations to verify that employees are complying with the organization's password policies. When an organization demands a high level of security, its workers are aware that their employment can be terminated for abuse of password policies.

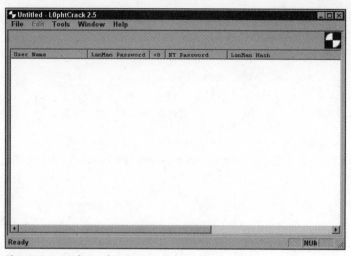

**Figure 8-1:** L0phtCrack 2.5 password-cracking program

# Incidence Response — The Response Makes the Difference

Properly responding to a computer security incident can save an organization time, money, and in some cases, their reputation. Nevertheless, incident response planning is an important practice that is rarely carried out — perhaps because incidence response is viewed as expensive and often perceived as an admission that something could go awry. While incident response plans may vary in their approach, their goals are essentially the same.

## Planning a Response

In general, the key incident response planning objectives are as follows:

✓ To help affected organizations recover from security incidents quickly and efficiently.

✓ To minimize the impact resulting from the loss or theft of information (classified or unclassified) or the disruption of critical computing services when incidents occur.

✓ To respond to incidents systematically, following proven procedures that dramatically decrease the likelihood of recurrence(s).

✓ To balance both the operational and security requirements of an organization while staying within realistic budgetary constraints.

✓ To deal with legal issues. A plethora of legal issues surrounds the computer security arena. Procedures that have been analyzed from a legal viewpoint can be followed with the assurance that legal statutes are not being violated.

Organizations may now find themselves legally liable if they haven't taken appropriate steps to secure themselves and their networks from malicious code.

Before I go further with my discussion of security incidence response, I want to define a few key terms that will make the discussion more understandable.

- ✓ An *event* is any observable occurrence in a system and/or network. Examples of events include:
  - The system boot sequence
  - A system crash
  - Data packet flooding within a network
- ✓ An *adverse event* is an event that affects your system or network in a negative way. Adverse events could include the following:
  - Floods
  - Fires
  - Electrical outages
  - Excessive heat that causes system crashes

  Adverse events such as natural disasters and power-related disruptions, though certainly undesirable incidents, are not generally within the scope of incident response planning teams, but should nevertheless be addressed in your organization's business contingency plans.
- ✓ The term *incident,* for the purposes of this discussion, refers to an adverse event in an information system or network or the threat of the occurrence of such an event. Examples of incidents include:
  - Unauthorized use of another user's account
  - Unauthorized use of system privileges
  - Execution of malicious code that destroys data

Events sometimes indicate that an incident is occurring. Typically, events caused by human error (for example, the unintentional deletion of a critical directory and all files contained therein) are the most costly and disruptive. Computer security–related events are attracting an increasing amount of attention within the Federal Government and the computing community in general. The explosive growth of networking has greatly exposed systems to the threat of unauthorized remote access, as does the abundance of malicious code that is readily available to perpetrators.

According to the Federal Computer Incidence Response Center (www.fedcirc.gov), incidents encompass the following general categories:

1. **Malicious code attacks.** Malicious code attacks include attacks by programs such as viruses, Trojan horse programs, worms, and scripts written by crackers/hackers to gain privileges, capture passwords, and/or modify audit logs to exclude records revealing unauthorized activity. Malicious code is particularly troublesome because it is typically written in such a way that it masquerades its presence, making it difficult to detect. Furthermore, self-replicating malicious code (such as viruses and worms) can replicate rapidly, making containment an especially difficult task.

2. **Unauthorized access.** This category encompasses a range of incidents, from improperly logging into a user's account (for instance, when a hacker logs into a legitimate user's account) to the unauthorized accessing of files and directories stored on a system or storage media by obtaining superuser privileges. Unauthorized access can also entail gaining access to network data by planting an illicit "sniffer" program or a device that captures all packets traversing the network at a particular point.

3. **Unauthorized utilization of services.** It is not absolutely necessary to access another user's account to perpetrate an attack on a system or network. An intruder can access information and plant Trojan horse programs, for instance, by misusing available services.

4. **Disruption of service.** Users rely heavily on services provided by network and computing services. With their malicious code, perpetrators can disrupt these services in a number of ways — for example, by erasing a critical program, using *mail spamming* (flooding a user account with e-mail messages), or altering the system's ability to function by installing a Trojan horse program.

5. **Misuse.** Misuse occurs when someone uses a computer system for other than its intended purpose, as when a legitimate user uses a computer to store personal records.

6. **Espionage.** Espionage is the act of stealing information to subvert the interests of a corporation or government. Many of the cases of unauthorized access to U.S. government systems during Operation Desert Storm and Operation Desert Shield were the manifestation of espionage activity against the United States.

7. **Hoaxes.** Hoaxes occur when false information about incidents or vulnerabilities is spread. In early 1995, for example, several users with Internet access distributed information about a so-called Good Times virus, even though no such virus existed.

## Responding to Events

Despite the implementation of security and anti-virus policies, some companies are still targeted by malicious code attacks. When malicious code bypasses security barriers, the execution of a well-planned response can both limit the code's proliferation and return the network to normal operation. Organizations should take the following basic steps once a virus has been detected on their network(s).

1. **Immediately notify all members of the organization.** By failing to quickly notify all employees, malicious code can continue to spread, dramatically increasing the potential for company losses. Failing to make timely notifications may hinder an organization's ability to remain fully (or even partially) operational.

2. **Limit the scope of the attack.** After all interested parties have been notified, you must limit the scope of damage. The idea is to prevent additional information from being discharged, thereby preventing additional damage to the system. Even if a company computer is not rendered completely inoperable by malicious code, the potential for further damage may necessitate a complete shutdown. Remember, malicious code cannot damage a computer that has been turned off.

3. **Cut the cord.** Even after disconnecting the LAN from the Internet, users will still be able to use their network workstations to conduct business while the malicious code threat is fully examined and analyzed. While this alternative might be effective if, for example, a Trojan horse program was transmitting information from your company's LAN to some outside party, this option does have one serious shortcoming: Depending on the extent to which an organization relies on the Internet for business operations, disconnection could result in a significant loss of revenue.

4. **Clean and/or modify infected systems.** Once the malicious code threat has been isolated and contained, the next step is removal. Some forms of malicious code intentionally install backdoors, which allow them to re-enter your system. The infamous BackOrifice Trojan used this method to gain access to a seldom-monitored port (#31337). By examining the ports commonly used by malicious code, those in charge of network security can uncover illicit activity and quickly close those ports.

5. **Reinstall operating systems or applications.** When areas of the operating systems or applications that have been attacked by malicious code cannot be specifically isolated and repaired, you may need to re-enter user information and actively reinstall your operating system. This procedure is usually resorted to when operating systems or applications will no longer function otherwise.

6. **Conduct a security audit.** Organizations that want to perform security audits of their networks have a variety of software programs at their disposal. Companies such as Vigilante (`www.vigilante.com`) can provide the necessary tools and security professionals for carrying out complete audit and vulnerability scans of computer networks.

7. **Get the network back online.** By returning the affected computers to normal operation, employees regain access to the network resources they need to perform their duties. Obviously, it is best to perform this step after *all* threats from hackers or malicious code have been eliminated.

8. **Document and Check.** Organizations should ensure that they document spare parts and business continuity procedures and that they prepare a checklist of the most important and critical considerations well in advance.

9. **Monitor network activity.** Organizations can often collect a good deal more information about hackers or virus writers when they *continue* to examine the scene after the intrusion. Typically, organizations implement improved security and monitoring procedures

(and equipment) in the aftermath of an attack. By monitoring failed login attempts or any attempts to access backdoor programs, companies may be able to "catch" the original intruder red-handed. Each such subsequent incident should be further evaluated. Once a computer system has been infiltrated by intruders, word gets out and it becomes known in the hacker population. As a result, compromised systems become larger targets for subsequent attacks.

# Security Awareness — Those Who Learn Avoid the Worm

Despite the plethora of worms and Trojans that continually plague the corporate landscape, many employees in the workforce rarely take the time to think about security. Communication between management and rank-and-file employees frequently falls short when it comes to complex issues such as computer security. The opinions and expectations at different levels of the corporate chain of command can differ so widely that consistent security policies may seem impossible to achieve. Heightened security awareness requires unambiguous communication so that all members of an organization are following the same security procedures.

It is essential that everyone in the organization comprehend the potential problems that can result from inadequate computer and information security. All computer users must understand how their computers and information are vulnerable to damage, and how their actions (individually and as a group) protect the organization's systems.

## Sending Security Reminders

Employees must understand that letting down their guard just once can result in a substantial security breach that may affect more than just their segment of the company. While employees in general are aware of the need to maintain vigilance regarding potential security threats, reminders are warranted. Whether they are subtle or blatant, such reminders can encourage increased awareness and turn security procedures into a positive habit. Reminders may be circulated in any number of ways throughout the organization, including:

- ✓ Interoffice memos and newsletters — especially when a specific, new threat has arisen
- ✓ E-mail messages
- ✓ Announcements during office meetings and assemblies
- ✓ Employee and contractor awareness presentations

The reminders can also take the form of short, printed "prompts" on objects displayed or used throughout the company, such as:

- ✓ Screen savers
- ✓ Mouse pads
- ✓ Calendars

✓ Notepads

✓ Posters

✓ Pens and pencils

✓ Mugs

## Realizing That a Threat to One Means a Threat to All

Proper security awareness dictates that all employees remain attentive to the hazards that can affect their individual computers. Desktop computers and the information stored on their hard drives *are* vulnerable to damage. Organizations have experienced data loss stemming from accidental deletion to floods and fire, any of which has the potential to destroy computers containing years of data.

Many computer users do not know that computer systems at organizations are constantly under attack. Every day, attempts are made to break into computer systems, or a virus turns up on someone's computer. Such attacks are a constant threat, and they make the need for security even more critical. Cracking into computer systems seems to have become an international sport. Computer intruders from all over the world are continually attempting to break into computer systems via the Internet. Once they (or their malicious code) get into a system, data theft or destruction can result.

Intruders use a variety of techniques to gain unauthorized access to computer systems. It *is* possible to thwart intruders' attacks, but only when employees take the proper precautions. The following examples demonstrate the importance of network administrator and end user cooperation in this process:

✓ A password cracker uses a program that automatically makes continual attempts to log in to the system by using a series of easily deduced passwords, or by using a dictionary as a source of guesses. This type of approach can be defeated if users follow the guidelines for password selection and security mentioned earlier in this chapter.

✓ An intruder sometimes takes advantage of common vulnerabilities, such as a configuration error that grants file access to *all* users, or makes use of backdoors that were originally left open by developers for the purpose of system maintenance. Network administrators or engineers are cautioned to stay alert to these types of threats and to stay one step ahead of the intruders by repairing known errors and closing the backdoors.

✓ Network spoofing is another ingenious way for intruders to gain access. The intruder sets up a malicious program that impersonates the logon routine for another system. When a user attempts to log on to the system, the intruder's program collects the user's password and then returns a bogus message that the system is currently unavailable. Malicious programs collect hundreds of valid passwords using this method. Frequent password modification can defeat this type of attack.

All of these types of attacks are illegal. Unfortunately, legal action taken against these attackers (assuming they can be apprehended) will not restore lost critical information. As a result, active steps must be taken to protect systems, including:

✓ Recognizing and reporting suspicious computer operations

✓ Guarding passwords and changing them frequently

✓ Never e-mailing passwords unencrypted across a network (Internet included)

While private organizations must ensure that their members and employees are "security-aware," the government is also not immune to this obligation. In a statement issued on February 14, 2002, the U.S. Department of State elucidated that requirement, as follows:

Richard Clarke, White House special advisor for Cyberspace Security, met February 13 with the Senate Judiciary subcommittee on Administrative Oversight and the Courts to discuss the status of cyberspace security in the United States.

Senator Charles Schumer (Democrat-New York), chairman of the subcommittee, described the answers to the questions he has researched about cybersecurity as "very, very worrisome." Access to servers, networks, digital controls, air traffic control, and entire regional power grids is entirely too easy, he said.

Schumer said these problems must be fought on two fronts. First, the United States must protect against physical vulnerability — in other words, the fact that the hardware (servers, networks, cables) is amassed in very few places. The Senator used the example of last year's train accident in Baltimore that slowed considerably the Internet traffic in Chicago. Furthermore, all the fiber optic cables that traverse the Atlantic Ocean come together in only one or two places on Manhattan Island.

Secondly, the U.S. must protect against technological vulnerability. Both the public and private sector must safeguard themselves against viruses that affect or have the capability to shut down commerce. The last four viruses have caused over $12 billion worth of damage. One virus in particular took down over 350,000 servers.

In his briefing for the committee, White House advisor Clarke outlined what the Critical Infrastructure Board has done in the past 90 days to begin strengthening cybersecurity. The Critical Infrastructure Board is composed of 10 operating committees and 23 federal agencies. Like the Homeland Security Council, the Critical Infrastructure Board coordinates the cybersecurity activities of government agencies already underway.

Clarke outlined 10 programs that have been implemented or adjusted in the past 90 days:

- A national strategy for cybersecurity in accordance with the private sector and the academic community. This strategy will be formulated through an open, transparent process. The result will be a living document that can change as rapidly as Internet technology.

- The President's proposed FY-2003 budget includes a dramatic 64 percent increase for network security, now approaching about $4 billion.

- A fundamental change of thinking has occurred within IT firms to alter products to give more attention to security.

- Security of IT Internet Services has also improved.

- Due to the Critical Infrastructure Board, bureaucracies are coordinated better and are working together more closely now.

- Implementation of a "Cybercorps," or IT security scholarships, granted by the government. These scholarships work toward a bachelor or master's degree in IT security. For every year of scholarship granted, one year of service in the federal government is required.

- Implementation of a cyberintelligence warning network to bring to light extraordinary and specific vulnerabilities in the cybersystem. This information is shared between the public and private sector.

- Over 150 private IT companies are working together to further enhance cybersecurity.

- Implementation of a modeling and simulation center to plan reactions to attacks on the cybersystem and failure of cybersecurity.

- Implementation of a cyberspace security public campaign, with help from such IT firms as AOL, Cisco, and Microsoft, to educate, warn, and prevent the public from cyberspace attacks.

Clarke said he prefers not to use the term "cyberterrorism," but instead favors use of the term "information security" or "cyberspace security." Most terrorist groups have not engaged in information warfare, Clarke said, except for some very minor infractions. Instead, terrorist groups have thus far only used the Internet for propaganda, communications, or fundraising.

Instead of concentrating on who may engage in information warfare, Clarke said, one must concentrate on the vulnerabilities of cyberspace security. The spectrum of who can hack into vital information systems is enormous. It can range from a 14-year-old boy to a nation-state. So worrying about who could do such a thing is much less efficient than taking care of cyberspace vulnerabilities.

Clarke also pointed out the extreme significance of the cyberspace infrastructure. In the past ten years, every sector of the U.S. economy and government has moved onto network systems. Everybody relies on networks, and nothing can operate unless the networks are functioning correctly. However, Clarke said, none of these things were designed "with security in mind."

In the private sector, the amount of money spent on IT security is roughly .0025 percent of total revenue, said Clarke. That is less than the amount of money spent on coffee in the same companies.

There is "lots of low-hanging fruit," said Clarke, meaning there are many very easy things that can be done to disrupt the cybersystem. Changes need to be made.

One example is Microsoft. Bill Gates, head of Microsoft, ordered his company to stop writing and designing new products for 30 days, Clarke said. Instead, the company must retool their existing products to become more secure. Even if 30 days does not seem to be long enough to accomplish that task, it will make program designers concentrate more on security when writing future products.

To illustrate the possible effect of a cyberattack, Clarke pointed to his discussion with the CEO of a major railroad company. Even an enterprise as old as railroads is based on electronic controls. The company's network lets them know the necessary information regarding where every train and boxcar is at every minute. If this network were attacked and the relaying of information stopped, the CEO said that he would be forced to order every train to stop, completely devastating the railroad system.

Senator Schumer noted that if this were the expected effect for a railroad company, the effects of a network shutdown of a regional power grid or an air traffic control grid would be staggering.

The need for security awareness reaches beyond the private sector. A security issue may begin in one sector but in short order affects all networks linked via the Internet. In tandem with the government, organizations *can* make inroads toward maintaining their network viability. Threats to security arrive from a variety of sources.

# Educating End Users

As the initial chapters of this book discuss, computer viruses—programs that can "infect" other programs, damage hard drives, erase critical information, and knock systems offline—are a serious threat. Literally thousands of viruses can get on your system. They can come from anywhere and can steal or destroy data.

The types of threats that malicious codes pose to networks are discussed in Chapter 1. Specific types of malicious code are examined in more detail in Chapter 4.

The symptoms of an infected system may include any of the following:

- ✓ Unusual items that appear on the display, including graphics, odd messages, or system error messages
- ✓ Corrupted or inaccessible program files, hard disks, or diskettes
- ✓ Programs that take longer to start up, run more slowly than usual, or do not run at all
- ✓ Unexplained decreases in the amount of available system memory

Unfortunately, once symptoms appear, it may be too late to save valuable data. The key is to stop malicious code *before* it has the opportunity to damage a system. Employees should be educated to follow these guidelines:

- ✓ Use anti-virus software to scan for viruses on *all* new software prior to loading them on to a system (even "off-the-shelf" software).
- ✓ Do *not* run programs obtained from unfamiliar Bulletin Board systems or the Internet without first scanning them for viruses.
- ✓ Secure physical access to your computer.
- ✓ Back up your files frequently, so you can restore damaged information.
- ✓ If you think that your computer is infected, take immediate action.
- ✓ Close all files and programs.
- ✓ Document what symptoms were observed.
- ✓ Shut down the system.

# Proactive versus Reactive Malicious Code Defense

All computers can be victimized by security incidents. Although these incidents take many forms, they can all exploit system vulnerabilities at a tremendous rate. Companies must respond to attacks at an equal or greater speed in order to limit the scope of their security weaknesses, as well as to limit the damage caused by these incidents. Security incidents are addressed by two methods or approaches:

✓ **The proactive approach.** This approach encompasses all steps taken to avert security incidents that compromise the organization's computer systems.

✓ **The reactive approach.** Although successful implementation of the proactive policies appears to negate the need for other security measures, security professionals agree that the additional implementation of a *reactive* approach provides the broadest coverage. The reactive approach consists of measures taken by an organization after their systems have been besieged by a security incident(s).

The incidence response methods examined earlier in this chapter are part of the reactive approach.

At one time, it was enough that an organization subscribe to the CERT mailing list and follow their recommended course of action in order to preserve the security of the company computer networks. As security incidents continue to multiply, as well as increase in destructiveness, such a simple security approach is no longer adequate. No single approach can defend against penetration by every hacker. An approach using a well-balanced mix of both proactive and reactive procedures is warranted.

## Patches

Organizations must patch susceptible systems. This proactive approach to malicious code defense is, by far, the most important step organizations can take as part of an optimal defense against network breaches. To ensure that the patching is carried out effectively, management must be prepared to devote sufficient staff and man-hours to the task. This strategy may become an expensive endeavor depending upon the size of the organization, since it may have hundreds — even thousands — of computers located on several sites using more than one operating system. Regardless of the organization's size, the following patching guidelines should be followed:

✓ When a new operating system has been installed, consider any available security patches as part of that system and install them, as well. To exclude them is to install an incomplete, flawed system. Patch information and updates are available from most vendors at their Web site. Remember to patch other applications, as well.

✓ Keep records of all areas where patches have been applied.

✓ Make sure the organization's computers are updating virus definitions regularly using their automated processes.

✓ Make sure that all of the organization's computers are using the most recent anti-virus software available.

✓ Visit www.cert.org and request to be included on their mailing list so that you are informed of patches as soon as they become available.

✓ Request to be included on the security-related e-mail lists of your software vendors (most are free-of-charge) so that you may remain informed about recommended patches.

# Vulnerability Assessment

An integral aspect of the proactive approach includes gauging the organization's susceptibility to security attacks. In order to discover where vulnerabilities lie, the organization may use programs to methodically scan their networks and computers (an *automated* vulnerability assessment). By the same token, malicious coders use similar programs to identify shortcomings in their victims' systems. If no patch has been developed for those hacker-exposed flaws, they will surely be exploited.

Nonetheless, automated vulnerability assessment programs are effective. However, because these programs can be difficult to configure, can produce outcomes that are sometimes hard to understand, and require periodic updates, some companies may want to have the assessment made by an outside service.

Another part of the proactive method is the attempt to understand how a malicious code writer approaches a targeted network. By examining the system in the same way a malicious coder would, the organization can better anticipate where the system will be targeted and thus take the necessary precautions.

# Proactive Limitations

The trouble with malicious code defense is that modern-day Web browsers, e-mail, and instant messaging programs expose computers and the networks that connect them to self-executing code, leaving companies vulnerable to a wide variety of attacks. Many computer users and corporate employees don't realize that when they visit Web sites or open e-mail messages, much of the content executes automatically on their computer. The organizational workforce is exposed to this new technology on a daily basis when using the Web to conduct research or communicating with business associates and friends by e-mail or instant messaging. Despite the use of intrusion detection systems, powerful firewalls, and updated anti-virus software, users remain vulnerable to the "new generation" of attacks coming from both e-mail messages and the Web. While firewalls can protect a company's trusted internal network from the untrusted Internet, it is not uncommon for malicious code attacks to arrive on trusted ports using *approved* protocols.

# Proactive Anti-Virus Products

Most of the anti-virus products in use today are reactive in nature and rely upon a continuously updated database of "known" viruses (called *virus signatures*) to detect and protect computer systems. It is reactive by design, offering protection after other users have been affected and the developer has had the opportunity to examine the viral signature and develop a suitable defense. It is analogous to getting inoculated *after* you've been infected. Computer users have little or no protection from new attacks until after their anti-virus vendor receives the new attack sample, creates a new signature, and delivers that patch to their product's anti-virus database. This leaves organizations and computer users vulnerable until the new updates are delivered hours, sometimes days, later.

Because of this deficiency, many anti-virus vendors now focus on developing content monitoring proactive anti-virus defense. They base this approach on the assumption that by monitoring how code "behaves," rather than relying on a "known" signature for detection, malicious code will be stopped before it can damage computer systems. Products like Surfin Guard Pro by Finjan Software Ltd. (www.finjan.com) or Trojan Trap by Tiny Software, Inc. (www.tinysoftware.com) operate using this method of malicious code defense.

These proactive anti-virus programs and hybrid anti-virus products are covered in greater detail in Chapter 9.

# Identifying Internet Hoaxes and False Alarms

Among the unsolicited messages that fill Internet users' e-mail inboxes are ominous warnings about devastating new viruses like Trojans that steal passwords and malicious code that threatens to wipe all the data from a user's hard drive. Besides these warnings, users may also find messages touting free money, appeals on behalf of missing or sick children, and a host of other subject matters specifically designed to garner attention, persuading users to forward the message on to everyone for whom they have an address. The vast majority of these messages are hoaxes and chain letters. While hoaxes do not automatically infect systems as Trojans or worms would, they are nevertheless time-consuming and can be costly to remove from all the systems. Organizations may find that they spend more time investigating and then discrediting hoaxes than handling bona fide malicious code attacks. Keep in mind that hoax warnings are, in most instances, simply scare tactics started by malicious people that are then circulated by innocent end users who think they are helping the Internet community by distributing these spurious warnings.

## The Cost of Hoaxes

On the surface, the cost and risks associated with hoaxes may appear to be incidental, especially if you consider the cost of handling only one hoax on one machine. The true cost, however, is significant when your tally includes all computers and systems that have been victimized. The actual time spent by employees reading bogus messages adds up in man-hours—hours for (and during) which an employee is being paid by the organization.

Imagine if each of the 20,000 employees of a large organization received just one hoax message and spent just one minute reading and then discarding it. The cost associated with this hoax would be as follows:

20,000 people x .01667 hours x $25/hour = $8,335 per hoax

While $8,335 may not seem like a considerable amount of money for a large company to lose, remember that organizations are plagued by many hoax messages. Furthermore, many employees are paid more than $25 per hour (especially when you factor in additional costs such as medical, dental, and disability benefits).

Now imagine the costs associated with a hoax when recipients believe and then act upon bogus messages. Some hoaxes instruct users to scan their PCs for viruses using the built-in Windows file find utility. The alleged malicious files are actually critical system files needed for proper operation of the computer. If users delete them, they are, in effect, being tricked into damaging their own PCs. Depending upon the scope and extent of damage to the system(s), the repairs may cost an organization a substantial amount of time and money.

## Recognizing Hoaxes and False Alarms

Some detective work may be required to determining whether a warning is based on fact or fiction. Warning messages (designed to spread panic or fear) are common and must be cleverly worded to be perceived as legitimate. It is impossible to list each of the hoax messages that are in existence, as new ones are put into global circulation on a daily basis. However, users should be aware of several traits that are common to all hoaxes.

✓ The message usually begins by urging recipients to forward the message (about a serious threat) to all of their family, friends, and co-workers.

✓ The message cites or quotes a person with an important-sounding title or even a government agency as the source of the information.

✓ There are no links to an outside source. Prominent news services, magazine publishers, and software companies inform the public very quickly about problems or risks as well as hoaxes, and are glad to take credit for doing so. Refer to your favorite news source's online Web site to determine if a threat is real and has been reported by a reliable source.

✓ The message warns users not to open incoming messages with specific wording in the subject line. Ostensibly, to do so will result in terrible damage to your computer or network. This is classic hoax terminology.

One of the best ways to determine if a warning is a hoax is to look it up on one of the Web sites that monitors these events. Such sites have sensors out all over the world, and concerned users can be confident that these experts have heard of the hoax (if it exists). The following Web sites help users determine the validity of virus warnings:

✓ www.vmyths.com

✓ http://hoaxbusters.ciac.org/

✓ www.symantec.com/avcenter/hoax.html

✓ www.commandcom.com/virus/virus_hoaxes.html

# Summary

One of the best ways an organization can defend against the threat of malicious code is by tapping its human resources. Even hackers use human resources, in the form of social engineering. Despite regularly updated anti-virus software, companies still experience the adverse effects of viruses, worms, and Trojan horse programs on their computer systems. Through the application of various security policies and employee education, organizations can minimize the dangers posed by hackers and malicious code. Key points covered in this chapter include:

✓ How well-planned and properly designed security, anti-virus, and password policies supply the backbone of malicious code defense

✓ What the dangers of corporate e-mail messaging and the rules for safe e-mail messaging are

✓ What the benefits of incidence response plans are and why they are so critical in an organization's overall computer security plan

✓ How security awareness through employee education can save organizations time and money by eliminating costly mistakes

✓ Why a customized, well-balanced blend of proactive and reactive security measures provides the highest level of protection

✓ How to identify and prevent the threats caused by virus hoaxes

# Chapter 9

# Hardware and Software Protective Measures

## In This Chapter

✓ Exploring firewalls

✓ Employing intrusion detection

✓ Selecting anti-virus products

✓ Choosing "hybrid" code behavior monitoring products

✓ Protecting Web servers

✓ Blocking code at the Internet gateway

✓ Blocking ports

✓ Updating and patching OSs/browsers

✓ Backing up and recovering data

✓ Protecting the Registry (Windows OS)

WHILE THE IMPLEMENTATION OF SECURITY policies and increased security awareness go a long way towards protecting computer systems from the many threats posed by malicious code, hardware and software devices are an organization's first line of defense. Firewalls, anti-virus products, and intrusion detection systems all play important, yet diverse, roles in an organization's overall security plan. Individual security devices exhibit a specific purpose and function, but when they work together, they provide multiple layers of protection. As the rate of computer security breaches surges, the cost to businesses and government organizations has proportionately increased.

The only way to make computers completely hacker- or virus-proof is to turn them off. Since this is not a viable solution, the real issue is how to make your computer as secure as possible. Leaving an unguarded computer connected to the Internet via broadband (for example, ISDN, DSL, or cable) is akin to leaving the door to your home or business unlocked. Hackers are opportunists who furtively "walk" around, jiggling doorknobs until they find an unlocked door. In the case of computer systems, the unlocked door might be an open port. By "locking the door"—installing a security system—entry becomes much more difficult.

Organizations must keep in mind that broadband Internet connections, which are "always-on," are easier to hack into because they have a static (fixed) IP address. This means that once a hacker discovers your computer on the Internet, he or she can easily find it again. Dial-up Internet connections are issued a new IP address each time your computer connects, which makes it much harder to locate your computer again (unless, of course, malicious code has already plagued your system by "phoning home" each time you connect).

Internet security products can provide individuals and organizations with adequate protection because the vast majority of attacks are "general" in nature; in other words, they do not specifically target any one company. When individuals or organizations make it difficult for hackers to find and gain entry into their computer systems, they will most likely be left alone. This chapter covers the various security devices that are available to individuals and companies that wish to protect their computers from the threats of Internet marauders and malicious code.

# Firewalls — Gatekeepers of the Internet

Firewalls are the gatekeepers of the Internet. Similar to "bouncers" at a nightclub, they decide who is given permission to enter and who is not. A *firewall* is essentially a software or hardware device that filters the information coming into a private network or computer system through the Internet connection. When the firewall filters flag an incoming packet of data as "suspicious," it is not permitted to pass through. Firewalls can use one or more methods to monitor and control the traffic traveling in and out of the network:

   ✓ **Proxy service** — Data from the Internet is intercepted by the firewall and then sent to the requesting computer, and vice versa.

   ✓ **Packet filtering** — Data packets are examined against a set of filters. Data packets passing inspection are permitted to pass through the filters and are then forwarded to the requesting system. Packets that do not pass inspection are quickly discarded.

   ✓ **Stateful inspection** — This method doesn't examine the actual contents of each data packet; instead, it compares certain key components of the packet to a database of trusted information. Data traveling from inside the organization (LAN) to the outside (Internet) is monitored for specific characteristics. When the data is returned from the Internet, the incoming information is compared to these characteristics. When the comparison yields a reasonable match, the information is allowed through. Otherwise, it is discarded.

Since firewalls scrutinize *every* data packet that arrives at the computer (before it is "seen" by any other programs), they have complete discretion over what data may be received by the computer from the Internet. Bear in mind that TCP/IP ports are only "open" on a computer when the first arriving packet, requesting the establishment of a connection, is answered by your computer. If the arriving packet is ignored, the computer port effectively "disappears" from the Internet. When this happens, no connections are permitted.

The true benefit of a firewall lies in its ability to be discerning about what data it lets through and what it blocks. Since every incoming packet must contain the correct IP address of the sender's machine (so the receiver can send back a receipt acknowledgement), the firewall can be selective about which packets are admitted and which are dropped. It can filter packets based upon any combination of the originating computer's IP address and port and the destination computer's IP address and port.

# Using Firewalls for Malicious Code Defense

While firewalls successfully keep hackers and script kiddies out, they also have the added benefit of preventing Trojan horse programs from communicating with an outside party. Although Trojans are often lumped in the same category as viruses and worms, they display distinct differences. Once executed, these innocent-looking programs allow intruders to assume control of an Internet-enabled computer remotely, from their own PCs.

Firewalls block the vulnerable or open ports that are commonly used by hackers to commandeer your system. Firewalls are particularly useful in preventing your computer from unwittingly taking part in a DDoS (distributed denial-of-service attack) or from being accessed by hackers even if a user has already installed a Trojan unintentionally.

Remember, some Trojans installed from e-mail attachments and downloads do not phone home and inform the hacker where the Trojan is located. Hackers must probe a range of IP addresses in the hope of finding existing installed Trojans. Table 9-1 contains a brief list of some of the more common Trojans and the ports they use. A more complete list is provided in Chapter 7.

**TABLE 9-1 Ports Commonly Used by Trojans**

| Port | Trojan |
| --- | --- |
| 555 | phAse zero |
| 1243 | Sub-7, SubSeven |
| 3129 | Masters Paradise |
| 6670 | DeepThroat |
| 6711 | Sub-7, SubSeven |
| 6969 | Gate Crasher |
| 12345 | NetBus |
| 21544 | GirlFriend |
| 23456 | Evil FTP |
| 27374 | Sub-7, SubSeven |
| 30100 | NetSphere |
| 31337 | BackOrifice |
| 31789 | Hack'a'Tack |
| 50505 | Sockets de Troie |

A simple tip: Windows users can check for these Trojans in the following way:

1. Start a DOS session and enter the command `netstat -an` on your computer.

2. Check the ports on the entries that are marked "listening". IP addresses are followed by a colon and the port (see Figure 9-1). Users are concerned with the "local" ports on the list.

3. If any ports on the above list are found to be open or active, they should be considered hostile ports. Hostile ports should be closed, filtered, or monitored since they are mostly used for Trojan and intrusion programs. Monitoring and blocking of ports is covered later in this chapter.

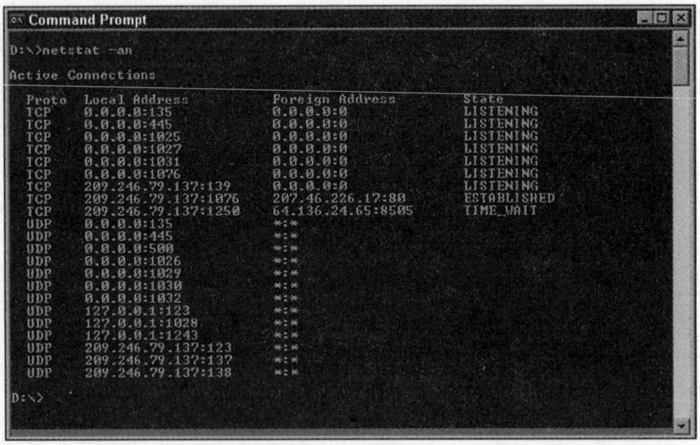

**Figure 9-1:** Netstat running in a DOS session (Windows XP)

In addition to using firewalls and intrusion detection systems as tools for malicious code defense, many network operating systems allow for the filtering of ports by controlling inbound TCP/IP traffic. While the exact procedure varies between operating systems, the following steps demonstrate how to accomplish TCP/IP filtering for Windows 2000–based computers. TCP/IP filtering is useful from a security standpoint because it works in Kernel (root) mode and can only be altered by those with root privileges.

Follow these steps to configure TCP/IP filtering in Windows 2000:

1. Click the Start menu.

2. Click Settings.

3. Click Control Panel.

4. Double-click the Network and Dial-up Connections option.

5. Select and right-click the interface on which you wish to configure incoming access control.

6. Click Properties.

7. Click Internet Protocol (TCP/IP) in the Components box.

8. Click Properties.

9. Click the Advanced tab in the Internet Protocol (TCP/IP) Properties dialog box.

10. Choose the Options tab.

11. Click TCP/IP Filtering.

12. Click Properties.

13. Check the Enable TCP/IP Filtering (All adapters) box.

14. You now have two choices, Permit All and Permit Only, for each of three columns:

   ■ TCP Ports

   ■ UDP Ports

   ■ IP Protocols

> **note**
>
> To allow all packets for TCP and UDP traffic, select the Permit All option. To allow only selected TCP and UDP traffic, select Permit Only. Click Add and then key in the port number in the Add Filter dialog box. If you do not want to allow *any* UDP or TCP traffic, simply click Permit Only without keying in any port numbers.

# Hardware Firewalls

A hardware-based firewall is essentially a physical piece of equipment that is located between a computer network (for example, a LAN) and the Internet. In the case of a cable or DSL connection, this hardware device is located between the DSL/cable modem and a network hub or a switch. Hardware firewalls are sometimes favored over software firewalls for a number of reasons:

   ✓ A hardware firewall is designed to be just that: a firewall that does not run any other superfluous applications. This simplifies the software required inside the firewall device.

   ✓ On some hardware firewalls, the software is contained in ROM (read-only memory) chips. Since special equipment is needed to modify these chips, the use of ROM chips helps deflect any tampering attempts made by hackers from the Internet.

   ✓ Another benefit is that the software is usually smaller in size and is therefore less prone to flaws or bugs.

Hardware firewalls are typically employed in a networked environment. The vast majority of broadband routers use a technology called NAT (Network Address Translation). Network Address Translation allows a single device, such as a router, to act as an agent between a local (private) network and the Internet (public network). Such an arrangement means that only a single, unique IP address is required to represent an entire group of computers. Simply put, users can utilize NAT to hide their internal network from the Internet—the same way a broadband router performs firewall security. One broadband router that uses NAT for firewall protection is the Linksys EtherFast Cable/DSL router (www.linksys.com). This router is quite popular with small/office home/office (SOHO) users. While very effective at keeping hackers and script kiddies out of a network, hardware firewalls offer users little protection from malicious code.

## Personal Software Firewalls

It has become increasingly apparent that the Internet is not as harmless as it once seemed. Denial-of-service (DoS) attacks, Internet worms, and major Web site break-ins have become commonplace. Due to the heightened level of public awareness regarding these risks, users are now looking for ways to protect themselves from all manner of threats.

Traditionally, the best approach for individual protection encompasses the following steps:

✓ Run reputable anti-virus software on a regular basis and keep it current with regular anti-virus updates.

✓ Be sure to always maintain a current backup of all critical files.

While these two practices remain excellent forms of protection, personal firewall software is now freely available to average users and should be considered mandatory for all cable and DSL users, especially those not already using a hardware firewall. Personal software firewalls are different from their industrial-strength brethren. They are mostly used in standalone computers directly connected to the Internet. Hackers no longer target only large organizations for cyberattacks. Modern-day hackers seek out the home or SOHO user in search of bank account numbers, income tax returns, or passwords. In addition, users need to protect their PCs hijacked as unwilling participants in denial-of-service attacks on the Internet. Now that "always-on" broadband connections are more affordable, they are becoming increasingly popular with home users, leaving them at risk. Fortunately, users are presented with a variety of tools available for protecting their data. Personal software firewalls can block certain types of malicious code attacks and protect PCs from Internet threats.

The benefit of personal firewalls is that they can filter both inbound and outbound data. Without this bidirectional monitoring feature, users would not be able to effectively protect themselves from spyware programs and Trojan horses. Once users inadvertently install them on their PCs, both spyware and Trojan horses attempt to communicate information from the user's PC (information such as account numbers, passwords, or Web usage) back to the originating party. Without the ability to monitor and control *outbound* transmissions, users are powerless against such programs. Here are some popular and free *bidirectional* personal software firewalls:

✓ **ZoneAlarm** by Zone Labs, Inc. (www.zonelabs.com), is a bidirectional personal software firewall that comes in two varieties: a limited free version or the full-featured ZoneAlarm Pro, which costs $50.

✓ **Tiny Personal Firewall** by Tiny Software, Inc. (www.tinysoftware.com), is a full-featured and robust personal firewall. It is a free download for personal users. Business and institutional customers are required to purchase the multiple user licenses for the product.

✓ **Agnitum Outpost Firewall** by Agnitum Ltd. (www.agnitum.com) is one of the most fea-ture-packed personal firewalls available for the Windows platform. It offers peace of mind from any threats by cookies, advertisements, e-mail viruses, backdoors, spyware, crackers, adware, and virtually every other Internet danger. Agnitum Outpost is the first firewall that can support plug-in components so its capabilities are easily extended.

After installing any one of the preceding products, users are alerted the first time an outbound connection is attempted by *any* application in their PCs (malicious code included). Any time an outbound connection is requested for which the firewall has no rule, the personal firewall "asks" the user for permission (that is, to create a rule) to either permit or deny the outbound request. After the rule has been set by the user, the firewall stores that rule in a database for future refer-ence. This prevents the firewall from "barking away" each time the same application is launched.

## Built-in Windows XP Firewall

Microsoft Windows XP provides basic Internet security in the form of a built-in firewall, known as the *Internet Connection Firewall (ICF)*. This feature is designed for home and small business use and it provides protection for computers directly connected to the Internet. ICF is available for local area network or dial-up connections. It also prevents the scanning of ports and resources (file and printer shares) from external sources.

## Enabling the XP Internet Connection Firewall

The Internet Connection Firewall is useful for protecting a dial-up connection when your operat-ing system is linked directly into an ISP, or for protecting a LAN connection that is connected to an asymmetric digital subscriber line (ADSL) or cable modem. The Internet Connection Firewall feature may also be enabled on the Internet connection of an Internet Connection Sharing (ICS) host computer to provide protection to that ICS host computer.

Use the Network Setup wizard in the following way to enable the Internet Connection Firewall:

1. Click the Start menu.
2. Click Control Panel.
3. Double-click the Network and Internet Connections option.
4. Click Setup, or change your home or small office network.
5. When you select a configuration in the wizard that indicates your computer is con-nected to the Internet, the Internet Connection Firewall will be enabled.

To manually configure the Internet Connection Firewall:

1. Click the Start menu.
2. Click Control Panel.
3. Double-click the Network and Internet Connections option.

4. Click Network Connections.

5. Select the connection on which you wish to enable Internet Connection Firewall and right-click it.

6. Click Properties.

7. Choose the Advanced tab.

8. Click "Protect my computer or network".

9. To allow applications and services to pass through the firewall, they must be enabled by clicking Settings and by selecting the appropriate items to be allowed for the Internet Connection Firewall configuration.

If your LAN uses Internet Connection Sharing (ICS) to supply Internet access to several computers, you should use ICF only on the shared Internet connection. You should not enable the firewall on any connection that does not directly connect to the Internet. The ICF feature of Windows XP is not needed if your network already uses a third-party firewall or a proxy server

# Industrial-Strength Firewalls

While personal software firewalls are designed for single computer protection, larger organizations with networks of multiple users require a more powerful and sophisticated firewall and malicious code protection. Most of these products are designed for larger organizations with sensitive data that requires a high level of security. Several powerful hardware and software-based products have become popular. Keep in mind that some of these products can be tricky to configure and may require special training by company personnel for proper operation and maintenance. Two are presented here, one software-based and the other hardware-based, with a brief explanation of some of their advanced features.

✓ **FireWall-1** by Check Point Software (www.checkpoint.com) is a complete software firewall with an inventive design that helps organizations set up and enforce a comprehensive security policy that protects *all* of their network resources. According to its manufacturer, Firewall-1 boasts a number of features. First, it uses a central management system for all firewalls (one screen to manage all network firewalls). Second, its security policy interface clearly illustrates all firewall rules in an easy to understand tabular format. Additionally, FireWall-1's content security capabilities elevate data inspection to the highest level, protecting users from various hazards (including computer viruses and malicious Java or ActiveX applets), while providing access control to the Internet. Check Point's integrated Security Servers employ multiple methods of enforcing content security, such as file name matching for FTP, e-mail address translation for SMTP, and stripping of Java script tags for HTTP.

✓ **SonicWALL, Inc.** (www.sonicsys.com) offers companies of all sizes robust hardware-based Internet security solutions. SonicWALL offers organizations a complete line of powerful Internet security solutions to protect the single telecommuter up to the large network hub. SonicWALL Internet security appliances are powerful, easy-to-use, afford-able security platforms that include, among other features, an ICSA-certified firewall, network anti-virus protection, and content filtering.

Other companies, such as Cisco Systems, Inc. (www.cisco.com) and Internet Security Systems, Inc. (www.iss.net), should also be considered when searching for a complete firewall security solution. Cisco's PIX products are hardware-based firewalls, while Internet Security Systems offers a suite of powerful software security solutions for organizations of any size.

# Employing Intrusion Detection

The Internet is a public network. The tremendous growth and popularity of the Internet has been accompanied by a gradual evolution of the standard business model of organizations around the globe. Increasingly, individuals and companies are connecting to the Internet on a daily basis to benefit from the new approach to conducting business, known as *e-commerce*. Because Internet connectivity has become vital to modern day organizations, concerns over network security have also become central. At present, nearly all discussions on computer security are focused on the techniques or tools used in defending computer networks. Simply put, an intrusion detection system is analogous to a burglar alarm. A strong door lock can help protect a jewelry store from rob-bery. However, if somebody breaks the lock in an attempt to steal the jewels, it is the burglar alarm that detects the broken lock and alerts the authorities and owner by sounding the alarm.

Similarly, network intrusion detection systems complement firewall security. The firewall, like the lock on the door, protects an organization from malicious Internet attacks, while the intru-sion detection system, like the alarm system, detects when someone has infiltrated the network by breaking through the firewall.

While most firewalls effectively filter incoming traffic from the Internet, they can be circum-vented. External users, for example, can connect to the company's private network by dialing in via modem. Because some networks are configured to permit this type of outside access, the fire-wall would not interpret this type of connection as a threat.

This is where intrusion detection systems (IDSs) are beneficial. The IDS monitors network traffic and analyzes that traffic for hostile attacks originating from inside or outside of the organi-zation. Intrusion detection systems have been around for many years and have evolved into prac-tical (and highly recommended) security tools. An IDS is not a panacea for securing network infrastructure. Instead, it should be applied as an integral part of an organization's overall security plan, consisting of several security tools deployed throughout the networked environment.

For the most part, IDSs currently come in two varieties: the computer-based intrusion detec-tion system and the network-based intrusion detection system.

✓ With a **computer-based (host-based) IDS**, a user installs the IDS software program directly on the computer that is to be monitored. Host-based IDS is a software program that is installed on *each* computer that requires protection. The key difference between the host-based and network-based solutions is the data source, or the location from which each system receives the information used to determine that an attack is in progress. Host-based intrusion detection systems primarily use audit logs directly from the server's operating system. The benefit of this type of system is that the audit logs contain information about events that have already become apparent; host-based systems are able to determine the success of a security breach with more detail and accuracy than a network-based intrusion detection system. On the other hand, because a host-based IDS operates using log files, security events will have already transpired by the time they are detected. This makes response time an important issue. Significantly, response time can be improved if the system is properly configured. For example, a host-based intrusion detection system can be set to receive an alert from the operating system whenever there is a *new* log entry, rather than merely check for entries at periodic intervals.

✓ **Network-based intrusion detection systems** employ raw network packets as their data source. A network IDS monitors these packets traveling across the network in an attempt to discover if an intruder is attempting to break into a system. A typical example is a system that watches for large numbers of TCP connection requests to many different ports on a target machine. In this manner, the system discovers if someone is attempting a TCP port scan. A network IDS may run either on the target machine watching its own traffic or on a stand-alone computer watching all network traffic (hub, router, switches).

Note that a network-based IDS monitors several computers, while a host-based IDS monitors only a single computer. In short, when an IDS looks for attack signatures in the operating system log files, it is *host-based,* and when it looks for these patterns in network traffic, it is *network-based.*

Snort is a free, open source, lightweight network intrusion detection system that was originally designed primarily for Linux and UNIX operating systems. Snort has now been engineered to be compatible with the Windows family of operating systems, as well. It is capable of performing real-time traffic analysis and packet logging on IP networks. Snort can perform many functions, including protocol analysis and content searching/matching. It can be used to detect a variety of attacks and probes, such as buffer overflows, stealth port scans, CGI attacks, SMB probes, and OS fingerprinting attempts. Like most programs written for UNIX and Linux, Snort is open source code and is free for download at www.snort.org, the home page of the Snort development team. There, users can find specific instructions on how to download and install a copy of Snort for their particular Linux, UNIX, or Windows operating system.

# Selecting Anti-Virus Products — The Good, the Bad, and the Free

Anti-virus products have changed dramatically over the last several years. With the tremendous growth of the Internet and the widespread, nearly universal use of e-mail, viruses, worms, and Trojan horses have flourished. In the "old" days of computing, viruses spread via floppy disks. The rate of transmission was slow and often stayed within the confines of a single organization. Today's malicious code, however, rides the information superhighway at breakneck speed.

Virus spread is so rapid that many anti-virus vendors cannot develop signatures fast enough to immediately protect all users. To combat this limitation, high-quality anti-virus products put into effect a process called heuristics to help detect unknown malicious code. *Heuristics,* a type of artificial intelligence, enables anti-virus software products to detect malicious code even when there is not yet a signature for it in its database. Heuristics, however, can create false positive outcomes. As a result, some vendors have scaled back the level of heuristic capability in their products, making them somewhat less effective at detecting newly released malicious code.

# Choosing the Right Product

Remember that anti-virus software is *mandatory*. However, such an abundance of quality anti-virus products exist on the market today that choosing the right one to protect an organization's network infrastructure can be daunting. When choosing a product, ask yourself the following questions:

✓ Is the anti-virus product ICSA Labs (TruSecure)–certified? The answer to this question is especially important. Products that are ICSA Labs–certified by TruSecure Corporation have passed rigorous testing. According to TruSecure, the objective of their ICSA Labs' Anti-Virus Certification Program is to make available to the user community a selection of products that provide the following security services:

- Protection to computer systems and media from computer virus intrusion.

- Detection of computer viruses on an infected computer system or media.

- Recovery from a computer virus infection.

  Users can visit the TruSecure Web site (www.trusecure.com) for a list of anti-virus software products, as well as many other computer security products that have passed ICSA Labs' testing and obtained certified status.

✓ Does the product have heuristic capabilities? As I discussed in the previous section, heuristics help anti-virus software detect viruses for which they have no signature. Choose anti-virus software that has a good support and a proven track record, such as those that are offered by Symantec or McAfee.

✓ How often does the vendor make anti-virus signatures (updates) available (daily or weekly)?

✓ Does the vendor quickly issue warnings via e-mail to all registered product users once a new virus has been detected so that users can perform updates as soon as possible?

Another excellent source of information that can assist users in choosing anti-virus software is http://Helpvirus.com. Here, users are met with a wealth of information regarding anti-virus resources, as well as resources related to privacy and security.

# Name Brand versus Lesser-Known Products

Consumers often believe that "name brand" products offer a higher level of quality than lesser-known products. They assume that manufacturers of name brand products have an "image" to preserve and that they therefore work harder to maintain the quality of their merchandise. While many of the anti-virus software name brand products do provide a high degree of protection, many of the lesser-known products protect users equally well. Additionally, several of these lesser-known anti-virus products are available *at no cost* for personal use for an unlimited amount of time, allowing individuals and those on a budget to also benefit from high-quality anti-virus protection.

The following is a list of four vendors that provide anti-virus software free for personal use. While this short list is accurate as of the writing of this book, due to the dynamic nature of the Internet, some of these products may no longer be available or free. Please check the individual vendor's Web site for availability and additional, specific information.

✓  AVG Antivirus (www.grisoft.com)

✓  eScorcher by eScorcher Antivirus, LLC (www.escorcher.com)

✓  AntiVir by H+BEDV Datentechnik GmbH (www.free-av.com)

✓  SurfinGuard by Finjan Software (www.finjan.com)

# Choosing "Hybrid" Code Behavior Monitoring Products

Unfortunately, despite frequent signature updates and heuristics, many anti-virus products still "miss" the occasional worm, virus, or Trojan horse program. The reason is simple: it takes time (sometimes days) to analyze, develop, and then distribute new signature updates once a fast spreading malicious code has been detected. Recognizing this deficit, several vendors have developed a new breed of "hybrid" anti-virus products that does not rely solely on viral signatures for detection. Using digital "sandbox" technology, these products monitor code "behavior" in their attempt to determine whether a piece of software code is malicious or benign.

Sandbox techniques are proactive approaches to stopping the actions of malicious code. By using a digital sandbox, all active content (ActiveX, Java) is executed and run in a controlled environment. The purpose of the sandbox is to create an impassable barrier between all active content and the operating system. The sandbox tracks all active content whether it originates from the Web, e-mail messaging, or downloads. The sandbox virtually "surrounds" the active content and intercepts all requests for operating system resources and/or services. It evaluates the request in comparison to a set of "rules" established by the user that will either permit or deny the request. The behavior of active content determines whether it is permitted to function. When hostile activity is detected, the active content is immediately terminated. Three products that currently provide this type of protection for Windows-based computers are:

✓  SurfinGuard Pro by Finjan Software (www.finjan.com)

✓  Trojan Trap by TinySoftware, Inc. (www.tinysoftware.com)

✓  eSafe Enterprise by Alladin Knowledge Systems (www.esafe.com)

With both eSafe and Trojan Trap, a blended approach is used in which traditional signature-based reactive protection is coupled with proactive content monitoring. Each of these products uses sandbox technology to monitor code behavior. Users are encouraged to visit each vendor's Web site for pricing, availability, and specific details.

# Protecting Web Servers

Code Red and Code Red II taught us that Web servers are not immune to malicious code. While desktop PCs have been subjected to a glut of viruses, worms, and Trojans, Web servers have also been targeted by malicious code attacks. After being hit by a virus or hacker, companies usually suffer little more than humiliation. In some instances, however, that embarrassment is coupled with severe debilitation and economic loss. Security on the company Web server(s) should be incorporated as a basic component of the organization's standard operating procedure. Just as no organization would think of leaving their doors unlocked and unattended after hours, neither should the company Web site designers leave their site open to intrusion or malicious attack. While some companies may need to leave their doors unlocked after hours, they do so only *when protected by security personnel*. Likewise, Web sites may be left open to "visitors" provided that all that enters is authorized and adequately monitored.

The following methods are used most frequently by businesses seeking to protect their Web servers and sites:

✓ Repairing known software flaws and plugging network holes

✓ Deleting unused, superfluous software

✓ Recognizing attacks to the Web site

✓ Limiting any malicious code movement once it has been acknowledged

✓ Safeguarding the rest of the network after an attack is detected

✓ Scanning for potential vulnerabilities, prioritizing and mitigating risk

Assessing an organization's sensitivity to risk determines the best security plan to implement. Economics plays a large role in how organizations conduct business, particularly in a tight economy. The amount of available business capital must be weighed against the cost of potential security breaches before settling on a security plan. Monetary expenditures for protective security measures should be concentrated on the areas considered *most sensitive* to an organization. Since the value of the data contained on Web servers is far more costly to reproduce or replace than the actual server, sound hacker and malicious code defense measures are paramount in importance.

The two facets of securing a Web server are:

✓ The securing of the data so that it may not be viewed or modified by malicious code.

✓ The security of the content itself, or the authorization and authentication of the individuals who are permitted to view and modify that content.

Since the latter aspect is beyond the scope of this book, it will not be covered in detail.

Hackers often try to compromise Web servers with various types of attacks, such as buffer overflows and Trojan horses (two common varieties). While dozens of available software products and hardware devices provide high levels of Web server protection, they all share some common goals:

✓ Eliminating loss of business through Web site defacement or penetration

✓ Providing protection behind the firewall

✓ Containing an automatic update mechanism to ensure the best protection at all times

✓ Preventing Web servers from being compromised from both known and unknown attacks

✓ Saving time through reduction in false positives

✓ Creating a secure environment for all Web server applications

✓ Ensuring maximum uptime for valuable corporate Web servers

✓ Minimizing the need for dedicated security personnel

Web servers such as Microsoft's IIS (Internet Information Server) have been the target of several worm attacks over the last few years as a result of flaws in the operating system code, permitting the worm to exploit this *known* vulnerability. In fact, one of the ways the infamous Nimda worm of 2001 was able to propagate was by taking advantage of the vulnerability in Microsoft's IIS servers, which allowed unauthorized users to gain control of system-level (root) commands. The Nimda worm, for example, alters the system in the following manner:

✓ By creating Trojan horse versions of applications, such as Internet Explorer, which helps the worm spread and further infect other computers

✓ By creating a "guest" account on Windows NT and 2000 systems and then adding this account to the "administrator" group, providing full access to the compromised system to any machine accessing the application

✓ By enabling file sharing of the C: drive

## Keeping Informed of Server Threats

By keeping Web server and workstation operating systems up-to-date and patched, users can avoid malicious code exploitation of known vulnerabilities. One Web site that offers an excellent resource for information, advisories, and warnings on malicious code attacks and operating system flaws is www.cert.org, the CERT Coordination Center at Carnegie Mellon. CERT studies Internet security vulnerabilities, handles computer security incidents, publishes security alerts, researches long-term changes in networked systems, and provides information and training to users who want to improve their computer security. Users can stay abreast of Microsoft-related security issues and fixes by subscribing to the Microsoft Security Notification Services at http://www.microsoft.com/technet/security/notify.asp. Once enrolled, users receive automatic e-mail notification of security issues directly from Microsoft.

Users may also want to consider placing a shortcut to the Microsoft Security Advisor Program on their desktops. To do so, follow these steps:

**1.** Open Internet Explorer.

**2.** Navigate to www.microsoft.com/technet/security/notify.asp

3. Choose Add To Favorites from the Favorites menu.

4. Check the Make Available Offline check box.

5. Click Customize.

6. Click Next in the Offline Favorite wizard.

7. Select the Yes option button and specify to download pages two links deep from this page.

8. Click Next.

9. Select the "I Would Like To Create A New Schedule" option button, and click Next.

10. Accept the default settings, and click Next.

11. Click Finish.

12. Click OK.

13. Choose Organize Favorites from the Favorites menu.

14. Select the Microsoft TechNet Security shortcut in the Organize Favorites dialog box.

15. Click Properties.

16. Click the Download tab of the Microsoft TechNet Security Properties dialog box.

17. Uncheck the Follow Links Outside Of This Page's Web Site check box.

18. Click OK, and then Close.

The Microsoft TechNet Security shortcut can now be dragged from your Favorites menu to your desktop. A small red mark will appear on the icon when there is new security news.

# Choosing Web Server Anti-Virus Software

Increased use of networked computers makes the rapid distribution of viruses and other malicious code almost effortless. This is, in most part, due to Internet-connected machines predominantly running one version or another of the popular 32-bit Windows operating systems. In turn, the majority of malicious code is specifically targeted at the Windows platform. With a large percentage of the machines on the Internet running closely compatible operating systems, an environment now exists where a small number of users can unleash network pandemonium once one malcontent develops malicious code and then deceives a few inexperienced users into executing it. In this situation, policies and user education enter into play as a first line of defense.

However, just as anti-virus software is necessary for individual workstations, the use of anti-virus software for Web servers is indispensable. When choosing Web server anti-virus software, users should follow the same criteria specified earlier in this chapter in "Choosing the Right Product." Several of the more popular companies providing a wide range of anti-virus products, including products specifically designed for Web servers, are:

✓ Symantec Corporation (www.symantec.com)

✓ McAfee.com Corporation (www.mcafee.com)

✓ Computer Associates International, Inc. (`www.cai.com`)

✓ Finjan Software (`www.finjan.com`)

All of the aforementioned organizations specialize in computer security, are well-known, and have been around for many years.

# Blocking Code at the Internet Gateway

When they first emerged, Internet worms such as Code Red, I Love You, and Nimda propagated at theretofore-unparalleled speed. This trend in virus distribution abilities forces organizations to continue seeking out cost-effective ways to deal with all types of malicious code outbreaks. The only way to effectively prevent much of today's costly, debilitating Internet-borne malicious code is by *increasing compliance* of strictly defined anti-virus and security policies. Internet gateway protection is a key component of an organization's overall anti-virus solution. By scanning for viruses at the Internet gateway, malicious code can be blocked before it enters the company network. This helps diminish any damage to network workstations and servers.

Internet gateways are used to connect all networked computers securely to the Internet through a single account using connection types ranging from analog modems to broadband. All Internet gateways:

✓ Allow the sharing of a single high-speed Internet account across an organization's entire internal network

✓ Permit easy upgrades as the organization's needs grow

✓ Set access and time controls and monitor network activity

✓ Stop unwanted access from Internet marauders or hackers by using a firewall

An Internet gateway can be set up as a Web server with special "gateway" software installed to monitor Internet traffic into and out of a company network, or it can be a separate, standalone hardware device. Hardware solutions pose a slight advantage over software-only solutions in that they are *dedicated* security appliances; they don't consume additional network resources or overburden an already taxed network server.

Whether it is a standalone hardware device or a software program, the Internet gateway must provide protection for three basic protocols. The protocols are defined as follows:

✓ **HTTP protection** keeps infected files from being downloaded via the Web by protecting users against malicious Java and ActiveX programs.

✓ **FTP protection** works transparently, ensuring that infected files are not inadvertently downloaded from unsecured remote sites.

✓ **SMTP protection** complements the mail server by scanning for viruses in all inbound and outbound Simple Mail Transport Protocol (SMTP) traffic.

Several companies provide both hardware and software gateway protection solutions. Choosing the best solution requires striking a balance between an organization's security needs and how much it is willing to pay for that security. Nearly all of the major Internet security and anti-virus software companies (such as Symantec, McAfee, Computer Associates, and Trend Micro) provide powerful hardware and software gateway security solutions. Users are encouraged to visit the manufacturers' Web sites for pricing and availability.

# Blocking Ports

In order to surf the World Wide Web or send and receive e-mail messages, users must have *some* open ports on their PCs. Web pages, for example, use port 80, and e-mail messages travel via ports 25, 110, or 143. Although over 65,000 ports are available for Internet use, the vast majority of these are *not* in use at any given time. Time and again, users install a firewall only to discover that ports they didn't even know existed *are open*. Blocking unused ports and services is the foundation upon which to construct an effective security barrier. When users do not need a particular service, it should be disabled. Fortunately, users can retain considerable control over their PCs by monitoring and restricting the data traffic flowing through their open ports. By installing a desktop firewall program such as ZoneAlarm, Tiny Personal Firewall, or Agnitum's Outpost, users immediately know which ports are open and which programs (malicious code included) attempt to send data to and from their PCs.

# Applying OS/Browser Patches and Updates

In truth, careless programming and idle Internet users are the true culprits in virus attacks. Most of the worms making headlines in the recent past could have been avoided if operating systems or browser programs were properly updated and patched. Software flaws are routinely discovered by security experts, prompting manufacturers to scramble and issue a patch or fix. However, with a tight economy, some network administrators are finding that monetary constraints or staffing cutbacks make it difficult or impossible to remain vigilant about security procedures. As a consequence, security patches are not being applied as routinely as they should be.

To effectively protect an organization against hackers and malicious code, anti-virus software, virus definitions, *and* applications must be kept up-to-date. New viruses are routinely discovered, along with security holes in operating systems, browsers, and other applications. This often leaves computers vulnerable to hacker and malicious code attacks.

Another potential security issue is the early release of programs. Early versions routinely contain bugs that do not appear until the program is used more extensively. Patches, which are made widely available after the product is released, repair flawed applications by covering security holes and other security issues. By *always* using the most recent version of a software product, users are provided with the highest degree of reliability and security currently available. In new versions, patches that corrected old problems have been integrated into the program. One of the most important upgrades users can make is in their Web browser. Browser upgrades and enhancements can be downloaded (usually free of charge) at the manufacturer's Web site.

Patches are invariably released each time flaws or security holes are discovered. To ensure that users are always up-to-date, they must regularly check the manufacturer's Web site. Numerous product manufacturers offer a notification service so that users of their products can remain current without having to worry about missing a patch when it becomes available. When they are enrolled for this service, users are notified via e-mail each time a security threat is discovered or when new product updates or patches become available.

# Detecting Unauthorized Access Using Logs

Logs are a critical component of successful Internet security. Log files reveal what is and what is not happening. All popular networking operating systems such as UNIX, Linux, Netware, and Windows NT employ logs. Two of the most widely used networking operating systems are Windows 2000 and Windows XP, and the heart of their Web and Application services is the built-in Web server Internet Information Server (IIS). This full-featured server lets anyone host Web sites that can take advantage of interactive applications. Because of its popularity and widespread use, IIS has been the subject of malicious code attacks on several occasions (Code Red, Code Red II, and SirCam, for example). The monitoring of IIS and Windows log files can be a useful and important component of an organization's overall security plan.

Both IIS logs and Windows security logs are useful for monitoring various security events over an extended time period. The easiest way to view these log files is to use the Microsoft Management Console. The IIS logs can also be viewed by using any standard text editor, such as Windows Notepad.

The Windows Security Log is also useful to detect unauthorized access attempts. These attempts often appear as warnings or errors directly in the log entries. For an extra measure of security, you may wish to archive these logs for later use. Additional information about log auditing can be found in your Windows documentation. When examining the security log, you will see events according to the event category to which they pertain. According to the Microsoft 2000 Advanced Server documentation Web site, the following types of events can be audited and appear in the security log as follows:

- ✓ System restart
- ✓ System shutdown
- ✓ Authentication package loading
- ✓ Registered logon process
- ✓ Audit log cleared
- ✓ Number of audits discarded
- ✓ Logon successful
- ✓ Unknown user name or password
- ✓ Time restricted logon failure

✓ Account disabled

✓ Account expired

✓ Invalid workstation

✓ Logon type restricted

✓ Password expired

✓ Failed logon

✓ Logoff

✓ Open object

✓ Close handle

✓ Assign special privilege

✓ Privileged service

✓ Privileged object access

✓ Process created

✓ Process exit

✓ Duplicate handle

✓ Indirect reference

✓ Privilege assigned

✓ Audit policy change

✓ Domain changed

✓ User changed

✓ User created

✓ User deleted

✓ Global group member removed

✓ Global group member added

✓ Domain local group changed

✓ Domain local group created

✓ Domain local group member removed

✓ Domain local group member added

✓ Domain local group member deleted

You can check the Windows Security Log to uncover security glitches as follows (when using Windows 2000):

1. Click Start and navigate to Settings.

2. Select Control Panel.

3. Double-click Administrative Tools.

4. Double-click Computer Management.

5. Expand System Tools.

6. Expand Event Viewer.

7. Choose Security Log. (If the Security Log is not displayed, then the user account used is unauthorized.)

8. The Security Log should be inspected for evidence of failed attempts to:

   ■ Log on

   ■ Use privileges

   ■ Access files (or modify them)

9. The Security Log should be checked for evidence of attempts to:

   ■ Shut down the server, or

   ■ Make changes to security privileges or the audit log.

You may store (archive) a Windows Security Log as follows:

1. Click Start and navigate to Settings.

2. Select Control Panel.

3. Double-click Administrative Tools.

4. Double-click Computer Management.

5. Expand System Tools.

6. Expand Event Viewer.

7. Choose Security.

8. Click Save Log File As under the Action menu.

9. In the dialog box called Save As, choose which directory you are saving the file to and enter the name you're giving it.

You may go back and open a file you've archived as follows:

1. Click Start and navigate to Settings.

2. Select Control Panel.

3. Double-click Administrative Tools.

4. Double-click Computer Management.

5. Expand System Tools.

6. Expand Event Viewer.

7. Choose Security.

8. Choose New and select Log View under the Action menu.

9. To open a previously saved log, click Saved under the Add Another Log View box. Scroll to the file you're seeking.

10. Choose Security under the Log type list.

11. Click OK to display your file.

Reviewing the IIS log files may also alert you to security issues. The following incidents should raise your suspicions:

✓ Failed attempts to launch executable scripts or files.

✓ Attempts (unauthorized) to upload files to a directory that contains executable files.

✓ Numerous failed attempts to access files (or modify them).

✓ Numerous failed attempts to log on from one IP address (which may signal an attempt to deny other users access).

You can access IIS logs by using built-in text editors such as Windows Notepad or Wordpad to open and view the log file.

# Data Backup and Disaster Recovery

Despite the implementation of sound security policies and the use of the best and most up-to-date anti-virus products, data damage or loss continues to occur. While hardware devices can easily be replaced, data often cannot. Far too many users wait until problems arise or malicious code assails their PC before they take action. Once the presence of a virus is detected on a computer, it may be too late to recover damaged files. A number of viruses cannot be successfully removed as a result of the manner in which the virus infects the program. It is absolutely vital to have protection *before* the virus strikes. A comprehensive plan for backing up data is an essential component in any computer security arsenal.

## Creating a Backup Plan

The first step organizations should take is to designate one person as coordinator and record keeper of all backups. The backup plan should be put in writing and kept with an organization's security policies and procedures documentation. The following items should be included in the backup plan:

✓ The name of the backup coordinator and/or record keeper

✓ The type of data requiring backup

✓ The frequency of data backups

✓ The location of on-site data storage

✓ The location of off-site data storage

✓ The method used for backing up data, along with a checklist of procedures

## What to Backup

There are a number of ways users can select which files to designate for backup. The method used depends on the way an organization uses its network and how often its files change. Organizations ordinarily end up using a combination of these techniques:

✓ **Full backup** — Full backups are accomplished by selecting all files on a hard disk to be backed up. This is the easiest type of backup and yields the most complete backup package; however, it is the most costly technique, takes the most time, and requires the greatest amount of storage space.

✓ **Selective backup** — With a selective (partial) backup, users select only specific files and directories to be backed up. This type of backup gives organizations the most control over which data is backed up. This type of backup is the best option when backup space is limited or when certain data files change much more often than others.

✓ **Incremental backup** — Organizations that perform frequent backups may find that they end up backing up the same data repeatedly, even data that has not changed over time. A better alternative is to consider a mix of both full backups and incremental backups. An incremental backup is a type of backup where only files that have modified since the last backup are selected for backup. Similar to a selective backup, files are selected based on whether or not they have been recently modified, rather than by an arbitrary selection based on file names or directories. This yields the same advantages of a selective backup, while also ensuring that all *changed* files are covered.

## Tools for Data Backup

Numerous tools are available that will make the process of backing up data easy and painless. Nearly all of the available backup software programs allow the backup process to be automated.. The use of automation ensures that performing regular data backups is not put off or forgotten. Users of UNIX or Linux can find many freeware programs with this automation feature at www.storagemountain.com. For Macintosh users, freeware backup software can be found at www.versiontracker.com. Windows users, for the most part, need look no further than their own computer since backup software is provided with the Windows operating system. While the built-in Windows backup program may lack some of the advanced features of more advanced third-party backup products, it has enough functionality to make it very useful to individuals and organizations alike.

The backup programs provided by later versions of Windows such as 2000 and XP have dramatically improved over earlier versions. In Windows XP for example, the built-in backup software is located by navigating to the Start menu ⇨ Programs ⇨ Accessories ⇨ System Tools. For other Windows versions, users should check their manuals for the backup program's exact location. Once activated, the Backup and Restore wizard goes through the following steps:

**1.** It queries the user as to whether or not a backup or restoration of data is desired (see Figure 9-2).

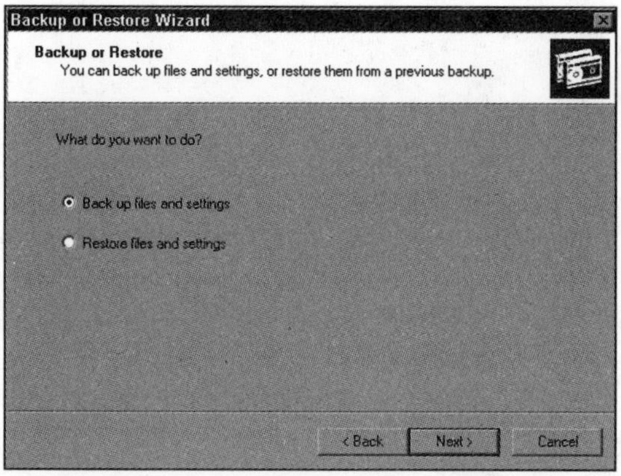

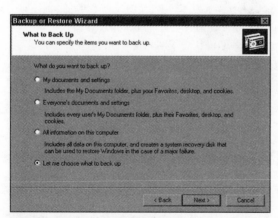

**Figure 9-2:** Selecting a backup or restoration of data

**2.** The next screen prompts users to select which files on their computer they wish to backup (see Figure 9-3). There are several options here.

**Figure 9-3:** Selecting what to backup

**3.** If the users select the last option, "Let me choose what to back up", they are then provided with a screen that requires them to check off or select which files they wish to backup (see Figure 9-4).

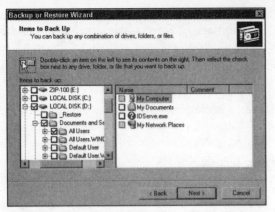

**Figure 9-4:** Choosing specific folders or files to backup

4. After selecting the appropriate files, users are prompted to choose a destination for their backup data (see Figure 9-5). In this illustration, the recipient of the backup data is an Iomega ZIP drive. Backups can be written to other media types, as well, such as a tape drive or a CD-R disk.

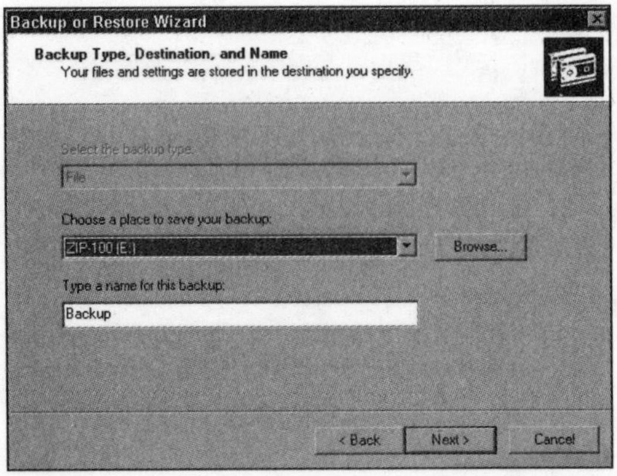

**Figure 9-5:** Selecting a backup destination and type

# Registry Backup and Protection (Windows OS)

One of the most misunderstood components within the Windows operating system is the Registry. In Chapter 5, I examined the location and function of the Registry, as well as the reason malicious code often tries to exploit this powerful database. Regular Registry backups can save hours of frustration by allowing the user to easily restore the Registry in case it ever becomes accidentally damaged by the users themselves or after being corrupted by malicious code. The process of backing up the Registry varies among Windows versions. Rather than list them all here, users interested in learning how to manually back up under their particular Windows version can find lengthy instructions at `http://support.microsoft.com/`.

Later versions of Windows have a built-in Restore utility that takes periodic snapshots of the Registry and other critical files and saves them in a special location. This allows users to "roll back" the OS configuration to a working copy in the event the Registry becomes corrupted or altered by malicious code. Fortunately, you can find dozens of freeware and shareware utilities that can easily perform Registry backup and restoration with only a few mouse clicks. For those who are interested, the following three Web sites contain Registry backup and restoration freeware and shareware programs, along with numerous other utilities:

✓ `http://freeware.intrastar.net/registry.htm`

✓ `http://www.webattack.com/`

✓ `http://www.davecentral.com/`

Users are advised to use discretion when deciding whether or not to download and install freeware or shareware from the Internet. As with any downloaded materials, all freeware and shareware must be scanned for viruses using up-to-date anti-virus software prior to installing them on any computer.

Manually backing up the Windows Registry allows users to restore the Registry if they choose to reverse changes they've made while editing it (or to restore the Registry when it has become corrupted by malicious code). The general procedure for manually backing up a Windows Registry and saving it to the Windows desktop is as follows:

1. Click Start, and then click Run. The Run dialog box appears.

2. Type `regedit` and then click OK. The Registry Editor opens.

3. Select My Computer at the top of the left pane.

4. Click Registry, and then click Export Registry File (Windows 95/98/Me/NT/2000), or click File, and then click Export (Windows XP).

The remainder of this procedure is operating system–specific. Therefore, the following steps are broken down in accordance with the version of Windows being used. In Windows 95/98/NT:

1. Select "Desktop" in the Save In box of the dialog box.

2. In the File name box, enter a name that you will remember, such as `registry backup`.

3. Click Save. The file is now saved to your Windows desktop.

In Windows Me/2000/XP:

1. Click the Desktop icon.

2. In the File name box, enter a name that you will remember, such as `registry backup`.

3. Click Save. The file is now saved to your Windows desktop.

To restore the Registry backup:

1. Locate the Registry backup file that you created. In our example, it will have an icon similar to the one shown in Figure 9-6 and will be located on the Windows desktop.

2. Double-click the icon. A message is displayed asking you to confirmation the restoration.

3. Click Yes. A confirmation that the Registry has been restored is displayed.

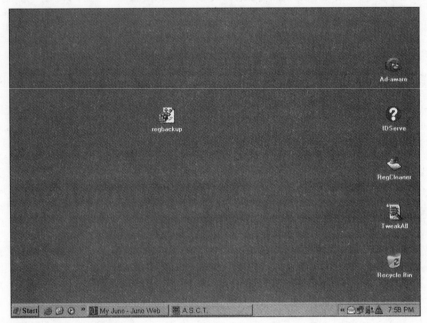

**Figure 9-6:** The Registry icon

# Summary

Firewalls and anti-virus and code behavior monitoring software provide individuals and organizations with powerful first lines of defense against the threat of malicious code. Because of the speed at which malicious code traverses the Internet and organizational network systems, a *combination* of defense products provides the most effective protection. With so many hardware and software products available, choosing the right combination of anti-virus products can be confusing.

Key points covered in this chapter include:

✓ Why firewalls are the "gatekeepers" of the Internet and how they are used to defend against Trojan horses

✓ How intrusion detection systems help with network security and malicious code defense

✓ What organizations should look for when choosing an anti-virus product and why the ICSA certification is so important

✓ How new proactive code behavior monitoring software complements traditional reactive anti-virus products

✓ Why Web servers are vulnerable and how to protect them from malicious code attack

✓ Why stopping viruses, worms, and Trojan horses at the Internet gateway is critical to network security

✓ Why regular patching and updating of browsers and operating systems must be part of an overall security plan

✓ Why data backup and recovery are crucial components in an organization's network security policy

✓ Why protecting and preserving the Windows Registry in servers and workstation computers is an important and integral part of an organization's overall security plan

# Chapter 10

# Server-Side Exploits

## In This Chapter

✓ Protecting yourself against CGI scripts

✓ Considering the dangers of server-side include statements (SSIs)

✓ The hazards of cross site scripting (CSS)

✓ Backdoors and debugging exploits

✓ Effects of cookie poisoning

✓ Parameter tampering

✓ Stealth commanding

✓ Hidden-field manipulation

✓ Combating buffer overflow

✓ Understanding known vulnerabilities

✓ The power of mail server bombs

✓ Raw sockets and associated dangers

A WEB SITE IS A powerful tool that enables businesses, government, and private users to share information and conduct business on the Internet. Organizations — small and large, private and public — are devoting many resources to creating attractive, attention-getting Web sites, but they may be neglecting basic security controls. Recent attacks on Web sites show that computers supporting Web sites are vulnerable to assaults that can range from minor nuisances to significant interruptions of service.

Many years ago, malicious code was largely confined to individual computers. With increased use of the Internet (in both commercial and personal applications), organizations around the world continually grapple for their "place" on the Internet bandwagon. In fact, creating and maintaining a Web presence is an integral part of today's business model. Organizations can take two approaches when opening a virtual shop. They can choose to maintain their own Web site with in-house servers, or they can choose to use an outside company that specializes in Web hosting. Companies that host Web sites often employ in-house security specialists to keep their servers secure from hackers and malicious code. Smaller companies or companies with limited IT budgets or personnel may not be fully aware of the risks involved with maintaining Internet-connected servers or with hosting their own Web sites.

In addition, vulnerabilities that stem from the use of the World Wide Web are associated with browser software and server software. The vulnerabilities introduced by the use of browser software in searching for and retrieving information over the Internet are generally less severe than those posed by servers. However, Web browsing programs are complex and are becoming more so. The more intricate a program, the less secure it generally is. Consequently, flaws may be exploited by network-based attacks.

Web pages often include forms. As with e-mail messaging, data sent from a Web browser to a Web server may pass through many interconnected computers and networks before reaching its final destination. Users should be aware that the privacy of their personal or valuable information sent using a Web page entry cannot be assured.

Web servers are vulnerable to threats, especially malicious threats. Web servers may be attacked directly or they can be used as launching points for attacks made on an organization's internal networks. Organizations must examine the underlying operating system of their Web server, the Web server software, server scripts, and other software for vulnerabilities.

The 2001 Code Red, Code Red II, and Nimda worms explicitly showed the vulnerability of certain Web servers running Microsoft's IIS. After the "success" of the Code Red worms, a new worm called "Nimda" ("admin" spelled backwards) made its rounds, quickly infecting large numbers of vulnerable systems. The increasing trend in attacks made by worms on vulnerable servers aroused the concern of security personnel the world over. In the *Highlights* publication #12-01 of January 15, 2002, the NIPC addressed the progression of worms, including those targeting servers in 2001, as follows:

**Evolution of Malicious Code During 2001: Increasing Role of Worms and Malicious Code Packages with Multiple Capabilities**

Technical professionals have noted a significant new development in malicious code trends. This trend is the rise in prominence of worms (self-propagating malicious code) in the "top ten" list reported monthly by major computer security and anti-virus vendors. Computer viruses had, until recent years, dominated the "top ten."

**Tracking the trend**

Three worms emerged during 1999 on the top ten "infectors" list. By the beginning of 2000, computer viruses and worms each accounted for approximately half of the list. The number of worms rose to eight of the top ten "infectors" by the end of 2000, and this pattern continued into 2001. In July and August 2001, it was observed that worms accounted for all of the top ten malicious code attacks.

**Worms as the "weapon of choice" for computer attacks**

Articles by security and anti-virus technical professionals often disagree on specific details in discussing malicious code complexities. The differences include different views on the severity of individual malicious code attacks compared to those of other attacks, and on how to rank specific attacks within the overall scope of attacks. Additionally, several technical professionals have referred to the increase of malicious code attacks incorporating worm attributes as worms becoming the "weapon of choice" for computer attacks during 2001.

Increased capabilities of malicious code packages have resulted in more devastating impacts. Several other trends were also noted in 2001. Most significant is the incorporation of the capabilities of worms, Trojan horses (backdoors), and viruses in a single package. Malicious code attacks during 2001 also included techniques for propagating more rapidly than ever before. The brief interval between the Code Red worm and the release of Nimda worm continued the long-established trend of malicious code packages being modified based on "lessons learned" from previous attacks. This resulted in a more advanced malicious code package. Initial analysis of the "VBS/Mass-Mailing Worm, W32/Goner.A" that appeared on or about December 4, 2001, is in progress, and we are currently evaluating the degree to which the Goner worm may incorporate capabilities not emphasized in earlier packages.

Many technical professionals believe that the increasingly difficult challenges presented by malicious code will continue to be an emerging trend. However, aggressive and up-to-date security practices and policies can mitigate such impacts. While new defensive approaches are being developed to deal with the increasingly powerful, fast-spreading malicious code attacks, immediate attention by system administrators is needed.

In this bulletin, the NIPC states that worms such as Nimda were modified based upon "lessons learned" from previous attacks, resulting in the development of "advanced" propagation techniques. While many of these worm attacks could have been prevented if the operating systems in the servers they infected had been properly updated and patched, other server-side exploits should also be a concern to organizations with servers connected to the Internet. This chapter focuses on various server-side exploits and the procedures organizations must follow to mitigate their risk.

# CGI Scripts

Standard Web pages are, fundamentally, static files written in Hypertext Markup Language (HTML). A user simply requests a Web page, and the Web browser displays the downloaded HTML document. However, there are times when "static" Web pages are not sufficient for an organization's needs. Web browsers are also designed to display "Web forms," allowing users to enter data dynamically. In some instances, organizations may want to collect user data and have that data "returned" to the organization. Instead of serving a static file, you want the Web server to run a program and feed the result of that program back to the user's Web browser. Such a program is called a *CGI program,* or *CGI script.*

CGI (Common Gateway Interface) is sometimes used to add "dynamic" content to standard HTML Web pages. Although it is extremely helpful, the use of CGI can pose certain security risks.

- ✓ It is extremely easy to write vulnerable scripts, allowing hackers or malicious code to gather information submitted by users. For example, it is a common CGI scripting mistake to allow the script to intentionally or unintentionally leak information about the host system that will help hackers break in.

- ✓ CGI scripts can use up a server's valuable disk space with useless or erroneous files and consume much of the Web server's resources.

- ✓ It is easy for files to become corrupted, even those not attacked by hackers or malicious code.

- ✓ Even the most innocuous scripts can be exceptionally dangerous to the integrity of a server. Any time a server is "interacting" with a client, the client can potentially attack the server to gain unauthorized access.

✓ Scripts that process remote user input, such as the contents of a form or a "searchable index" command, may be vulnerable to attack in cases where a remote user succeeds in "tricking" them into executing commands.

✓ CGI scripts may intentionally (or unintentionally) leak information about the host system that could assist attackers in the event they attempt to "hack" in.

## Other CGI Dangers

Poorly written CGI scripts are a major source of security holes on servers on the World Wide Web. The majority of contemporary Web browsers can interpret scripts embedded in HTML pages downloaded from Web servers. Such scripts are written in any one of the many scripting languages (Vbs, Java, and CGI) and are executed directly by the client's Web browser. Many browsers are set up by default with the ability to run these scripts automatically.

One of the biggest dangers faced by users is that Web sites may unintentionally include malicious HTML tags or scripts in dynamically generated Web pages based upon invalidated input from unreliable sources. This problem occurs most often when a Web server does not adequately ensure that generated pages are properly encoded to prevent the unintended execution of scripts, or when user input has not been validated to prevent the display of malicious HTML.

Protecting Web servers against the threats of malicious CGI scripts in servers that use Windows NT, 2000, or XP requires confining the execution of those scripts to certain directories. Server administrators should consider allowing all scripts to reside in and execute from a single directory. Then, they should consider configuring that directory's permissions to allow access only by the Web server and the administrator.

To configure your Windows 2000 or XP server to confine CGI scripts in this manner, follow the steps that are outlined at the Microsoft Windows 2000 Server documentation Web site at this URL:

```
http://www.microsoft.com/windows2000/en/server/iis/default.asp?url=/
windows2000/en/server/iis/htm/core/iicacgia.htm
```

These measures give greater control over all scripts that are placed on the Web server by requiring users to ask the administrator for permission to place them in the designated directory. All scripts should be tested before they are allowed to be used in the Web server.

## Solutions for End Users

While many of the solutions available to Web users are very useful, the final solution lies with Web page developers. They must modify their pages to completely eliminate these types of problems. Web users, nevertheless, can take advantage of three basic options to reduce their risk of being attacked through scripting vulnerabilities. These options are as follows:

✓ Being careful or choosy about which Web sites they visit. This approach significantly reduces the user's exposure to possible malicious scripts while still allowing the browser to execute scripts, thereby maintaining functionality. Users must understand that they are accepting more risk when they select this option, but are doing so in order to preserve important Web browser functionality.

✓ **Disabling the use of scripting languages in Web browsers altogether.** While this option affords the greatest degree of protection, it has the unwanted effect of disabling Web page functionality. This option is best selected when users require the highest degree of security and are not concerned with any loss of functionality.

✓ **Installing a product (such as SurfinGuard Pro) that is specifically designed to prevent the harmful effects of any downloaded or HTML-embedded malicious scripts.** Such programs run scripts in a controlled "sandbox" environment, away from critical OS components, thereby protecting the end user from malicious activity. This protects the user while simultaneously providing the full dynamic Web content the user requires.

SurfinGuard Pro is intended for Windows operating systems only. For UNIX users, a free download called sbox by Lincoln D. Stein can be found at `http://stein.cshl.org/software/sbox/`.

# Server-Side Include Statements

Similar to CGI scripts, server-side include (SSI) statements are a simpler way to make Web site pages interactive. *Server-side includes (SSIs)* use straightforward HTML-embedded directives that impel the Web server to execute a program or include data in an HTML document. As a shorthand alternative to CGI, server-side includes can be a practical programming tool. However, like CGI, they should be used with caution because of their potential to introduce security risks. Since server-side includes are directives designed for the Web server, they must first be parsed (trimmed down) each time the requested document is delivered to a Web browser. Server-side includes are placed directly in HTML pages and are then evaluated on the server while the pages are being served. In short, SSIs add dynamically generated content to an existing HTML page *without* having to serve the entire page via a CGI program or any other dynamic technology.

Nevertheless, Web sites that use SSI should understand the risks they impose. The weakness in using SSI lies largely in cases where SSI is used to execute programs on the server using the `exec` directive. This command allows the server to execute files and can act like an "open door." Once the door is opened, hackers or malicious code can potentially direct the server to divulge personal information or issue commands that could destroy the system. Web server administrators may wish to disable any `exec` directives to mitigate any risk posed by using them.

# Cross Site Scripting

*Cross site scripting (CSS)* is the name given to an entire class of vulnerabilities affecting Web servers and browsers in which one client can, in effect, control the actions of another client's browser by posting malicious code to a Web site. While this security issue has received extensive attention, the problem is particularly alarming because it arises from a simple and common oversight. Thousands of server-side programs contain this problem, and no particular programming language is exempt.

## Identifying the Problem

Web pages contain HTML code that is created by the server and read by the client's Web browser. Servers that produce static pages have complete control over how the client interprets the pages that the server provides. Conversely, servers that generate dynamic pages do not control how the output they generate is interpreted by the client's Web browser. The core component of the cross site scripting security issue is that if malicious Web content can be introduced into a dynamic page, neither the server nor the client would have adequate information to identify what has transpired and take defensive actions.

The key component of a cross site scripting attack is the attackers' ability to inject their *own* malicious HTML code into pages on a Web site. Unless Web pages are specifically constructed to guard against the placing of these types of scripts, they permit a hacker to insert malicious code that can expose secure Internet connections, poison cookies, or cause the user to access restricted sites.

## How Cross Site Scripting Affects Web Users

Hackers may attach malicious script to data sent to a Web site, such as a Web address, an element in a form, or even a database inquiry. Whenever the Web site responds to a user's request for data, the malicious script "tags along," infecting the recipient's Web browser.

Web browsers can be exposed to malicious scripts in three ways:

✓ Through viewing dynamically generated pages that contain content developed by malicious individuals

✓ By following untrusted links in e-mail messages, Web pages, or newsgroup postings

✓ By using interactive forms on unreliable Web sites

## What Can Malicious Scripts Do?

Malicious scripts possess many "talents," including:

✓ The ability to capture passwords and other confidential information that users erroneously believe is under protection. Companies should be concerned because malicious scripts can be used to expose an organization's local network to all comers on the Internet.

✓ The ability to use malicious scripts to infect cookies with copies of themselves. When the "poisoned" cookie is sent back to a vulnerable Web site and subsequently passed back to the user's browser, the malicious script may re-execute. Keep in mind that this is not a flaw in cookies; rather, it is malicious script exploiting the functionality provided by cookies. Cookie poisoning is covered later in this chapter.

## Restricting the Malicious Script

As with any type of malicious script, the end result of the cross site scripting vulnerability can be avoided by disabling all scripting languages in the user's Web browser. Microsoft Internet Explorer enables the automatic execution of active content by default, which makes these applications particularly vulnerable to certain kinds of viruses and worms. Web pages and e-mail messages can contain embedded scripts that will be executed when the page or message is accessed.

Many Web sites use scripting to enhance their content. By disabling the automatic execution of scripts, users are prevented from accessing many Web sites. While this may seem a drastic tactic, it reduces the opportunity for certain viruses and worms to infect user computers. If users do not want to disable scripting completely, the next best option is to adjust the browser to issue a prompt before it executes the script. This scenario allows users to choose whether they trust the Web site before they allow the script to run.

The following steps must be taken in order to adjust the browser options in both Microsoft's IE (5.0 or later) and Netscape (3.0 or later) Web browsers, altering how those browsers allow active scripts to execute.

To disable active scripting in Internet Explorer 5 or later:

1. Start the Internet Explorer browser.

2. From the Tools menu, select Internet Options. The Internet Options dialog box appears.

3. Select the Security tab. The Security Options panel appears.

4. Click the Internet zone to select it.

5. Click the Custom Level button. The Security Settings dialog box appears.

6. Select the High option from the Settings pull-down list.

7. Click the Reset button. A dialog box appears, asking if you are sure you want to change the security settings for this zone.

8. Click Yes. You must now scroll through the Settings list and make the following changes:

    a. For the setting "Scripting ActiveX controls marked safe for Scripting," check the radio button for Disable.

    b. If you decide to disable Java, for the setting Java permissions, check the radio button for Disable Java.

If you have Microsoft Virtual Machine installed, this setting is found under the Microsoft VM section. If you do not have a Java permissions setting, then Java is already disabled.

    c. For the setting "Active scripting under the Scripting section," check the radio button for Disable.

9. Click OK to accept these changes. A dialog box appears, asking if you are sure you want to make these changes. Click Yes.

10. In the Internet Options dialog box, click the Advanced tab. The Advanced Options list appears.

11. Make sure the setting "Warn if changing between secure and not secure mode" under the Security heading is checked.

**12.** Click Apply to save your changes.

**13.** Click OK to close the Internet Options dialog box.

To disable active scripting in Netscape Navigator 3.0 or later:

**1.** Start the Netscape Communicator browser.

**2.** From the Edit menu, select Preferences. The Preferences dialog box appears.

**3.** From the Category list, click Advanced. (Do not click the plus sign.) The Advanced Preferences panel appears.

**4.** Uncheck Enable Java and uncheck Enable JavaScript.

**5.** Click OK to accept the changes.

**6.** Click the Padlock icon in the lower left-hand corner of your browser. The Security Info dialog box appears.

**7.** Click the Navigator link from the list on the left. The "Navigator Security Settings" panel appears.

**8.** In the "Show a warning before:" section, make sure the options "Viewing a page with encrypted/unencrypted mix" and "Leaving an encrypted site" are checked.

**9.** Click OK to accept the changes and close the dialog box.

# Backdoors and Debugging — How Malicious Code Gets in

In the field of information technology, the term *backdoor* can have two different meanings. It can be defined as a secret opening that a programmer intentionally engineers into code in order to provide a way into the system without knowledge of the administrator's password. Alternatively, it can be defined as a "hole" surreptitiously generated by malicious code with the intent of allowing a hacker to gain future entry into a system. Software developers often create backdoors and turn on debugging to help troubleshoot the applications they develop. Such strategies work well and are advantageous during the development process, but these items are often left in the final version of the application. Backdoors that let a user log in with no password or a special URL that allows direct access to application configurations are quite popular. The following list provides examples of various backdoors:

✓ A technician comes to install new software and leaves behind something in the software that allows him or her to log into a network server.

✓ A hacker infiltrates a UNIX or Linux computer and installs what is known as a *rootkit* — a series of programs and configuration errors that allows the hacker to gain re-entry into the system.

✓ When a hacker breaks into your system, he or she installs an application that allows him or her to log in with a unique username and password.

✓ Somebody passing by an unattended computer and noticing that the computer is logged in with root/administrator privileges quickly creates his or her own account that permits him to re-enter the system at a later time.

✓ A hacker sends a Trojan horse that installs a backdoor component when the user runs it.

# Backdoor Programs

A *backdoor program* is a hacking tool that takes control of a victim's computer. There are two components to backdoor programs:

✓ The **client component**, which is installed on the victim's computer

✓ The **remote control component**, which resides on the hacker's machine

Sometimes, people mean both components when they refer to a backdoor program; at other times, they mean only the client element. Backdoors are sometimes used by hackers to gain unauthorized entry into a computer or network and are often a component of Trojan horse programs. A backdoor program is designed to hide itself inside a target host. It allows the installing user to access the targeted system at a later time without using the normal authorization process or vulnerability exploitation.

NIPC's *CyberNotes* (issue #2002-04; dated February 25, 2002), lists a few of the currently known backdoors and some of their capabilities (just four are included here for illustrative purposes):

**Backdoor.EggHead:** This is a backdoor Trojan horse program that uses a freeware IRC bot as its core component. This backdoor works only under Windows NT/2000/XP. Once activated, this backdoor gives a third party unrestricted access to the client's computer.

**Backdoor.IISCrack.dll:** This backdoor Trojan is a Dynamic Link Library (DLL) that is used to attack and exploit IIS servers. If the attack is successful, then the attacker will have gained System level access to the server. For this backdoor to work, the attacker must be able to copy it to the server's scripts directory. Once there, the attacker just uploads the DLL using his Web browser (for example, URL/scripts/backdoor.dll), and uses the DLL to give commands to the system.

**Backdoor.NetDevil:** Backdoor.NetDevil allows a malicious user to remotely control an infected computer. When Backdoor.NetDevil is run, it copies itself to the %System% folder. The file name that it uses may vary, because the malicious user who creates this backdoor Trojan can choose any desired file name. It adds a value that refers to the dropped file to one of the following Registry keys:

```
HKEY_LOCAL_MACHINE\Software\Microsoft\Windows\Current Version\Run

HKEY_LOCAL_MACHINE\Software\Microsoft\Windows\Current Version\Run
Services
```

When the malicious user creates the BackDoor.NetDevil server file, there are many functions that can be added. It can be programmed to:

- Display a fake error message to conceal its true nature
- Choose the ports that are used by the backdoor to communicate with the malicious user. By default, it uses port 901 for direct control, port 902 for communicating logged key strokes, and port 903 for file transfer
- Use different notification methods to send information to the malicious user about the compromised computer
- Attempt to kill running firewall and anti-virus processes

If Backdoor.NetDevil is run, it allows the malicious user to remotely take control over the compromised computer, and can include:

- Full control over the file system
- Upload to and download from the host computer
- Run files of the malicious user's choice
- Kill running processes
- Display messages
- View the screen
- Log key strokes
- Annoying actions, such as manipulate the mouse, open and close the CD-ROM drive, turn the monitor on and off, and so on

**BKDR_SMALLFEG.A (Alias: SMALLFEG.A):** This backdoor Trojan is dropped by TROJ_SMALLFEG. DR, and executes as a service process. It attempts to establish a connection to several remote IRC servers, all with the domain name `undernet.org`. It attacks IRC servers by sending foul messages.

Backdoors will continue to be popular with malicious coders as long as uninformed (or over-confident) users continue to ignore the need to:

- ✓ Consistently update and maintain proper patches
- ✓ Regularly update their anti-virus software
- ✓ Periodically scan common Trojan ports for activity

# Debugging

A standard practice applied during the developmental stage of any software product is the use of debugging. *Debugging,* as the name implies, is the practice of removing bugs or flaws in programs by program developers using any one of several programming tools (such as memory dumps or break points). While this practice is useful for programming, extreme care must be taken by software developers to ensure that all debugging structures (or constructs) are removed and not erroneously left in the final product. Hackers usually try several obvious debug constructs to see if the removal of all debug commands in the final product was carried out successfully. Any lapse can result in devastating vulnerabilities due to the sheer power that most debug constructs possess.

Sometimes hackers scan random Internet addresses looking for a specific hole. For example, they may attempt to scan the entire Internet for machines that have the SendMail DEBUG hole and then exploit any vulnerable computers that they encounter. This is known as a "birthday attack." Armed with a list of "well-known" security holes and a list of IP addresses, a hacker will most likely locate some computers somewhere that have one of those holes. Regular patching of software products is essential to prevent this type of attack, particularly where known vulnerabilities exist.

# Cookie Poisoning

*Cookies* are small text files generated by a Web server and stored in the client user's computer for future access. Cookies are contained in the information flowing between the user's computer and Web servers and are used to provide customization of the client-side of Web information. Cookies personalize a user's Web experiences and store short-term information, such as the items selected and checked while browsing through an online merchant's Web site.

Cookies provide the means of easier Internet navigation. Designers of nearly every major Web site use them because they:

✓ Provide users with a richer surfing experience

✓ Make it less complicated to gather accurate information about visitors to the site

Cookies are not executable files. Generally, they are stored as text files and do not possess the ability to pass along viruses. Even if a cookie *were* an executable file, it could not automatically spread a virus unless it was executed by the user. Essentially, cookies cannot harm your computer. The common argument against cookies does not concern what they can do to computers, but what information they can store, and what they can pass on to servers.

Two types of cookies exist: *persistent* and *non-persistent.*

✓ **Persistent cookies** are stored on users' computers, where they reside until they are deleted or they reach a predetermined expiration date. Persistent cookies are most commonly used to provide visitors with a customized Web experience by recording their preferences (such as how they choose to have their Web pages displayed). Additionally, cookies are used to gather statistical information (such as the average time spent viewing a particular page). This type of information is valuable for many reasons, such as providing sponsors with insight on how to improve the design, content, and navigational properties of a Web site.

✓ **Non-persistent (or per-session) cookies** do not permanently record data, and they are not stored on the user's hard drive. Rather, non-persistent cookies are stored in memory and are only available during an active browser session. Once the browser is closed, the cookie disappears. Non-persistent cookies are used primarily for technical reasons (such as providing seamless navigation).

If a hacker can capture cookies by monitoring network data transmissions, he or she theoretically gains unauthorized access to personal information, including a user's credit card numbers, passwords, identifying information, and mailing address.

To identify a user, a Web server downloads a cookie to the client's computer. That cookie is then used as a form of identification whenever the client communicates back to the server. *Cookie poisoning* is a term that signifies the "modification" of a cookie text file. Malicious coders can alter information that is stored on system cookies (passwords, account numbers, and the like) so that unauthorized information is sent back to the installer of the cookie, thereby giving the coder control over someone else's account.

Users can take several preventative security measures with regard to cookies:

✓ Using non-persistent cookies instead of persistent cookies.

✓ When using persistent cookies, specifying a short duration for the cookie's lifespan (the longer the time, the bigger the risk).

✓ Using the "secure tag" so that the cookie is sent *only* if a secure channel is being used. Secure channels are indicated by Web addresses that begin with https instead of http.

✓ Avoiding applications that use persistent cookies to store privacy-related information. For example, checking a box like "Please check box to remember user name and password" might allow an application to store the user's ID or password in the form of a cookie, creating a potential security threat.

For Windows users, a handy freeware program called CookieWall (see Figure 10-1) by AnalogX (www.analogx.com) is available. This program acts as a cookie "firewall" and simplifies cookie monitoring and management.

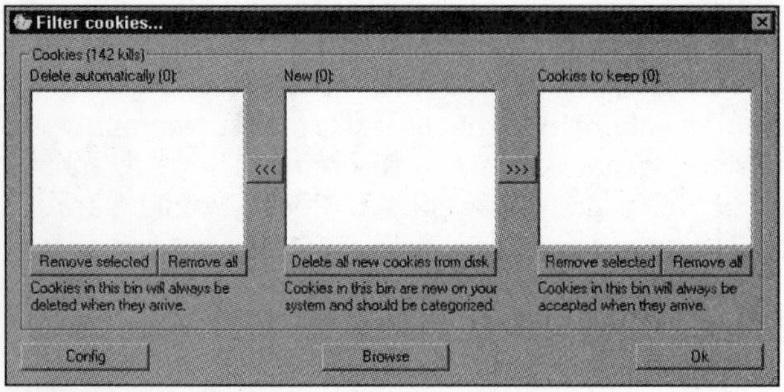

**Figure 10-1:** CookieWall by AnalogX

# Parameter Tampering

*Parameter tampering* involves the exploitation of insecure Web address parameters to retrieve information that would otherwise be unavailable to the user. Many online Web merchants use databases to store personal customer information and provide a Web address that links to that database.

Malicious users can exploit insecure programming code (such as incorrect CGI parameters) to potentially retrieve a listing of all users, passwords, credit card numbers, or any other personal data stored in the database.

In fact, in October 2000, a security flaw in Internet superstore buy.com's computer system let anyone view the name, address, and phone number of customers who returned products to the company, simply by manipulating a URL (Web address string). The breach was relatively straight-forward. buy.com provides a special URL (including a customer number) to its customers who wish to make returns so that they can easily print a mailing label to place on their parcel. The label includes the customer's return address and phone number. By changing the customer number in the URL, any user could view other customers' return labels. Fortunately, buy.com quickly patched the problem before any widespread abuse occurred.

The best defense is a good offense. While designing Web applications with security in mind can help prevent this type of exploit in the first place, it can lead to a more complex application and extend development time, two factors sometimes not deemed cost-effective by software developers anxious to put out their product.

# Stealth Commanding

Hackers often put script commands in the input fields of Web forms via Trojan horses with the intent to run malicious code that is damaging to Web sites. Poorly written applications that do not guard against this type of attack allow the malicious script commands to be entered in the form fields, which are then transmitted back and executed on the server. For example, a hacker could add malicious code that would trick a user into clicking a URL that would then send the user's session cookie — perhaps containing a username and password — to a hacker.

# Hidden-Field Manipulation

Hackers can sometimes access and then alter hidden fields in a Web page in order to change the price of items that are being sold via the Internet. In this manner, they can set their own prices and then continue to the checkout to complete their purchase.

Hidden fields in a Web page are often used to save information about the client's session without having to maintain a complex database on the server-side. Their name notwithstanding, these fields aren't truly hidden; they can be seen by viewing the source code contained within a Web page. To perform this action using Internet Explorer:

1. Open the Web browser and click View.
2. Click "Source" near the bottom of the drop-down menu.

As shown in Figure 10-2, the HTML programming code that constitutes the Web page appears (not so hidden, after all).

These manipulations are successful because most applications don't bother to authenticate the returning Web page; instead, they assume that the incoming data is the same as the outgoing data.

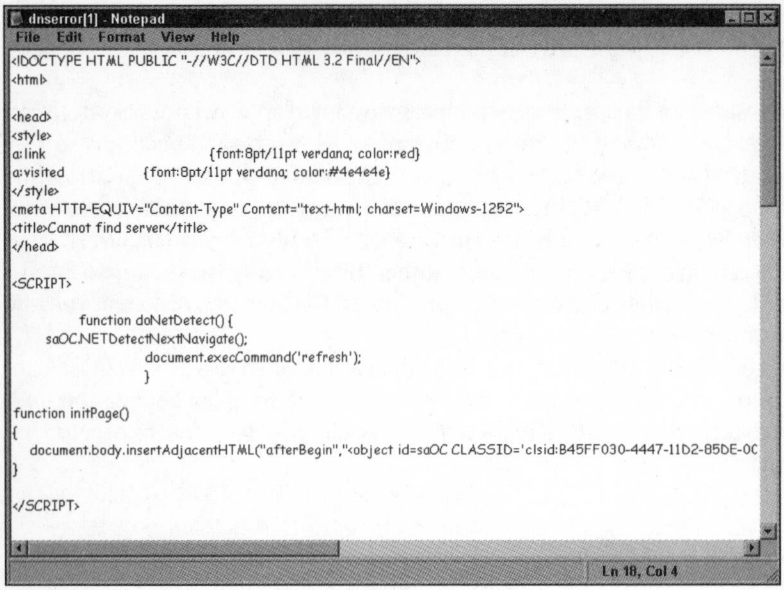

```
dnserror[1] - Notepad                                          _ □ ×
 File   Edit   Format   View   Help
<!DOCTYPE HTML PUBLIC "-//W3C//DTD HTML 3.2 Final//EN">
<html>

<head>
<style>
a:link                      {font:8pt/11pt verdana; color:red}
a:visited            {font:8pt/11pt verdana; color:#4e4e4e}
</style>
<meta HTTP-EQUIV="Content-Type" Content="text-html; charset=Windows-1252">
<title>Cannot find server</title>
</head>

<SCRIPT>

        function doNetDetect() {
    saOC.NETDetectNextNavigate();
                document.execCommand('refresh');
                }

function initPage()
{
    document.body.insertAdjacentHTML("afterBegin","<object id=saOC CLASSID='clsid:B45FF030-4447-11D2-85DE-0C
}

</SCRIPT>

                                                        Ln 18, Col 4
```

**Figure 10-2:** Internet Explorer showing HTML source code

# Combatting Buffer Overflow

A *buffer overflow* occurs when a malicious user sends more data than an application expects, thereby causing a buffer overrun. A buffer is a specially selected area of computer memory or disk space reserved for temporary data storage. This type of attack can be directed to the application or any of its components. It is used to crash the system, or to gain complete control over it by having it execute the attacker's malicious code. Buffer overflow vulnerabilities are quite common. These code-based attacks allow malicious code to be executed on vulnerable systems. In-depth details regarding these exploits are easily obtained and publicly available for any interested parties at the CERT Coordination Center Web site (www.cert.org) or at the Microsoft Web site (www.microsoft.com).

Buffer overflow attacks are often used by malicious code, as evidenced in recent years by the Code Red and Code Red II worms. However, Code Red I and II were not the first pieces of malicious code to use buffer overflows to their advantage. The Morris worm of 1988 exploited a flaw in a UNIX service called *finger*. When you "finger" a user, the finger service returns information about the user. This includes data such as the user's true name and phone number. With the Morris worm, the buffer overflow attack replaces the server's finger program with a UNIX command interpreter program, sometimes referred to as a "shell." This shell is then used to replicate the program that links, uploads, and executes additional new copies of the worm.

By 1998, buffer overflow exploits had become a familiar woe in the computing community, primarily targeting UNIX/Linux systems. While various UNIX and Linux distributors were quick to release patches, the number of exploits remained astonishing. In August 2001, the NIPC released the following bulletin regarding yet another exploit of the UNIX operating system:

ASSESSMENT 01-019
"Buffer Overflow Vulnerability in Telnet Daemon"
August 30, 2001

Synopsis: Recently, the cybersecurity community received numerous reports of intruders using the buffer overflow vulnerability in the telnet daemon program. Security organizations, such as CERT/Coordination Center, cited this vulnerability in a July advisory (http://www.cert.org/advisories/CA-2001-21.html) outlining the vulnerability and solutions to address this problem. Due to the increase of these reports and with the activity of a new worm that has targeted this vulnerability, the NIPC urges the consumers to contact their vendors to obtain the appropriate fix. This vulnerability has the potential to impact the victim by allowing an intruder to copy, delete, or execute any program on the victim's system.

A new worm called "x.c," designed to exploit this vulnerability, has been discovered. Although that specific worm has been disabled, other malicious code variants could take advantage of the same vulnerability. Vendor patches are available and NIPC urges consumers to contact their vendor to obtain the appropriate fix for their operating system.

This vulnerability affects primarily FreeBSD-derived telnet daemons (including Solaris, AIX, and several versions of Linux), but some information suggests other vendors' telnet daemons may also be subject to attack using the same method.

A list of vulnerable systems, along with links to vendor patches, can be obtained at http://www.securityfocus.com/bid/3064. It is recommended that users of these operating systems check with their vendor for applicable patches, or disable the telnet daemon entirely.

The distressing aspect of buffer overflow exploits is that proper programming practices have the ability to wipe out even potential exploits. Defense against this type of attack should revolve around:

- ✓ Controlling access to sensitive systems
- ✓ Installing software updates that replace exploitable software
- ✓ Routinely patching operating systems and applications, or patching anytime a program update becomes available.

Firewalls may or may not be effective against buffer overflow attacks. Today's most commonly used firewalls, stateful inspection firewalls, do not protect against the majority of buffer overflow exploits. On the other hand, application gateway firewalls *can*, but only when properly configured with the application gateway enabled.

# Defending Known Vulnerabilities

The computer systems of today's organizations come under attack from a multitude of sources. These range from malicious code, such as viruses and worms, to human threats, such as hackers and phone "phreaks." Attacks target different characteristics of a system, which leads to the possibility that a particular system will be more susceptible to a certain kind of attack. Malicious code attacks a system in one of two ways, either internally or externally. Traditionally, the virus has been an internal threat, while the worm has generally been a threat from an external source.

Although the entire hacker population has grown considerably over the past few years, the vast majority of hackers are not the seasoned professionals depicted by Hollywood; rather, they are less knowledgeable neophytes called "script kiddies" or "ankle biters." To guard against hackers or the threats posed by malicious code, administrators should make sure systems are always configured for *maximum* security. Unfortunately, system administrators are seldom told that, in addition to keeping the network operating smoothly, they must also make sure it's secure. When they *are* presented with the task of network security, it usually comes in the form of a simple requirement to prevent old user accounts from being reactivated or to enforce strong password policies.

In order to control and minimize the risk of threats faced by those operating an information system, both managers and users must know the system's vulnerabilities, as well as the threats that can exploit them. Knowledge of the "threat environment" allows the organization's system manager to implement the most cost-effective security measures. In some cases, managers may find it more cost-effective to simply tolerate the expected losses.

I should mention that the following threats and associated losses are based on their prevalence and significance in the current computing landscape. This list is not exhaustive, as some threats may combine elements from more than one area.

- ✓ **Errors and omissions:** Users, data entry clerks, system operators, and programmers frequently make unintentional errors that contribute to security problems, both directly and indirectly. Sometimes the error is the threat, such as a mistake made in entering data or a programming error that crashes the system. In other cases, errors create vulnerabilities. Errors can occur in any segment of the system.

- ✓ **Programming and development errors (otherwise known as bugs)** range from benign or harmless to catastrophic in their severity. In the past decade, software quality has improved significantly to reduce this type of threat, yet software "horror stories" still abound.

- ✓ **Installation and maintenance errors** also cause security problems.

Errors and omissions are important threats to data integrity. Errors are caused not only by data entry clerks processing hundreds of transactions daily, but also by all of an organization's system users who create and edit data. Many programs, especially those that are designed by users for personal computers, lack quality control measures. Even the most sophisticated programs, however, cannot detect all types of input errors or omissions.

People often assume that the information they receive from an organization's computer system is more accurate than it really is. Errors and omissions concerns should be included in an organization's computer security, software quality, and data quality programs.

## Malicious Code and Known Vulnerabilities

Recent surveys call attention to the growing number of companies that are being subjected to unauthorized use of their systems by outsiders. The number of Web site defacements is escalating at an accelerated rate. The risk from malicious code (such as the Code Red and Nimda worms) remains the primary concern in connection with computer security. Typically, malicious code is specifically written to take advantage of known vulnerabilities in operating systems and applications. That code writers specifically have these weaknesses in mind when developing their programs is evidenced by the recent Nimda worm, which tests for a total of 16 *known vulnerabilities* in anticipation of exploiting them.

The NIPC recommends that all organizations follow these steps to minimize their potential vulnerability:

- ✓ Join their local InfraGard chapter (contact the local FBI field office for details)
- ✓ Establish a liaison with law enforcement
- ✓ Educate their users
- ✓ Maintain backups of all original operating system software
- ✓ Maintain current backups of all important data
- ✓ Maintain and enforce the organization's information systems security policies
- ✓ Install adequate security software to recognize attacks
- ✓ Enable packet filtering and access control list on routers
- ✓ Track/audit defensive steps
- ✓ Ensure audit trails are turned on
- ✓ Place a banner on the organization's system to notify unauthorized users that they may be subject to monitoring
- ✓ Routinely test the network for vulnerabilities
- ✓ Change logins/passwords frequently
- ✓ Require use of passwords containing alphanumeric-special character combinations and/or one-time tokens
- ✓ Cancel logins/passwords when employees leave the organization
- ✓ Install vendor patches for known vulnerabilities
- ✓ Maintain the most current updates to anti-virus software
- ✓ Restrict/monitor network access to internal hosts
- ✓ Utilize remote access/authorization tools
- ✓ Consider establishing an emergency response team or contact with an existing incident response organization
- ✓ Develop an organizational computer incident response plan/policy

Additional information regarding known software vulnerabilities can be found at http://icat.nist.gov/icat.cfm, the National Institute of Standards and Technology ICAT Web site, a searchable index of information regarding computer vulnerabilities. It contains a search capability that links users to additional vulnerability and patch information.

# Universal Plug and Play

In December 2001, the NIPC issued the first of several bulletins regarding a "known" vulnerability of a component of Microsoft's new flagship operating system, Windows XP. Vulnerabilities in the Universal Plug and Play (UPnP) service, which is included by default on Microsoft Windows XP, and optionally on Windows Me and Windows 98, could allow an intruder to execute arbitrary code on vulnerable systems. According to Internet security analyst and programmer Steve Gibson, the reason the UPnP flaw occurred was as follows:

> The Universal Plug and Play service (UPnP), which is installed and running in all versions of Windows XP — and may be loaded into Windows 98 and ME — essentially turns every one of those systems into a wide-open Internet server. This server listens for TCP connections on port 5000 and for UDP "datagram" packets arriving on port 1900. This allows malicious hackers (or high-speed Internet worms) located anywhere in the world to scan for, and locate, individual Windows UPnP-equipped machines. Any vulnerability — known today or discovered tomorrow — can then be rapidly exploited.

The UPnP service identifies and uses network-based devices. According to the initial NIPC bulletin, UPnP exhibits two known vulnerabilities:

- ✓ An attacker may gain root level or system access as a result of a buffer overflow in the UPnP.

- ✓ The Simple Service Discovery Protocol (SSDP), which allows computers using UPnP to recognize new network devices, can also be used to send false packets to an address hosting exploitable Windows systems.

Organizations (and individuals) should monitor or entirely block ports 1900 and 5000. Any increase in traffic on those ports may indicate active scanning for this vulnerability. Ensure that a policy is in place that restricts access to the corporate network and to those machines that have not yet been patched. Set the UPnP service settings to Disable. They are set to Manual by default.

Users can also download a freeware product called "Unplug n' Pray" (see Figure 10-3) by Internet Security guru Steve Gibson at www.grc.com, which allows anyone to quickly disable (or subsequently re-enable) UPnP with the simple click of a mouse.

For more about the UPnP vulnerability, including further discussion of what the NIPC's recommendations concerning this vulnerability are, how to disable UPnP manually, and how to implement the Unplug n' Pray utility, see Chapter 5.

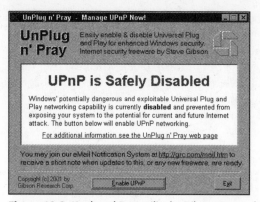

**Figure 10-3:** Unplug n' Pray utility by Gibson Research Corporation

# Mail Server Bombs

The inspiration behind a mail bomb is to choke the recipient's server with so many e-mail messages that it simply stops working. Mail servers are "bombarded" with e-mail messages. They can be sent as a single, extremely large e-mail message or as thousands of individual, small e-mail messages. Internet e-mail message bombs are considered cybercrimes and are the result of sending those e-mail messages to one mail server or servers. They are considered a form of cyberstalking. An enormous amount of duplicate e-mail is sent with the intention of inundating the servers (which cannot immediately process an onslaught of such magnitude). Consequently, most servers crash. Rebooting the server, however, typically resolves the problem.

While the individual e-mail message(s) within the mass mailing may be innocuous in and of itself, it is the *volume* of messages that causes detrimental effects with wide-scale reach. Not only does server downtime affect the individual recipient's account, but it can also shut down entire systems, leaving the server's other users cut off. Couple this with organizations that rely on the server to conduct e-commerce and the resulting monetary losses can be staggering. Furthermore, many employees may not be able to conduct their duties without use of their computer stations (for as long as it takes to get the server back to a fully functioning state), which means the scope of the damage broadens again.

Experienced hackers are not the only individuals who can send e-mail message bombs; any ordinary user can generate them. Worms and Trojan horses developed by hackers may be used to spawn them, as well. In June 2001, Microsoft's IIS (Internet Information Services) was subjected to a worm called DoS.Storm.Worm. The attack demonstrated the fact that worms and Trojans can be used to generate and trigger e-mail message bombs. DoS.Storm.Worm specifically targeted computer systems running IIS without its properly updated security patches. Such systems were infected with the worm, which then executed a denial-of-service attack on `www.microsoft.com`. Obscene e-mail messages sent to an address allegedly found at Microsoft completed the e-mail message bombing.

Popular e-mail programs such as Microsoft Outlook allow users to direct incoming mail to a specified folder. When users have been targeted by a mail bombing, they begin to receive the same message over and over again. One solution is to shut down their e-mail program and reset it to direct all incoming mail with that message to their Recycle Bin or trash folder. When the user logs back on, the reconfigured e-mail program automatically deletes multiple copies of e-mail messages. A second method to defend against mail bombing is to simply contact your ISP and ask them to automatically delete multiple copies of any messages (that is, dozens of the same message) found in your inbox located on their e-mail server.

# Raw Sockets and Associated Dangers

Circa 1981, the Computer Systems Research Group (CSRG) at the University of California, Berkeley created the TCP/IP protocols that the Internet relies upon for communication. Along with TCP/IP, they also created "Berkeley Sockets" for UNIX, which incorporated a "raw socket" component designed to assist in the task of creating Internet applications. Simply put, a *raw socket* bypasses the normal TCP/IP protocol stack by opening a backdoor directly into the underlying network transport system. The original Berkeley designers intended that raw sockets be used for Internet research and development purposes only.

Windows XP Home Edition allows full access to raw sockets. Winsock, as sockets are called when referring to older Windows operating systems, did not always allow full access to raw sockets. Raw sockets mean raw access to the Internet. Moreover, the problem of malicious agents getting into people's computers and launching denial-of-service (DOS) attacks with spoofed data packets increases significantly with the use of raw sockets.

In UNIX or Linux, raw sockets are protected from unauthorized access. Only those with full "root" privileges can utilize them. This security measure keeps raw socket access out of the hands of hackers and malicious code. User-level applications are thereby prevented from accessing (and potentially abusing) the raw sockets capability. The security features built into all other raw socket–capable operating systems (UNIX, Linux, and so on) deliberately restrict raw socket access to applications running with full "root" privileges. The Windows XP Home Edition, however, executes all applications with full administrative "root" privilege. Therefore, Windows XP eliminates the raw socket safety restrictions imposed by nearly every other operating system.

Because they avoid traditional TCP/IP protocols, hackers can use raw sockets to generate TCP packets, making it impossible for receiving networks to verify if those packets are genuine. Blocking the packets is impossible because that would entail blocking *all* TCP packets traveling on the network; effectively impeding all inbound data traffic. This vulnerability could permit malicious code to open a new backdoor into Windows via raw sockets, which has been included in Windows XP. This vulnerability was reported to Microsoft by Internet security expert Steve Gibson in the summer of 2001. Since Microsoft refused to remove raw socket support before shipping out its Windows XP Home Edition, Mr. Gibson and Jeremy Collake were motivated to create a freeware program called "SocketLock" to prevent Windows raw socket abuse (see Figure 10-4). This program, along with additional information on raw sockets, can be found at www.grc.com, the homepage of the Gibson Research Corporation.

**Figure 10-4:** SocketLock Raw Socket Abuse Prevention System

# Creating a Plan to Secure Your Web Server

While most security incidents cause minor embarrassment or inconvenience, it is possible for an intruder attack to cause real problems and severe losses. Every organization should establish a security program that assesses the risks of attacks and takes steps to reduce the risks to an acceptable level. Each organization has to determine its sensitivity to risk and must decide how open it wants to be to the external world. When resources are limited, the cost of security incidents should be considered, and the investment in protective measures should be concentrated on areas of highest sensitivity.

## Techniques to Secure Web Servers

The most common methods for protecting Web servers include:

- ✓ Removing unnecessary software
- ✓ Detecting attacks upon a Web server using intrusion detection
- ✓ Correcting flaws in remaining software
- ✓ Restricting an attacker's actions once a part of a Web server is compromised
- ✓ Protecting the rest of the network if the Web server is compromised

Those are basic steps. But as your organization determines its sensitivity to risk, three levels of Web security techniques can be applied:

- ✓ **Level 1, Minimum Security** — Applying Level 1 security involves the following techniques:
  - ▪ Upgrading software/installing patches
  - ▪ Using single-purpose servers
  - ▪ Removing unnecessary applications

✓ **Level 2, Penetration Resistance** — Applying Level 2 security involves the following techniques:

- Applying external firewalls

- Remote administration security

- Restricting server scripts

- Using Web server shields with packet filtering

- Considering issues of education and personnel resource allocation

- Applying those techniques listed in Level 1

✓ **Level 3: Attack Detection and Mitigation** — Applying Level 3 security involves the following techniques:

- Applying separation of privilege

- Enacting hardware-based solutions

- Installing internal firewalls

- Installing network-based intrusion detection

- Installing host-based intrusion detection

- Applying those techniques listed in Level 2

## Removing Unnecessary Applications

All privileged software not specifically required by the Web server should be removed. Privileged software can be considered software that runs with administrator privileges or that receives packets from the network. Operating systems often run a variety of privileged programs by default. Many system administrators are not even aware of the existence of many of these programs. Each privileged program provides another avenue by which an attacker can compromise a Web server. It is therefore crucial that Web servers be purged of unnecessary programs. For greater security and because it is often difficult to identify what software is privileged, many system administrators remove all software that is not needed by a Web server.

## Upgrading Software/Installing Patches

As with attacks on network workstations, one of the simplest and yet most effective techniques for reducing the risk of attack on Web servers is the installation of the latest software updates and patches. Web servers should be frequently (sometimes daily) examined to determine what software needs to be updated or patched. Any software on a Web server that an attacker could use to penetrate the system must be regularly updated. Software in this category includes the operating system, servers, or any software that receives network packets, software running as root or administrator, and security software.

The following process should be followed:

1. Make a list of software and write down the associated version numbers.

2. Find the Web page for each piece of software and make sure that you have installed the latest version.

3. Find and install the available patches for the applicable version of the software. Each software vendor provides unique instructions on how to install its patches (usually these instructions are very simple). Be careful to follow the vendor instructions, as patches must often be installed in a set sequence for the process to work.

4. Verify that patched software functions correctly.

## Using Single-Purpose Servers

Organizations should run Web servers on computers dedicated exclusively to that task. A common mistake organizations make is to try to save money by running multiple servers on the same host. For example, it is not uncommon to run an e-mail server, Web server, and database server on the same computer. However, each server run on a host provides an attacker with avenues for attack. Each newly installed server then increases the organization's reliance upon that host while simultaneously decreasing its security. Given the decreasing cost of hardware and the increasing importance of having fast Web servers, it is generally effective to buy a dedicated host for each Web server. In addition, in situations where a Web server constantly interacts with a database, it is best to use two separate hosts.

## Education and Personnel Resource Allocation

Attackers are able to penetrate most Web servers because the system administrators are either not knowledgeable about Web server security or did not take the time to properly secure the system. Web site administrators must be trained about Web server security techniques and rewarded for spending time securing the site. Several excellent books and training seminars exist to aid system administrators in the securing of their Web sites.

# Summary

Over the past few years, malicious code has expanded from targeting networked computers on the company LAN to attacking the servers that help drive the Internet. Server-side attacks cost organizations millions each year in lost revenues as a consequence of data loss and downtime. Web applications have unique security requirements, requiring organizations to continually examine Web server operating systems and applications for vulnerabilities.

Key points covered in this chapter include:

✓ What the security implications of using CGI scripts on Web servers are and how confining the execution of CGI scripts to certain directories can markedly increase security

✓ How server-side include statements (SSIs), while easier to use than CGI scripts, can also introduce serious security risks via `exec` directives

✓ What threats are posed by cross site scripting (CSS) and what steps are necessary to restrict scripts from malicious activities

✓ What dangers are posed by backdoors and debugging options and what measures are required to defend systems against those threats

✓ How ordinarily innocuous cookie files can be manipulated and poisoned by hackers or malicious code

✓ How hackers apply parameter-tampering techniques to gather personal information about Internet users

✓ How hackers put Trojan horses in the input forms of Web pages using a technique called stealth commanding, allowing them to steal a user's personal data

✓ How hackers can access and manipulate hidden fields in Web pages in order to change the price of items sold on the Internet

✓ Why buffer overflow attacks are the most common Internet exploit and what steps are necessary to limit or prevent them

✓ Why known vulnerabilities are frequently exploited by hackers and malicious code

✓ Mail server bombs and their potential to overload and crash Web servers

✓ What the dangers associated with raw socket availability are, including the importance of making them accessible only to those with "root" or administrative privileges

# Part III

## Looking Ahead

## IN THIS PART:

As a potent business tool, the public Internet is an essential component of the modern corporate landscape. However, the same technology in the wrong hands may produce costly and devastating results. This part explores how malevolent individuals exploit the Internet as a weapon of terrorism and what governments and organizations around the globe are doing to counter this trend. The book concludes with an evaluation of the future of malicious code combat.

# Chapter 11

# Cyberterrorism and Hacktivism—New Millennium, New Threats

## In This Chapter

✓ Exploring cyberterrorism and identifying cyberterrorists

✓ Defining hacktivism

✓ Considering the USA Patriot Act of 2001

✓ Engaging the ethical issues of cyberterrorism

✓ Feeling the effects of information warfare and identity theft

THERE IS NO SINGLE definition of terrorism. According to the FBI's Web site, terrorism is "the unlawful use of force or violence against persons or property to intimidate or coerce a Government, the civilian population, or any segment thereof, in furtherance of political or social objectives." The FBI further describes terrorism as either domestic or international, depending on the origin, base, and objectives of the terrorist organization.

✓ **Domestic terrorism** involves groups or individuals who are based and operate entirely within the United States and Puerto Rico, are without foreign direction, and whose acts are directed at elements of the U.S. government or population.

✓ **International terrorism** is the unlawful use of force or violence committed by a group or individual who has some connection to a foreign power or whose activities transcend national boundaries against persons or property to intimidate or coerce a government, the civilian population, or any segment thereof in furtherance of political or social objectives.

The FBI divides terrorist-related activity into three categories:

✓ A **terrorist incident** is a violent act or an act dangerous to human life, in violation of the criminal laws of the United States or of any state, to intimidate or coerce a government, the civilian population, or any segment thereof in furtherance of political or social objectives.

✓ **A suspected terrorist incident** is a potential act of terrorism in which responsibility for the act cannot be attributed at the time to a known or suspected terrorist group or individual.

✓ **Terrorism prevention** is a documented instance in which a violent act by a known or suspected terrorist group or individual with the means and a proven propensity for violence is successfully interdicted through investigative activity.

In July 1996, U.S. President Bill Clinton signed an executive order assembling a team of specialists to study the problem of cyberterrorism. Hopefully, the study would lead to the development of plans for protecting computer-reliant infrastructure (including electrical power systems, telecommunications, banking systems, transportation systems, water stores, and emergency services). Some questioned the need for such plans. They posited that computer failures, outages, and service disruptions are common occurrences — whether intentional or inadvertent. Although these unfortunate events are debilitating (transiently), they do not completely cripple our nation. Current trends indicate that the need for such plans must not be underestimated. Development of strategies must start with an understanding of cyberterrorism — where it is coming from and where it is headed.

# What Is Cyberterrorism?

As a communications medium, the Internet has proved to be the ultimate means for establishing contact. Not only is it affordable for a large segment of the population, it also provides nearly global delivery without time restrictions. The Internet's ability to dispense information in the form of the written word, digital images, and audio and video displays is enormously influential in the forming of public opinion and participation. Pair these features with its cloak of anonymity and its scope of global proportion and it is readily apparent why the Internet is an attractive tool for cyberterrorists.

Appropriately, cyberterrorism has grown into a major concern for governments as well as organizations in the private sector. Perpetrators may use specialized knowledge and skills to manipulate telecommunications systems in order to obtain extensive command of an infiltrated system. As with most weapons of destruction, a cyberterrorist can (through use of the Internet) inflict a tremendous amount of damage in a fraction of a second. In a January 28, 2002 press release from Senator John Edwards of North Carolina, Edwards states, "We live in a world where a terrorist can do as much damage with a keyboard and a modem as with a gun or a bomb."

*Cyberterrorism* is essentially an unlawful act that is carried out against computers and/or with the use of computers in order to coerce or intimidate others. Cyberterrorism encompasses attacks made on computer systems, networks, and the information stored on them. The unlawful act(s) may result in the suspension (or total destruction) of municipal services to a particular population, fomenting fear and insecurity in residents or outright violence. Ultimately, the objective of the unlawful act(s) is to influence a population or a government to conform to a particular political, social, or ideological agenda. A component of the cyberterrorist process is to provoke unrest and uncertainty about a government and its ability to guard and defend its populace. When the public becomes ill at ease, it is most vulnerable to outside influence. Cyberterrorism can also include unlawful acts of revenge carried out with the use of computers; for example, a malicious individual might hack into a hospital's computer system to change a patient's prescription order to a fatal dose.

The fundamental technique used by hackers to gain unlawful access to computer networks is as follows:

1. They start with intelligence gathering, which enables them to collect basic information about the networks they are targeting.

2. Then, they study the network to identify individual systems and to probe those systems for vulnerable sections.

3. The next step in the process of gaining entry is the attack.

4. If the attack is successful, hackers advance through the layers of a network, moving to systems that give them even more access to information and records.

5. Once they find what they are looking for, they obscure the system path they followed during the hack. This entails altering basic activity logs within each system.

Much terrorist activity revolves around disseminating propaganda, eliciting recruits, raising money, devising plans, and communicating amongst themselves and with others. However, even when these activities are carried out with the use of information technology, they do not constitute cyberterrorism in and of themselves. Attacks that are primarily costly nuisances, those that interfere with *non*essential services and simple computer deliveries of a terrorist organization's messages (over the Internet) for example, do not amount to cyberterrorism. Only when a destructive *act* itself is executed with the use of computers and other electronic means (using a technique like launching infected e-mail attachments) is it appropriate to use the term "cyberterrorism." To be thought of as such, attacks must effect considerable monetary losses and/or result in death or bodily injury (as a result of water contamination, plane crashes, bombings, and so on).

While disturbances in computer systems may not always result in physical violence against services, property, and/or human lives, the damage to computer systems (and, subsequently, to the other systems that rely on them) is intolerable in today's information-dependent, *inter*dependent society. Without resorting to the use of conventional weapons, cyberterrorists can manipulate computer systems to disrupt power grids and other elements of infrastructure.

Although today's technology can provide adequate security against cyberterrorism, it is frequently configured incorrectly or used in ways that leave it susceptible to attack. Additionally, the possibility remains that an insider, acting single-handedly or in conjunction with other terrorists, will exploit access capabilities. For example, in 1999, a Russian gas monopoly called Gazprom was hit by hackers who collaborated with a Gazprom insider. The hackers are said to have used a Trojan horse program to gain control of the central switchboard that controls gas flow in regional pipelines. The gas monopoly was quickly able to regain control of the switchboard, however. However, such quick regain of control may not always be the case.

Whether they originate from outsiders or from within an organization, such attacks are on the rise. Recently, an Australian gained access to a computerized waste management system and dumped millions of gallons of raw sewage on parks and in rivers in Queensland, Australia. The NATO computer system was crippled by e-mail bombs during the war in Kosovo. In the autumn of

2001, a "cyberjihad" was announced against the United States by a group called Gforce Pakistan when they commandeered the Department of Defense's Web pages.

In February 2000, Michael A. Vatis, Director of the National Infrastructure Protection Center, made the following statement before the Senate Judiciary Committee, Criminal Justice Oversight Subcommittee and House Judiciary Committee:

> Terrorist's groups are increasingly using new information technology and the Internet to formulate plans, raise funds, spread propaganda, and to communicate securely. In his statement on the worldwide threat in 2000, Director of Central Intelligence George Tenet testified that terrorist's groups, "including Hizbollah, HAMAS, the Abu Nidal organization, and Bin Laden's al Qa'ida organization are using computerized files, e-mail, and encryption to support their operations." In one example, convicted terrorist Ramzi Yousef, the mastermind of the World Trade Center bombing, stored detailed plans to destroy United States airliners on encrypted files on his laptop computer. While we have not yet seen these groups employ cybertools as a *weapon* to use against critical infrastructures, their reliance on information technology and acquisition of computer expertise are clear warning signs. Moreover, we have seen other terrorist groups, such as the Internet Black Tigers (who are reportedly affiliated with the Tamil Tigers) engage in attacks on foreign government Web sites and e-mail servers. "Cyberterrorism"—by which I mean the use of cybertools to shut down critical national infrastructures (such as energy, transportation, or government operations) for the purpose of coercing or intimidating a government or civilian population—is thus a very real, though still largely potential, threat.

Vatis' statement underscores the fact that, while specific terrorist groups have not yet used cybertools as weapons, the potential for this type of application and those groups' proficient use of information technology should remind governments and organizations to remain wary. The future threats posed by cybercrime, cyberterrorism, and hacktivism are daunting. As you read the following prepared statement by National Intelligence officer for Science and Technology Lawrence Gershwin to the Joint Economic Committee Cyberthreat Trends and U.S. Network Security, take note of the magnitude of the current and future challenges to be faced by both government and the private sector in securing IT infrastructure. The exploits of cyberterrorists, hacktivists, and hackers, if not fully acknowledged now, will most certainly become evident in the future.

June 21, 2001
Statement for the Record
for the Joint Economic Committee
Cyber Threat Trends and U.S. Network Security
Lawrence K. Gershwin
National Intelligence Officer
for Science and Technology
(as prepared for delivery)

Mr. Chairman, thank you for the opportunity to provide a statement on cyberthreat and critical infrastructure issues. Late last year, the NIC published a report called *Global Trends 2015,* which presented the results of a close collaboration between U.S. Government specialists and a wide range of experts outside the government on our best judgments of major drivers and trends that will shape the world of 2015.

In 2015, we anticipate that the world will almost certainly experience quantum leaps in information technology (IT) and in other areas of science and technology. IT will be the major building block for international commerce and for empowering nonstate actors. Most experts agree that the IT revolution represents the most significant global transformation since the Industrial Revolution beginning in the mid-eighteenth century.

■ The integration — or fusion — of continuing revolutions in information technology, biotechnology, materials science, and nanotechnology will generate dramatic increases in technology investments, which will further stimulate innovation in the more advanced countries.

The networked global economy will be driven by rapid and largely unrestricted flows of information, ideas, cultural values, capital, goods and services, and people: that is, globalization. This globalized economy will be a net contributor to increased political stability in the world in 2015, although its reach and benefits will not be universal. In contrast to the Industrial Revolution, the process of globalization will be more compressed. Its evolution will be rocky, marked by chronic financial volatility and a widening economic divide.

### Cyberthreat Concerns

As the Director of Central Intelligence testified to the Congress earlier this year, no country in the world rivals the U.S. in its reliance, dependence, and dominance of information systems. The great advantage we derive from this also presents us with unique vulnerabilities.

■ Indeed, computer-based information operations could provide our adversaries with an asymmetric response to U.S. military superiority by giving them the potential to degrade or circumvent our advantage in conventional military power.

■ Attacks on our military, economic, or telecommunications infrastructure can be launched from anywhere in the world, and they can be used to transport the problems of a distant conflict directly to America's heartland.

Hostile cyberactivity today is ballooning. The number of FBI computer network intrusion cases has doubled during each of the past two years. Information derived from the Internet indicates that, since last September, the number of hacker defacements on the Web have increased over tenfold.

Meanwhile, several highly publicized intrusions and computer virus incidents — such as the recent intrusion into the California Independent System Operator, the nonprofit corporation that controls the distribution of 75 percent of the state's power — have fed a public, and perhaps foreign government, perception that the networks upon which U.S. national security and economic well-being depend are vulnerable to attack by almost anyone with a computer, a modem, and a modicum of skill. This impression, of course, overstates the case.

### U.S. Networks as Targets

Information from industry security experts suggests that U.S. national information networks have become more vulnerable — and therefore more attractive as targets of foreign cyberattack. An independent group of security professionals created the "Honeynet Project," placing virtual computers on the Internet to evaluate threats and vulnerabilities that currently exist. The results were stunning: the average computer placed on the Internet will be hacked in about eight hours. University networks are even worse, with an unsecured computer system being hacked in only about 45 minutes.

- The growing connectivity among secure and insecure networks creates new opportunities for unauthorized intrusions into sensitive or proprietary computer systems within critical U.S. infrastructures, such as the nation's telephone system.

- The complexity of computer networks is growing faster than the ability to understand and protect them by identifying critical nodes, verifying security, and monitoring activity.

- Firms are dedicating growing, but still insufficient, resources to the defense of critical U.S. infrastructures against foreign cyberattack — perceived as a low likelihood threat compared to routine disruptions such as accidental damage to telecommunications lines.

Mainstream commercial software — whose vulnerabilities are widely known — is replacing relatively secure proprietary network systems by U.S. telecommunications providers and other operators of critical infrastructure. Such commercial software includes imported products that provide opportunities for foreign implantation of exploitation or attack tools.

U.S. government and defense networks similarly are increasing their reliance on commercial software.

Opportunities for foreign placement or recruitment of insiders have become legion. As part of an unprecedented churning of the global information technology workforce, U.S. firms are drawing on pools of computer expertise that reside in a number of potential threat countries.

- Access to U.S. proprietary networks by subcontractors of foreign partners is creating "virtual" insiders whose identity and nationality often remain unknown to U.S. network operators.

- Foreign or U.S. insiders were responsible for 71 percent of the unauthorized entries into U.S. corporate computer networks reported to an FBI-sponsored survey last year.

- Despite growing interconnectivity, control networks — whose compromise could disrupt critical U.S. infrastructures such as power or transportation — are designed to be less accessible from outside networks, according to industry experts. In addition, many control networks use unique, proprietary, or archaic programming languages thought to be — and clearly intended to be — poorly understood by hackers. Nonetheless, we remain concerned that increasing use of the Internet by critical infrastructures and the U.S. military, combined with increasing convergence to just a few software systems, could leave the U.S. open to more damaging attacks.

### Growing Foreign Capabilities

Advanced technologies and tools for computer network operations are becoming more widely available, resulting in a basic, but operationally significant, technical cybercapability for U.S. adversaries.

Most U.S. adversaries have access to the technology needed to pursue computer network operations. Computers are almost globally available, and Internet connectivity is both widespread and increasing. Both the technology and access to the Internet are inexpensive, relative to traditional weapons, and require no large industrial infrastructure.

- The tradecraft needed to employ technology and tools effectively however — particularly against more difficult targets such as classified networks or critical infrastructures — remains an important limiting factor for many of our adversaries.

Hackers since the mid-1990s have shared increasingly sophisticated and easy-to-use software on the Internet, providing tools that any computer-literate adversary could obtain and use for computer network reconnaissance, probing, penetration, exploitation, or attack. Moreover, programming aids are making it possible to develop sophisticated tools with only basic programming skills.

Globally available tools are particularly effective against the mechanisms of the Internet, but specialized tools would be needed against more difficult targets, such as many of the networks that control critical infrastructures.

Even with technology and tools, considerable tradecraft also is required to penetrate network security perimeters and defeat intrusion detection systems — particularly against defensive reactions by network security administrators. Tradecraft also will determine how well an adversary can achieve a targeted and reliable outcome, and how likely the perpetrator is to remain anonymous. Attackers must tailor strategies to specific target networks — requiring advanced and continued reconnaissance to characterize targets and ensure that exploitation tools remain effective in the face of subtle changes to computer systems and networks.

■ Cyberattacks against less well-defended networks still would require prior identification of critical nodes and a preplanned campaign, if the attacks were to achieve a strategic impact.

### Potential Actors and Threats

Let me talk about some of the groups that will challenge us on the cyberfront.

### Hackers

Although the most numerous and publicized cyberintrusions and other incidents are ascribed to lone computer-hacking hobbyists, such hackers pose a negligible threat of widespread, long-duration damage to national-level infrastructures. The large majority of hackers do not have the requisite tradecraft to threaten difficult targets such as critical U.S. networks — and even fewer would have a motive to do so.

Nevertheless, the large worldwide population of hackers poses a relatively high threat of an isolated or brief disruption causing serious damage, including extensive property damage or loss of life. As the hacker population grows, so does the likelihood of an exceptionally skilled and malicious hacker attempting and succeeding in such an attack.

■ In addition, the huge worldwide volume of relatively less skilled hacking activity raises the possibility of inadvertent disruption of a critical infrastructure.

### Hacktivists

A smaller foreign population of politically active hackers — which includes individuals and groups with anti-U.S. motives — poses a medium-level threat of carrying out an isolated but damaging attack. Most international hacktivist groups appear bent on propaganda rather than damage to critical infrastructures.

Pro-Beijing Chinese hackers over the past two years have conducted mass cyberprotests in response to events such as the 1999 NATO bombing of China's embassy in Belgrade. Pro-Serbian hacktivists attacked a NATO Web site during Operation Allied Force. Similar hacktivism accompanied the rise in Israeli-Palestinian clashes last year and several thousand Web page defacements and some successful denial-of-service attacks were associated with the recent EP-3 incident.

### Industrial Spies and Organized Crime Groups

International corporate spies and organized crime organizations pose a medium-level threat to the United States through their ability to conduct industrial espionage and large-scale monetary theft, respectively, and through their ability to hire or develop hacker talent.

- Japanese syndicates used Russian hackers to gain access to law enforcement databases, evidently to monitor police investigations of their operations and members, according to a press report last year.

- According to press reports, a Mafia-led syndicate this year used banking and telecommunications insiders to break into an Italian bank's computer network. The syndicate diverted the equivalent of $115 million in European Union aid, to Mafia-controlled bank accounts overseas before Italian authorities detected the activity.

Foreign corporations also could use computer intrusions to tamper with competitors' business proposals, in order to defeat competing bids or unfairly position products in the marketplace.

- Computer network espionage or sabotage can affect U.S. economic competitiveness and result in technology transfer directly through product sales, or indirectly to U.S. adversaries.

Because cybercriminals' central objectives are to steal, and to do so with as little attention from law enforcement as possible, they are not apt to undertake operations leading to high-profile network disruptions, such as damage to U.S. critical infrastructures.

Major drug trafficking groups, however, could turn to computer network attacks in an attempt to disrupt U.S. law enforcement or local government counternarcotics efforts.

Organized crime groups with cybercapabilities conceivably could threaten attacks against critical infrastructure for purposes of extortion.

# Who Are Cyberterrorists?

One of the most frightening aspects of cyberterrorism is that virtually anyone can commit such acts. Unlike the suicide missions of the September 11th terrorists, cyberterrorism can be accomplished remotely and anonymously. Anyone can don the cyberterrorist costume — disgruntled employees, foreign spies, perpetrators of fraud, political activists, conventional criminals, and even juveniles with a minimal amount of computer knowledge. With the growth of the Internet, the pool of potential cyberterrorists has grown, and hacker tools and information can be easily accessed online.

The cyberterrorist's primary goal is to gain exposure at almost any cost. Short of being identified individually, such terrorists seek any type of publicity for their cause. Not only do they gain media hype for their protests, they also attain notoriety for their skills. Their virus-writing and Internet warfare procedures provide them with a chance to demonstrate their computer expertise and their ability to fell, or at least cripple, sometimes-giant organizations.

These terrorists disregard the trickle-down effect of their attack, which may initially be invisible but later result in serious losses. Those who rely on the targeted organization for goods or services are directly affected, as are those who are dependent upon *them*. Such consequences may not have been foreseen by the terrorists and can have unpredictable and devastating outcomes.

The cyberterrorist may forgo the usual techniques used in terrorism, instead applying technology to obtain ransoms, impose demands, or otherwise wreak havoc upon and intimidate targeted populations. The cyberterrorist can often accomplish these goals without exposing himself to harm. Although the "pure" cyberterrorist has not yet made headlines, current hacker and denial-of-service attacks may provide a preview as to what the pure cyberterrorist is capable of doing.

Cyberspace is continuously being used to launch all manner of serious attacks. Whether the source of attack is a hacker or cyberterrorist, the threat is real — and costly to society. The recent I Love You virus (and its variants), for example, hit an estimated tens of millions of users and cost billions of dollars in damage. Denial-of-service attacks against Yahoo!, CNN, eBay, and other e-commerce Web sites are estimated to have caused over a billion dollars in losses. Consequently, they undermine the confidence of businesses and individuals engaging in e-commerce.

Terrorists are not only exploring the use of weapons of destruction, they are also investigating the use of weapons of mass disruption. Cyberspies, cyberthieves, saboteurs, and thrill seekers regularly infiltrate computer systems, steal personal data and trade secrets, vandalize Web sites, disrupt service, sabotage data and systems, initiate computer viruses and worms, conduct fraudulent transactions, and harass individuals and companies. These attacks are facilitated with increasingly powerful and easy-to-use software tools, which are obtained readily (and for free) from thousands of Web sites on the Internet.

The hacking community, based for the most part in the United States, Europe, the nations of the former Soviet Union, the Middle East, and Asia, is composed of individuals who see the hacking process merely as a challenge, a brain tease, and a diversionary puzzle. They may not think they have committed any crime, perceiving their acts as virtuous and honorable. They sometimes consider themselves victims of persecution and at times do not believe that what they are doing causes real damage. At their most harmless, these individuals (or groups) simply examine and gather information; however, privacy issues and military secrecy can render such infiltrations acts of terror.

# The Cyberterrorist and the Typical Hacker

Hackers are primarily motivated by a desire to make themselves infamous. They exploit the infrastructure of the Internet for their personal gratification. As discussed in Chapter 2, many hackers hack simply for the thrill of the challenge, to garner the respect of fellow hackers, or for public recognition of their abilities. On the other hand, one can study traditional terrorist movements to know that the cyberterrorist is inspired by a different agenda. Successful terrorist attacks are well-coordinated and well-planned and subtle at their onset. It is precisely these attributes that makes the terrorist attacks of September 11, 2001 so terrifying. A great amount of planned and organized coordination was required to implement the attacks. The cyberterrorist attempts highly planned, well-researched attacks on critical pieces of information infrastructure rather than aiming at indiscriminate targets over a wide variety of sources (for instance, widespread denial-of-service attacks or an attack on an electrical power plant).

# Computer Sabotage

Using the Internet to achieve a disruption in the normal operation of a computer or computer network through the introduction of worms, viruses, or logic bombs is referred to as *computer sabotage*. Computer sabotage can be carried out in a number of ways, and may be motivated by the saboteur's desire:

✓ To gain economic advantage over a competitor

✓ For sport

✓ For revenge

✓ To promote the illegal activities of terrorists

✓ To steal data or programs for extortion purposes.

One recent case of computer sabotage involved a Maryland man named Claude R. Carpenter, II, who pleaded guilty to intentionally causing damage to a protected computer in July 2001. According to the Statement of Facts presented by Assistant U.S. Attorney Stuart A. Berman and Department of Justice Trial Attorney Michael O'Leary, Claude Carpenter started working as a systems administrator for Network Resources on March 13, 2000. Network Resources is a subcontractor to the Internal Revenue Service (IRS), and Carpenter was responsible for performing work on the Integrated Network Operations Management System (INOMS) database, the inventory system for all hardware and software within the IRS. More specifically, Carpenter's responsibilities included monitoring three computer servers maintained at the IRS' computer center at the New Carrollton Federal Building in Lanham, Fort Worth, Texas. Within a brief period of time, Carpenter was admonished for inappropriate actions and comments, for repeatedly arriving at work late, leaving before the end of his shift, and not being available for system responses and customer requests. His supervisor discussed these issues with him on April 3, 2000. Carpenter met with supervisors two more times in the month of April; they warned him that any further problems with attitude or timeliness would be grounds for dismissal. Carpenter continued to be late for work. Thus, on May 4th, his root access — the level of complete control over a computer system utilized by system administrators — was limited to work performed directly on one server, not on the other two servers or through any remote work. On May 18th, following a dispute between Carpenter and a co-worker, Carpenter's supervisor prepared and sent to the project manager a draft letter of dismissal for Carpenter. Carpenter's supervisor did not print out the letter or give it to Carpenter.

Carpenter was assigned to work a shift from 2:00 p.m. to 12:30 a.m. During that shift, he logged into one of the servers to which he had no right to possess root access and proceeded to access his supervisor's computer profile, modifying the profile and inserting several lines of destructive computer code. Carpenter then "commented out" the code in his supervisor's profile so that it would not execute. However, he subsequently inserted the same lines of active destructive code onto all three servers, so that once executed, it would wipe out the data on all three servers. Carpenter tried to conceal his activities by turning off system logs, removing history files, and seeking to have the destructive code overwritten after execution so that it would be impossible for system administrators to determine why the data was deleted.

The day after Carpenter committed these destructive acts, he was dismissed, after describing to the project manager the draft dismissal letter that was located on his supervisor's computer. During the following two weeks, Carpenter called the system administrator room several times to ask if "Everything was OK," "If the machines were running OK," or "If anything was wrong with the servers." After Carpenter's activities were discovered, the IRS and the project managers shut down the three computer servers in order to remove the destructive code and reestablish the security and integrity of the system. In November 2001, Carpenter was sentenced to 15 months in prison and fined $109,000.

The preceding example illustrates how organizations like the IRS are becoming increasingly dependent on interconnected information systems to conduct business and to provide information and services to their customers. While the vulnerabilities of systems are getting increasing attention, many organizations have not adopted systematic, thorough practices for evaluating their systems' vulnerabilities and for reducing the risks. Furthermore, individuals in charge of maintaining these systems require extensive background checks and periodic review, since insiders are often in the best position to cause harm to critical system components.

# Hacktivism — Where Hacking, Activism, and Cyberterrorism Meet

An activist is an individual who takes action in an attempt to improve situations or conditions that he or she perceives as wrong. While anyone can call themselves an activist, activists generally get involved in political and economic matters, such as social justice or environmental issues. They are usually fervent about one or more issues, and are also usually well-versed in one or more subjects. Contrary to popular opinion, activists are not always zealots aggressively seeking to destroy the government. They do not all espouse the same beliefs, yet most believe in equality for all people. For the most part, they may be considered liberal-minded. Change is often inspired by their ability to act on their convictions.

Hackers are individuals who take pleasure in manipulating and learning from technology. The correct term for security breaking is *cracking*. The term *hacker,* however, is often used in this regard, as well. Although the media often portrays hackers as social misfits bent on destruction, hackers are more accurately described as computer enthusiasts. Contrary to legend, hackers are usually intelligent, sociable individuals who enjoy a sense of community.

More information on hackers and their motivations can be found in Chapter 2.

There are different types of hackers. Amateurs, also known as *ankle biters,* possess few skills and little technical knowledge and are situated at the bottom (ankle height) of the hacker hierarchy. Experienced hackers — those individuals who don't promote particular political or ideological agendas but who possess superb skills and extensive knowledge—are positioned at the top of the hacking hierarchy. At yet another level, you find the hackers who engage in corporate espionage. These hackers can be described as disgruntled employees with an ax to grind. Within this group, a more recent brand of hacker—known as a hacktivist—exists. As you may have surmised, a *hacktivist* is the result of crossing an activist with a hacker. Hacktivists engage in a form of cyber-terrorism known as *hacktivism* in their efforts to topple organizations with ideologies contrary to their own.

Hacktivism refers to the merging of political activism and computer hacking. The use of hacktivism has been noted in protest activities since the Electronic Disturbance Theater (EDT) launched a series of so-called "network direct actions" against the Mexican government in 1998. These actions primarily took the form of defacements of the Mexican government's Web sites and DOS attacks. The EDT sought to gain the public's attention regarding confrontations between the Mexican government and certain fringe groups, such as the Zapatista rebels, with the use of electronic actions against the Mexican, as well as the U.S., government.

Since then, the larger protest community has shown its computer skills in supporting protest events in general and network direct actions in particular, both of which have been steadily on the increase. Where protestors once organized rallies and handed out pamphlets, virtual sit-ins are now being staged and programmers enlisted to produce code that will attack certain Web sites.

Hacktivist activities may occur in connection with or directly following certain national and international events. The NIPC issued the following bulletin on September 14, 2001, three days after the attacks on New York's World Trade Center:

Increased Cyberawareness

The National Infrastructure Protection Center (NIPC) expects to see an upswing in incidents as a result of the tragic events of September 11, 2001. Increased hacking attacks are likely to have two motivations:

- Political hacktivism by self-described "patriot" hackers targeted at those perceived to be responsible for the terrorist attacks. NIPC has already received reports of individuals encouraging vigilante hacking activity.

- Virus propagation in which old viruses are renamed to appear related to recent events. One such incident has already been reported in which a new version of the life_stages.txt.shs virus was renamed wtc.txt.vbs to appear to be related to the World Trade Center.

The NIPC reiterates that the above conduct is illegal and punishable as a felony, with penalties extending to five years in prison. Those individuals who believe they are doing a service to this nation by engaging in acts of vigilantism should know that they are actually doing a disservice to the country.

To limit the potential damage from any cyberattacks, system administrators are encouraged to follow best practices to ensure the security of their networks. Some of the most basic measures are outlined below:

- Increase user awareness
- Update anti-virus software
- Stop hostile attachments at the e-mail server
- Utilize ingress and egress filtering (filtering of data coming onto and out of the network)
- Establish policy and procedures for responding and recovery

In conclusion, civil disobedience and activism has not changed a great deal since the days of the Vietnam War protests. What *has* changed is the type of medium used by dissenters. Back in the 1960s, protesters hoped to make enough of a racket that their particular cause would attract television reporters, who would then broadcast the event to the entire world. Nowadays, all it takes is a computer and a modem to become the focus of attention; *plus,* it can be done by anyone anonymously.

## Who Are Hacktivists?

Despite the fact that the media often portrays hackers as mysterious, malevolent intruders, various individuals and groups have candidly committed cyberattacks in the name of furthering a particular cause. Such attacks can take the form of a DOS attack on a Web site, wherein enough "participants" make that Web site inaccessible to normal traffic. Other attackers just want to circumvent government restrictions they see as inequitable. Nevertheless, all hacktivists try to combine their zeal with technology by using the power of the Internet to apply new forms of social dissent.

## Reverend Billy's Starbucks Invasion and the EDT

In May 2000, actor and activist Bill Talen, who goes by the moniker "Reverend Billy," called for thousands of Internet users to empower their personal computers for an assault on the Starbucks' Web site. From the hidden corners of the globe, they would converge on the company's Web site, overloading it in a classic distributed denial-of-service (DDoS) attack.

Reverend Billy seems to think that Starbucks' soft earth approach and tone masks its true corporate callousness. He hands out leaflets that say that Starbucks is screwing the planet, the farmers, the baristas, and New York's neighborhoods. Reverend Billy and his Church of Stop Shopping have been preaching the anticorporatism gospel to New Yorkers for the past several years. Followers of his cause are encouraged to visit `www.revbilly.com` and download a small malicious software program that will help carry out the attack against Starbucks. The software works only with Netscape 4.0 or higher Web browsers, perhaps as an additional protest against corporate giant Microsoft and their Internet Explorer Web browser. The offending software was designed by the Electronic Disturbance Theater hacktivist group.

The goal of the EDT, made up of cyberactivists and artists who combine their radical political views with software design and artistry (performance art and recombinant art), is to develop the theory and practice of *ECD (electronic civil disobedience).* Flood Net, a Uniform Resource Locator (URL)–based software (JavaScript), is a device produced by the EDT, used, as its name implies, to flood and block Web sites by repeatedly requesting a specific Web page on a server. EDT members stress that the software they use in their attacks is disruptive to Internet traffic, but that it does not wipe out data.

## Hacktivists and China — Hong Kong Blondes, LoU, and Yellow Pages

Several hacktivist movements have targeted the Chinese government. Whether these groups are real or fraudulent, the media attention they have received is noteworthy. One such group, which calls itself the Hong Kong Blondes and is supposedly made up of Chinese computer scientists, physicists, and human rights activists, seeks to topple the Chinese government with the Internet as their weapon. Several of their members are purportedly part of the Chinese government, some lost relatives in Tiananmen Square, and other associates are across the globe, including those in the U.S., Europe, and Canada. With human rights issues at the center of their grievances, they claim to have temporarily disabled a Chinese communications satellite and to have already hacked into every major Chinese government network. The Chinese government has never confirmed these claims.

Another hacktivist group, called the Legion of the Underground (LoU), is said to have been influenced by the Hong Kong Blondes. Based in the U.S., this band hacked into several Chinese sites to voice their objection to the manner in which the Chinese government penalizes those who commit computer crimes. After being denounced by several hacker groups, LoU suspended their Internet attack on China.

Another offshoot of the Hong Kong Blondes is known as the Yellow Pages, also supposedly comprised of members with superb hacking skills. The aim of this group is to oppose companies who do business with China (especially American corporations) by using network attacks. In particular, it wants to denounce investments made by western companies in China.

Shortly after a U.S. intelligence plane and a Chinese fighter plane collided in midair over the South China Sea, the Chinese were victimized by Internet protestors who "sided" with the U.S. The U.S. claimed its aircraft was flying over international waters, while China maintained that it has territorial rights over the western half of the sea (this is disputed by bordering nations).

Within hours of debuting its new Web site, China's human rights agency had the site invaded by a protestor. The protestor replaced the nation's proclamation of its human rights record with the following words: "China's people have no rights at all, never mind human rights. How can the United States trade millions and millions of dollars with them and give them most-favored trade status when they know what is happening?" The words "Boycott China" also appeared, as did obscenities and links to valid sites, such as that of Amnesty International. While such actions are condemned by "legitimate" old school hackers, and even by other protestors who are more diffident, there is no doubt that interest in and attention to the Chinese human rights cause was raised.

Another high-profile incident occurred during a NATO air campaign in May 1999 after the United States accidentally bombed the Chinese embassy in Belgrade, Yugoslavia. In retaliation, U.S. Web sites were defaced in the name of China, and massive e-mail campaigns were executed to gain sympathy and support for the Chinese cause. U.S. government Web sites were the primary targets. The U.S. Departments of Energy and the Interior and the National Park Service all suffered defacements of their Web pages. Even the White House Web site was taken down for three days after it was continually mail bombed.

## The Injustice Worm

Hacktivists sometimes resort to the use of malicious code to get their message across. In March 2001, for example, a worm called Injustice was released onto the Internet; it causes the victim's computer to send pro-Palestinian messages to 25 Israeli organizations and government agencies.

Anti-virus firms have indicated that Injustice is relatively benign because it does not damage users' machines and its outbreak has been contained. The main interest in the Injustice outbreak is in its use of malicious code to deliver a political message.

Like the Anna bug, Injustice is a Visual Basic Script (VBS) worm that uses Microsoft Outlook to replicate. The worm arrives in an e-mail message with the subject line "RE:Injustice" and an attachment, INJUSTICE.TXT.VBS. Opening the attachment causes a user's machine to become infected and sends the worm to 50 users in the victim's Outlook address book as well as 25 or so other e-mail addresses affiliated with Israel, including that of the Webmaster of the country's official Web site and 13 other government addresses. Next, the worm runs Internet Explorer and opens the URLs of six pro-Palestinian Web sites, each in a new window. It then displays a message criticizing the Israeli soldiers. The attachment works only on computers using Microsoft's Windows operating system. When opened, the virus presents the following message:

```
PLEASE ACCEPT MY APOLOGIES FOR DISTURBING YOU.
```

The message continues by describing the death of a 12-year-old Palestinian boy during a violent clash between Palestinian protestors and Israeli troops.

## The WANK Worm of '89

Hacktivism is not a new concept. One of the first hacktivist incidents dates back to October 1989, when the WANK (Worms Against Nuclear Killers) worm attacked SPAN (NASA's own wide area network). As a result of this attack, the following message was displayed on infected computers' login screens:

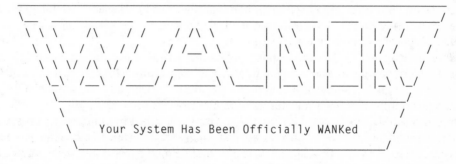

```
You talk of times of peace for all, and then prepare for war.
```

The WANK worm attacked only a small number of accounts on each computer in an attempt to avoid detection. When it found a privileged account, it would invade that system and then begin again, targeting other systems reachable from the new host. Within a few weeks, countermeasures were developed and installed to stop the WANK worm. The attackers responded with an improved version, called the OILZ worm. The OILZ worm repaired some of the problems associated with the WANK worm and added exploitation of other vulnerable points. The NASA WANK and OILZ worms caused a major loss of availability along two large government networks, resulting in significant expense and prompting investigations by the GAO (General Accounting Office) into network management and security.

# Cult of the Dead Cow

The Cult of the Dead Cow (cDc) is a group that has been hacking for nearly two decades. It embraces the right of Internet users the world over to have unfettered access to Web sites. cDc is especially displeased with China, Iran, and Cuba, and condemns those nations for not allowing their citizens to view sites that they consider unsuitable.

OXblood Ruffin, known as the foreign minister of cDc (and believed by many to have coined the term *hacktivism*), differentiates ordinary hacking from cracking. Ruffin believes hacking has been degraded to incorporate acts that would better fall under the term cracking. He regards crackers as those who invade a computer system with the *intent to wreak havoc* (through malicious, destructive actions), as opposed to hackers, who do not necessarily work against computer security. He also makes a distinction between hacktivism and cracktivism. "The former seeks to remedy the Internet of bad code, restrictions, lack of access, and so forth. The latter seeks to use the Net through various protest actions or as a publicity medium," according to Ruffin. "I very much disagree with [cracktivism] methodology." He further states, "Hacktivism is about using more eloquent arguments—whether of code or words—to construct a more perfect system. One does not become a hacktivist merely by inserting an 'h' in front of the word 'activist' or by looking backward to paradigms associated with industrial organization."

# Other Hacktivities

The government of India has experienced several Web site infiltrations by groups that support the Kashmiri people and separatist groups of Pakistan in their conflict with Indian military forces. The attacks cause photographs and comments protesting the Indian government to be displayed on the sites' opening screens. College students maintain that they have defaced an Indian nuclear weapons research center's Web site by having it display a mushroom cloud image. They were protesting India's performance of nuclear tests.

In 1997, five Portuguese hacktivists (supposedly named Kaotik Team) began a hacking campaign against Indonesian government and military Web pages, protesting the invasion of East Timor, a former Portuguese colony. Anti-Indonesia slogans and reworked photographs of the foreign minister and members of the armed forces were plastered on the Web pages.

Former Mexican President Ernesto Zedillo's Web site was hacked by protestors who support the fight of the indigenous people of Chiapas against the Mexican government. While the Flood Net attack was thwarted by the Pentagon, the protestors claimed success because it drew additional attention to their cause.

# The Pro-U.S. Hackers

Beginning on September 11, 2001, on bulletin boards, IRC and newsgroups, hackers and hacking groups fueled by U.S. patriotism called for attacks to be made on Pakistani and Afghani Web sites. They promoted active retaliation for the terrorist attacks on the World Trade Center and Pentagon. A Web site concerning Afghan dogs was reportedly the first victim of pro-U.S. cyberprotesters. On September 12, the Pakistani government's official Web site was defaced. Other Web sites that were defaced belonged to the Afghan News Network, Afghan Politics, Taleban.com, and Talibanonline.com. Spam (unwanted mass e-mail messages) was also used to encourage hackers to join together in attacking the Web sites of Islamic fundamentalists and those supporting terrorism. The spam recipients were encouraged to further disseminate the message to persuade others to join the fight in any way they could, either through active hacking or in support roles such as information gathering.

Denial-of-service (DoS) attacks were also used by pro-U.S. hackers. E-mail bombing is a popular form of DoS attack. Massive amounts of e-mail or Web traffic are directed against a specific site, overloading it and causing it to crash. On September 12th, the official Web site of the Presidential Palace of Afghanistan was affected by a DoS attack that rendered it inaccessible. Usenet newsgroups dealing with Islam have also experienced DoS attacks. The newsgroup `soc.religion.islam` was e-mail-bombed by hackers and crashed as a result.

The call for hackers to unite forces has succeeded. Palestinian and Afghani Web sites have been attacked by a pro-U.S. group called the Dispatchers. Led by a hacker named The Rev, who has defaced a number of Web sites, the Dispatchers have vowed to target those responsible for the September 11th terrorist attacks. Their first known defacement was carried out on September 16th, with the Iranian Ministry of the Interior as their target.

A prominent pro-U.S. hacking group known as YIHAT (Young Intelligent Hackers Against Terror) was formed in late September 2001 by the wealthy German hacker Kim Schmitz. YIHAT's goal is to gather information on terrorists and give that information to the proper U.S. authorities. YIHAT claims to have hacked into a Sudanese bank and uncovered records linking bank accounts to Al-Qa'ida and Osama bin Laden. YIHAT has created a Web site called `www.kill.net` for recruiting purposes. That site has suffered DoS attacks from opposing hackers and hacking groups supporting anti-U.S. sentiments, including Fluffi Bunni, a hacker well-known in the hacking community. This has forced YIHAT to move its activities "underground" and operate covertly in an effort to protect its members. As of this writing, they seem to have discontinued use of the `www.kill.net` Web site. Although YIHAT publicly denounces Web defacements, numerous defacements have been committed in its name that appear to be the work of either a fringe element of the group, an outsider wishing to be accepted into the group, or someone wanting to discredit it. YIHAT has announced plans to seek sponsorship from a nation that would look favorably on their hacking activities in the effort to fight terrorism. They are also preparing to open a hacking training center in order to better instruct their members. The group's expanding number has been listed at 800 registered members, although press accounts have placed the number at 25 to 35 active members.

While the damages of cyberterrorism have thus far been minimal, cyberprotestors and hacktivists will almost certainly target the Internet's infrastructure in the future, the goal being intentional destruction rather than public embarrassment or simple political statements. Pro-active network defense and security management are imperative to the prevention of more serious damage to infrastructure assets. International cooperation and private-public cooperation within the United States is necessary to ensure that critical IT infrastructure systems remain fully operational.

# The USA Patriot Act of 2001

In 1986, Congress passed the Electronic Communications Privacy Act (ECPA), which outlawed the unauthorized interception of digital communications. This act was soon followed by the Federal Computer Fraud and Abuse Act (CFAA). Prior to the CFAA, it was considered a misdemeanor offense to traffic in computer passwords from governmental computers "knowingly and with intent" when it "affects interstate or foreign commerce." Under the CFAA, accessing federal computer systems without authorization and with the intent to commit fraudulent theft or "malicious damage" became a felony offense. Penalties ranged from a prison term of five years for a first offense to ten years for a second.

Robert Morris and Kevin Mitnick were participants in two celebrated cases involving the Federal Computer Fraud and Abuse Act. Unfortunately, Morris miscalculated how rapidly his worm would replicate. He was the first person to be prosecuted under this act and was convicted of violating the CFAA. He received a fine of $10,050 and a sentence of three years probation that included 400 hours of community service. Kevin Mitnick, one of the most infamous hackers of the twentieth century, was arrested in 1995 for computer fraud and intercepting communications. Kevin, who was also convicted under the CFAA, was sentenced to 46 months in a federal prison.

## Enacting the USA Patriot Act

As part of the rush to protect America from acts of terror following September 11, 2001, the United States government enacted new legislation giving the government additional tools to help combat terrorist acts. On October 26, 2001, President Bush signed the "Uniting and Strengthening America by Providing Appropriate Tools Required to Intercept and Obstruct Terrorism Act of 2001" (known as USAPA and also as the USA Patriot Act) into law. This bill, 342 pages long, makes changes to over 15 different statutes already in existence. According to the bill's stated intent, the USAPA is designed "to deter and punish terrorist acts in the United States and around the world, to enhance law enforcement investigative tools, and for other purposes."

This innovative bill is not entirely intended to address terrorism. It may also be used for investigative purposes in nonviolent domestic computer crimes, not only for federal law enforcement officials but also for local system administrators. With this law, the United States has given sweeping new powers to both domestic law enforcement and international intelligence agencies, and has eliminated the checks and balances that previously gave courts the opportunity to ensure that these powers were not abused. This aspect of USAPA has resulted in some controversy.

## USAPA's Effect on Information Technology

Superficially, the greater part of USAPA amends many of the preexisting laws regarding surveillance, money laundering, immigration, victim compensation, and intelligence gathering and sharing. The core of this act grants additional powers to law enforcement and intelligence agencies, both domestic and international, while removing numerous obstacles that formerly plagued them. Many of USAPA's provisions are centered on Internet Service Providers. In a statement before the House Judiciary Committee's Subcommittee on Crime on February 12, 2002, the president of the United States Internet Service Providers Association, Clint N. Smith, said the following regarding USAPA:

> First, the USA Patriot Act authorized an ISP to disclose customer records or communications if the ISP *reasonably* believes there is an *immediate* risk of death or personal injury, such as with an e-mail bomb threat. This was a positive change for both law enforcement and ISPs. But it put ISPs in the odd position of having to determine whether the danger was "immediate," and the "reasonable" belief standard may require an ISP to research whether an emergency situation is a bona fide emergency prior to alerting law enforcement. HR 3482 removes the requirement that the danger be

"immediate" and allows ISPs to act on a "good faith" belief rather than the higher standard of a "reasonable" belief. These changes will encourage ISPs to promptly report threats of death or personal injury to law enforcement.

The USA Patriot Act expanded law enforcement investigative powers to fight terrorism but did not explicitly grant ISPs immunity from liability in all cases for their role in this fight. HR 3482 clarifies that ISPs are immune from liability for acting in good faith (1) when they turn over information to law enforcement in emergency situations and (2) when they invite law enforcement to monitor the communications of a computer trespasser. Equivalent statutory immunity applies in other contexts involving ISP involvement in electronic surveillance conducted under statutory authorization. Making such immunity explicit will remove an ambiguity that might otherwise reduce cooperation between ISPs and law enforcement.

Among USAPA's provisions is a new definition of terrorism, which now includes computer hacking. Crimes now covered under the new law include unleashing malware that can destroy critical infrastructure systems, hacking into a government system, and damaging Internet-connected computers. The act, created in the wake of the September 11th tragedies, also defines cyberterrorism to include computer crimes that cause at least $5,000 in damage or destroy medical equipment.

In addition, as a result of USAPA, biometrics will be increasingly applied in the identification of visa holders who try to enter the United States. More federal agents will be trained in new, innovative computer forensics labs used to seize and intercept evidence related to cyberterrorism.

The most controversial provisions of USAPA deal with surveillance. Civil liberties activists were among the first to question the broader search and seizure powers permitted by the USA Patriot Act, believing it to be more of an FBI "wish list" than a legitimate means of putting an end to terrorism. In certain circumstances, local authorities can now search homes and offices without being required to notify the subject of the inquiry or obtain a court order.

USAPA also permits the FBI to freely employ the DCS 1000 wiretap technology, formerly called Carnivore, to capture Web browsing habits and the e-mail correspondence of suspected criminals without a judge's order. To assuage the fears of privacy activists, Congress implemented a December 2005 expiration date for certain USAPA provisions, but reserved the right to renew that date if warranted by future circumstances.

# Ethical Issues Surrounding Cyberterrorism

The ethical issues concerning cyberterrorism are diverse. A large assortment of ethical transgressions can be carried out through the use of a computer. When financial institutions fall victim to extortion, they not only suffer losses, but inadvertently cause their customers to be victimized as well. Those institutions are challenged with a moral obligation to instill a sense of security in their victimized clientele and their potential future clients. The illegal altering medical records is unethical, as it can quickly and easily cause harm to another. Spreading misinformation is unethical in its lack of regard for the truth, and also because it can negatively impact the safety of those who believe the information. Altering, destroying, or stealing others' data is a violation of privacy. The ordinary hacker is guilty of a lack of regard for other people's privacy. Hacking-for-hire is illicit because hackers openly sell their services to break into others' systems.

Cyberterrorists are often interested in gaining publicity in any possible way. For example, information warfare techniques such as Trojan horse viruses and network worms not only cause damage to computing resources, they also help the virus designer "show off." This is a serious ethical issue because so many people are affected. For one, the viruses can consume system resources until networks become useless, costing companies time and money. Also, depending on the type of work performed on the affected computers, the damage to the beneficiaries of that work could be lethal. Even if a virus designer never meant to harm anyone, the virus may produce unpredictable effects with, ultimately, disastrous results.

# Information Warfare

According to the U.S. Department of Defense, *information warfare* is defined as, "Actions taken to achieve information superiority in support of national military strategy by affecting adversary information and information systems while leveraging and defending our information and systems."

The competition for information is as old as human conflict. It is virtually a defining characteristic of humanity. Nations, corporations, and individuals each seek to increase and protect their own store of information and simultaneously try to limit, penetrate, and obtain their adversary's. Since around 1970, extraordinary improvements in the technical means of collecting, storing, analyzing, and transmitting information have been made. In the past, a spy had to physically tap phone lines and use miniature cameras and microphones to obtain desired information about a person. While today's spy can still employ these utilities (now more miniaturized and easier to use than ever), most of the information he needs is available in existing databases. Today's information warrior doesn't have to survey someone for months; he can simply get the desired information with the help of a computer over the telephone line.

Information warfare, in a wider sense, is used daily between individuals and organizations. Emergency report teams poised to take countermeasures are notified every day about computer system penetrations. Often, attackers argue that they are not committing a crime, but rather improving the security of a system by exposing its weaknesses.

Viruses are well-known in every computer-based environment, so it is not astonishing that this type of computer program is used in the information warfare arena. One can easily envision the CIA or any covert agency inserting malicious code into the switching networks of the enemy's telephone system. As today's telephone systems are switched by computers, they can be shut down (or at least experience massive failures) by a virus with the same ease used to shut down an ordinary computer.

The U.S. and other high-tech societies are especially vulnerable to information warfare attacks. They rely heavily on today's electronic communication and data exchange. An offender can attack these information backbones with low financial and equipment investments (low, that is, in comparison to their resultant damage).

Terrorism does not always aim to destroy the enemy's armed might, but it always aims to undermine his will to fight. In an effort to bring about societal change, the terrorist seeks to disrupt the daily life of his target population by striking at the most vulnerable segments of its society. Such vulnerable areas include transportation networks and public events, which ensure broad media coverage. By hitting the citizen when he feels himself the safest, the terrorist causes the greatest confusion and loss of morale.

Today, with nearly every aspect of our lives dependent on information networks, terrorists can take advantage of a whole new field of action. While the technology needed to operate and protect these networks is costly, the means required to attack them are comparatively cheap. In the simplest case, one needs only a computer, a modem, and a willing hacker.

# Cyberterrorism Defense

The first line of defense against cyberterrorism is a solid foundation of awareness. If a technological environment is to be adequately protected, a solid security foundation must begin with heightened organizational awareness, active vulnerability management, and comprehensive disaster recovery planning. Guarding against cyberterrorism means adhering to the following fundamental security guidelines:

✓ Protect those aspects considered the most critical to operations (whether individual, business, or organizational) and continuity.

✓ Notify all users on the network never to open any suspicious e-mail attachments.

✓ Force anti-virus updates throughout the network and direct all users to update their anti-virus software before conducting any business on their computers.

✓ Enforce strict rules for all inbound Internet traffic.

✓ Organize a response plan and a response team.

✓ Remember that ports are critical in any defensive strategy and must be carefully monitored. Unused ports should be closed or blocked by a firewall.

✓ Install and maintain an intrusion detection system.

✓ Establish adequate security and disaster-recovery network procedures.

✓ Consider purchasing insurance specifically designed to cover Internet- and/or network-related losses.

# Identity Theft — The Crime of the New Millennium

The 1990s spawned a new variety of criminal, called the *identity thief,* whose stock in trade lies in everyday business transactions. Each transaction requires people to share personal information: bank and credit card account numbers, annual income, Social Security numbers (SSNs), and name, address, and phone numbers. An identity thief co-opts some piece of personal information and appropriates it without the true owner's knowledge to commit a theft or fraudulent act. An all-too-common example is when an identity thief uses personal information to open (and use) a credit card account in someone else's name.

Because of the increased use of personal computers for conducting all manner of business transactions, identity theft occurs more frequently over the Internet. Online banking has become an accepted practice, and individuals and businesses are using financial management software programs such as Quicken to handle recordkeeping, accounting, and taxes. When malevolent hackers are permitted to access computers containing this type of information, they seize the opportunity to pilfer it. The most common motivations for identity theft are:

✓ Taking over financial accounts

✓ Opening new bank accounts

✓ Applying for loans

✓ Applying for credit cards

✓ Applying for Social Security and other benefits

✓ Purchasing property

✓ Renting property

✓ Establishing services (phone, utilities, and so on)

While the Internet simplifies the process of applying for credit cards, managing bank accounts, and making sales and purchases, it also offers thieves a cloak of invisibility. Criminals need not be physically present to make fraudulent purchases or apply for credit online. As the Internet makes it easier for malicious hackers and crackers to infiltrate and appropriate, it also makes them more difficult for law enforcement to locate.

In a March 2001 U.S. Department of Justice Bulletin titled *Identity Theft: The Crime of the New Millennium,* Assistant United States Attorney for the District of Oregon, Sean B. Hoar, defines identity theft in the following way:

> Identity theft has been referred to by some as the crime of the new millennium. It can be accomplished anonymously, easily, with a variety of means, and the impact upon the victim can be devastating. Identity theft is simply the theft of identity information such as a name, date of birth, Social Security number (SSN), or a credit card number. The mundane activities of a typical consumer during the course of a regular day may provide tremendous opportunities for an identity thief: purchasing gasoline, meals, clothes, or tickets to an athletic event; renting a car, video, or home improvement tools; purchasing gifts or trading stock online; receiving mail; or taking out the garbage or recycling. Any activity in which identity information is shared or made available to others creates an opportunity for identity theft.
>
> It is estimated that identity theft has become the fastest-growing financial crime in America and perhaps the fastest-growing crime of any kind in our society. (*Identity Theft: Is There Another You?: Joint hearing before the House Subcomms. on Telecommunications, Trade and Consumer Protection, and on Finance and Hazardous Materials, of the Comm. on Commerce,* 106th Cong. 16 (1999) (testimony of Rep. John B. Shadegg)). The illegal use of identity information has increased exponentially in recent years. In fiscal year 1999 alone, the Social Security Administration (SSA) Office of Inspector General (OIG) Fraud Hotline received approximately 62,000 allegations involving SSN misuse. The widespread use of SSNs as identifiers has reduced their security and increased the likelihood that they

will be the object of identity theft. The expansion and popularity of the Internet to effect commercial transactions has increased the opportunities to commit crimes involving identity theft. The expansion and popularity of the Internet to post official information for the benefit of citizens and customers has also increased opportunities to obtain SSNs for illegal purposes.

On May 31, 1998, in support of the Identity Theft and Assumption Deterrence Act, the General Accounting Office (GAO) released a briefing report on issues relating to identity fraud entitled "Identity Fraud: Information on Prevalence, Cost, and Internet Impact is Limited". The report found that methods used to obtain identity information ranged from basic street theft to sophisticated, organized crime schemes involving the use of computerized databases or the bribing of employees with access to personal information on customer or personnel records. The report also found the following: In 1995, 93 percent of arrests made by the U.S. Secret Service Financial Crimes Division involved identity theft. In 1996 and 1997, 94 percent of financial crimes arrests involved identity theft. The Secret Service stated that actual losses to individuals and financial institutions which the Secret Service had tracked involving identity fraud totaled $442 million in fiscal year 1995, $450 million in fiscal year 1996, and $745 million in fiscal year 1997. The SSA OIG stated that SSN misuse in connection with program fraud increased from 305 in fiscal year 1996 to 1,153 in fiscal year 1997. Postal Inspection investigations showed that identity fraud was perpetrated by organized crime syndicates, especially to support drug trafficking, and had a nationwide scope. Trans Union Corporation, one of the three major national credit bureaus, stated that two-thirds of its consumer inquiries to its fraud victim department involved identity fraud. Such inquiries had increased from an average of less than 3,000 a month in 1992 to over 43,000 a month in 1997. VISA U.S.A., Inc., and MasterCard International, Inc., both stated that overall fraud losses from their member banks were in the hundreds of millions of dollars annually. MasterCard stated that dollar losses relating to identity fraud represented about 96 percent of its member banks' overall fraud losses of $407 million in 1997.

Victims of identity theft often do not realize they have become victims until they attempt to obtain financing on a home or a vehicle. Only then, when the lender tells them that their credit history makes them ineligible for a loan, do they realize something is terribly wrong. When they review their credit report, they first become aware of credit cards for which they have never applied, bills long overdue, unfamiliar billing addresses, and inquiries from unfamiliar creditors. Even if they are able to identify the culprit, it may take months or years, tremendous emotional anguish, many lost financial opportunities, and large legal fees, to clear up their credit history.

Many who conduct personal business over the Internet feel confident that it is a safe practice. The bottom line is that as long as a computer is connected to the Internet, it should *not* be considered safe unless it uses firewall and up-to-date anti-virus software protection.

# Defending against Identity Theft on the Internet

Firewalls and anti-virus software are an organization's first line of defense regarding identity theft from the Internet. Firewalls hide the organization's network computers from Internet marauders, while anti-virus software helps prevent attacks from "password-stealing" Trojans. Organizations may even use firewalls in multiple layers so that it is nearly impossible to access any personal information. Every person or group with high-speed Internet access should absolutely have a firewall and anti-virus software. Without a firewall, hackers can gain easy entry into a system. Once inside, they are free to steal personal information (for instance, by accessing a tax program account like Turbo Tax or Quicken to get a bank password or account number).

Another danger not considered by most users is that hackers can use someone else's computer as a staging area to commit crimes. If such a situation occurs, the victimized computer's owner may find himself involved in a criminal investigation at some point (which may become costly, inconvenient, and damaging to his reputation).

## What to Do and Where to Turn

Victims of identity theft or fraud must act immediately to minimize the damage to personal correspondence, funds, and financial accounts, as well as to their reputation. The U.S. Federal Trade Commission (`www.ftc.gov`) recommends that the following actions be taken immediately if you learn (or even suspect) that identity theft has occurred:

✓ Contact the fraud departments of each of the three major credit bureaus and report that your identity has been stolen. Ask that a "fraud alert" be placed on your file and that no new credit be granted without your approval. Contact information for the three major credit bureaus is as follows:

- Equifax, Inc., P.O. Box 740123, Atlanta, GA 30374-0123; `www.econsumer.equifax.com`

- Experian Information Solutions, Inc., 701 Experian Parkway, Allen, TX 75013; `www.experian.com/`

- Trans Union LLC, P.O. Box 97328, Jackson, MS 39288-7328; `www.transunion.com/`

✓ For any accounts that have been fraudulently accessed or opened, contact the security departments of the appropriate creditors or financial institutions. Close these accounts. Put passwords (not your mother's maiden name) on any new accounts you open.

✓ File a report with your local police or the police where the identity theft took place. Get a copy of the report in case banks, credit card companies, or others need proof of the crime at a later time.

The FTC established an Identity Theft Toll-Free Hotline at 1-877-IDTHEFT (438-4338) and the ID Theft Web site (`http://consumer.gov.ftc.gov/idtheft`) to give victims of identity theft a central location within the federal government to report their cases and receive helpful information.

# Summary

As a result of the September 11th, 2001 terrorist attacks on the United States, government, corporate, and private sectors are more concerned with security than ever before. While the U.S. and its allies have markedly increased their security measures both domestically and abroad, the nearly universal reliance on computers and the Internet has opened the door to new threats of cyberterrorism, hacktivist attacks, and identity theft. Fortunately, the use of firewalls, intrusion detection systems, and anti-virus software can help reduce these threats.

Key points covered in this chapter include:

- ✓ What cyberterrorism and hacktivism are and what costs they impose on society
- ✓ Who cyberterrorists and hacktivists are and what type of threats they pose
- ✓ The USA Patriot Act of 2001 and its dramatic effects on information technology
- ✓ Computer sabotage and its relationship to both cyberterrorism and hacktivism
- ✓ Information warfare and the U.S. government plans for cyberdefense
- ✓ Malicious code as it relates to cyberterrorism and hacktivism
- ✓ The security measures effective against threats posed by cyberterrorism
- ✓ How the Internet has made identity theft the crime of the new millennium, and what to do and where to turn if you become a victim of this crime

# Chapter 12

# Cyberforensics and the Future of Virus Warfare

## In This Chapter

✓ Exploring PDA viruses

✓ Considering wireless protection

✓ Defining blended threats and multiplatform viruses

✓ Examining digital warfare and future viruses

✓ Utilizing cyberforensics

WITH SOCIETY'S EVER-INCREASING reliance on computers, experts now face a number of new challenges related to the computer security landscape. Unlawful disclosures of information, wide-scale computer break-ins, and the exponential growth in the number of computer viruses being written, unleashed, and discovered are all indicative of the increasing threats to effective use of computing resources. Untold numbers of computer crimes go undetected, and still others go unreported — sometimes because the victim fears that publicity about their losses may reduce the amount of consumer confidence in their business practices. The various threats to computer security include:

✓ Fraud

✓ Theft

✓ Espionage (economic and international)

✓ Sabotage

✓ Cyberterrorism

✓ Computer viruses

✓ Cybervandalism

Additionally, not all cybercriminal activities are directed at government, commerce, and other organizations. Violations of personal privacy, harassment, and cyberstalking threaten individual computer users, as well.

# Personal Digital Assistant Viruses

Historically, malicious code has been one of the biggest threats to corporate networks. Viruses have evolved from simple "tomfoolery" to mechanisms capable of international devastation. When computer sales skyrocketed in the early 1980s, the public emphasized the benefits that computers could bring to businesses and individuals. The threat of viruses wiping out mission-critical data and causing trillions of dollars in damage was rarely mentioned. Today, the threat posed by malicious code affects every aspect of Information Technology (IT) planning and operations.

On the whole, a good number of IT managers and system administrators have understood and reacted to the ongoing threats presented from viruses by implementing network anti-virus policies and procedures. However, vendors of nearly all major anti-virus software products must first obtain a copy of the virus, examine its signature, and then distribute a cure via the Internet. The downside to this process is that the end user must regularly update the program so that it continues to be effective.

Undeniably, the growth of the Internet has directly contributed to a rise in the speed at which malicious code traverses the globe and spawns variants. These variants, along with the originals, are often inserted into e-mail messages, downloads, and other popular browser-based applications. Furthermore, the applications and services that can be targeted by viruses are now expanding to include mobile devices such as cellular telephones, personal digital assistant (PDA) devices, and computer appliances, which are increasingly interfacing with business and government computer networks. This extension of organizational networks into novel areas like wireless and PDAs challenges system administrators to adapt to increasingly sophisticated anti-virus deployments.

Personal digital assistants seem to be everywhere these days. They are made by different manufacturers, and are thus available in a variety of styles. Typically, PDAs are some form of small, hand-held device that combines computing functions with telephone/fax and networking features. Even cellular phone companies have joined the fray by combining hand-held computer technology with their existing product lines (another reason for the recent dramatic rise in cellular phone use).

PDAs have become an invaluable tool for remotely getting e-mail, maintaining calendars, to-do lists, and address books, and taking notes. They have blurred the partition between work and personal information because people use them to do their jobs as well as to record an abundance of personal information. They often contain confidential data—identification information such as birthdays, personal preferences, Internet addresses, and even passwords.

A number of security issues and areas of vulnerability are found in the typical PDA system. Despite their tremendous popularity, PDA devices currently have very few built-in security features. Any pre-programmed security features consist of little more than password-based authentication. To make matters worse, programs are publicly available that allow users to bypass the built-in security system.

Many organizations and individuals have neglected to address the security threat of virus attacks on personal digital assistants. As mobile devices become an integral part of everyday life in the twenty-first century, however, the threat of attacks on these devices will grow. Whether contracted through wireless e-mail messages and news services, or simply through synchronization with another computer, dangerous viruses can invade PDAs and worm their way into an individual's or organization's computer and network.

# Exploring PDA Vulnerabilities

A recent omen of future security problems for PDAs was the appearance in August 2000 of the "Liberty Crack" program, the first Trojan horse targeted specifically at PDAs. Liberty Crack Trojan, widely available for download, was written by a software programmer and disguised as a legitimate program. In this instance, the Trojan appeared to be a free version of Liberty GameBoy emulation software for the Palm Pilot PDA. Once Liberty Crack is executed, it can delete all of the applications on the handheld device. Fortunately, most PDAs automatically back themselves up when they are synchronized with a computer. Thus, if the PDA shows symptoms of malicious code infection, it can simply upload the data from the computer back onto the handheld.

PalmOS/Vapor.741 was the second Trojan to hit the Palm OS. When this Trojan is first run, all third-party application icons disappear as if deleted. The files still exist, yet their icons are missing from the available applications icons. Recovery requires a hard reset (rebooting the device) and hot-sync (resynchronization).

Although neither of these Trojan attacks caused widespread damage, they serve as a wake-up call to PDA users who have previously paid no attention to security. These breaches also indicate that PDAs have garnered the attention of virus writers, who may well view the handheld operating system as a new challenge. It is safe to presume that new viruses, Trojan horses, and worms are currently being created and will be unleashed on the handheld community in the near future.

Users could also unintentionally, yet easily, download a virus through infected Word or Excel files. They might download infected files *to* their PDA *from* their home PC, and then introduce the virus into their corporate network when they synchronize the device with their computer at work. There are four common methods of transmission by which a virus can infect a PDA:

✓ Through infected e-mail messaging when using a PDA over a wired or wireless Internet connection

✓ When synchronizing with an infected computer

✓ Through an infected file that is transferred (beamed) from another PDA via a built-in infrared (IR) port

✓ By downloading infected files from the Internet

One example that demonstrates the type of damage a sophisticated virus might inflict on a wireless network occurred recently in Japan. In August 2000, a virus spread to some 100,000 mobile cell phones, which then began dialing Japan's 110 emergency network (equivalent to North America's 9-1-1 system). People had used their cell phones to surf a particular Web site containing a questionnaire on personal relationships, and when they did so, they unsuspectingly downloaded a Trojan horse program. The Trojan lay dormant on the infected phones until a predetermined time.

The potential for in-the-wild viruses, Trojans, and worms to be directed specifically at PDAs is very real; however, the spread of such viruses will not be nearly as fast as conventional computer-based viruses. The number of PDA users is significantly lower than the number of desktop computer users. PDA users still download applications and data from a few sources, rather than exchanging information with other PDA users. Once PDA-to-PDA or PDA networking is commonplace, you will more than likely see a significant rise in the spread of PDA viruses.

# Malicious Code Software Solutions

Most major anti-virus vendors offer products specifically designed for PDAs. McAfee (www.mcafee.com), for example, offers a product called McAfee VirusScan Handheld that is installed on a user's desktop computer at work and also on their PDA device. It scans all files for viruses as the files are transferred to and from the desktop computer. The software checks for the same types of viruses that users can check for using a desktop version of this product. McAfee's VirusScan Handheld product can be downloaded to a laptop or desktop computer from the Internet. It then performs a self-installation the next time the PDA and the computer are synchronized. The software provides for automatic updates via the Internet. It is available for each of the four major device platforms:

- ✓ Palm Inc.'s Palm OS

- ✓ Microsoft Corp.'s Pocket PC and Windows CE

- ✓ Symbian Ltd.'s EPOC

Another anti-virus vendor called Symantec (www.symantec.com) offers a similar product for PDAs—Symantec AntiVirus for Palm OS. This software resides directly on the PDA device and protects users from viruses entering from synchronization, infrared beaming, and network access.

In addition to the installation of anti-virus software, the following steps should be observed in order to broaden overall wireless security, as outlined by the U.S. Government's Center for Information Technology, National Institutes for Health:

- ✓ **Guard against theft**—Think of portable devices as cash; don't tempt people. Easily stolen and concealed, these items make prime targets. When traveling, consider storing these devices where a thief would not look (in a sports bag, for example, rather than a computer bag).

- ✓ **Keep the data safe**—Your first defense is a strong password. If the device came with a default password, change it immediately. Never store passwords, especially on a PDA. Sensitive information should be encrypted when stored. If using a laptop, sensitive data should never be saved on the hard drive. It is a good practice to store data disks apart from the laptop.

  Because viruses can be received or given each time you make a connection to the network, or when you transfer data through an infrared port, make sure that anti-virus software is up-to-date, and be careful with whom data is exchanged. As with desktop computers, beware of downloading freeware or shareware software from untrusted sources, since they may contain viruses or other malicious code.

  Check out the security features on your portable device and enable them (using "private" or "hide" features). Third-party vendors have already developed PDA biometric safeguards, like fingerprint readers, and a variety of encryption password technologies exist, as well. However, while the information is encrypted or marked "private" on the handheld, it may not be encrypted on the desktop unless additional software is used. Opening the database for the address book, memo pad, or other files in the PDA directory with Notepad can allow a person to display and copy contents of these files. This is of particular concern if the PDA is lost, or if it is synchronized to a laptop that is stolen or lost. Including some contact information at the login prompt enables an honest person to return a lost device to its owner.

✓ **Be careful when synchronizing PDAs with PCs** — It is unwise to leave a PDA in its cradle connected to a desktop computer. Someone could enter and replace the PDA with their own. They could start sending inappropriate e-mail (with you as the sender), and they could download information from your computer. Using a screen saver password on the desktop computer is advised. If the PDA is synchronized with a home computer, be careful that sensitive information is not being transferred between the two.

✓ **Backup important information** — Should a portable device be lost, a recent backup of the information will help restore files. Note, however, that a backup of a device may not always back up third-party applications installed on the PDA. Consider using products such as BackupBuddy (from Bluenomad) or backing up the PDA to a secure digital/-multimedia card, compact flash or memory stick device, available for most recent hardware releases from virtually all PDA manufacturers.

In summary, PDA security is an important issue. PDAs are as much of a security risk, if not more so, than desktop computers. Consequently, all PDA users should take it upon themselves to implement appropriate security measures and to follow any and all applicable security policies.

# Wireless LANs

The deployment of wireless networking systems is proceeding rapidly. Technological advancements and reductions in the cost of ownership have converged so that wireless systems are becoming a measurable part of the national information infrastructure. The growth of booked and projected sales indicates that wireless networking qualifies as a technology megatrend. Along with their convenience and popularity, however, wireless systems provide new and attractive opportunities for those seeking to exploit them maliciously. "Raising the security bar" by reducing wireless network vulnerabilities, therefore, becomes an important consideration for any organization that adopts wireless systems.

The wireless LAN is a new way to extend the reach of local area networks (LANs). Instead of plugging into a LAN wall outlet, the connection is made wirelessly to a LAN access point. All that is needed is a wireless LAN card for the user and an access point connected to the wireless LAN. This enables truly wireless access to the LAN and the Internet. Wireless LAN users enjoy the freedom of being automatically connected to the LAN and of mobile computing without being tethered to wires and cables. Wireless LAN is speedy as well as convenient: no more cables or searching for LAN outlets.

# Benefits of Wireless LANs

The widespread reliance on networking in business and the impressive growth of the Internet and online services are powerful evidence to the benefits of shared data and shared resources. With wireless LANs, users can access shared information without looking for a place to plug in, and network managers can set up or augment networks without installing or relocating wires. Wireless LANs offer the following productivity, convenience, and cost advantages over traditional wired networks:

✓ **Mobility** — Wireless LAN systems provide users with access to real-time information anywhere in their organization. This mobility supports productivity and service opportunities not possible with wired networks.

✓ **Speed and simplicity** — Installing a wireless LAN system can be quick and uncomplicated and eliminates the need to pull cable through walls and ceilings.

✓ **Flexibility** — Wireless technology allows the network to travel where wired networks cannot.

✓ **Scalability** — Wireless LAN systems can be configured in a variety of layouts to meet the needs of an organization's specific applications and installations. Configurations are changed easily and range from peer-to-peer networks suitable for a small number of users to full infrastructure networks serving thousands of users that enable roaming over a broad area.

In 1999, the Institute of Electrical and Electronics Engineers (IEEE) approved a specification for wireless LANs called 802.11b. An 802.11b wireless LAN (WLAN) works by using Radio Frequency (RF) to transmit and receive data through the air without the need for cables. It passes through walls and ceilings. Building on a previous wireless standard called 802.11, this new extension defines the standard for wireless LAN products that operate at speeds of 11 Mbps. This speed is necessary to make wireless LAN technology practical for use in larger organizations.

An independent organization called the Wireless Ethernet Compatibility Alliance (WECA) (www.wi-fi.com) ensures that wireless LAN products from different vendors are interoperable using the 802.11b standard. WECA brands 802.11b–compliant products as "Wi-Fi", with dozens of vendors promoting Wi-Fi products. As a result, organizations of every size and type are either considering or deploying wireless LANs. Other wireless standards, such as 802.11a and the newer 802.11g, offer LAN speeds greater than 802.11b but have not yet been widely adopted because the hardware they require is more expensive.

Wireless LANs typically enhance rather than replace wired LAN networks. The following list describes some of the many advantages made possible through the flexibility of wireless LANs:

✓ Consulting or small workgroups can increase productivity via quick network setup.

✓ Network managers can minimize the overhead caused by moves or extensions to networks.

✓ Executives can make quicker decisions because they have real-time information at their fingertips.

✓ Training sites at corporations and students at universities now use wireless connectivity to ease access to information.

✓ Warehouse workers use wireless LANs to exchange information with central databases, increasing their productivity.

✓ Branch office workers can minimize setup requirements by installing preconfigured wireless LANs that require little support.

# Bluetooth

The increased use of wireless devices brought about the development of a tool that could link those devices together. In May 1998, telecommunications giants including Ericsson, IBM, Intel, Nokia, and Toshiba formed a group called the Bluetooth Special Interest Group, or Bluetooth SIG. As the developer of new emerging technology for wireless communications, Bluetooth SIG now comprises almost all of the largest companies in the telecommunications industry, including Microsoft and Motorola.

Bluetooth (named after King Harold Bluetooth of 10th century Denmark) provides a radio link between wireless devices. It is fundamentally a radio transceiver that operates over a spread-spectrum. The inexpensive Bluetooth offers a short-range radio link between devices such as mobile phones, PDAs, laptops, fax machines, network access points, and other devices and peripherals. Bluetooth's appeal stems from its ability to connect virtually any device. It is used most frequently to link mobile phones to laptops and PDAs. Networks can be created as the need arises and without the use of cables. Bluetooth provides a standard way to link devices all over the world. Bluetooth alters its frequency for every data packet 1,600 times every second. Those frequency changes, coupled with Bluetooth's short-range limit of a few feet (due to its low power signals), enable it to make its connections without interfering with other Bluetooth-connected devices.

The low power signals used by Bluetooth are in the same unlicensed radio spectrum (2.40–2.48 gigahertz) as microwave ovens and some security tags used by department stores. In addition to certain problems caused by this signal interference, Bluetooth's ability to interoperate amongst a number of devices has been questioned. Bluetooth claims that "up to seven simultaneous connections can [be] established and maintained."

When introduced, the wireless Bluetooth suffered some of the same security problems evidenced in its wired network counterparts. Questions of password confidentiality and the preservation of data privacy arose due to issues regarding the manner in which connections were established amongst the wireless devices. This thwarted the widespread application and use of Bluetooth. Bluetooth was, however, able to revamp their product (known as Bluetooth 1.1) by revising its authentication synchronization process. It continues to be the predominant technology for short-range wireless intercommunication.

# Wireless LAN Security Issues

Traditionally, networked devices had to be physically connected to a network before its resources could be accessed. That allowed organizations to physically restrict those who had access to the network. This level of restriction is not the case with wireless networking. Due to the open nature of a wireless network and the relative anonymity of wireless connections, wireless networks are becoming a popular backdoor into networks. When the door is left open, malicious hackers are free to plant viruses that can easily spread to the organization's entire network when an infected computer connects to the LAN.

Viruses that attack wireless devices and LANs are an emerging reality in the future of virus warfare. Like their corded cousins, wireless viruses can erase data or damage devices such as mobile phones, PDAs, and laptops hooked up to wireless LANs. Currently, wireless viruses are not exceedingly widespread because such a large number of different wireless device types exist. In the future, however, the number of viruses and the rates of infection will undoubtedly increase due to widespread adaptation of cross-platform operating systems like Java.

Because wireless technologies are in a nascent stage of development, users must be aware of some of the *other* security risks concerning wireless networks. In October 2001, the NIPC released the following information in their 09-01 *Highlights* bulletin regarding the dangers of 802.11b:

Wireless Networking: Security Concerns

*Wireless networking offers great convenience for mobile users, although the technology's immaturity has led to serious security concerns that must be addressed.*

Numerous corporations around the country, including operators of critical infrastructures, are implementing wireless networks in an effort to extend the benefits of their enterprise computer networks to an increasingly mobile workforce. However, researchers and attackers alike have found several security-related design flaws in protocols that serve as the basis for most wireless networks.

Drive-by Surfing

The media, for example, has reported instances of external computer users being able to access wireless networks, in a phenomenon that has been dubbed "drive-by surfing." The following reports graphically illustrate the relative ease in which such access can be achieved:

- A computer consultant in the Silicon Valley reported that he was able to map several computer networks merely by driving down the street with a wireless-enabled laptop.

- One individual stated that while sitting in a cab in New York, he was able to browse a portion of the network of a nearby financial institution through his laptop.

- One large technology-based company found that unauthorized wireless access points within its facilities could be accessed from public roads running near its headquarters.

As with the appearance of any new technology, wireless network access will require close monitoring until its security features mature. When one combines the immaturity of wireless security features, a lack of understanding and experience regarding the proper configuration and management of wireless networks, and the readily available attack tools now available over the Internet, the growing concerns surrounding current implementations of wireless networking become self-evident.

At the present time, critical infrastructure operators should consider enhancing their security posture with regard to wireless networking by taking steps such as the following:

- Developing or updating enterprise-wide wireless access policies and standards

- Demanding products that resist casual snooping

■ Monitoring for any unauthorized wireless access points that a department or user may establish on their own initiative

■ Utilizing application-layer security products to protect data in transit

■ Centrally managing wireless access using network access control, authentication of users, encryption, desktop firewalls, and intrusion detection

In the above list, the NIPC suggests that users purchase products that resist casual snooping. One of the easiest ways to defy snooping is by using encryption. *WEP*, short for *Wired Equivalent Privacy*, is a security protocol for wireless LANs defined in the 802.11b standard. WEP is designed to provide the same level of security as that of a regular wired LAN. Naturally, wired LANs are more secure than WLANs because they are inherently protected by the nature of their design. By placing some (or all) of the network inside a building, it can be protected from unauthorized access. WLANs, operating over radio waves, do not have the same physical protection as wired LANs and are therefore more vulnerable to tampering. WEP was designed to provide security by encrypting the data traversing radio waves.

However, it was recently discovered that WEP is not as secure as once believed. Because WEP specifies only a 40-bit key, several 802.11b products claim to provide additional encryption. Companies can get away with claiming that their encryption goes further if it goes over and beyond the standard 40-bit key. In 2001, several people wrote hacking programs for 802.11b's WEP. More recently, hackers and script kiddies have employed one of several tools, such as WEPCrack or AirSnort. AirSnort is a program that runs on the Linux operating system and takes advantage of an exploit outlined in a paper published by Scott Fluherer, Itsik Mantin, and Adi Shamir. AirSnort can discover a WEP key after passively monitoring a wireless network. According to the SourceForge.net Web site at `http://sourceforge.net`, AirSnort can determine the WEP key within seconds after "listening" to 100MB–1GB of traffic. In addition, since the current implementation of WEP is based on static keys (never changing over time), hackers eventually flush out the data they need to crack the encryption key if they persist long enough. Nearly all 802.11b vendors offer 128-bit key extensions to WEP, so most would implement the 128-bit version.

Besides using a higher encryption scheme, the following three security points should be observed when implementing a wireless LAN:

✓ **Change the location of wireless access points.** When performing a site survey for access point deployment, administrators should consider locating the access points toward the middle of their building rather than near the perimeter or windows. Coverage should radiate out to the perimeter, not beyond it.

✓ **Conduct preventative scans.** Network administrators should survey their site(s) periodically using a freeware utility such as NetStumbler (see Figure 12-1), found at `www.nets tumbler.com`. This utility allows the network administrator to see whether any rogue access points pop up on the network. Because 802.11b wireless hardware is both inexpensive and widely available, it is more likely that a malicious hacker will purchase a wireless network interface card (NIC) and access point and use them to access an organization's network without authorization. Network administrators should also check to see if *any* wireless access is possible from outside the organization's physical building.

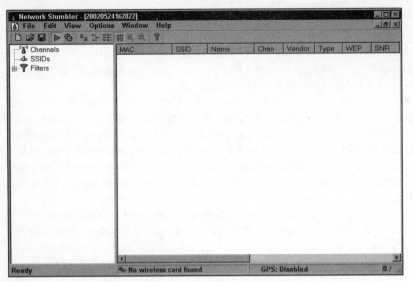

**Figure 12-1:** NetStumbler freeware program

✓ **Change the default password on your access point or wireless router.** Hackers know the manufacturers' default passwords and usually try those first. Programs such as the aforementioned NetStumbler can identify the manufacturer of wireless adapters, making it an easy task to figure out who made a particular device.

While e-mail messaging remains the most popular avenue for virus attacks, the Web and wireless LANs are rapidly becoming areas of concern. Corporations should incorporate all network-connected devices, including those that are wireless, in their anti-virus policies.

# Blended Threats

Blended malicious code threats of the future will combine characteristics of viruses, worms, and Trojan horses. In fact, blended threats have already begun to surface—witness Code Red, Nimda, and the more recent Goner worm. By utilizing multiple methods and techniques, blended threats spread rapidly and cause pervasive damage. Characteristics of blended threats include:

✓ Using several methods to spread, first scanning for vulnerabilities to compromise a system.

✓ Causing damage by defacing a Web server or launching a denial-of-service attack at a particular Web address. Perhaps also planting a Trojan horse program for delayed execution.

✓ Exploiting weaknesses by taking advantage of known vulnerabilities such as buffer overflows and known default passwords to gain unauthorized access.

✓ Spreading without the aid of human intervention.

✓ Attacking from multiple points and inserting malicious code into executable (`.exe`) files on a system. Perhaps also making Registry changes or inserting malicious script code into HTML files.

The Goner worm demonstrates that virus writers have become more skilled at constructing blended threats. While its method of infection is similar to previous mass-mailing worms, Goner carries a destructive payload that not only disables the user's anti-virus protection, but also installs a DDoS client on infected machines, causing them to attack other computers. Such blended threats are the unfortunate consequence of the ready availability of virus-writing programs on the Internet. Blended threats will, without question, become increasingly prevalent in the future.

Effective protection from blended threats requires a comprehensive security solution that contains multiple layers of defenses such as a firewall, intrusion detection, and anti-virus software. Companies like Symantec (`www.symantec.com`) and Network Associates (`www.nai.com`) are just two examples of a number of organizations that provide comprehensive network security solutions against the multiple threats posed by blended malicious code.

# Multiplatform Malicious Code

Like humans, malicious code can be "taught" to speak different languages. Equal opportunity malicious code can infect two or more computer operating system platforms such as Windows, Linux, or the MacOS. One of the first multiplatform viruses, dubbed W32.Winux, was discovered in March 2001. It could be described as a proof-of-concept virus since it did not affect very many computers. It was not able to spread quickly, because most people do not tend to share executable programs between computers running Linux operating systems and Windows operating systems. It did, however, set the stage for future malicious code to simultaneously target several different operating systems.

It is not uncommon to find several different operating systems communicating across an organization's LAN. Advances in computer networking make it possible for Linux, UNIX, Windows, and Macintosh computers to effortlessly share information throughout an organization's network. The concept of a multiplatform virus is not new. Back in 1995, the first multiplatform macro virus was discovered and given the name WinWord.Concept. It was capable of infecting Windows 95, Windows NT, and Apple Macintosh computers, as well as Windows 3.$x$ running Microsoft Word 6. The nondestructive WinWord.Concept was the first virus to infect documents rather than executable code.

At present, operating systems such as Linux and UNIX have not gained popularity because they are more difficult to configure than Windows and Macintosh systems. This situation is likely to change in the future as UNIX and Linux become easier to set up and use. When this occurs, virus writers will no doubt construct viruses that can infect a wide variety of operating systems, making the challenge of malicious code defense, particularly across a multiplatform network, considerably more demanding.

# Digital Warfare — Malicious Code as a Weapon

Forget conventional weapons: future conflicts will largely be fought by cyberwarriors seated at computers. In a cyberwar, victory will lie with the side that succeeds in shutting down the enemy's computers. The U.S. (and other countries around the globe) is gearing up to fight future cyberwars while simultaneously doing its best to keep present and future foes from invading and destroying its cyberinfrastructure.

In the era of digital warfare, malicious computer code will be covertly introduced by an attacker into one or more computer systems or networks to meet military, political, economic, or personal objectives. The motivation may be financial gain or perhaps a desire to make a political statement. Whatever the reason, malicious code will certainly play an important role in this arena. In the future, digital weapons may take the form of a virus, worm, logic bomb, time bomb, Trojan horse, or some combination thereof, depending on the desired outcome. These digital weapons differ from the ordinary "hacker" variety insofar as they target a *specific system* or network of systems, with *a specific objective,* in a manner that is predictable to the attacker. Within this context, the attacker could be a military or national organization, a terrorist organization, a multinational or private corporation, or even an individual with the knowledge and means to develop and install such code.

In February 2001, in a public press release titled "Cyber Attack: The National Protection Plan and its Privacy Implications", Senator Jon Kyl made the following statement:

> The United States is the most technologically sophisticated country in the world. Today, virtually every key service in our society is dependent on computer technology: electric power grids, air traffic control, nuclear warning, and banking, to name a few examples. Highly interdependent information systems control these infrastructures. With the benefits of technological advances comes a new set of vulnerabilities that can be exploited by individuals, terrorists, and foreign nations.
>
> Our enemies don't need to risk confronting our powerful military if they can attack vulnerabilities in our critical information infrastructure. According to the National Security Agency, more than 100 nations are working on information warfare tactics. There have already been a disturbing number of attacks on U.S. information systems, exposing our "Achilles Heel" to any potential adversary.
>
> At our last hearing, Michael Vatis from the FBI described how Russia conducted a "series of widespread intrusions, into Defense Department, other federal government agencies, and private-sector computer networks." Additionally, China is reportedly considering forming an entirely new branch of the military for information warriors. A recent article in the Chinese Liberation Army Daily assessed that the integration of Web warfare with ground combat will be essential to winning future conflicts. Moreover, a recent book titled "Unrestricted Warfare", written by two Chinese Army Colonels, proposes tactics for developing countries like China to use to compensate for their military inferiority vs. the U.S. One scenario described in the book envisions a situation where the attacking country causes panic through cyberattacks on civilian electricity, telecommunications, and financial markets. These examples underscore the severity of the threat facing the U.S.
>
> In light of these concerns, I authored an amendment to the 1996 Defense Authorization Act, directing the President to submit a report to Congress "setting forth the results of a review of the national policy on protecting the national information infrastructure against strategic attacks." This ultimately culminated in the National Plan before us today, which is more than a year overdue.

I am pleased the Plan calls for specific milestones with timetables for securing our nation's information systems, although its goals are modest and merely a first step. I hope the Administration considers the Plan a living document that must be reviewed and revised with new technological advances and discovered vulnerabilities. This will be a complicated and expensive process, but it is a vital one to protect our nation's security and way of life. To support the effort, I am encouraged that news reports indicate the President's budget will include a $160 million increase in spending on cybersecurity initiatives.

In securing the critical infrastructures that provide our way of life, we must be careful that it doesn't occur at the expense of civil liberties. We need to update our current legal framework to reflect the revolution in information technology — to strike the right balance between security and civil liberties. The reality is that doing nothing to enhance our cybersecurity in fact erodes the privacy and civil liberties of Americans by making private information accessible to any hacker with a computer and a modem. The National Plan's implementation must consider the reasonable privacy issues that need to be discussed and appropriately balance them with security interests.

Senator Kyl's statement makes it clear that both government and organizations in the private sector must prepare now for cyberwarfare by developing appropriate digital weaponry. Revisions in our nation's legal framework — especially as it relates to privacy issues and civil liberties — will have to accompany our emergent posture in the cyberwarfare realm. Kyl's concerns regarding American civil liberties illustrate the need for a balanced approach to cyberwarfare defense, one that both protects our country's digital infrastructure and our citizens' constitutional right to privacy.

# Future Viruses — Bigger Payloads, Better Social Engineering

Making predictions about the future of malicious code is at best difficult, if not impossible. Virus writing and anti-virus software are persistently changing; however, if the past is used as a guide, some general assumptions about viruses of the future can be made. Besides a shift towards targeting wireless and handheld devices, the biggest change in malicious code of the future may be in the level of damage it will have the potential to exact. As more organizations, governments, and military agencies migrate to the Internet, the risk posed by virus outbreaks increases. In point of fact, the Nimda virus contained computer code that could have permitted it to erase an infected machine's hard drive. Thankfully, its authors chose not to active it. By extension, this means that future malicious code carrying a destructive payload could have the ability to cripple infrastructure components that are controlled by various online systems (such as telecommunications systems, power generation, and transportation systems).

Another likely trend in the future of malicious code is the increased use of social engineering. As I have discussed in earlier chapters of this book, malicious code can be introduced into a computer system by tricking or tempting a user into opening an infected e-mail attachment. Whenever a wide-scale viral (computer) outbreak garners a great deal of press, many users immediately seek to either update the anti-virus software already installed on their computers, or install some if they were surfing unprotected. During a malicious code outbreak, malicious individuals may circulate e-mail messages with executable programs attached that claim to remedy a particular virus. Upon activation, the so-called "antidote" is actually the virus itself (or some other destructive variant), helping to perpetuate the vicious cycle.

# Internet Banking

*Internet banking* enables consumers to access a host of banking services from a personal computer by connecting to the bank's computers via the Internet. Not only is travel time eliminated, but using ATM machines, banking by telephone, and banking by mail also become unnecessary. While this type of service is compelling because of its convenience, it also opens the door to the possibility of theft and fraud via the Internet.

In February 2001, the NIPC released the following information in their 02-01 *Highlights* bulletin concerning the dangers of online banking:

Internet Banking and Security

The use of the Internet as a remote delivery channel to conduct transactions has proven alluring for both financial institutions and their customers. Security features are an integral part of Internet Banking.

In May 2000, the "On-line Banking Report" estimated that 7 million Web banking users in the U.S. conducted $19 million worth of transactions on average per month. The market research firm International Data Corporation (IDC) has concluded that consumer interest in on-line banking will continue to rise, and the firm projects that the number of households conducting banking on-line will exceed 22 million within a few years. All of the large U.S. banks and many of the smaller financial institutions offer some means of conducting transactions over the Internet. These transactions range from transferring funds, applying for a loan, and electronic bill presentment and payment.

The benefits of Internet banking include: convenience, time and money-saving factors, ease of access, and opportunities for aggregation of services. These benefits are offset in part by the exposure to the same risks faced by other on-line activities such as: technical factors, server outages, or malicious activity. Robust authentication of users, combined with the speed and volume at which on-line financial operations are conducted, has the potential to make Internet banks vulnerable to schemes such as those in which large numbers of bogus transactions are submitted in an attempt to defraud the institution. Arrests reportedly involving such a plot against the on-line bank Egg were recently made in the United Kingdom. The security of customer accounts may also be compromised either through user error (e.g., if the customer leaves his banking software active on a computer that others may access) or through poor configuration management on the server. A British on-line bank had to briefly suspend operations this past summer after users reportedly were able to view other customers' account information.

Security features are an integral part of Internet banking. U.S. financial regulatory guidelines mandate review of a bank's information systems as part of its regular auditing process. Federal bank examinations also evaluate key aspects of information technology risk management practices. Most Internet-based banking systems use encryption protocols such as Secure Socket Layer (SSL) to protect sensitive data in transit over the Internet, as well as to prevent a third party from spoofing the bank's identity.

One important Internet banking component which is not subject to the same degree of rigorous security auditing as the other components is the customer's personal computer (PC). Unlike computers on a corporate network, home computers are not subject to a formal security regime, anti-virus measures may be more lax, most data stored on the typical user's computer is not protected by encryption, and a home PC is usually not behind a firewall. These factors collectively make the user's PC the weak link in an on-line banking environment.

In August 2000, a Visual Basic Script (VBS) worm circulating on the Internet affected customers of a Swiss bank. The worm, based loosely on the infamous VBS/Loveletter worm, distributed itself via e-mail. When a Windows-based computer became infected, the worm attempted to download a Trojan component to the victim's computer via FTP. After the infected computer was restarted, the Trojan accessed the computer's registry and copied sensitive PIN information relating to the on-line banking software used by the bank and sent the information to three e-mail addresses. (For more information on this worm, please refer to NIPC Alert 00-053 of August 17, 2000 at `http://www.nipc.gov/warnings/alerts/2000/00-053.htm.`) Although the bank stated that no customers had reported any damage as a result of this attack, the incident gained widespread attention as proof that attacks on users of home banking software do not occur only in staged demonstrations.

The financial industry is responding to these types of threats by increasingly supplying their on-line customers with extra security software to help protect their PCs, and offering their customers a personal firewall that will limit access to a user's PC from the Internet. Security-conscious computer users can also select from a wide range of commercial software packages to protect their PCs and the data on them.

Given the growth forecast for Internet banking, the security of this delivery channel will gain in importance as it becomes an integral part of the banking system. Participants need to ensure that financial information and funds transferred over the Internet are safe from malicious diversion or alteration. The increasing use of home PCs for high-value financial transactions requires adequate measures to secure them from attack via viruses and Trojan horses. An effective anti-virus package as well as personal firewalls can mitigate the risks posed by Internet banking. No single solution will provide an all-encompassing secure environment for a transaction involving two or more parties. Security on the Internet is a shared responsibility borne by all who use the network, including the home PC banker.

In the preceding bulletin, the NIPC points out that the personal computer is the weakest link in conducting online banking. Due to the security considerations of online banking, some individuals and organizations remain reluctant to fully utilize all the benefits that it offers. As a service to the public, the Federal Deposit Insurance Corporation (`www.fdic.gov`) offers information to consumers who wish to conduct their banking transactions over the Internet.

The Federal Deposit Insurance Corporation, or FDIC, was created in 1933 to insure deposits and promote safe and sound banking practices. Its main function is to maintain the stability of (and hence the public's confidence in) the nation's financial system. Due to persistent concerns over the dangers of online banking, the FDIC provides the following tips to on their Web site to anyone interested in engaging in Internet banking:

How to Keep Your Transaction Secure

- The Internet is a public network. Therefore, it is important to learn how to safeguard your banking information, credit card numbers, Social Security Number and other personal data.
- Look at your bank's Web site for information about its security practices, or contact the bank directly.

Also learn about and take advantage of security features. Some examples are:

- Encryption is the process of scrambling private information to prevent unauthorized access. To show that your transmission is encrypted, some browsers display a small icon on your screen that looks like a "lock or a "key" whenever you conduct secure transactions online. Avoid sending sensitive information, such as account numbers, through unsecured e-mail.

- Passwords or personal identification numbers (PINs) should be used when accessing an account online. Your password should be unique to you and you should change it regularly. Do not use birthdates or other numbers or words that may be easy for others to guess. Always carefully control to whom you give your password. For example, if you use a financial company that requires your passwords in order to gather your financial data from various sources, make sure you learn about the company's privacy and security practices.

- General security over your personal computer, such as virus protection and physical access controls, should be used and updated regularly. Contact your hardware and software suppliers or Internet service provider to ensure you have the latest in security updates.

- If you have a security concern about your online accounts, contact your bank to discuss possible problems and remedies.

- Remember that nonfinancial Web sites that are linked to your bank's site are not FDIC-insured.

- As an added convenience to their customers, some banks offer online links to merchants, retail stores, travel agents and other nonfinancial sites. An outside company's products and services are not insured by the FDIC, and your bank may not guarantee the products and services.

- As in everyday business, before you order a product or service online, make sure you are comfortable with the reputation of the company making the offer. Only then should you give out your credit card or debit card number. And never give the number unless you initiated the transaction.

As a way to attract new customers and to reduce some of the costs associated with routine banking, many financial institutions are now seeking to use wireless technology when implementing new networks. In light of this trend, the FDIC has provided Financial Institution Letters regarding Internet banking issues. The following is an excerpt from their February 2002 Financial Institution Letter (FIL-08-2002) outlining some of the risks associated with wireless technology, along with some useful suggestions on how to manage and mitigate those risks.

### Wireless Technology and the Risks of Implementation

Wireless networks are rapidly becoming a cost-effective alternative for providing network connectivity to financial institution information systems. Institutions that are installing new networks are finding the installation costs of wireless networks competitive compared with traditional network wiring. Performance enhancements in wireless technology have also made the adoption of wireless networks attractive to institutions. Wireless networks operate at speeds that are sufficient to meet the needs of many institutions and can be seamlessly integrated into existing networks. Wireless networks can also be used to provide connectivity between geographically close locations without having to install dedicated lines.

Wireless Internet access to banking applications is also becoming attractive to financial institutions. It offers customers the ability to perform routine banking tasks while away from the bank branch, automated teller machines, or their own personal computers. Wireless Internet access is a standard feature on many new cellular phones and hand-held computers.

Wireless technology carries additional risks that financial institutions should consider when designing, implementing, and operating a wireless network. Common risks include the potential:

- Compromise of customer information and transactions over the wireless network
- Disruption of wireless service from radio transmissions of other wireless devices
- Intrusion into the institution's network through wireless network connections
- Obsolescence of current systems due to rapidly changing standards

These risks could ultimately compromise the bank's computer system, potentially causing:

- Financial loss due to the execution of unauthorized transactions
- Disclosure of confidential customer information, resulting in — among other things — identity theft
- Negative media attention, resulting in harm to the institution's reputation
- Loss of customer confidence

### Risk Mitigation

Security should not be compromised when offering wireless financial services to customers or deploying wireless internal networks. Financial institutions should carefully consider the risks of wireless technology and take appropriate steps to mitigate those risks before deploying either wireless networks or applications. As wireless technologies evolve, the security and control features available to financial institutions will make the process of risk mitigation easier. Steps that can be taken immediately in wireless implementation include:

- Establishing a minimum set of security requirements for wireless networks and applications
- Adopting proven security policies and procedures to address the security weaknesses of the wireless environment
- Adopting strong encryption methods that encompass end-to-end encryption of information as it passes throughout the wireless network
- Adopting authentication protocols for customers using wireless applications that are separate and distinct from those provided by the wireless network operator
- Ensuring that the wireless software includes appropriate audit capabilities (for such things as recording dropped transactions)
- Providing appropriate training to IT personnel on network, application, and security controls so that they understand and can respond to potential risks
- Performing independent security testing of wireless network and application implementations

# Cyberforensics

Nearly every computer crime leaves some type of evidence. Computer forensics, also referred to as cyberforensics, deals with the gathering of evidence from computer media (for example, floppy or hard disks) apprehended at the crime scene. Judd Robbins, a computer forensics investigator, defines computer forensics as "Simply the application of computer investigation and analysis techniques in the interest of determining potential legal evidence." Whereas a forensics specialist may study a crime scene in an attempt to "re-create" a crime, computer forensics specialists attempt to piece together the details of a computer crime by studying a suspect's computer and its contents. Key objectives of cyberforensics include rapid discovery of evidence (before it becomes tainted or disappears altogether), an estimate of the potential impact on the victim, and an assessment of the intent and identity of the perpetrator(s).

Evidence may be sought in a wide range of computer crime or misuse, including but not limited to theft of trade secrets, theft (or destruction) of intellectual property, and fraud. Computer specialists can draw on a variety of methods for discovering data that resides in a computer system, or recovering deleted, encrypted, or damaged file information. Any or all of this information may help during discovery, depositions, or actual litigation procedures.

## Conducting Cyberforensic Examinations

The International Association of Computer Investigative Specialists (IACIS) lists the following three essential requirements for a competent forensic examination:

✓ Forensically sterile examination media must be used.

✓ The examination must maintain the integrity of the original media.

✓ Printouts, copies of data, and exhibits resulting from the examination must be properly marked, controlled, and transmitted.

In some cases, an organization may become involved in an investigation carried out by a local, state, or federal law enforcement agency. A suspect may have used the organization's computers to launch an attack on a computer located at another site, or law enforcement may suspect that data is being stored on a workstation or server by an employee suspected of committing a crime. Anyone with a modem and access to an organization's resources can use those resources to store data associated with criminal activity. If an organization is asked to cooperate in an ongoing investigation, law enforcement will most likely use their own experts to conduct the forensic process.

The primary role of cyberforensics is to investigate and elicit evidence from electronic devices — not just limited to desktop computers — in an admissible fashion. While the evidence may never be presented in court, it should be collected in such a way that it could be used in court if required.

In some circumstances, a company-directed investigation is warranted. For example, a business may call in computer forensics specialists if it experiences problems with:

✓ Inappropriate use of e-mail messaging and Internet access by employees (for example, pornography, sexual harassment, and abuse)

✓ Illegal dissemination of corporate information to individuals, other companies, or organizations

✓ Theft of confidential information

✓ Corporate fraud and sabotage for personal gain or revenge

Evidence of a computer criminal's incursion can, for the most part, be found in the following three segments of a computer:

✓ **Log files** — Log files are the records computers maintain to monitor machine activities. A determined and patient cybersleuth can tap a computer's log files to piece together a comprehensive picture of the user's activities.

✓ **Computer files** — When any new file is created using an operating system such as Linux, UNIX, or Windows, the operating system notes the time the file was created. Furthermore, the operating system indicates when a file was last modified or accessed by a user. By carefully examining this information, particularly when used in conjunction with data derived from the log files, a forensic investigator determine a great deal about the nature of a user's activity.

✓ **Hard disk** — Any data placed on a computer's hard disk remains intact until the operating system overwrites it. For example, under the FAT file system, only the data's corresponding FAT entry is removed (not the actual data) when a file is deleted. The actual data stored on the disk remains until new data overwrites it. The fact is that most computer users — including criminals — rarely use all the space available on their hard drives. As a result, an investigator can find incriminating evidence on the hard drive that the user thought was deleted long ago.

## Outsourcing a Specialist

When an organization is financially constrained from setting up an in-house forensic team or investigation, or when an organization does not want to devote its resources to doing so, outside security and computer forensic services may be called upon as an alternative. When selecting computer forensic expert(s) in the event of a considerable intrusion, the organization should look for the following credentials:

✓ Precise recordkeeping

✓ A thorough knowledge of hardware and software subsystems

✓ A thorough understanding of evidence collection and maintenance

✓ A thorough knowledge of legal procedures

✓ Access to and the ability to use appropriate cyberforensic utilities

Pinkerton Consulting and Investigations, Inc. (www.psg-pinkerton.com) and Data Recovery Services, Inc. (www.legalforensics.com) are just two companies among many that can be called upon for computer forensic services. Users can search through a list of other organizations that provide computer forensic and security services at www.expertisesearch.com.

# Summary

One cannot accurately predict the future of malicious code, but as long as computers and the Internet are an important part of daily life, malicious code will follow to infect them. While no method of malicious code defense is one hundred percent effective, a comprehensive approach, using up-to-date anti-virus programs, network security policies and user education is the best defense. Key points covered in this chapter include:

- ✓ Considering Personal Digital Assistants and the dangers they pose to an organization's LAN

- ✓ Exposing the dangers of wireless LANs and how they will be the target of future malicious code attacks

- ✓ Exploring the future of blended malicious code and how it uses several different attack methodologies

- ✓ Explaining how multiplatform malicious code can attack several different types of operating systems

- ✓ Examining digital warfare and how the U.S. plans to maintain its dominance in this emerging field

- ✓ Discussing how future viruses will take old tricks and successfully use them with a new slant

- ✓ Exploring the future of and perceived dangers of Internet banking

- ✓ Defining cyberforensics and its use in the field of virus writers and malicious code

- ✓ Outsourcing a cyberforensic specialist

# Appendix A

# What's on the Web Site

You can find a Web site with links leading you to some of the software solutions discussed in this book at www.wiley.com/compbooks/schweitzer. This appendix provides you with information on the contents of that Web site. Specifically, this appendix includes:

- ✓ System requirements
- ✓ Application links on the Web site
- ✓ Troubleshooting

## System Requirements

Make sure that your computer meets the minimum system requirements listed in this section. If your computer doesn't match up to most of these requirements, you may have a problem using some of the suggested applications. You should have:

- ✓ A PC running Windows 9x or higher with a Pentium processor running at 120 MHz or faster.
- ✓ At least 32MB of total RAM installed on your computer; for best performance, we recommend at least 64MB.
- ✓ A modem with a speed of at least 28,800 bps.
- ✓ Internet access.

## Application Links on the Web Site

The Web site contains links to the following applications:

- ✓ Ad-aware

    Freeware. Freely downloadable at www.lavasoftusa.com, Ad-aware is spyware removal utility. It scans your PC's hard drives, memory, and registry for known spyware components. If it finds any, it helps you eliminate them. This utility boasts numerous features and a wizard-style interface to assist you with the scanning and removal procedures. Ad-aware is compatible with Windows 98, 2000, NT4, Me, and XP.

✓ **Agnitum Outpost Firewall**

Freeware. Downloadable at `www.agnitum.com`, Agnitum Outpost is a personal firewall containing such security features as Full Stealth Mode, Anti-Leak, and MD5 Authentication. Outpost Firewall protects against numerous Internet threats, including adware, backdoors, crackers, cookies, spyware, e-mail viruses, and advertisements. Also, as the first personal firewall to utilize plug-ins, Outpost uses that feature to employ such tasks as intrusion detection, content filtering, and e-mail guard. This firewall requires little or no configuration by the user and starts protecting the moment it is installed. Agnitum Outpost is compatible with Windows 95, 98, 98SE, Me, NT, 2000, and XP.

✓ **AVG 6.0 (Free Edition)**

Freeware. Freely downloadable at `www.grisoft.com`, the anti-virus system AVG 6.0 Free Edition provides protection against viruses, worms, and Trojan horses and is an ICSA (TruSecure)–certified product. Some of its most important features include free virus database updates, an Automatic Update feature, the AVG E-mail Scanner, the automatic healing of infected files, and the AVG Virus Vault for the safe handling of infected files. AVG is compatible with Windows-based computers.

✓ **eScorcher Anti-Virus**

Freeware. Promoting itself as one of the most user-friendly anti-virus programs for the Windows platform, eScorcher can find and eliminate popular Trojans, worms, and viruses. eScorcher is designed as anti-virus protection for computers using Windows 95/98/Me/2000/NT4/XP operating systems. You don't need a lot of technical knowledge to learn how to use it. eScorcher can be downloaded at `www.escorcher.com`.

✓ **ID Serve**

Freeware. Downloadable at `www.grc.com`, ID Serve is an Internet server identification utility. With Internet activity on the increase, malicious hackers have become more interested in breaking into Internet servers. Because some Web servers are more secure than others, this utility can help users to easily determine what type of Internet servers Web sites are using. AVG is compatible with Windows-based computers.

✓ **LeakTest**

Freeware. LeakTest is downloadable at `www.grc.com`. Any comprehensive security pro-gram must safeguard its owner by preventing Trojan horses, viruses, and spyware from using the system's Internet connection without the owner's knowledge. Scanning for the presence of Trojans, viruses, and spyware is important and effective, but if a piece of mal-ware does get into your computer, you want to expose it immediately by detecting its communication attempts and cutting off its communication with external agencies. LeakTest is a small utility that can be used to simulate the presence and effect of Trojan horses, viruses, and adware/spyware running in a computer. It tells the user whether it has been able to slip out past a firewall's outbound Trojan/virus/spyware protection mechanism and establish a standard TCP connection. LeakTest is compatible with Windows-based computers.

✓ **SocketLock**

Freeware. Downloadable at `www.grc.com`, SocketLock is a raw socket abuse prevention system for Windows 2000– and XP-based computers. With SocketLock installed, all system processes continue to enjoy complete and unrestricted access to full raw sockets; however, users are not permitted to access raw socket features.

✓ **SuperScan**

Freeware. Downloadable at `www.webattack.com`, SuperScan is a TCP port scanner, pinger, and hostname resolver that can perform ping scans and port scans using any IP address range. Users can specify and scan a variety of port ranges or perform scans using those provided by the program's built-in port lists, and they can use this program to ping remote computers to test responses from connected hosts. SuperScan provides a built-in editor that enables users to change the port list or port descriptions, and the program allows users to assign a custom "helper" application to any port and then connect to any open ports that are discovered using the user-defined "helper" applications. SuperScan is user-friendly and contains a comprehensive help file. SuperScan is compatible with Windows 9$x$, Me, NT, and 2000.

✓ **SurfinGuard Pro**

Freeware. Found at `www.finjan.com` and representing a proactive approach to defending your systems, SurfinGuard Pro watches and restricts the behavior of downloaded programs and active content in an effort to protect users from unknown threats. By running active content such as executables or ActiveX or Java content in a protected SafeZone, SurfinGuard Pro automatically prevents potentially harmful actions. SurfinGuard Pro bases its actions on code behavior, rather than on signature recognition, and can therefore defend effectively against new attacks without relying on database updates. SurfinGuard Pro is compatible with Windows 9$x$, Me, NT, 2000, and XP.

✓ **Tiny Personal Firewall 2.0**

Freeware. Downloadable at `www.tinysoftware.com`, Tiny Personal Firewall 2.0 is a free, ICSA-certified, bi-directional, Windows-based firewall that is useful to both novice and expert users. Although small in size, this firewall offers a great deal of functionality and even supports dual processor computers. Tiny Personal Firewall 2.0 is compatible with Windows 9$x$, Me, NT, 2000, and XP.

✓ **Unplug n' Pray**

Freeware. Downloadable at `www.grc.com`, the Unplug n' Pray utility allows users to check their Windows-based computers for the presence of the UPnP service and permits users to easily and safely enable and disable it as needed. Unplug n' Pray is compatible with all versions of Windows.

✓ **ZoneAlarm**

Freeware. Found at `www.zonealarm.com`, the freeware version of this personal firewall blocks Internet threats and protects Windows-based PCs. ZoneAlarm provides the basic protection that individuals need to secure their PC and keep valuable information private, and it protects automatically from the moment it is installed, requiring no programming knowledge on your part. A built-in tutorial allows users to get ZoneAlarm up and running quickly. It's compatible with Windows 95, 98, Me, NT, 2000, and XP.

*Shareware programs* are fully functional, trial versions of copyrighted programs. If you like particular programs, register with their authors for a nominal fee and receive licenses, enhanced versions, and technical support. *Freeware programs* are copyrighted games, applications, and utilities that are free for personal use. Unlike shareware, these programs do not require a fee or provide technical support. *GNU software* is governed by its own license, which is included inside the folder of the GNU product. See the GNU license for more details.

*Trial, demo,* or *evaluation versions* are usually limited either by time or functionality (such as being unable to save projects). Some trial versions are very sensitive to system date changes. If you alter your computer's date, the programs will "time out" and will no longer be functional.

# Troubleshooting

If you have trouble with the Web site, please call the Wiley Customer Care phone number: 1-800-762-2974. Outside the United States, call 1-317-572-3994. You can also contact Wiley Customer Service by e-mail at `techsupdum@wiley.com`. Wiley Publishing, Inc., will provide technical support only for general quality control items; for technical support on the applications themselves, consult the program's vendor or author.

# Appendix B

# Cybercrime before Congress

The following statement was made on May 25, 2000, by James K. Robinson, Assistant Attorney General for the Criminal Division. He spoke before the Senate Judiciary Committee on Cybercrime regarding cybercrimes and The Internet Integrity and Critical Infrastructure Act. Robinson's statement clearly shows that, along with the increase in legitimate Internet users, cybercrimes are on the increase, as well. Furthermore, Mr. Robinson contends that current laws are ill-equipped and were never designed for the information age.

## Statement on Cybercrime and The Internet Integrity and Critical Infrastructure Act

Mr. Chairman, Senator Leahy, and Members of the Committee, I thank you for this opportunity to testify on the topic of cybercrime and S. 2448, The Internet Integrity and Critical Infrastructure Act sponsored by Chairman Hatch and Senator Schumer. The issue before this Committee today is one of singular importance, and I commend the Committee for holding this hearing today. I also want to thank you personally Mr. Chairman and Senator Leahy for your leadership, not just on this issue, but on many matters dealing with public safety over the years.

Chairman Hatch, we have been pleased to work with you on a number of initiatives to help law enforcement, and we sincerely appreciate your efforts to address the current challenges facing us in cyberspace by introducing S. 2448, along with Senator Schumer, and for holding this hearing today. Senator Leahy, you have been a pivotal person in the development of many of the most prominent statutes utilized today against online criminals, such as the Electronic Communications Privacy Act, and the Computer Fraud and Abuse Act. Your efforts to protect the online public have continued recently with the introduction of S. 2430, The Internet Security Act of 2000. The Department of Justice appreciates the continued dedication and leadership of you both to these important issues. It is my sincere hope that we will all be able to work together in the remaining days of this Congress to help ensure the safety of all Americans who use the Internet.

### The Internet and Public Safety

Over the last decade, use of computers and the Internet has grown exponentially, and individuals have increasingly come to depend on this use in their daily lives. The Internet has resulted in new and exciting ways for people to communicate, transfer information, engage in commerce, and expand their educational opportunities. These are but a few of the wonderful benefits of this rapidly changing technology. There is no question that the Internet has changed the way we live today. Yet, as people have increasingly used computers for lawful purposes, so too have criminals increasingly exploited computers to commit crimes and to harm the safety, security, and privacy of others.

In just the past few months, for example, legitimate e-commerce has been the target of malicious computer hackers in the form of denial-of-service attacks. These unlawful attacks involve the intrusion into an unknown number of computers, which are in turn used to launch attacks on several, target computers, such as Yahoo, eBay, CNN, and ZDNET. In these cases, the number of victims can be substantial, as can the collective loss and cost to respond to these attacks. We have also seen the emergence of fast-moving viruses that have caused damages to computer systems around the world and have disrupted the computer systems of consumers, businesses, and governments.

In April 1999, the Melissa virus was released. Through the cooperative efforts of state and federal law enforcement, as well as the contributions of antiviral companies and Internet service providers, the perpetrator of the virus was found within a few days of the virus's dissemination. He pled guilty in December, admitting that his actions caused over $80 million in damages.

A few weeks ago, the I Love You virus began infecting systems around the world. While there is not yet any official assessment of the damages caused by this virus, antiviral companies have estimated that the damages are in the billions. As with the Melissa virus, law enforcement agencies on all levels have been cooperating with the private sector to determine who released this virus. The FBI is now working closely with the National Bureau of Investigation of the Philippines to pursue leads in that country. While I cannot comment directly on that investigation, I will say that the FBI and the Department of Justice will continue to provide whatever technical, investigative, or prosecutorial assistance is needed by the Philippine government.

Frighteningly, the I Love You virus was followed almost immediately by copycat variants. At last count, there were almost 30 of these variants that had been identified. They were followed last Thursday by the New Love virus, a virus that self-replicated, mutated in name and size, and destroyed the computer systems affected by it. The FBI, again working with the private sector, is investigating.

The new crop of viruses are becoming more sophisticated and difficult to detect. If we are going to control this epidemic of viruses and denial-of-service attacks, U.S. law enforcement must continue to work with the private sector and with law enforcement in other countries. As all these cases demonstrate, computer crime is a global problem. In this regard, we are making important progress. Last week, I returned from a meeting in Paris at which the government and industry of the G8 nations, along with representatives of other nations and groups, sat down to discuss how we can work together to identify the source of criminal behavior on the Internet, as well as trace those responsible for committing crime over the Internet. We are also involved in similar efforts with the Council of Europe. Efforts are underway, which are nearing completion, to develop a cybercrime convention that will create minimum standards for defining crimes committed over computer networks. The convention will also establish minimum standards for international cooperation and domestic law enforcement powers. The draft convention also would further expand the 24/7 point of contact network that was begun by the G8. This network of experienced law enforcement officials capable of dealing with computer crime has been steadily expanding beyond its original eight members, and we are working to further develop the network so that we are better prepared to address crimes committed using computer networks wherever and whenever they occur.

Fostering better international understanding and response to computer crimes has been a priority for over a decade and we are making significant progress. We will continue to build on the successes of the past and capitalize on worldwide attention brought about by the I Love You virus to continue working with nations across the globe on this vital issue.

While the denial-of-service attacks and the recent viruses have received a great deal of attention and are cause for concern, they are but one facet of the criminal activity that occurs online today. Criminals use computers to send child pornography to each other using anonymous, encrypted communications; hackers illegally break into financial computers and steal sensitive, personal information of private consumers, such as name, address, social security number, and credit card information; criminals use the Internet's inexpensive and easy means of communication to commit large-scale fraud on victims all over the globe. Simply put, criminals are exploiting the Internet and victimizing people, worldwide, every day.

It is important to note, Mr. Chairman, that when law enforcement successfully investigates, apprehends, and prosecutes a criminal who has stolen a citizen's personal information from a computer system, law enforcement is undeniably working, not just to apprehend the offender, but to protect privacy and deter further privacy violations at the hands of criminals. The same is true when law enforcement apprehends a hacker who compromised the financial records of a bank customer.

# Responding to the Challenge of Unlawful Conduct on the Internet

The growing threat of illicit conduct online was made clear in the findings and conclusions reached in the recently released report of the President's Working Group on Unlawful Conduct on the Internet, entitled, "The Electronic Frontier: The Challenge of Unlawful Conduct Involving the Use of the Internet." This extensive report highlights in detail the significant challenges facing law enforcement in cyberspace. As the report states, the needs and challenges confronting law enforcement "are neither trivial nor theoretical." The Report outlines a three-pronged approach for responding to unlawful activity on the Internet:

1. Conduct on the Internet should be treated in the same manner as similar conduct offline, in a technology-neutral manner.

2. The needs and challenges of law enforcement posed by the Internet — including the need for resources, up-to-date investigative tools, and enhanced multi-jurisdictional cooperation — are significant.

3. Finally, continued support for private sector leadership in developing tools and methods to help Internet users to prevent and minimize the risks of unlawful conduct online.

I would encourage anyone with an interest in this important topic to review carefully the report of the Working Group. The report can be found on the Internet by visiting the Web site of the Department of Justice's Computer Crime and Intellectual Property Section, located at www.cybercrime.gov. That Web site also contains a great deal of other information relating to cybercrime and to the laws protecting intellectual property.

The migration of criminality to cyberspace accelerates with each passing day, and the threat to public safety is becoming increasingly significant. As Deputy Attorney General Eric Holder told a joint hearing of House and Senate Judiciary Subcommittees in February, this nation's vulnerability to computer crime is astonishingly high and threatens not only our financial well-being and our privacy, but also this nation's critical infrastructure.

However, Mr. Chairman, the laws defining computer offenses — and the legal tools needed to investigate criminals using the Internet — have lagged behind technological and social changes, leaving them out-of-date and, in some instances, ineffective. In short, law enforcement today does not have the tools we need to fully protect the Internet-using public from criminal activity online.

We must confront this problem on two fronts simultaneously. First, we must make certain that the substantive laws defining which conduct is criminal, such as the Computer Fraud and Abuse Act (Title 18 section 1030), are adequately refined and updated. Second, we must look critically at the tools law enforcement uses to investigate and prosecute computer crimes — such as the Electronic Communications Privacy Act and the pen register and trap and trace statutes — to ensure that they are cast in terms that fully account for the rapid advances in technology. Failure to do both will render our efforts meaningless. If we have the appropriate substantive laws, but no means to effectuate them, we will be stymied in our pursuit of online criminals. Conversely, if the conduct in question is not covered by the criminal law, the ability to gather evidence is of no value in protecting the safety and privacy of people who use the Internet. It is not a coincidence, Mr. Chairman, that today marks the fourth time, since February of this year, that the Department of Justice has provided testimony on this issue to Congress. This issue — the safety of the Internet-using public — is and will remain a priority of the Justice Department. I would note, for example, that earlier this month the Attorney General and the Director of the FBI participated in the creation of the Internet Fraud Complaint Center, which gives consumers the ability to go online and file complaints with the Center. This is but one aspect of the approach we are taking to make cyberspace safe for everyone.

# Department of Justice Views on S. 2448

At this point, I am pleased to offer the preliminary views of the Department of Justice on S. 2448, "The Internet Integrity and Critical Infrastructure Protection Act," that is the subject of today's hearing.

At the outset, let me say that the proposed legislation appropriately focuses on several very important public safety goals. As I mentioned earlier, the ability to fully protect public safety online requires that the substantive laws utilized to define criminal activity be fine-tuned. The proposed legislation, S. 2448, offers a number of provisions that address the substantive laws.

## A. REFINING THE SUBSTANTIVE LAW FOR THE INFORMATION AGE:

First, the legislation addresses the ability of federal investigators and prosecutors to bring online criminals to justice by removing the $5,000 "damage" threshold for federal jurisdiction. The Department has encountered numerous instances in which computer intruders have gained unauthorized access to computers used in the provision of "critical infrastructure" systems and services, which include, for example, computers that run 9-1-1 emergency services.

Yet, in several investigations, proof of damage in excess of $5000 — the amount presently required to allow federal investigation and prosecution — has not been readily available. Given the risks posed by the initial act of gaining unauthorized access to these vital computers, federal jurisdiction should not be restricted to those instances in which damage of $5,000 or more can be readily demonstrated, under the current definition of "damage". S. 2448 acknowledges and solves this problem by making federal jurisdiction clearly attach at the outset of an unauthorized intrusion into interstate systems, rather than requiring investigators to wait for estimates of damage to confer jurisdiction. While the Justice Department has some concern about treating the newly covered crimes as felonies in every instance, we strongly support this idea, and would like to work with Congress to best determine the appropriate classification of offenses below the $5,000 damage amount. It is, however, vital to our ability to respond to criminal activity that the jurisdictional threshold be removed.

Second, the bill enhances the deterrent effect of the Computer Fraud and Abuse Act — the primary statute used to prosecute computer hackers — by raising the maximum penalties for various categories of violations, such as those that occurred in the recent denial-of-service attacks discussed earlier. At present, the statutory maximum penalty for these violations is five years. Given the scope and severity of the damage to protected computers that hackers have been doing recently, the current five-year maximum does not adequately take into account the seriousness of their crimes.

For example, as I mentioned earlier, David Smith recently pled guilty to violating Title 18, subsection 1030(a)(5)(A), for releasing the Melissa virus that caused massive damage to thousands of computers across the Internet. Although Smith agreed, as part of his plea, that his conduct caused over $80,000,000 worth of damage (the maximum dollar figure contained in the Sentencing Guidelines), experts estimate that the actual amount of damage may have been as much as ten times that amount. Depending on the circumstances of the offense, the amount of loss and the criminal history of the offender, the Sentencing Guidelines may call for a sentence of greater than five years. However, such a sentence cannot be imposed at this time. We support the goal of raising penalties for violations of the Computer Fraud and Abuse Act and will work with the Committee to determine the appropriate increase.

S. 2448 also provides for increased punishment for computer criminals that "use" minors to help in the commission of the crime. The Department shares your concern that adults that exploit children to aid in the furtherance of their own criminal activity deserve special condemnation. We might explore whether this provision be applied to all of 18 U.S.C. 1030 and not just subsection (a)(5). The Department points out, however, that the provision only be applicable to adults who use juveniles and not to juvenile co-conspirators, and we look forward to working with you to ensure the provision is tailored appropriately.

Third, S. 2448 takes important steps to provide greater deterrence to would-be juvenile hackers. We are increasingly encountering juveniles committing crimes and creating risks to the public via the Internet. For example, a juvenile was recently charged with the recent denial-of-service attack on CNN. This juvenile, known as "Mafiaboy," is currently being prosecuted in Canada. We have also seen juvenile hackers penetrate numerous sensitive computers, including computers run by the Defense Department, even as military operations were being planned. In addition, in March of 1998, a juvenile hacker interfered with a computer that provided telecommunications of a town in central Massachusetts, including the regional airport. This action cut off telephone service to the airport's control tower, fire department, and security services.

To address this important problem, the bill provides that juvenile adjudications for violations of the Computer Fraud and Abuse Act count as prior convictions if such juveniles continue to violate section 1030 as adults. Thus, any juvenile who is arrested and adjudicated delinquent for such a crime would face a stiffer penalty if he or she does not reform. The bill also modifies federal law to allow the federal government to investigate and prosecute juveniles who commit certain serious computer offenses. As S. 2448 recognizes, when an individual attacks a federal computer, or when a hacker uses interstate communications or the Internet to compromise the health, safety, or security of the public, it clearly raises substantial federal interests and warrants federal jurisdiction.

Mr. Chairman, we support your efforts to address these issues and assist law enforcement to combat crime effectively and promote public safety online. As mentioned earlier, however, revision of the substantive law is but one much needed part of the response to cybercrime. The balance of my testimony, and the views of the Department of Justice on S. 2448, will focus on the second prong — making certain that law enforcement has the tools necessary to investigate and build cases against online criminals.

## B. UPDATING THE TOOLS NEEDED TO PROTECT PUBLIC SAFETY ONLINE:

Section 301 of the proposed legislation attempts to solve several important problems relating to the use of pen registers and trap and trace devices in the investigation of computer crime. The Justice Department is concerned, however, that as introduced, this section of the bill does not address several problems in the existing statute that have been caused by changes in telecommunications technology and the telecommunications industry. First, the language of the existing law is obsolete. The definition of "pen register," for example, refers to a "device" that is "attached" to a telephone "line." Telephone companies, however, no longer accomplish these functions using physical hardware attached to an actual telephone line. Moreover, the existing statute refers specifically to telephone "numbers," a concept made out-of-date by the need to trace communications over the Internet that use other means to identify users' accounts. The Department strongly recommends that these provisions be amended to clarify that pen/trap orders apply equally to the tracing of communications in the computer network context. Indeed, S. 2092, introduced by Senators Schumer and Kyl, would amend the statute in these important ways.

In addition to amending the language of the statute to reflect the technological changes that have and will continue to occur, the Justice Department also recommends that the statute be amended to ensure that federal courts have the authority to order all telecommunications carriers providing service in the United States — whether within a particular judicial jurisdiction or not — to provide law enforcement authorities the information needed to trace both voice and electronic communications to their source. The deregulation of the telecommunications industry has created unprecedented hurdles in tracing multiprovider communications to their ultimate source and destination. Many different companies, located in a variety of judicial districts, may handle a single communication as it crosses the country. Under the existing statute, however, a court can only order the installation of a pen/trap device within the jurisdiction of that court. As a result, investigators often have to apply for multiple court orders in multiple jurisdictions in order to trace a single communication, causing a needless waste of resources and delaying and impeding important investigations. Given that time is of the essence in the vast majority of computer hacking cases, this delay may be fatal to the investigation. S 2092 addresses this problem as well.

Section 302 of the proposed legislation regulates the release of personally identifiable information by providers of satellite television services. Although the protection of the privacy of satellite subscribers' information is a laudable goal, the manner in which this provision seeks to address this issue creates serious concerns. This provision is drafted in "technology-specific" terms. The Justice Department has consistently argued, and does so today, that in order to be effective, statutes must remain technology-neutral. By creating a standard exclusively for one form of technology — in this case, satellite television service — the provision restricts the activities of certain companies and individuals based on an arbitrary criterion. If a company chooses to provide its television programming over cable lines or over the Internet, it would not be bound by these restrictions.

The law should not treat companies differently based on the various ways in which they provide the identical service. Further, the Justice Department is concerned about the scope of services — beyond simply providing television service — that would be covered by this provision, thus compounding the disparate treatment noted above. Given the fact that the old distinctions between communications providers and their respective services are rapidly falling away — with each industry crossing over into other areas and offering multiple communications services — technology-specific statutes simply become unworkable. We believe that ECPA governs all communication providers without regard to specific technology used to provide the services.

Another portion of S. 2448 which raises significant concerns for the Department of Justice is Title V, regarding International Computer Crime Enforcement. International cooperation in computer crime cases — as highlighted in recent weeks — is extremely important, and strengthening international cooperation mechanisms is a high priority for the Department. As I noted earlier, we are making significant progress in this area, and any new proposals have to be fashioned extremely carefully so as not to undermine the valuable avenues of cooperation already in place. The Department is concerned that Title V would not significantly promote international cooperation on computer crime investigations, and it has the potential to damage existing agreements and legal authorities. The Department, therefore, opposes inclusion of this provision in the bill.

Before concluding my testimony, let me make some brief remarks on two issues that have principally been handled by parts of the Administration other than the Department of Justice. Concerning the anti-spamming provision in S. 2448, the Administration agrees that the use of deceptive identification information in connection with unsolicited commercial e-mail raises serious concerns. While the Administration has not endorsed any currently proposed approach to this problem, we support continued examination of this issue and note that comprehensive anti-spamming legislation has been proposed in and is being considered by both the House and the Senate at this time.

Concerning the online collection and dissemination of personally identifiable information on the Internet, I draw your attention to the statement on that subject earlier this week by Secretary of Commerce Daley. Secretary Daley expressed the hope that we will continue to see improvement in the quantity and quality of online privacy policies. He stated that, "if we do not see such progress, then we may eventually need to consider whether legislation would provide companies with the right incentives to have good policies and participate in an effective self-regulatory program." Secretary Daley added that any such legislation, if it becomes necessary "should recognize and provide incentives for self-regulation, such as by granting participants in effective self-regulatory programs a "safe harbor" from regulation. Such incentives are not currently included in S. 2448.

# Conclusion

Mr. Chairman, my testimony today is necessarily focused upon the more significant portions of the proposed legislation and is not intended to be all-inclusive. It is my sincere hope that through this and other hearings that have been held, those of us who are concerned about public safety and want to see the Internet continue to flourish and thrive, can come together and forge responses to the problems that I have outlined here today. I again want to commend this Committee for its continued leadership on the issues of technology and public safety and pledge to you today that the Department of Justice stands ready to work with all concerned to make the Internet safe for all Americans.

If we fail in our responsibility to respond to criminal conduct online, we will, in effect, render cyberspace a safe haven for criminals. If we do not make the Internet safe, people's confidence in using the Internet and e-commerce will decline, parents will no longer let their children use the Internet for the wonderful learning tool that it is, and people worlds apart will no longer use the Internet to communicate and the flow of information will slow. By failing to ensure the public's safety online, we are effectively endangering the very benefits born of the Information Age. The Internet Integrity and Critical Infrastructure Protection Act is a positive step in avoiding that unfortunate and unnecessary result, and we look forward to working with the Committee and the Congress on this matter in the weeks ahead.

# Summary

In October 2000, a watered-down version of the aforementioned Internet Integrity and Critical Infrastructure Protection Act was passed by the U.S. Senate Judiciary Committee. However, many of its tougher provisions were amended or deleted at the request of Vermont Senator Patrick Leahy, the ranking Democrat on the committee. Leahy said that, in its original form, the bill would have over-federalized minor computer abuses.

One of the amended provisions deals with the current federal law's $5,000 damage threshold for cybercrimes. Current law places a crime that causes less than $5,000 in damage outside federal jurisdiction, unless the crime causes injury to a person, is a threat to public safety, or in some way hampers medical treatment. The original bill would have eliminated the $5,000 threshold, raising a variety of minor computer crimes to the level of federal offenses. While the amended bill retains the $5,000 threshold for federal jurisdiction over hacker attacks, the release of viruses, and other common computer crimes, it clarifies how the $5,000 in damage is calculated and limits civil damage actions to exclude negligent design or manufacture of computer hardware, software, and firmware.

## Appendix C

# It's Not Just Fun and "War Games" — Juveniles and Computer Crime

Joseph V. DeMarco
Assistant United States Attorney
Southern District of New York
Computer and Telecommunications Coordinator

## I. Introduction

In the 1983 movie *War Games*, Matthew Broderick and Ally Sheedy play high school students who inadvertently access the NORAD computer network, thinking that they are merely playing a "war game" with the computers. As a consequence, Broderick and Sheedy come Hollywood-close to initiating a nuclear exchange between the United States and the Soviet Union. In order to accomplish this hack, Broderick configures his PC's modem to automatically dial random telephone numbers in the city where the computers he hopes to break into are located. When Sheedy asks Broderick how he pays for all the telephone calls, Broderick coyly tells her that "there are ways around" paying for the phone service. Sheedy asks: *"Isn't that a crime"?* Broderick's reply: *"Not if you are under eighteen."*

This article demonstrates why Broderick was wrong, for, while the movie may have seemed to be pure science fiction, the increased reliance on computers at all levels of society, coupled with the explosive growth in the use of personal computers and the Internet by teens, has made the scenario portrayed by the film seem to be not so fictional. Consider the following cases:

✓ A juvenile in Massachusetts pleads guilty to charges he disabled a key telephone company computer servicing the Worcester airport control tower, thereby disabling both the main radio transmitter, as well as a circuit which enabled aircraft on approach to send signals activating the runway lights.

✓ A 16-year-old from Florida pleads guilty and is sentenced to six months in a detention facility for intercepting electronic communications on military computer networks and for illegally obtaining information from a NASA computer network.

✓ A 16-year-old in Virginia pleads guilty to computer trespassing after hacking into a Massachusetts Internet Service Provider's (ISP's) computer system, causing $20,000 in damages.

✓ A 13-year-old California boy pleads guilty to making threats directed against a 13-year-old girl over the Internet. The boy had created a Web site which included a game featuring the girl's picture over a caption which read: "Hurry! Click on the trigger to kill her." The Web site included a petition calling for the girl's death.

*See* www.cybercrime.gov/juvenilepld.htm (Worcester airport); cybercrime.gov/comrade.htm (NASA case); Arthur L. Bowker, *Juveniles and Computers: Should We Be Concerned,* Federal Probation, December 1999, at 40 (Virginia and California cases). This article seeks to explain: (1) why and how the rise of the computer culture and Internet generation presents opportunities for juveniles to commit crimes distinctly different from those traditionally committed by minors; (2) the statutory framework governing prosecution of computer delinquents in federal court; and (3) special considerations which pertain to the prosecution of computer crimes by juveniles. At a time when a *Newsweek* survey estimates that almost eighty percent of children regularly go online, the incidence of computer crime committed by juveniles will, increasingly, come to a prosecutor's attention.

# II. Kids and Computer Crime

As has been documented in other articles in this publication (a bulletin that can be found at www.cybercrime.gov), the rapid growth in the use of personal computers (PCs) and the advent of the Internet have made it possible for persons of all ages to commit serious crimes — including extortion, computer hacking, and credit card fraud — without ever leaving the comfort of home. In addition, difficulties in obtaining electronic evidence and tracing back to the electronic wrong-doer present unique challenges to law enforcement investigating computer crimes committed by persons of any age. In the context of juveniles who engage in criminally antisocial computer behavior, these problems take on special significance. This is true for several reasons.

First, the enormous computing power of today's PCs make it possible for minors to commit offenses which are disproportionately serious to their age. For example, while property offenses committed by minors in the "brick and mortar" world typically include shoplifting or other forms of simple theft, the advent of computer technology has made it possible for minors in the "point and click" world to engage in highly complex fraud schemes. "Typical" computer crimes committed by minors include trading stolen credit card numbers and amassing thousands of dollars worth of fraudulent purchases on those cards, or large-scale pirating of copyrighted computer software which is later sold or bartered to other minors in exchange for other pirated software. A Canadian juvenile has already been held responsible for launching a massive denial-of-service attack costing American companies millions of dollars. Likewise, there is, in principle, no reason why a juvenile could not release a computer virus, infecting tens of thousands of computers, or engage in large-scale securities manipulation, causing six- and seven-figure damages to investors. Indeed, given the technological sophistication of today's youth (evident to any parent who has relied on their fourteen-year-old to set up the family computer), it is possible for a teenager to commit computer-related property offenses on a scale to which, prior to the 1980s, only seasoned veterans of the criminal justice system could aspire.

Second, the ability of a juvenile to portray himself or herself as an adult in the online world means that juveniles have access to fora in which to engage in criminal activity — for example, auction Web sites, financial services Web sites, and chat rooms — that in the physical world would quickly deny them any access at all. This access opens doors to criminality previously closed to minors. In a similar vein, kids who are too young to drive can use a PC connected to the Internet to access computers worldwide, adding to their ability to commit serious and far-reaching offenses and to confederate with other computer delinquents. Not only is it difficult for parents to deny their children access to computers — necessary for much legitimate schoolwork — even were parental control at home practicable, the ubiquitous (and often free) computer access provided by high schools, public libraries, and friends make "computer curfews" an oxymoron.

Third, juveniles appear to have an ethical "deficit" when it comes to computer crimes. In one study, 34 percent of university undergraduates admitted to illegally pirating copyrighted software, and 16 percent admitted to gaining illegal access to a computer system to browse or exchange information. *See* Bowker, *Juveniles and Computers*, at 41 (citing surveys). Moreover, a recent poll of 47,235 elementary and middle school students conducted by Scholastic, Inc., revealed that 48 percent of juveniles do not consider hacking to be a crime. This ethical deficit increases the likelihood that even "good kids" who are ordinarily unlikely to commit crimes such as robbery, burglary, or assault, may not be as disinclined to commit online crimes.

# III. Prosecuting Juveniles in Federal Court

Against this backdrop, federal prosecutors bringing computer delinquents to justice must master the provisions of the criminal code applicable to those actions. Specifically, they must understand the Juvenile Justice and Delinquency Prevention Act (the "Act"), codified at 18 U.S.C. §§ 5031 to 5042 of Title 18, which governs both the criminal prosecution or the delinquent adjudication of minors in federal court. While a complete analysis of the Act is beyond the scope of this article, certain of its provisions bear discussion, for proceedings against juveniles in federal court differ in significant respects from the prosecution of adults, and the prosecution of computer delinquents presents special considerations different from that of juveniles involved in other delinquencies. Specifically, as described below, the Act creates a unique procedure for delinquency proceedings against juveniles — a process quasi-criminal and quasi-civil in nature, replete with its own procedural complexities and particular rules. In their totality, these unique provisions seek to take account not only of the special protections provided to minors but also of the fact that even persons under 18 can commit "adult" crimes.

As a threshold matter, it is important to note that a juvenile proceeding is not the same as a criminal prosecution. Rather, it is a proceeding in which the issue to be determined is whether the minor is a "juvenile delinquent" as a matter of status, not whether he or she is guilty of committing a crime. Thus, a finding against the juvenile does not result in a criminal conviction; instead, it results in a finding of "delinquency." Indeed, the juvenile proceeding is specifically designed to *lessen* the amount of stigma that attaches to the act of delinquency compared to a criminal conviction, and to emphasize the rehabilitation, rather than punishment, of the juvenile. *See, e.g., United States v. Hill,* 538 F.2d 1072, 1074 (4th Cir. 1976). With that background in mind, several aspects of the Act can be examined.

## A. Who Is a Juvenile?

Under the Act, a "juvenile" is a person who has not yet reached the age of eighteen at the time of the commission of the offense *and* is under twenty-one as of the time of the filing of formal juvenile charges. *See* 18 U.S.C. § 5031. Thus, a person who committed the offense before his eighteenth birthday but is over twenty-one on the date formal charges are filed may be prosecuted as an adult; the juvenile delinquency proceedings do not apply at all. This is true even where the government could have charged the juvenile prior to his twenty-first birthday but did not. *See In re Jack Glenn Martin,* 788 F.2d 696, 698 (11th Cir. 1986) (determinative date is date of filing of formal indictment or information, fact that Government could have brought charges against defendant prior to his twenty-first birthday held to be "irrelevant"); *see also United States v. Hoo,* 825 F.2d 667 (2d Cir. 1987) (absent improper delay by government, age at time of filing of formal charges determines whether the Act applies).

## B. Does Federal Jurisdiction Exist?

As is true in the case of adults, not every criminal act violates federal law. Only where Congress has determined that a particular federal interest is at stake, and has passed appropriate legislation, can a federal criminal prosecution go forward. In general, under the Act, there are three situations where federal delinquency jurisdiction over a juvenile exists. *First,* where the state court lacks jurisdiction, or refuses to assume jurisdiction. *See* 18 U.S.C. § 5032. *Second,* where the state does not have available programs and services adequate for the needs of juveniles. *See id. Third,* where the crime is a federal felony crime of violence or one of several enumerated federal offenses (principally relating to narcotics and firearm offenses), and there exists a sufficient federal interest to warrant exercise of federal jurisdiction. *See id.* These three jurisdictional bases are discussed below.

1.   No State Statute, or State Refuses Jurisdiction: This first basis for federal jurisdiction will be the most frequently used basis in the context of juvenile computer delinquents. It encompasses situations where a state has no law criminalizing the specific conduct, or does have a law but, for whatever reason, indicates that it will not pursue a proceeding under its law against the minor. With regard to the former, although many states have enacted laws analogous to the general federal computer crime statute (18 U.S.C. § 1030), the electronic eavesdropping statute (18 U.S.C. § 2511), and the access device fraud statute (18 U.S.C. § 1029), to pick the most commonly prosecuted cybercrimes, some states do not have laws under which the crime in question can be prosecuted. In these cases, under the Act, the juvenile, nevertheless, can be held to account for his or her act of delinquency under federal law.

More commonly, however, a state will have a statute which does cover the cybercrime in question — *see, e.g.,* N.Y. Penal Law § 156.10 (computer trespass); *id.* § 156.27 (computer tampering in the first degree); *id.* § 250.05 (intercepting or accessing electronic communications) — but will be unwilling to assume jurisdiction over the juvenile, perhaps because of a shortage of resources, or a dearth of technical and/or prosecutorial expertise. In such cases, upon certification by the United States Attorney that pertinent state officials do *not* wish to proceed against the juvenile, the Federal Government may assume jurisdiction. *See* 18 U.S.C. § 5032.

In the context of cybercrime, certain offenses committed by juveniles may amount to crimes in multiple states. A crippling denial-of-service attack or the transmission of a computer virus can generate victims in numerous jurisdictions. The Act, however, does not appear to require that, in such cases, the government must certify that each and every state that could potentially have jurisdiction is unwilling to assume the jurisdiction at their disposal. The Act merely requires that the "juvenile court or other appropriate court of *a State* does not have jurisdiction or refuses to assume jurisdiction over [the] juvenile" (18 U.S.C. § 5032 [emphasis supplied]). Typically, the pertinent state will be the state contemplating proceedings against the minor which, in practice, will often be the state in which the federal prosecutor investigating the case sits. Of course, since federal criminal proceedings can often preclude state criminal proceedings under state double jeopardy principles, federal prosecutors faced with multistate cases should consult with prosecutors from all affected states in order to determine what, if any, effect a federal juvenile proceeding may have on a state's proceedings. Consultation is also warranted because certain states may provide for treatment of the juvenile as an adult more easily than the provisions of the Act (discussed below), which deal with transfer of a juvenile to adult status.

2. **The State Has No Programs or Inadequate Programs:** This second basis for federal jurisdiction arises infrequently, as most states do have programs and facilities which provide for the adjudication, detention, and rehabilitation of minors. (Indeed, as of the writing of this article, there are no federal detention facilities specifically designed for juveniles. Juveniles who are the subject of federal delinquency proceedings are housed in contract facilities run by state, local, or private entities.) However, in the event that state officials were, for any reason, unable to address the needs of a juvenile, this exception would apply.

3. **Enumerated Crimes and Crimes of Violence:** Finally, the Act also sets forth certain federal crimes for which jurisdiction is deemed to exist, and where there is a substantial federal interest to warrant jurisdiction. The enumerated offenses are controlled substance offenses arising under 21 U.S.C. §§ 841, 952(a), 953, 955, 959, 960(b)(1), (2), (3), as well as firearms-related offenses arising under 18 U.S.C. §§ 922(x), 924(b), (g), or (h). While these offenses are typically inapplicable to cybercrime, the statute also permits jurisdiction in cases of "crimes of violence" which are punishable as felonies. *See* 18 U.S.C. § 5032. Although the Act itself does not define it, 18 U.S.C. § 16 defines crimes of violence as offenses that "ha[ve] as an element the use, attempted use, or threatened use of physical force against the person or property of another," or any offense "that is a felony and that, by its nature, involves a substantial risk that physical force against the person or property of another may be used in the commission of committing the offense" (18 U.S.C. § 16). In the context of cybercrime, the statutes which implicate this basis of jurisdiction include 18 U.S.C. § 875(b) (transmission in interstate or foreign commerce of extortionate threats to injure another person), 18 U.S.C. § 1951(a) and (b)(2) (interference with commerce by extortion or threats of physical violence), and 18 U.S.C. § 844(e) (transmission of, *inter alia,* bomb threats).

Prosecutors relying on this third basis for jurisdiction should keep in mind that their certification must not only set forth a federal felony crime of violence, but must also certify that a substantial federal interest in the case or offense warrants assumption of federal jurisdiction. Eight of the nine circuits that have addressed the issue have held that the United States Attorney's certification of a substantial federal interest is not subject to appellate review for factual accuracy; only the Fourth Circuit has held otherwise. *See United States v. John Doe*, 226 F.3d 672, 676–78 (6th Cir. 2000) (collecting cases).

Where the Federal Government is the victim of a crime, the federal interest is apparent. Yet, even when it is not the victim, federal interests often exist, as cybercrime often involves conduct affecting critical infrastructures (e.g., telecommunications systems); industries, or technologies significant to the nation's economy (e.g., aerospace, computer software); or criminal groups operating in multiple states and/or foreign countries (e.g., identity theft and stolen credit card rings). It is precisely in these important and often hard-to-enforce-locally situations that federal jurisdiction is peculiarly appropriate.

## C. Delinquency Proceedings

Assuming that federal juvenile jurisdiction exists, prosecutors bringing such actions will typically commence the action with the filing, under seal, of a juvenile information and the jurisdictional certification. *See* 18 U.S.C. § 5032, ☐☐ 2–3. It is important to note that the certification must be signed by the United States Attorney personally, and a copy of the pertinent memorandum delegating authority from the Assistant Attorney General to the United States Attorneys to sign the certification should be attached to the submission. (A copy of the delegation memorandum, dated July 20, 1995, can be obtained from the Terrorism and Violent Crime Section of the Department of Justice.)

A juvenile has no Fifth Amendment right to have his or her case presented to a grand jury, nor does the juvenile have the right to a trial by jury. *See, e.g., United States v. Hill*, 538 F.2d 1072, 1075–76 (4th Cir. 1976); *United States v. Indian Boy*, 565 F.2d 585, 595 (9th cir. 1975). Instead, the "guilt" phase of a delinquency proceeding is essentially conducted as a bench trial. And in that trial — in which the government must prove that the juvenile has committed the act of delinquency beyond a reasonable doubt — the juvenile has many of the same rights as a criminal defendant. These include: (1) the right to notice of the charges; (2) the right to counsel; (3) the right to confront and cross-examine witnesses; and (4) the privilege against self-incrimination. *See Hill*, 538 F.2d at 1075, n.3 (collecting cases). Moreover, in the delinquency proceeding, the Federal Rules of Criminal Procedure apply — to the extent their application is not inconsistent with any provision of the Act. *See* Fed. R. Crim. P. 54(b)(5); *see also* Wright, *Federal Practice and Procedure: Criminal 2d* § 873. The Federal Rules of Evidence likewise apply to the delinquency trial; *see* F.R.E. 101, 1101, although courts have held them inapplicable to transfer proceedings, discussed below. *See Government of the Virgin Islands in the Interest of A.M., a Minor*, 34 F.3d 153, 160–62 (3rd Cir. 1994) (collecting cases).

In addition, the Act affords juveniles special protections not ordinarily applicable to adult defendants. Most notably, the juvenile's identity is to be protected from public disclosure. *See* 18 U.S.C. § 5038 (provisions concerning sealing and safeguarding of records generated and maintained in juvenile proceedings). Thus, court filings should refer to the juvenile by his or her initials and not by name, and routine booking photographs and fingerprints should not be made or kept. Moreover, whenever a juvenile is taken into custody for an alleged act of delinquency, the juvenile must be informed of his or her legal rights "in language comprehensible to [the] juvenile" (18 U.S.C. § 5033), and the juvenile's parent, guardian, or custodian must be notified immediately of the juvenile's arrest, the nature of the charges, and the juvenile's rights. *Id.* Upon arrest, the juvenile may not be detained for longer than a reasonable period of time before being brought before a magistrate. *Id.* When brought before a magistrate, the juvenile must be released to his or her parents or guardian upon their promise to bring the juvenile to court for future appearances, unless the magistrate determines that the detention of the juvenile is required to secure his or her appearance before the court, or to ensure the juvenile's safety or the safety of others. *See* 18 U.S.C. § 5034. At no time may a juvenile who is under twenty-one years of age and charged with an act of delinquency or adjudicated delinquent be housed in a facility where they would have regular contact with adults. *See* 18 U.S.C. §§ 5035, 5038. Under the Act, a juvenile has a right to counsel at all critical stages of the proceeding, and the Act authorizes the appointment of counsel where the juvenile's parents or guardians cannot afford to retain counsel. *Id.*

## D. Transfers From Juvenile Delinquency Proceedings to Adult Criminal Proceedings

As noted above, under certain circumstances, a juvenile's case may be transferred to adult status and the juvenile can be tried as an adult. In these situations, the case proceeds as any criminal case would with the exception that a juvenile under eighteen who is transferred to adult status may never be housed with adults, either pretrial or to serve a sentence. Most notably, a juvenile may transfer to adult status by waiving his juvenile status, upon written request and advice of counsel. *See* 18 U.S.C. § 5032, ☐4. In addition, the Act creates two forms of transfer which do not take into account the juvenile's wishes: discretionary transfer and mandatory transfer.

As the name implies, discretionary transfer is an option available, upon motion by the Government, in certain types of cases where the juvenile is age fifteen or older at the time of the commission of the act of delinquency. *See* 18 U.S.C. § 5032, ☐4. As applied to the field of cyberdelinquency, it is available in cases involving felony crimes of violence (e.g., extortion, bomb threats). Under the Act, a court must consider six factors in determining whether it is in the interest of justice to grant the Government's motion for discretionary transfer: (1) the age and social background of the juvenile; (2) the nature of the alleged offense, including the juvenile's leadership role in a criminal organization; (3) the nature and extent of the juvenile's prior delinquency record; (4) the juvenile's present intellectual development and psychological maturity; (5) the juvenile's response to past treatment efforts and the nature of those efforts; and (6) the availability of programs to treat the juvenile's behavioral problems. *See* 18 U.S.C. § 5032, ☐5. In the context of typical computer crimes committed by juveniles, several of the factors will often counsel in favor of transfer to adult status: many cyberdelinquents come from middle-class, or even affluent backgrounds; many commit their exploits with the assistance of other delinquents; and many are extremely intelligent. Moreover, many of the most sophisticated computer criminals are under eighteen by only a few months and, as verge-of-adult wrongdoers, may well merit adult justice.

Mandatory transfer is more circumscribed than discretionary transfer, and is limited to certain enumerated offenses (e.g., arson) which are not typically applicable in cyberprosecutions, or to violent felonies directed against other persons. *See* 18 U.S.C. § 5032, ☐4. Here, however, transfer is further limited to offenses committed by juveniles age sixteen and older who also have a prior criminal conviction or juvenile adjudication for which they could be subject to mandatory or discretionary transfer. As a practical matter, therefore, in the area of cybercrime the majority of proceedings begun as juvenile proceedings will likely remain as such, and will not be transferred to adult prosecutions.

## E. Sentencing and Detention

Under the Act, a court has several options in sentencing a juvenile adjudged to be delinquent. The court may suspend the finding(s) of delinquency; order restitution; place the juvenile on probation; or order that the juvenile be detained. *See* 18 U.S.C. § 5037(a). In cases where detention is ordered, such detention can never be longer than the period of detention the juvenile would have received had they been an adult. *See* 18 U.S.C. § 5037(b). Accordingly, the Sentencing Guidelines, although not controlling, must be consulted. U.S.S.G. § 1B1.12; *see United States v. R.L.C.,* 503 U.S. 291, 307 n.7 (1992). Finally, if the disposition hearing is before the juvenile's eighteenth birthday, he or she may be committed to official detention until his or her twenty-first birthday or the length of time they would have received as an adult under the Sentencing Guidelines, whichever term is less. If the juvenile is between eighteen and twenty-one at the time of the disposition, he or she may be detained for a maximum term of three or five years (depending on the type of felony relevant to the proceeding), but in no event can he or she be detained longer than they would be as an adult sentenced under the Guidelines. *See* 18 U.S.C. § 5037(b), (c).

# IV. Special Considerations

As demonstrated above, federal delinquency proceedings are unique from a legal point of view, and prosecutors initiating such proceedings would do well to consult closely with the United States Attorney's Manual provisions concerning delinquency proceedings, *see* USAM § 9-8.00, as well as the Terrorism and Violent Crime Section (TVCS), which serves as the Department's expert in this field. Prosecutors should also familiarize themselves with the legal issues typically litigated in this area in order to avoid common pitfalls. *See, e.g.,* Jean M. Radler, Annotation, *Treatment Under Federal Juvenile Delinquency Act (18 U.S.C. §§ 5031–5042) Of Juvenile Alleged To Have Violated Law of United States,* 137 ALR Fed. 481 (1997).

In addition to the novel nature of the proceedings themselves, however, crimes committed by juveniles pose unique investigative challenges. For example, common investigative techniques such as undercover operations and the use of cooperators and informants can raise difficult issues rarely present in the investigations of adults. Indeed, a seemingly routine post-arrest interview may raise issues of consent and voluntariness when the arrestee is a juvenile which are not present in the case of an adult arrestee. *Compare, e.g., United States v. John Doe,* 226 F.3d 672 (6th Cir. 2000) (affirming district court's refusal to suppress juvenile's confession notwithstanding arresting officer's failure to comply with parental notification provisions of Act, where circumstances surrounding confession demonstrated voluntariness of juvenile's confession) *with United States v. Juvenile (RRA-A),* 229 F.3d 737 (9th Cir. 2000) (ruling that juvenile's confession should be suppressed where arresting officer's failure to inform parents may have been a factor in confession, notwithstanding juvenile's request to arresting officers that her parent's *not* be contacted and informed of the arrest).

Alternatively, consider the case of a juvenile in a foreign country who, via the Internet, does serious damage to a United States Government computer or to an e-commerce Web server. Ordinarily, of course, extradition of foreign nationals to the United States is governed by treaty. Where they exist, treaties generally fall into two categories: "dual criminality" treaties, in which the signatories agree to extradite for offenses if the offenses are criminal in both nations, and "list" treaties, in which extradition is possible only for offenses enumerated in the treaty. Interestingly, however, some extradition treaties contain provisions which specifically permit the foreign sovereign to take account of the youth of the offender in deciding whether to extradite. *E.g.,* Convention on Extradition between the United States of America and Sweden, 14 UST 1845; TIAS 5496 (as supplemented by Supplementary Convention on Extradition, TIAS 10812). How these international juvenile delinquency situations will unfold in the future is unclear. What is clear is that as more and more of the planet becomes "wired," opportunities for cybercrime — including cybercrime by juveniles — will only increase. (Prosecutors who encounter situations involving juvenile's operating from abroad should, in addition to consulting with TVCS, consult with the Department's Office of International Affairs.)

# V. Conclusion

Whether investigating a juvenile who commits a cybercrime involving computers maintained by a private party or computers maintained by segments of the strategic triad, a prosecutor considering bringing a juvenile to justice must not only master a new area of law, but also must be aware that traditional approaches to a case bear reevaluation in light of the unique aspects and special considerations presented by a juvenile who engages in acts of cyberdelinquency.

# About the Author

Joseph V. DeMarco is an Assistant United States Attorney for the Southern District of New York, where he serves as Computer and Telecommunications Coordinator. Currently, he is on detail to the Department's Computer Crimes and Intellectual Property Section in Washington, D.C.

This bulletin, along with numerous cybercrime-related material, can be found at www.cyber crime.gov, the Computer Crime and Intellectual Property Section (CCIPS) of the Criminal Division of the U.S. Department of Justice.

# Appendix D

# National Infrastructure Protection Center Statement on Cybersecurity

The following statement on the issue of cybersecurity was delivered for the record by Leslie G. Wiser, Jr., Chief of the Training, Outreach, and Strategy Section of the National Infrastructure Protection Center of the Federal Bureau of Investigation on August 29, 2001. Wiser delivered the statement before the House Committee on Government Affairs, Subcommittee on Government Efficiency, Financial Management, and Intergovernmental Relations at a San Jose, California, field hearing. As you read this document, take note of the importance of the government's role in cybersecurity (hence its formation of the NIPC). Wiser emphasizes how cooperation between the NIPC, foreign governments, and the private sector is the foundation for a sound cybersecurity infrastructure.

## Statement on Cybersecurity

Good morning Chairman Horn, thank you for inviting me here today to discuss cybersecurity issues. While I am going to discuss broad aspects of cybersecurity and the role of the NIPC in helping to secure the nation's critical infrastructures, I am going to focus on some recent incidents that demonstrate the success we can have when government partners with other nations and with the private sector. I will then discuss the NIPC's role in cybersecurity with respect to predicting, preventing, detecting, and responding to incidents with an emphasis on computer viruses and worms. The final part of my statement will focus on some of the recent virus and worm cases we have faced.

A virus is malicious computer code embedded within an executable program that victims activate on their machines, usually by opening an e-mail attachment. Often viruses are sent with notes instructing recipients to open the attachment, such as the note with the Melissa macro virus which stated, "here is the document you requested," or with a tantalizing title such as "sexxxy.jpg," or "naked wife." Worms, on the other hand, require no action by the victims to activate. They spread on their own from system to system without the need for the victim to do anything. The Code Red Worm, for example, automatically sends itself to 99 IP addresses it generates. Once activated, viruses and worms can do anything from deleting files to sending themselves, together with documents on your hard drive, to some or all of the names in your address book or to any Internet Protocol address.

# Arrest in Leave Worm Case

On June 23, 2001, the NIPC issued "Advisory 01-014," "New Scanning Activity (with W32-Leave.worm) Exploiting SubSeven Victims," regarding the Leave worm activity. This particular worm allowed the intruder access to an infected system while the victim machine was connected to the Internet. It is believed that home users' computers, without updated anti-virus software, were the systems primarily infected by this worm. Current anti-virus software will detect the presence of the W32-Leave.worm. Full descriptions and removal instructions can be found at various anti-virus Web sites.

A 24-year-old male was arrested on July 23, 2001, in the United Kingdom for violation of its Computer Misuse Act 1990. The announcement of his arrest was delayed to avoid potentially compromising the ongoing investigation. This individual, who, under British Law, cannot be identified at this time, was arrested in connection with designing and propagating malicious code, known as the W32-Leave.worm, or Leave worm, into Windows-based computer systems. This individual has been released from custody and ordered to return to New Scotland Yard on September 24, 2001.

This malicious code was discovered by the analytical efforts of the employees of the Systems Administration and Network Security (SANS) Institute and reported by SANS to the NIPC. This arrest came as a result of a joint FBI/New Scotland Yard, UK, investigation, and illustrates the benefits of law enforcement and private industry working together.

# Ongoing Efforts on Code Red

The Code Red worm was discovered in the wild on July 13, 2001, by network administrators who were experiencing a large number of attacks targeting the buffer overflow vulnerability first reported in June 2001. On June 19, 2001, the NIPC and FedCIRC issued a joint advisory about the buffer overflow vulnerability that targeted Microsoft Windows NT and Microsoft Windows 2000 operating systems running IIS 4.0 and 5.0. On July 19, 2001, the NIPC issued an advisory on the Code Red worm. The advisory stated that, "The activity of the Ida Code Red worm has the potential to degrade services running on the Internet." In one day alone, the Code Red worm infected more than 250,000 systems in just nine hours. The Code Red worm, which was first reported by eEye Digital Security, takes advantage of known vulnerabilities in the Microsoft IIS Internet Server Application Program Interface (ISAPI) service. Unpatched systems are susceptible to a "buffer overflow" in the Idq.dll, which permits the attacker to run embedded code on the affected system. This memory-resident worm, once active on a system, first attempts to spread itself by creating a sequence of random IP addresses to infect unprotected Web servers. Each worm thread will then inspect the infected computer's time clock. The trigger time for the DOS execution of the Code Red worm was at midnight on July 20, 2001. Upon successful infection, the worm proceeded to use the time thread in an effort to bring down the www.whitehouse.gov domain by having the infected systems simultaneously send 100 connections to port 80 of the White House's Internet Protocol address.

The original variant of the worm also placed the words "Welcome to worm.com! Hacked by Chinese!" on the victim sites. Two other variants of the original worm do not deface victim Web sites. The NIPC, along with its government and private sector partners, realized that persons using Microsoft Windows NT and Microsoft Windows 2000 operating systems running IIS 4.0 and 5.0 needed to be warned to patch their systems for the safety of the entire Internet. Officials from the following organizations were all involved in the response effort working through the weekend of July 28–29: National Infrastructure Protection Center (NIPC) of the FBI, Critical Infrastructure Assurance Office (CIAO) of the Department of Commerce, Federal Computer Incident Response Center (FedCIRC) of the General Services Administration, Computer Emergency Response Team Coordination Center (CERT/CC) of Carnegie Mellon University, Systems Administration and Network Security (SANS) Institute, Microsoft, Internet Security Systems, Inc. (ISS), Cisco Systems, Inc., Partnership for Critical Infrastructure Security (PCIS), Information Technology Association of America (ITAA), Digital Island, Inc., Information Technology Information Sharing and Analysis Center (IT-ISAC), Internet Security Alliance (ISA), UUNet, and America Online.

On Sunday July 29, the NIPC, Microsoft Corporation, Federal Computer Incident Response Center (FedCIRC), the Information Technology Association of America (ITAA), CERT Coordination Center (CERT/CC), SANS Institute, Internet Security Systems (ISS), and the Internet Security Alliance (ISA) issued a joint warning message about Code Red.

The NIPC posted the warning and numerous updates on its public Web site (www.nipc.gov) and pushed the warning to InfraGard members through the InfraGard communications network, to state and local police through the National Threat Warning System, and to tens of thousands of private sector companies via the FBI's Awareness National Security Issues and Response (ANSIR) network. By forwarding the warning message to those who may need it, the NIPC strives to ensure that those who are part of its information sharing networks receive the information as quickly as possible with minimal effort on their part. In other cases, InfraGard has already prevented cyber-attacks by discretely alerting InfraGard members to compromises on their systems. For efforts such as the one made on Code Red, the InfraGard initiative recently received the 2001 WorldSafe Internet Safety Award from the Safe America Foundation.

On July 30th, a joint news conference was held at the Ronald Reagan Building in Washington, D.C. The presence of representatives of agencies, companies, and organizations which produced the Code Red warning demonstrated the seriousness of the threat and the public-private partnership that has developed with regard to protecting our information systems from attack. The urgency of the news conference lay in the fear that the spread of the worm could absorb so much bandwidth as to degrade the overall functioning of the Internet. Since business, medical, and government professionals increasingly depend on the Internet's functioning to conduct normal operations, service degradation poses an emerging threat to America's economy and security.

Microsoft has developed a patch for the identified vulnerability. According to Microsoft, over 2 million copies of the IIS patch have been downloaded. The July 30th news conference no doubt accelerated this process. Since the patches can be downloaded and installed on a number of machines, the actual number of systems patched may be higher than 2 million. The NIPC and its partners have received much positive feedback from the user community regarding these efforts on Code Red.

We are hopeful that the worst of the damage feared was averted based on this awareness campaign. Nevertheless, Computer Economics — a California-based Internet research organization — estimates that the worm has already cost $2.4 billion in economic impact, including $1 billion to cleanse, inspect, patch, and return systems to normal service, and $1.4 billion for other support functions related to lost productivity due to the worm. As of August 8th, the SANS Internet Storm Center noted that 661,044 unique IP addresses have been infected, with 150–175,000 machines infected (machines can have more than one associated IP address). While all of these figures are subject to revision, two trends seem clear. First, the rate of infections from the original worm have been substantial, although not at the same rate as in July. Second, the aggressive efforts on the part of the government and private sector urging computer users to patch their systems seems to have paid off.

Self-propagating worms that exploit vulnerabilities in commonly used software platforms will continue to pose a security challenge. These worms require no social engineering (i.e., no one needs to be tricked into revealing any information) and require no action on the part of users (i.e., the opening of attachments). As we saw with Code Red, they can hurt us in two ways: They can consume Internet bandwidth during their propagation phase if enough machines are infected, and they can carry harmful payloads, like the instructions to launch against a chosen target. Anyone can be the next target, as future worms may result in much more destructive activity.

There is another worm we have been tracking since early August, dubbed "Code Red II." This worm exploits the same vulnerability as the original Code Red worm and its variants, but instead of compromising a system to launch denial-of-service attacks, it installs a backdoor into infected systems that can be accessed by anyone knowing that the victim system has been compromised.

On August 16th, the NIPC released an assessment entitled "Code Red Reminder and Clarification, Assessment 01-018." That assessment clarifies issues related to which operating systems and software are vulnerable to Code Red and also makes clear that, contrary to some reports, we have not yet identified a Code Red III.

## The NIPC Approach to the Problem

Because the NIPC is an interagency Center, it could quickly react to the recent infections of the Leave and Code Red worms. Senior leadership positions in the NIPC are held by personnel from several agencies. The NIPC Director is a senior FBI executive. The Deputy Director of the NIPC is a two-star Navy Rear Admiral, and the Executive Director is detailed from the Air Force Office of Special Investigations. The Section and Unit Chiefs in the Computer Investigation and Operations Section and the Training, Outreach, and Strategy Section are from the FBI. The Assistant Section Chief for Training, Outreach, and Strategy is detailed from the Defense Criminal Investigative Service. The Section Chief of the Analysis and Warning Section is from the CIA, and his deputy is a senior FBI agent. The head of the NIPC Watch and Warning Unit is reserved for a uniformed service officer, and the head of the Analysis and Information Sharing Unit is reserved for a National Security Agency manager. This breadth of leadership has meant that when worms such as Code Red appear, coordination across the civilian and military agencies of the government is rapid and efficient.

But it is not just in the leadership ranks that the NIPC has broad representation. Currently, the Center has representatives from the following agencies: FBI, Office of the Secretary of Defense, Army, Air Force Office of Special Investigations, Defense Criminal Investigative Service, National Security Agency, United States Postal Service, Department of Transportation/Federal Aviation Administration, Central Intelligence Agency, Department of Commerce/Critical Infrastructure Assurance Office, and the Department of Energy. This representation has given us the unprecedented ability to reach back to the parent organizations of our interagency detailees on intrusions and infrastructure protection matters in order to provide and receive information. In addition, we have formed an interagency coordination cell at the Center which holds monthly meetings with U.S. Secret Service, U.S. Customs Service, representatives from DoD investigative agencies, the Offices of Inspector General of NASA, Social Security Administration, Departments of Energy, State, and Education, and the U.S. Postal Service, to discuss topics of mutual concern.

This representation is not enough, however. The NIPC would like to see all lead agencies represented in the Center. The more broadly representative the NIPC is, the better job it can do in responding to viruses, worms, and other intrusions into critical U.S. systems.

We have established four strategic directions for our capability growth: prediction, prevention, detection, and mitigation/response. None of these are new concepts, but the NIPC will renew its focus on each of them in order to strengthen our strategic analysis capabilities. The NIPC will work to further strengthen its longstanding efforts on the early detection and mitigation of cyber-attacks. These strategic directions will be significantly advanced by our intensified cooperation with federal agencies and the private sector.

## PREDICTION

Our most ambitious strategic directions, prediction and prevention, are intended to forestall attacks before they occur. We are seeking ways to forecast or predict hostile capabilities in much the same way that the military forecasts weapons threats. The goal here is to forecast these threats with sufficient warning to prevent them. A key to success in these areas will be strengthened cooperation with intelligence collectors and the application of sophisticated new analytic tools to better learn from day-to-day trends. The strategy of prevention is reminiscent of traditional community policing programs, but with our infrastructure partners and key systems vendors. As the recent Leave and Code Red worm incidents demonstrate, our working relations have never been closer with key federal agencies, like FedCIRC, NSA, CIA, and the Joint Task Force — Computer Network Operations (JTF-CNO), and private sector groups such as SANS, the anti-virus community, major Internet Service Providers, and the backbone companies. These close relationships aid in predicting events before they happen.

## PREVENTION

Our role in preventing the spread of computer viruses and worms as well as other cyberintrusions into critical U.S. systems is not to provide advice on what hardware or software to use or to act as a federal systems administrator. Rather, our role is to provide information about threats, ongoing incidents, and exploited vulnerabilities so that government and private sector system administrators can take the appropriate protective measures. The NIPC has a variety of products to inform the private sector and other domestic and foreign government agencies of the threat, including: alerts, advisories, and assessments; biweekly CyberNotes; monthly Highlights; and topical electronic reports. These products are designed for tiered distribution to both government and private sector entities consistent with applicable law and the need to protect intelligence sources and methods, and law enforcement investigations. For example, Highlights is a publication for sharing analysis and information on critical infrastructure issues. It provides analytical insights into major trends and events affecting the nation's critical infrastructures. It is usually published in an unclassified format and reaches national security and civilian government agency officials as well as infrastructure owners and operators. CyberNotes is another NIPC publication designed to provide security and information system professionals with timely information on cybervulnerabilities, hacker exploit scripts, hacker trends, virus information, and other critical infrastructure-related best practices. It is published on our Web site and disseminated in hard copy to government and private sector audiences.

The NIPC has elements responsible for both analysis and warning. What makes the NIPC unique is that it has access to law enforcement, intelligence, private sector, foreign liaison, and open source information. No other entity has this range of information. Complete and timely reporting of incidents from private industry and government agencies allows NIPC analysts to make the linkages between government and private sector intrusions. We are currently working on integrating our databases, consistent with the law, to allow us to more quickly make the linkages among seemingly disparate intrusions. This database will leverage both the unique information available to the NIPC through FBI investigations and information available from the intelligence community and open sources. Having these analytic functions at the NIPC is a central element of its ability to carry out its preventive mission.

The NIPC also shares information via its InfraGard Initiative. All 56 FBI field offices now have InfraGard chapters. Just in the last six months, the InfraGard Initiative has added over 1,000 new members to increase the overall membership to over 1,800. It is the most extensive government–private sector partnership for infrastructure protection in the world, and is a service we provide to InfraGard members free of charge. InfraGard expands direct contacts with the private sector infrastructure owners and operators and shares information about cyberintrusions and vulnerabilities through the formation of local InfraGard chapters within the jurisdiction of each of the 56 FBI Field Offices and several of its Resident Agencies (subdivisions of the larger field offices).

A key element of the InfraGard initiative is the confidentiality of reporting by members. The reporting members edit out the identifying information about themselves on the notices that are sent to other members of the InfraGard network. This process is called sanitization, and it protects the information provided by the victim of a cyberattack. Much of the information provided by the private sector is proprietary and is treated as such. InfraGard provides its membership with the capability to write an encrypted sanitized report for dissemination to other members. This measure helps to build a trusted relationship with the private sector and at the same time encourages other private sector companies to report cyberattacks to law enforcement.

InfraGard held its first national congress from June 12–14, 2001. This conclave provided an excellent forum for NIPC senior managers and InfraGard members to exchange ideas. InfraGard's success is directly related to private industry's involvement in protecting its critical systems, since private industry owns most of the infrastructures. The dedicated work of the NIPC and the InfraGard members is paying off. InfraGard has already prevented cyberattacks by discretely alerting InfraGard members to compromises on their systems.

The NIPC is also working with the Information Sharing and Analysis Centers (ISACS), established under the auspices of PDD-63. The North American Electric Reliability Council (NERC) serves as the electric power ISAC. The NIPC has developed a program with the NERC for an Indications and Warning System for physical and cyberattacks. Under the program, electric utility companies and other power entities transmit incident reports to the NIPC. These reports are analyzed and assessed to determine whether an NIPC alert, advisory, or assessment is warranted to the electric utility community. Electric power participants in the program have stated that the information and analysis provided by the NIPC makes this program especially worthwhile. NERC has recently decided to expand this initiative nationwide. This initiative will serve as a good example of government and industry working together to share information, and the Electric Power Indications and Warning System will provide a model for the other critical infrastructures.

With the assistance of NERC, the NIPC conducted a six-month pilot program and a series of workshops to familiarize participants with the program's operating procedures. The workshops included hands-on table-top exercises that required program participants to work through simulated scenarios dealing with credible cyber- and physical attacks directed against the power industry. In the summer of 2000, a half-day table-top exercise was held for companies in NERC's Mid-Atlantic region, allowing them to role-play in responding to simulated incidents pre-scripted by NIPC and company representatives. Since October 2000, the NIPC — supported by NERC — conducted three workshops around the country in order to provide program participants with hands-on experience in responding to attacks against the electric power grid. Eventually, the NIPC will strive to have similar models and exercises for all the infrastructures.

The NIPC serves as sector liaison for the Emergency Law Enforcement Services (ELES) Sector at the request of the FBI. The NIPC completed the ELES Sector Plan in February 2001. The ELES Sector Plan was the first completed sector report under PDD-63 and was delivered to the White House on March 2, 2001. At the Partnership for Critical Infrastructure Security in Washington, D.C., in March 2001, the ELES Plan was held up as a model for the other sectors. The NIPC also sponsored the formation of the Emergency Law Enforcement Services Sector Forum, which meets quarterly to discuss issues relevant to sector security planning. The Forum contains federal, state, and local representatives. The next meeting of the Forum is scheduled for September 2001.

The Plan was the result of two years' work in which the NIPC surveyed law enforcement agencies concerning the vulnerabilities of their infrastructure, in particular their data and communications systems. Following the receipt of the survey results, the NIPC and the ELES Forum produced the ELES Sector Plan. The NIPC also produced a companion "Guide for State and Local Law Enforcement Agencies" that provides guidance and a "toolkit" that law enforcement agencies can use when implementing the activities suggested in the Plan.

The importance of the ELES Sector Plan and the Guide cannot be overstated. These documents will aid some 18,000 police and sheriff's departments located in towns and neighborhoods to better protect themselves from attack by providing them with useful checklists and examples of procedures they can use to improve their security. Since the local police are usually among the first responders to any incident threatening public safety, their protection is vital.

Also, the NIPC has prepared model agreements to promote information sharing and has presented them for negotiation to the following existing or potential ISACs: Association of Metropolitan Water Agencies (AMWA), Financial Services, Information Technology, National Association of State Chief Information Officers (NASCIO), National Coordinating Center (NCC) for Telecommunications, National Emergency Management Association (NEMA), National Petroleum Council (NPC), and U.S. Fire Administration (USFA). Offers for information sharing arrangements will be made to the emerging Rail and Aviation ISACs. We are promoting the establishment of an ISAC for the Public Health Services Sector. With respect to the federal agencies, NIPC has developed a model agreement for use in promoting information sharing with the other 70-plus executive branch agencies, and will soon launch a campaign to formalize these arrangements.

## DETECTION

Given the ubiquitous vulnerabilities in existing Commercial Off-the-Shelf (COTS) software, intrusions into critical systems are inevitable for the foreseeable future. Thus, detection of these viruses, worms, and other intrusions is crucial if the U.S. Government and critical infrastructure owners and operators are going to be able to respond effectively. To improve our detection capabilities, we first need to ensure that we are fully collecting, sharing, and analyzing all extant information. It is often the case that intrusions can be discerned simply by collecting bits of information from various sources; conversely, if we do not collate these pieces of information for analysis, we might not detect the intrusions at all. Thus, the NIPC's role in collecting information from all sources and performing analysis in itself serves the role of detection.

Federal Agency system administrators need to work with NIPC. PDD-63 makes clear the importance of such reporting. It states, "All executive departments and agencies shall cooperate with the NIPC and provide such assistance, information, and advice that the NIPC may request, to the extent permitted by law. All executive departments shall also share with the NIPC information about threats and warning of attacks and about actual attacks on critical government and private sector infrastructures, to the extent permitted by law."

In order to carry out this mandate, the NIPC is working closely with FedCIRC and the anti-virus community. The NIPC and the Computer Emergency Response Team (CERT) at Carnegie Mellon University have formed a mutually beneficial contractual relationship. The NIPC receives information from the CERT that it incorporates into strategic and tactical analyses and utilizes as part of its warning function. The NIPC is routinely in telephonic contact with CERT/CC and the anti-virus community for purposes of sharing vulnerability and threat information on a real-time basis. CERT/CC input is often sought when an NIPC warning is in production. The NIPC also provides information to the CERT that it obtains through investigations and other sources, using CERT as one method for distributing information (normally with investigative sources sanitized) to security professionals in industry and to the public. The Watch also provides the NIPC Daily Report to the CERT/CC via Internet e-mail. On more than one occasion, the NIPC provided CERT with the first information regarding a new threat, and the two organizations have often collaborated in putting information out about incidents and threats.

The NIPC has an excellent relationship with the General Services Administration's Federal Computer Incident Response Center (FedCIRC). NIPC and FedCIRC are both crucial to effective cyberdefense but serve different roles. When an agency reports an incident, FedCIRC works with the agency to identify the type of incident, mitigate any damage to the agency's system, and provide guidance to the agency on recovering from the incident. FedCIRC has detailed a person to the NIPC Watch Center. In addition, the NIPC sends draft alerts, advisories, and assessments on a regular basis to FedCIRC for input and commentary prior to their release. NIPC and FedCIRC information exchange assists both centers with their analytic products. The NIPC and FedCIRC are currently discussing ways to improve the flow of information between the two organizations and encourage federal agency reporting of incident information to the NIPC.

In response to victim reports, the NIPC sponsored the development of tools to detect malicious software code. For example, in December 1999, in anticipation of possible Y2K-related malicious conduct, the NIPC posted a detection tool on its Web site that allowed systems administrators to detect the presence of certain distributed denial-of-service (DDoS) tools on their networks. In those cases, hackers planted tools named Trinoo, Tribal Flood Net (TFN), TFN2K, and Stacheldraht (German for "barbed wire") on a large number of unwitting victim systems. Then, when the hacker sent a particular command, the victim systems in turn began sending messages against target systems. The target systems became overwhelmed with the traffic and were unable to function. Users trying to access the victim system were denied its services. The NIPC's detection tools were downloaded thousands of times and have no doubt prevented many DDoS attacks. In fact, in this cutting edge area of network security, the NIPC's Special Technologies and Applications Unit (STAU) received the 2000 SANS Award.

If we determine that an intrusion is imminent or underway, the NIPC Watch is responsible for formulating assessments, advisories, and alerts, and quickly disseminating them. The substance of those products will come from work performed by NIPC analysts. We can notify both private sector and government entities using an array of mechanisms so they can take protective steps. In some cases, these warning products can prevent a wider attack; in other cases, warnings can mitigate an attack already underway. This was the case both with our warnings regarding e-commerce vulnerabilities and with the more recent warnings posted about Code Red. Finally, these notices can prevent attacks from ever happening in the first place. For example, the NIPC released an advisory on March 30, 2001, regarding the Lion Internet worm, which is a DDoS tool targeting UNIX-based systems. Based on all-source information and analysis, the NIPC alerted systems administrators how to look for this compromise of their system and what specific steps to take to remove the tools if they are found. This alert was issued after consultation with FedCIRC, JTF-CNO, a private sector ISAC, and other infrastructure partners.

## MITIGATION/RESPONSE

Despite our efforts, we know that critical U.S. systems will continue to be attacked. The perpetrators could be criminal hackers, teenagers, cyberprotestors, terrorists, or foreign intelligence services. In order to identify an intruder, the NIPC coordinates an investigation that gathers information using either criminal investigative or foreign counter-intelligence authorities, depending on the circumstances. We also rely on the assistance of other nations when appropriate.

In the cyberworld, determining the "who, what, where, when, and how" is difficult. An event could be a system probe to find vulnerabilities or entry points, an intrusion to steal data or plant sniffers or malicious code, the spreading of a virus or worm, an act of teenage vandalism, an attack to disrupt or deny service, or even an act of war. The crime scene itself is totally different from the physical world in that it is dynamic—it grows, contracts, and can change shape. Further, the tools used to perpetrate a major infrastructure attack can be the same ones that are freely available on the Internet and used for other cyberintrusions (such as simple hacking, foreign intelligence gathering, or organized crime activity to steal property), making identification more difficult. Obtaining reliable information is necessary not only to identify the perpetrator but also to determine the size and nature of the intrusion and what information security response may prevent further attack: how many systems are affected, what techniques are being used, and what is the purpose of the intrusions—disruption, economic espionage, theft of money, etc.

Relevant information could come from existing criminal investigations or other contacts at the FBI Field Office level. It could come from the U.S. Intelligence Community, other U.S. Government agency information, private sector contacts, the media, other open sources, or foreign law enforcement contacts. The NIPC's role is to coordinate, collect, analyze, and disseminate this information. Indeed, this is one of the principal reasons the NIPC was created.

Because the Internet by its nature embodies a degree of anonymity, our government's proper response to an attack first requires significant investigative steps. Investigators typically need a full range of criminal and/or national security authorities to determine who launched the attack or authored the malicious code. There are many federal statutes that criminalize unauthorized conduct over the Internet. The law prohibits a wide variety of acts conducted with computers, some of which are traditional crimes (such as wire fraud and pornography) and others of which are more technology-specific crimes, such as hacking.

The primary Federal statute that criminalizes breaking into computers and spreading malicious viruses and worms is the Computer Fraud and Abuse Act, codified at Title 18 of the United States Code, Section 1030. Other statutes that are typically implicated in a hacking case include Section 1029 of Title 18, which criminalizes the misuse of computer passwords, and Section 2511 of Title 18, which criminalizes those hackers that break into systems and install "sniffers" to illegally intercept electronic communications. In order to investigate these violations, law enforcement relies on traditional sources and techniques to gather evidence, ranging from the public's voluntary assistance to court-authorized searches and court-authorized surveillance. We have similar investigative capabilities when pursuing cases in which foreign powers or terrorist organizations are impairing the confidentiality, integrity, or availability of our networks, although in these cases our legal authority typically is derived from the National Security Act of 1947 and the Foreign Intelligence Surveillance Act (FISA), both codified in Title 50 of the United States Code, rather than pursuant to the Federal Criminal Code.

The FBI has designated the NIPC to act as the program manager for all of its computer intrusion investigations, and the NIPC has made enormous strides in developing this critical nationwide program. In that connection, the NIPC works closely with the Department of Justice Criminal Division's Computer Crime and Intellectual Property Section, Office of Intelligence Policy and Review, and the U.S. Attorney's Offices in coordinating legal responses.

In the event of a national-level set of intrusions into significant systems or a major virus outbreak, the NIPC will form a CyberCrisis Action Team (C-CAT) to coordinate response activities and use the facilities of the FBI's Strategic Information and Operations Center (SIOC). The team will have expert investigators, computer scientists, analysts, watch standers, and other U.S. government agency representatives. Part of the U.S. government team might be physically located at FBI Headquarters, and part of the team may be just electronically connected. The C-CAT will immediately contact field offices responsible for the jurisdictions where the attacks are occurring and where the attacks may be originating. The C-CAT will continually assess the situation and support/coordinate investigative activities, issue updated warnings, as necessary, to all those affected by or responding to the crisis. The C-CAT will then coordinate the investigative effort to discern the scope of the attack, the technology being used, and the possible source and purpose of the attack.

The NIPC's placement in the FBI's Counterterrorism Division will allow for a seamless FBI response in the event of a terrorist action that encompasses both cyber- and physical attacks. The NIPC and the other elements of the FBI's Counterterrorism Division have conducted joint operations and readiness exercises in the FBI's SIOC. We are prepared to respond when called upon.

## As the Worm Turns

Over the past several years, we have seen a wide range of cyberthreats ranging from defacement of Web sites by juveniles to devastating worms and viruses released on the Internet. Some of these are obviously more significant than others. The theft of national security information from a government agency, or the interruption of electrical power to a major metropolitan area would have greater consequences for national security, public safety, and the economy than the defacement of a Web site. But even the less serious categories have real consequences and, ultimately, can undermine confidence in e-commerce and violate privacy or property rights. A Web site hack that shuts down an e-commerce site can have disastrous consequences for a business. An intrusion that results in the theft of credit card numbers from an online vendor can result in significant financial loss and, more broadly, reduce consumers' willingness to engage in e-commerce. Because of these implications, it is critical that we have in place the programs and resources to investigate and, ultimately, to deter these sorts of crimes.

Virus attacks have become more prevalent in recent years. While tens of thousands of viruses and worms exist in the wild, the vast majority of them are not serious threats. But just a few of them have unleashed havoc on the networks. A survey by InformationWeek and PriceWaterhouseCoopers conducted in the summer of 2000 estimated viruses would cause $1.6 trillion worth of damage in the year 2000 worldwide. That figure is larger than the gross domestic product of all but a handful of nations and demonstrates the huge economic costs that viruses and worms can have on the global economy.

In addition, because it is often difficult to determine whether a virus outbreak or worm propagation is the work of an individual with criminal motives or a foreign power, we must treat certain cases for their potential as a national security matter until we gather sufficient information to determine the nature, purpose, scope, and perpetrator of the attack. While we cannot discuss ongoing investigations, we can discuss closed cases that involve FBI and other agency investigations in which the intruder's methods and motivation were similar to what we are currently seeing. A few illustrative cases are described below.

As discussed above, Code Red infected over 150,000 systems and has yet to be stopped. But this is only the most recent in a growing list of computer worms. The first worm to get the attention of the computer users community was the Morris worm, released on November 2, 1988, by Robert Tappan Morris, a 23-year-old graduate student at Cornell University. The infant Internet community had never seen anything like this worm. In a matter of hours, it had infected 6,000 machines and, while it did not damage files, it clogged the machines and made them unusable. The machines had to be disconnected from the Internet and repaired. Morris was convicted of violating the Computer Fraud and Abuse Act and sentenced to three years probation, 400 hours of community service, and fined $10,500.

In May 2000, companies and individuals around the world were stricken by the "Love Bug," a virus (or, technically, a "worm") that traveled as an attachment to an e-mail message and propagated itself extremely rapidly through the victim's address books. The virus/worm also reportedly penetrated at least 14 federal agencies, including the Department of Defense (DOD), the Social Security Administration, the Central Intelligence Agency, the Immigration and Naturalization Service, the Department of Energy, the Department of Agriculture, the Department of Education, the National Aeronautics and Space Administration (NASA), along with the House and Senate.

Investigative work by the FBI's New York Field Office, with assistance from the NIPC, traced the source of the virus to the Philippines within 24 hours. The FBI then worked, through the FBI Legal Attaché in Manila, with the Philippines' National Bureau of Investigation, to identify the perpetrator. The speed with which the virus was traced back to its source is unprecedented. The prosecution in the Philippines was hampered by the lack of a specific computer crime statute. Nevertheless, Onel de Guzman was charged on June 29, 2000, with fraud, theft, malicious mischief, and violation of the Devices Regulation Act. However, those charges were dropped in August by Philippine judicial authorities. As a postscript, it is important to note that the Philippines' government on June 14, 2000, reacted quickly and approved the E-Commerce Act, which now specifically criminalizes computer hacking and virus propagation. Also, the NIPC continues to work with other nations to provide guidance on the need to update criminal law statutes.

In some cases, we have been able to prevent the release of malicious code viruses against public systems. On March 29, 2000, FBI Houston initiated an investigation when it was discovered that certain small businesses in the Houston area had been targeted by someone who was using their Internet accounts in an unauthorized manner and causing their hard drives to be erased. The next day, FBI Houston conducted a search warrant on the residence of an individual who allegedly created a computer "worm" that seeks out computers on the Internet. This "worm" looked for computer networks that have certain enabled sharing capabilities, and uses them for the mass replication of the worm. The worm caused the hard drives of randomly selected computers to be erased. The computers whose hard drives are not erased actively scan the Internet for other computers to infect and force the infected computers to use their modems to dial 911. Because each infected computer can scan approximately 2,550 computers at a time, this worm could have the potential to create a denial-of-service attack against the 911 system. The NIPC issued a warning to the public through the NIPC Web page, SANS, InfraGard, and teletypes to government agencies. On May 15, 2000, Franklin Wayne Adams of Houston was charged by a federal grand jury with knowingly causing the transmission of a program onto the Internet that caused damage to a protected computer system by threatening public health and safety and by causing loss aggregated to at least $5,000. Adams was also charged with unauthorized access to electronic or wire communications while those communications were in electronic storage. On April 5, 2001, Adams was sentenced to 5 years probation and fined $12,353 restitution. Under the terms of his sentencing, Adams is restricted to using a computer only for work and educational purposes.

National security threats remain our top concern. As Dr. Lawrence Gershwin, National Intelligence Officer for Science and Technology, told the Joint Economic Committee in June 2001, "For attackers, viruses and worms are likely to become more controllable, precise, and predictable — making them more suitable for weaponization. Advanced modeling and simulation technologies are likely to assist in identifying critical nodes for an attack and conducting battle damage assessments." The NIPC is concerned about three specific categories of national security intruders: terrorists, foreign intelligence services, and information warriors. As Gershwin noted in June, "Most U.S. adversaries have access to the technology needed to pursue computer network operations."

Terrorist groups are increasingly using new information technology and the Internet to formulate plans, raise funds, spread propaganda, and to communicate securely. In his statement on the worldwide threat in 2000, Director of Central Intelligence George Tenet testified that terrorist groups, "including Hizbollah, HAMAS, the Abu Nidal organization, and Bin Laden's al Qa'ida organization are using computerized files, e-mail, and encryption to support their operations." In one example, convicted terrorist Ramzi Yousef, the mastermind of the World Trade Center bombing, stored detailed plans to destroy United States airliners on encrypted files on his laptop computer. While we have not yet seen these groups employ cybertools as a weapon to use against critical infrastructures, their reliance on information technology and acquisition of computer expertise are clear warning signs. During the riots on the West Bank in the fall of 2000, Israeli government sites were subjected to e-mail flooding and "ping" attacks. The attacks originated with sympathetic Islamic elements trying to inundate the systems with e-mail messages. As one can see from these examples overseas, "cyberterrorism" — which refers to malicious conduct in cyberspace to commit or threaten to commit acts dangerous to human life, or against a nation's critical infrastructures, such as energy, transportation, or government operations, in order to intimidate or coerce a government or civilian population, or any segment thereof, in furtherance of political or social objectives — is a very real threat.

Foreign intelligence services have adapted to using cybertools as part of their information gathering tradecraft. While I cannot go into specific cases, there are overseas probes against U.S. government systems every day. It would be naive to ignore the possibility or even probability that foreign powers were behind some or all of these probes. The motivation of such intelligence gathering is obvious. By coordinating law enforcement and intelligence community assets and authorities in one Center, the NIPC can work with other agencies of the U.S. government to detect these foreign intrusion attempts.

The prospect of "information warfare" by foreign militaries against our critical infrastructures is perhaps the greatest potential cyberthreat to our national security. We know that many foreign nations are developing information warfare doctrine, programs, and capabilities for use against the United States or other nations. In testimony in June 2001, National Intelligence Officer Gershwin stated that "for the next 5 to 10 years or so, only nation states appear to have the discipline, commitment, and resources to fully develop the capabilities to attack critical infrastructures."

# Conclusion

While the NIPC has accomplished much over the last three years in building the first national-level operational capability to respond to cyberintrusions, much work remains. We have learned from cases that successful network investigation is highly dependent on expert investigators and analysts, with state-of-the-art equipment and training. We have had the resources to build some of that capability both in the FBI Field Offices and at the NIPC, but we have much work ahead if we are to build our resources and capability to keep pace with the changing technology and growing threat environment, while at the same time being able to respond to several major incidents at once.

We are building the agency-to-agency, government-to-private sector, foreign liaison, and law enforcement partnerships that are vital to this effort. The NIPC is well-suited to foster these partnerships since it has analysis, information sharing, outreach, and investigative missions. We are working with the executives in the infrastructure protection community to foster the development of safe and secure networks for our critical infrastructures. While this is a daunting task, we are making progress.

Within the federal sector, we have seen how much can be accomplished when agencies work together, share information, and coordinate their activities as much as is legally permissible. But on this score, too, more can be done to achieve the interagency and public-private partnerships called for by PDD-63. We need to ensure that all relevant agencies are sharing information about threats and incidents with the NIPC and devoting personnel and other resources to the Center so that we can continue to build a truly interagency, "national" Center. Finally, we must work with Congress to make sure that policymakers understand the threats we face in the Information Age and what measures are necessary to secure our Nation against them. I look forward to working with the Members and Staff of this Subcommittee to address these vitally important issues.

Thank you.

# National Infrastructure Protection Center Statement on Cybercrime

The following statement on the issue of cybercrime was delivered by Michael A. Vatis, Director of the National Infrastructure Protection Center of the Federal Bureau of Investigation on February 29, 2000. Vatis delivered this statement in Washington D.C. before the Senate Judiciary Committee, Criminal Justice Oversight Subcommittee, and House Judiciary Committee, Crime Subcommittee. As you read this document, you might take note of the steps being taken by the U.S. government in its effort to be ready for both current and future cybercrimes, regardless of the categories they fall into and the place from which they originate. Vatis' statement emphasizes the importance of cooperation between the three sections of the NIPC and the private sector as well as the role that law enforcement needs to play in the combat against cybercrime.

## Statement on Cybercrime

Good afternoon, Chairman Thurmond, Chairman McCollum, and members of the subcommittees. I am pleased to be testifying today before this special joint hearing. Addressing the problem of cybercrime requires dynamic new working relationships in both the government and private sector. This joint meeting symbolizes in part those new relationships. Our ability in law enforcement to deal with this crime problem will also require the support of Congress, and I want to express my appreciation for your subcommittees' longstanding support for the work of the FBI, and for your acknowledgment of the importance of the issue of cybercrime. The recent denial-of-service attacks against Yahoo!, Amazon.com, eBay, CNN, Buy.com, and other e-commerce Web sites have thrust the security of our information infrastructure into the spotlight. I look forward to discussing the steps we have taken to tackle this issue to date, and the measures that are necessary to ensure that we retain the ability to deal with this problem in the future.

The changes wrought by the Internet to our society — including business, education, government, and personal communication — are evident all around us, and still very much in flux. The cyberrevolution has permeated virtually every facet of our lives. Unfortunately, that revolution has entered the criminal arena as well. For just as millions of people around the globe have incorporated the Internet and advanced information technology into their daily endeavors, so have criminals, terrorists, and adversarial foreign nations. Whether we like it or not, cybercrime presents the most fundamental challenge for law enforcement in the 21st century. By its very nature, the cyberenvironment is borderless, affords easy anonymity and methods of concealment to bad actors, and provides new tools to engage in criminal activity. A criminal sitting on the other side of the planet is now capable of stealthily infiltrating a computer network in this country to steal money, abscond with proprietary information, or shut down e-commerce sites. To deal with this problem, law enforcement must retool its work force, its equipment, and its own information infrastructure. It must also forge new partnerships with private industry, other agencies, and our international counterparts. We have been doing all of these things for the last two years. But we must continue to build upon our progress to ensure that we can perform our responsibilities to protect public safety and national security in the Information Age. These are some of the issues I would like to focus on today.

# The NIPC

Let me begin with some background about the National Infrastructure Protection Center, or "NIPC." The NIPC is an interagency center located at the FBI. Created in 1998, the NIPC serves as the focal point for the government's efforts to warn of and respond to cyberattacks, particularly those that are directed at our nation's "critical infrastructures." These infrastructures include telecommunications and information, energy, banking and finance, transportation, government operations, and emergency services. In Presidential Decision Directive (PDD) 63, the President directed that the NIPC serve as a "national critical infrastructure threat assessment, warning, vulnerability, and law enforcement investigation and response entity." The PDD further states that the mission of the NIPC "will include providing timely warnings of intentional threats, comprehensive analyses, and law enforcement investigation and response."

To accomplish its goals, the NIPC is organized into three sections:

✓ The **Computer Investigations and Operations Section (CIOS)** is the operational response arm of the Center. It supports and, where necessary, coordinates computer investigations conducted by FBI field offices throughout the country, provides expert technical assistance to network investigations, and provides a cyberemergency response capability to coordinate the response to a national-level cyberincident.

✓ The **Analysis and Warning Section (AWS)** serves as the "indications and warning" arm of the NIPC. It provides tactical, analytical support during a cyberincident, and also develops strategic analyses of threats for dissemination to both government and private sector entities so that they can take appropriate steps to protect themselves. Through its 24/7 watch and warning operation, it maintains a real-time situational awareness by reviewing numerous governmental and "open" sources of information and by maintaining communications with partner entities in the government and private sector. Through its efforts, the AWS strives to acquire indications of a possible attack, assess the information, and issue appropriate warnings to government and private sector partners as quickly as possible

✓ The **Training, Outreach, and Strategy Section (TOSS)** coordinates the vital training of cyberinvestigators in the FBI field offices, other federal agencies, and state and local law enforcement. It also coordinates outreach to private industry and government agencies to build the partnerships that are key to both our investigative and our warning missions. In addition, this section manages our efforts to catalogue information about individual "key assets" across the country which, if successfully attacked, could have significant repercussions on our economy or national security. Finally, the TOSS handles the development of strategy and policy in conjunction with other agencies and the Congress.

Beyond the NIPC at FBI Headquarters, we have also created a cybercrime investigative program in all FBI Field Offices called the National Infrastructure Protection and Computer Intrusion (NIPCI) Program. This program, managed by the NIPC, consists of special agents in each FBI Field Office who are responsible for investigating computer intrusions, viruses, or denial-of-service attacks, for implementing our key asset initiative, and for conducting critical liaison activities with private industry. They are also developing cybercrime task forces in partnership with state and local law enforcement entities within their jurisdiction to leverage the limited resources in this area.

# The Broad Spectrum of Cyberthreats

Over the past several years, we have seen a range of computer crimes, ranging from defacement of Web sites by juveniles to sophisticated intrusions that we suspect may be sponsored by foreign powers, and everything inbetween. Some of these are obviously more significant than others. The theft of national security information from a government agency or the interruption of electrical power to a major metropolitan area would have greater consequences for national security, public safety, and the economy than the defacement of a Web site. But even the less serious categories have real consequences and, ultimately, can undermine confidence in e-commerce and violate privacy or property rights. A Web site hack that shuts down an e-commerce site can have disastrous consequences for a business. An intrusion that results in the theft of credit card numbers from an online vendor can result in significant financial loss and, more broadly, reduce consumers' willingness to engage in e-commerce. Because of these implications, it is critical that we have in place the programs and resources to investigate and, ultimately, to deter these sorts of crimes.

The following are some of the categories of cyberthreats that we confront today.

✓ **Insiders.** The disgruntled insider (a current or former employee of a company) is a principal source of computer crimes for many companies. Insiders' knowledge of the target company's network often allows them to gain unrestricted access to cause damage to the system or to steal proprietary data. The 1999 Computer Security Institute/FBI report notes that 55 percent of respondents reported malicious activity by insiders.

One example of an insider was George Parente. In 1997, Parente was arrested for causing five network servers at the publishing company Forbes, Inc., to crash. Parente was a former Forbes computer technician who had been terminated from temporary employment. In what appears to have been a vengeful act against the company and his supervisors, Parente dialed into the Forbes computer system from his residence and gained access through a co-worker's log-in and password. Once online, he caused five of the eight Forbes computer network servers to crash, and erased all of the server volume on each of the affected servers. No data could be restored. Parente's sabotage resulted in a two-day shutdown in Forbes' New York operations, with losses exceeding $100,000. Parente pleaded guilty to one count of violating the Computer Fraud and Abuse Act, Title 18 U.S.C. 1030.

✓ **Hackers.** Hackers (or "crackers") are also a common threat. They sometimes crack into networks simply for the thrill of the challenge or for bragging rights in the hacker community. Recently, however, we have seen more cases of hacking for illicit financial gain or other malicious purposes. While remote cracking once required a fair amount of skill or computer knowledge, hackers can now download attack scripts and protocols from the World Wide Web and launch them against victim sites. Thus, while attack tools have become more sophisticated, they have also become easier to use. The distributed denial-of-service (DDOS) attacks earlier this month are only the most recent illustration of the economic disruption that can be caused by tools now readily available on the Internet.

We have also seen a rise recently in politically motivated attacks on Web pages or e-mail servers, which some have dubbed "hacktivism." In these incidents, groups and individuals overload e-mail servers or deface Web sites to send a political message. While these attacks generally have not altered operating systems or networks, they have disrupted services, caused monetary loss, and denied the public access to Web sites containing valuable information, thereby infringing on others' rights to disseminate and receive information. Examples of "hacktivism" include a case in 1996, in which an unknown subject gained unauthorized access to the computer system hosting the Department of Justice Internet Web site. The intruders deleted over 200 directories and their contents on the computer system and installed their own pages. The installed pages were critical of the Communications Decency Act (CDA) and included pictures of Adolf Hitler, swastikas, pictures of sexual bondage scenes, a speech falsely attributed to President Clinton, and fabricated CDA text.

✓ **Virus writers.** Virus writers are posing an increasingly serious threat to networks and systems worldwide. Last year saw the proliferation of several destructive computer viruses or "worms," including the Melissa macro virus, the Explore.Zip worm, and the CIH (Chernobyl) virus. The NIPC frequently sends out warnings or advisories regarding particularly dangerous viruses, which can allow potential victims to take protective steps and minimize the destructive consequences of a virus.

The Melissa macro virus was a good example of our two-fold response — encompassing both warning and investigation — to a virus spreading in the networks. The NIPC sent out warnings as soon as it had solid information on the virus and its effects; these warnings helped alert the public and reduce the potential destructive impact of the virus. On the investigative side, the NIPC acted as a central point of contact for the field offices who worked leads on the case. A tip received by the New Jersey State Police from America Online, and their follow-up investigation with the FBI's Newark Division, led to the April 1, 1999, arrest of David L. Smith. Mr. Smith pleaded guilty to one count of violating 18 U.S.C. § 1030 in Federal Court, and to four state felony counts. As part of his guilty plea, Smith stipulated to affecting one million computer systems and causing $80 million in damage. Smith is awaiting sentencing.

✓ **Criminal groups.** We are also seeing the increased use of cyberintrusions by criminal groups who attack systems for purposes of monetary gain. In September 1999, two members of a group dubbed the "Phonemasters" were sentenced after their conviction for theft and possession of unauthorized access devices (18 USC § 1029) and unauthorized access to a federal interest computer (18 USC § 1030). The "Phonemasters" were an international group of criminals who penetrated the computer systems of MCI, Sprint, AT&T, Equifax, and even the National Crime Information Center. Under judicially approved electronic surveillance orders, the FBI's Dallas Division made use of new data intercept technology to monitor the calling activity and modem pulses of one of the suspects, Calvin Cantrell. Mr. Cantrell downloaded thousands of Sprint calling card numbers, which he sold to a Canadian individual, who passed them on to someone in Ohio. These numbers made their way to an individual in Switzerland and eventually ended up in the hands of organized crime groups in Italy. Cantrell was sentenced to two years as a result of his guilty plea, while one of his associates, Cory Lindsay, was sentenced to 41 months.

The Phonemasters' methods included "dumpster diving" to gather old phone books and technical manuals for systems. They used this information to trick employees into giving up their logon and password information. The group then used this information to break into victim systems. It is important to remember that often, "cybercrimes" are facilitated by old-fashioned guile, such as calling employees and tricking them into giving up passwords. Good cybersecurity practices must therefore address personnel security and "social engineering" in addition to instituting electronic security measures.

Another example of cyberintrusions used to implement a criminal conspiracy involved Vladimir L. Levin and numerous accomplices, who illegally transferred more than $10 million in funds from three Citibank corporate customers to bank accounts in California, Finland, Germany, the Netherlands, Switzerland, and Israel between June and October 1994. Levin, a Russian computer expert, gained access over 40 times to Citibank's cash management system using a personal computer and stolen passwords and identification numbers. Russian telephone company employees working with Citibank were able to trace the source of the transfers to Levin's employer in St. Petersburg, Russia. Levin was arrested in March 1995 in London and subsequently extradited to the U.S. On February 24, 1998, he was sentenced to three years in prison and ordered to pay Citibank $240,000 in restitution. Four of Levin's accomplices pleaded guilty, and one was arrested but could not be extradited. Citibank was able to recover all but $400,000 of the $10 million illegally transferred funds.

Unfortunately, cyberspace provides new tools not only for criminals, but for national security threats as well. These include terrorists, foreign intelligence agencies, and foreign militaries.

✓ **Terrorists.** Terrorist groups are increasingly using new information technology and the Internet to formulate plans, raise funds, spread propaganda, and communicate securely. In his statement on the worldwide threat in 2000, Director of Central Intelligence George Tenet testified that terrorist groups, "including Hizbollah, HAMAS, the Abu Nidal organization, and Bin Laden's al Qa'ida organization, are using computerized files, e-mail, and encryption to support their operations." In one example, convicted terrorist Ramzi Yousef, the mastermind of the World Trade Center bombing, stored detailed plans to destroy United States airliners on encrypted files on his laptop computer. While we have not yet seen these groups employ cybertools as a weapon to use against critical infrastructures, their reliance on information technology and acquisition of computer expertise are clear warning signs. Moreover, we have seen other terrorist groups, such as the Internet Black Tigers (who are reportedly affiliated with the Tamil Tigers), engage in attacks on foreign government Web sites and e-mail servers. "Cyber terrorism"—by which I mean the use of cybertools to shut down critical national infrastructures (such as energy, transportation, or government operations) for the purpose of coercing or intimidating a government or civilian population—is thus a very real, though still largely potential, threat.

✓ **Foreign intelligence services.** Not surprisingly, foreign intelligence services have adapted to using cybertools as part of their espionage tradecraft. Even as far back as 1986, before the worldwide surge in Internet use, the KGB employed West German hackers to access Department of Defense systems in the well-known "Cuckoo's Egg" case. While I cannot go into specifics about more recent developments in an open hearing, it should not surprise anyone to hear that foreign intelligence services increasingly view computer intrusions as a useful tool for acquiring sensitive U.S. government and private sector information.

✓ **Information warfare.** The prospect of "information warfare" by foreign militaries against our critical infrastructures is perhaps the greatest potential cyberthreat to our national security. We know that several foreign nations are developing information warfare doctrine, programs, and capabilities for use against the United States or other nations. Knowing that they cannot match our military might with conventional or "kinetic" weapons, nations see cyberattacks on our critical infrastructures or military operations as a way to hit what they perceive as America's Achilles heel—our growing dependence on information technology in government and commercial operations.

## Distributed Denial-of-Service Attacks

The recent distributed denial-of-service (DDOS) attacks have garnered a tremendous amount of interest in the public and in the Congress. Because we are actively investigating these attacks, I cannot provide a detailed briefing on the status of our efforts. However, I can provide an overview of our activities to deal with the DDOS threat beginning last year and of our investigative efforts over the last three weeks.

In the fall of last year, the NIPC began receiving reports about a new set of "exploits," or attack tools, collectively called distributed denial-of-service (DDOS) tools. DDOS variants include tools known as "Trinoo," "Tribal Flood Net" (TFN), "TFN2K," and "Stacheldraht" (German for "barbed wire"). These tools essentially work as follows: Hackers gain unauthorized access to a computer system(s) and place software code on it that renders that system a "master" (or a "handler"). The hackers also intrude into other networks and place malicious code which makes those systems into agents (also known as "zombies" or "daemons" or "slaves"). Each master is capable of controlling multiple agents. In both cases, the network owners normally are not aware that dangerous tools have been placed and reside on their systems, thus becoming third-party victims to the intended crime.

The masters are activated either remotely or by internal programming (such as a command to begin an attack at a prescribed time) and are used to send information to the agents, activating their DDOS ability. The agents then generate numerous requests to connect with the attack's ultimate target(s), typically using a fictitious or "spoofed" IP (Internet Protocol) address, thus providing a falsified identity as to the source of the request. The agents act in unison to generate a high volume of traffic from several sources. This type of attack is referred to as a SYN flood, as the SYN is the initial effort by the sending computer to make a connection with the destination computer. Due to the volume of SYN requests, the destination computer becomes overwhelmed in its efforts to acknowledge and complete a transaction with the sending computers, degrading or denying its ability to complete service with legitimate customers — hence the term "denial-of-service". These attacks are especially damaging when they are coordinated from multiple sites — hence the term "distributed denial-of-service."

An analogy would be if someone launched an automated program to have hundreds of phone calls placed to the Capitol switchboard at the same time. All of the good efforts of the staff would be overcome. Many callers would receive busy signals due to the high volume of telephone traffic.

In November and December, the NIPC received reports that universities and others were detecting the presence of hundreds of agents on their networks. The number of agents detected clearly could have been only a small subset of the total number of agents actually deployed. In addition, we were concerned that some malicious actors might choose to launch a DDOS attack around New Year's Eve in order to cause disruption and gain notoriety due to the great deal of attention that was being payed to the Y2K rollover. Accordingly, we decided to issue a series of alerts in December to government agencies, industry, and the public about the DDOS threat.

Moreover, in late December, we determined that a detection tool that we had developed for investigative purposes might also be used by network operators to detect the presence of DDOS agents or masters on their operating systems, and thus would enable them to remove an agent or master and prevent the network from being unwittingly utilized in a DDOS attack. Moreover, at that time there was, to our knowledge, no similar detection tool available commercially. We therefore decided to take the unusual step of releasing the tool to other agencies and to the public in an effort to reduce the level of the threat. We made the first variant of our software available on the NIPC Web site on December 30, 1999. To maximize public awareness of this tool, we announced its availability in an FBI press release that same date. Since the first posting of the tool, we have posted three updated versions that have perfected the software and made it applicable to different operating systems.

The public has downloaded these tools tens of thousands of times from the Web site, and has responded by reporting many installations of the DDOS software, thereby preventing their networks from being used in attacks and leading to the opening of criminal investigations, both before and after the widely publicized attacks of the last few weeks. Our work with private companies has been so well-received that the trade group SANS awarded their yearly Security Technology Leadership Award to members of the NIPC's Special Technologies Applications Unit.

Recently, we received reports that a new variation of DDOS tools was being found on Windows operating systems. One victim entity provided us with the object code to the tool found on its network. On February 18, we made the binaries available to anti-virus companies (through an industry association) and the Computer Emergency Response Team (CERT) at Carnegie Mellon University for analysis and so that commercial vendors could create or adjust their products to detect the new DDOS variant. Given the attention that DDOS tools have received in recent weeks, there are now numerous detection and security products to address this threat, so we determined that we could be most helpful by giving them the necessary code rather than deploying a detection tool ourselves.

Unfortunately, the warnings that we and others in the security community had issued about DDOS tools last year, while alerting many potential victims and reducing the threat, did not eliminate the threat. Quite frequently, even when a threat is known and patches or detection tools are available, network operators either remain unaware of the problem or fail to take necessary protective steps. In addition, in the cyberequivalent of an arms race, exploits evolve as hackers design variations to evade or overcome detection software and filters. Even security-conscious companies that put in place all available security measures therefore are not invulnerable. And, particularly with DDOS tools, one organization might be the victim of a successful attack despite its best efforts, because another organization failed to take steps to keep itself from being made the unwitting participant in an attack.

On February 7, 2000, the NIPC received reports that Yahoo had experienced a denial-of-service attack. In a display of the close cooperative relationship that we have developed with the private sector, in the days that followed, several other companies (including Cable News Network, eBay, Amazon.com, Buy.com, and ZDNET) also reported denial-of-service outages to the NIPC or FBI field offices. These companies cooperated with us by providing critical logs and other information. Still, the challenges to apprehending the suspects are substantial. In many cases, the attackers used "spoofed" IP addresses, meaning that the address that appeared on the target's log was not the true address of the system that sent the messages. In addition, many victims do not keep complete network logs.

The resources required in an investigation of this type are substantial. Companies have been victimized or used as "hop sites" in numerous places across the country, meaning that we must deploy special agents nationwide to work leads. We currently have seven FBI field offices with cases opened, and all the remaining offices are supporting the offices that have opened cases. Agents from these offices are following up literally hundreds of leads. The NIPC is coordinating the nationwide investigative effort, performing technical analysis of logs from victims' sites and Internet Service Providers (ISPs), and providing all-source analytical assistance to field offices. Moreover, parts of the evidentiary trail have led overseas, requiring us to work with our foreign counterparts in several countries through our Legal Attaches (Legats) in U.S. embassies.

While the crime may be high-tech, investigating it involves a substantial amount of traditional investigative work as well as highly technical work. Interviews of network operators and confidential sources can provide very useful information, which leads to still more interviews and leads to follow up. And victim sites and ISPs provide an enormous amount of log information that needs to be processed and analyzed by human analysts.

Despite these challenges, I am optimistic that the hard work of our agents, analysts, and computer scientists; the excellent cooperation and collaboration we have with private industry and universities; and the teamwork we are engaged in with foreign partners will, in the end, prove successful.

## Interagency Cooperation

The broad spectrum of cyberthreats described earlier, ranging from hacking to foreign espionage and information warfare, requires not just new technologies and skills on the part of investigators, but new organizational constructs as well. In most cyberattacks, the identity, location, and objective of the perpetrator are not immediately apparent. Nor is the scope of his attack—that is, whether an intrusion is isolated or part of a broader pattern affecting numerous targets. This means it is often impossible to determine at the outset if an intrusion is an act of cybervandalism, organized crime, domestic or foreign terrorism, economic or traditional espionage, or some form of strategic military attack. The only way to determine the source, nature, and scope of the incident is to gather information from the victim sites and intermediate sites, such as ISPs and telecommunications carriers. Under our constitutional system, such information typically can be gathered only pursuant to criminal investigative authorities. This is why the NIPC is part of the FBI, allowing us to utilize the FBI's legal authorities to gather and retain information and to act on it, consistent with constitutional and statutory requirements.

But the dimension and varied nature of the threats also means that this is an issue that concerns not just the FBI and law enforcement agencies, but also the Department of Defense, the Intelligence Community, and civilian agencies with infrastructure-focused responsibility such as the Departments of Energy and Transportation. It also is a matter that greatly affects state and local law enforcement. This is why the NIPC is an interagency center, with representatives detailed to the FBI from numerous federal agencies and representation from state and local law enforcement as well. These representatives operate under the direction and authority of the FBI, but bring with them expertise and skills from their respective home agencies that enable better coordination and cooperation among all relevant agencies, consistent with applicable laws.

We have had many instances in the last two years where this interagency cooperation has proven critical. As mentioned earlier, the case of the Melissa virus was successfully resolved with the first successful federal prosecution of a virus propagator in over a decade because of close teamwork between the NIPCI squad in the FBI's Newark Division and other field offices, the New Jersey State Police, and the NIPC.

The "Solar Sunrise" case is another example of close teamwork with other agencies. In 1998, computer intrusions into U.S. military computer systems occurred during the Iraq weapons inspection crisis. Hackers exploited known vulnerabilities in Sun Solaris operating systems. Some of the intrusions appeared to be coming from the Middle East. The timing, nature, and apparent source of some of the attacks raised concerns in the Pentagon that this could be a concerted effort by Iraq to interfere with U.S. troop deployments. NIPC coordinated a multiagency investigation which included the FBI, the Air Force Office of Special Investigations, the National Aeronautics and Space Administration, the Department of Justice, the Defense Information Systems Agency, the National Security Agency, and the Central Intelligence Agency. Within several days, the investigation determined that the intrusions were not the work of Iraq, but of several teenagers in the U.S. and Israel. Two juveniles in California pleaded guilty to the intrusions, and several Israelis still await trial. The leader of the Israeli group, Ehud Tenenbaum, has been indicted and is currently scheduled for trial in Israel in April.

More recently, we observed a series of intrusions into numerous Department of Defense and other federal government computer networks and private sector entities. Investigation last year determined that the intrusions appear to have originated in Russia. The intruder successfully accessed U.S. Government networks and took large amounts of unclassified but sensitive information, including defense technical research information. The NIPC coordinated a multiagency investigation, working closely with FBI field offices, the Department of Defense, and the Intelligence Community. While I cannot go into more detail about this case here, it demonstrates the very real threat we face in the cyberrealm, and the need for good teamwork and coordination among government agencies responsible for responding to the threat.

# Private Sector Cooperation

Most importantly, however, our success in battling cybercrime depends on close cooperation with private industry. This is the case for several reasons. First, most of the victims of cybercrimes are private companies. Therefore, successful investigation and prosecution of cybercrimes depends on private victims reporting incidents to law enforcement and cooperating with the investigators. Contrary to press statements by companies offering security services that private companies won't share information with law enforcement, private companies have reported incidents and threats to the NIPC or FBI field offices. The number of victims who have voluntarily reported DDOS attacks to us over the last few weeks is ample proof of this. While there are undoubtedly companies that would prefer not to report a crime because of fear of public embarrassment over a security lapse, the situation has improved markedly. Companies increasingly realize that deterrence of crime depends on effective law enforcement, and that the long-term interests of industry depend on establishing a good working relationship with government to prevent and investigate crime.

Testimony two weeks ago before the Senate Appropriations Subcommittee for Commerce, State, and Justice by Robert Chesnut, Associate General Counsel for eBay, illustrates this point:

> Prior to last week's attacks, eBay had established a close working relationship with the computer crimes squad within the Northern California office of the Federal Bureau of Investigation ("FBI"). eBay has long recognized that the best way to combat cybercrime, whether it's fraud or hacking, is by working cooperatively with law enforcement. Therefore, last year we established procedures for notifying the FBI in the event of such an attack on our Web site. As a result of this preparation, we were able to contact the FBI computer intrusion squad during the attack and provide them with information that we expect will assist in their investigation. In the aftermath of the attack, eBay has also been able to provide the FBI with additional leads that have come to our attention.

Second, the network administrator at a victim company or ISP is critical to the success of an investigation. Only that administrator knows the unique configuration of her system, and she typically must work with an investigator to find critical transactional data that will yield evidence of a criminal's activity.

Third, the private sector has the technical expertise that is often critical to resolving an investigation. It would be impossible for us to retain experts in every possible operating system or network configuration, so private sector assistance is critical. In addition, many investigations require the development of unique technical tools to deal with novel problems. Private sector assistance has been critical there as well.

To encourage private sector cooperation, we have engaged in a concerted outreach effort to private industry, providing threat briefings, issuing analyses and threat warnings, and speaking at industry conferences. In another example of cooperation, the Attorney General and the Information Technology Association of America announced a set of initiatives last year as part of a "Cybercitizens Partnership" between the government and the information technology (IT) industry. One initiative involves providing IT industry representatives to serve in the NIPC to enhance our technical expertise and our understanding of the information and communications infrastructure.

We have several other initiatives devoted to private sector outreach that bear mentioning here. The first is called "InfraGard." This is an initiative that we have developed in concert with private companies and academia to encourage information-sharing about cyberintrusions, exploited vulnerabilities, and physical infrastructure threats. A vital component of InfraGard is the ability of industry to provide information on intrusions to the local FBI field office using secure e-mail communications in both a "sanitized" and detailed format. The local FBI field offices can, if appropriate, use the detailed version to initiate an investigation; while NIPC Headquarters can analyze that information in conjunction with other information we obtain to determine if the intrusion is part of a broader attack on numerous sites. The NIPC can simultaneously use the sanitized version to inform other members of the intrusion without compromising the confidentiality of the reporting company. The key to this system is that whether, and what, to report is entirely up to the reporting company. A secure Web site also contains a variety of analytic and warning products that we make available to the InfraGard community. The success of InfraGard is premised on the notion that sharing is a two-way street: The NIPC will provide threat information that companies can use to protect their systems, while companies will provide incident information that can be used to initiate an investigation and to warn other companies.

Our Key Asset Initiative (KAI) is focused more specifically on the owners and operators of critical components of each of the infrastructure sectors. It facilitates response to threats and incidents by building liaison and communications links with the owners and operators of individual companies and enabling contingency planning. The KAI began in the 1980s and focused on physical vulnerabilities to terrorism. Under the NIPC, the KAI has been reinvigorated and expanded to focus on cybervulnerabilities as well. The KAI currently involves determining which assets are key within the jurisdiction of each FBI Field Office and obtaining 24-hour points of contact at each asset in cases of emergency. Eventually, if future resources permit, the initiative will include the development of contingency plans to respond to attacks on each asset, exercises to test response plans, and modeling to determine the effects of an attack on particular assets. FBI field offices are responsible for developing a list of the assets within their respective jurisdictions, while the NIPC maintains the national database. The KAI is being developed in coordination with DOD and other agencies. Currently, the database has about 2,400 entries. This represents 2,400 contacts with key private sector nodes made by the NIPC and FBI field offices.

A third initiative is a pilot program we have begun with the North American Electrical Reliability Council (NERC). Under the pilot program, electric utility companies and other power entities transmit cyberincident reports in near real-time to the NIPC. These reports are analyzed and assessed to determine whether an NIPC warning, alert, or advisory is warranted. Electric power participants in the pilot program have stated that the information and analysis provided by the NIPC back to the power companies fully justify their participation in the program. It is our expectation that the Electrical Power Indications and Warning System will provide a full-fledged model for the other critical infrastructures.

Much has been said over the last few years about the importance of information sharing. Since our founding, the NIPC has been actively engaged in building concrete mechanisms and initiatives to make this sharing a reality, and we have built up a track record of actually sharing useful information. These efforts belie the notions that private industry won't share with law enforcement in this area, or that the government won't provide meaningful threat data to industry. As companies continue to gain experience in dealing with the NIPC and FBI field offices, as we continue to provide them with important and useful threat information, and as companies recognize that cybercrime requires a joint effort by industry and government together, we will continue to make real progress in this area.

# Keeping Law Enforcement on the Cutting Edge of Cybercrime

As Internet use continues to soar, cybercrime is also increasing exponentially. Our caseload reflects this growth. In FY 1998, we opened 547 computer intrusion cases; in FY 1999, that number jumped to 1,154. Similarly, the number of pending cases increased from 206 at the end of FY 1997 to 601 at the end of FY 1998, to 834 at the end of FY 99, and to over 900 currently. These statistics include only computer intrusion cases, and do not account for computer-facilitated crimes such as Internet fraud, child pornography, or e-mail extortion efforts. In these cases, the NIPC and NIPCI squads often provide technical assistance to traditional investigative programs responsible for these categories of crime.

We can clearly expect these upward trends to continue. To meet this challenge, we must ensure that we have adequate resources, including both personnel and equipment, both at the NIPC and in FBI field offices. We currently have 193 agents nationwide dedicated to investigating computer intrusion and virus cases. In order to maximize investigative resources, the FBI has taken the approach of creating regional squads in 16 field offices that have sufficient size to work complex intrusion cases and to assist those field offices without a NIPCI squad. In those field offices without squads, the FBI is building a baseline capability by having one or two agents to work NIPC matters — that is, computer intrusions (criminal and national security), viruses, InfraGard, state and local liaison, and so on.

At the NIPC, we currently have 101 personnel on board, including 82 FBI employees and 19 detailees from other government agencies. This cadre of investigators, computer scientists, and analysts performs the numerous and complex tasks outlined above, and provides critical coordination and support to field office investigations. As the crime problem grows, we need to make sure that we keep pace by bringing on board additional personnel, including from other agencies and the private sector.

In addition to putting in place the requisite number of agents, analysts, and computer scientists in the NIPC and in FBI field offices, we must fill those positions by recruiting and retaining personnel who have the appropriate technical, analytical, and investigative skills. This includes personnel who can read and analyze complex log files, perform all-source analysis to look for correlations between events or attack signatures and glean indications of a threat, develop technical tools to address the constantly changing technological environment, and conduct complex network investigations.

Training and continuing education are also critical, and we have made this a top priority at the NIPC. In FY 1999, we trained 383 FBI and other government agency students in NIPC-sponsored training classes on network investigations and infrastructure protection.

The emphasis for 2000 is on continuing to train federal personnel while expanding training opportunities for state and local law enforcement personnel. During FY 2000, we plan to train approximately 740 personnel from the FBI, other federal agencies, and state and local law enforcement.

Developing and deploying the best equipment in support of the mission is also very important. Not only do investigators and analysts need the best equipment to conduct investigations in the rapidly evolving cybersystem, but the NIPC must be on the cutting edge of cyberresearch and development. Conducting a network intrusion or denial-of-service investigation often requires analysis of voluminous amounts of data. For example, one network intrusion case involving an espionage matter currently being investigated has required the analysis of 17.5 terabytes of data. To place this into perspective, the entire collection of the Library of Congress, if digitized, would comprise only 10 terabytes. The Yahoo! DDOS attack involved approximately 630 gigabytes of data, which is equivalent to enough printed pages to fill 630 pickup trucks with paper. Technical analysis requires high capacity equipment to store, process, analyze, and display data. Again, as the crime problem grows, we must ensure that our technical capacity keeps pace.

Finally, we must look at whether changes to the legal procedures governing investigation and prosecution of cybercrimes are warranted. The problem of Internet crime has grown at such a rapid pace that the laws have not kept up with the technology. The FBI is working with the Department of Justice to propose a legislative package for your review to help keep our laws in step with these advances.

One example of some of the problems law enforcement is facing is the jurisdictional limitation of pen registers and trap-and-trace orders issued by federal district courts. These orders allow only the capturing of tracing information, not the content of communications. Currently, in order to track back a hacking episode in which a single communication is purposely routed through a number of Internet Service Providers that are located in different states, we generally have to get multiple court orders. This is because, under current law, a federal court can order communications carriers only within its district to provide tracing information to law enforcement. As a result of the fact that investigators typically have to apply for numerous court orders to trace a single communication, there is a needless waste of time and resources, and a number of important investigations are either hampered or derailed entirely in those instances where law enforcement gets to a communications carrier after that carrier has already discarded the necessary information.

Other laws may be in need of revision because they are decades old and did not anticipate current technology. Many laws were not drafted in a technology-neutral way, and do not make much sense in today's world where telephone carriers, Internet Service Providers, and cable operators are all providing ways to communicate both electronically and by voice over the Internet. We are reviewing the pen register, trap-and-trace statutes, the Computer Fraud and Abuse Act, and the Cable Communications Policy Act to ensure that the laws make sense in the current environment.

There are also issues that we must readdress with respect to the need, under current law, to demonstrate at least $5,000 in damage for certain hacking crimes enumerated under 18 U.S.C. 1030(a)(5). In some of the cases we investigate, proof of damage in excess of $5,000 on a particular system is difficult to show, although the crime of breaking into numerous systems and obtaining root access, with the ability to destroy the confidentiality or accuracy of information remains very real and extremely serious.

Finally, we should consider whether current sentencing provisions for computer crimes provide an adequate deterrence. Given the degree of harm that can be caused by a virus, intrusion, or a denial-of-service — in terms of monetary loss to business and consumers, infringement of privacy, or threats to public safety when critical infrastructures are affected — it would be appropriate to consider whether penalties established years ago remain adequate.

# The Role of Law Enforcement

Finally, I would like to conclude by emphasizing two key points. The first is that our role in combating cybercrime is essentially two-fold: (1) preventing cyberattacks before they occur or limiting their scope by disseminating warnings and advisories about threats so that potential victims can protect themselves; and (2) responding to attacks that do occur by investigating and identifying the perpetrator. This is very much an operational role. Our role is not to determine what security measures private industry should take, or to ensure that companies or individuals take them. It is the responsibility of industry to ensure that appropriate security tools are made available and are implemented. We certainly can assist industry by alerting them to the actual threats that they need to be concerned about, and by providing information about the exploits that we are seeing criminals use. But network administrators, whether in the private sector or in government, are the first line of defense.

Second, in gathering information as part of our warning and response missions, we rigorously adhere to constitutional and statutory requirements. Our conduct is strictly limited by the Fourth Amendment, statutes such as Title III and ECPA, and the Attorney General Guidelines. These rules are founded first and foremost on the protection of privacy inherent in our constitutional system. Respect for privacy is thus a fundamental guidepost in all of our activities.

# Conclusion

I want to thank the subcommittees again for giving me the opportunity to testify here today. The cybercrime problem is real and growing. The NIPC is moving aggressively to meet this challenge by training FBI agents and investigators from other agencies on how to investigate computer intrusion cases, equipping them with the latest technology and technical assistance, developing our analytic capabilities and warning mechanisms to head off or mitigate attacks, and closely cooperating with the private sector. We have already had significant successes in the fight. I look forward to working with Congress to ensure that we continue to be able to meet the threat as it evolves and grows. Thank you.

# Appendix F

# Glossary — Worm Words and Virus Vocabulary

**Activation**   A term that refers to damage routines that viruses sometimes have that activate only when specific conditions have been met, such as the arrival of a certain calendar date or the performance of a particular action.

**ActiveX**   Controls Software components based on Microsoft's Component Object Model (COM) architecture. This technology provides tools for linking desktop applications to the World Wide Web.

**Backdoor**   A "hole" that programmers deliberately build into programs so that certain personnel, such as service technicians, can more easily access the system. Sometimes software programmers build in backdoors so that they (and system administrators) can easily enter the system and repair bugs or flaws. In some instances, backdoors are created unintentionally, the result of poor or sloppy programming.

**Back Orifice**   A program developed and released by a hacker group called "The Cult of the Dead Cow". Not a virus, this remote administration tool has the potential for malicious exploitation. BackOrifice gives a remote attacker the ability to gain full system administrator privileges on an infected computer. Its many other features include the ability to "sniff" passwords and other confidential data and then surreptitiously e-mail the collected data to a remote location on the Web.

**Basic Input Output System**   See *BIOS*.

**Behavior Blocking**   A set of actions designed to detect and prevent "virus-like" behavior from occurring. Some of the behaviors that should normally be blocked in a computer include the unauthorized formatting of disks or writing to the master boot record.

**BIOS, or Basic Input Output System**   The part of the system, located in the ROM (read-only memory) area of the computer, that identifies all the hardware devices and programs used to boot the computer before the locating and loading of the operating system.

**Boot Sector**   Hard disk drives, floppy diskettes, and logical drives (partitions) all have boot sectors where critical drive information is stored. It is located in a specially designated area on the first sector of a disk.

**Boot Sector Virus**   A type of virus that infects the boot sector of a fixed or floppy disk. Any formatted disk, even one that has no data on it, can harbor a boot sector virus. Any attempt to boot from a disk infected with a boot sector virus will cause the virus to become active in memory. Boot sector viruses are very common, and any attempt to remove them while they are active in memory is pointless, as they re-write themselves to the disk as soon as they have been removed.

**Bug**   An unintended fault or flaw in a computer program or application.

**Cavity Infectors**   A type of virus that attempts to maintain a constant file size when infecting. Each time an ordinary virus attaches itself to a program, the virus can usually be detected by observing an increase in file size. Cavity infectors locate a "hole" or "empty space" in the programming code and place themselves there so the actual file size doesn't increase.

**Circular Infection**   A type of infection that occurs when two separate viruses infect the boot sector of a disk, rendering the disk unbootable. Removing only one of the viruses will generally cause re-infection by the remaining virus.

**CMOS, or Complementary Metal Oxide Semiconductor**   A battery-powered memory chip that stores critical BIOS configuration information about the computer. Computer viruses sometimes try to alter this data in an attempt to render the computer inoperable.

**Companion Virus**   A type of virus that infects executable (`.exe`) files by creating a "companion" file with the same name as the original but with a `.com` extension. Because DOS executes `.com` files first (before `.exe` files or `.bat` files), the virus can load before any of these other executable files.

**Complementary Metal Oxide Semiconductor**   See *CMOS.*

**Cookies**   Small (around 4K in size) text files placed on a user computer's hard disk. Web sites use cookies to identify users who revisit their sites. Cookies sometimes contain personal information regarding specific user preferences. When a server receives a browser request that includes a cookie, the server can use the information stored in the cookie to customize the Web site for the user.

**Creation**   As recently as a few years ago, creating a virus required knowledge of computer programming. Today, anyone with little or even no programming knowledge can create a virus by using programs developed for this purpose.

**Cross Site Scripting, or CSS**   A Web browser and Web server vulnerability wherein one client is able to control another client's browser by posting malicious code to a Web site.

**CSS**   See *Cross Site Scripting.*

**DDoS Attack**   See *Distributed Denial-of-Service Attack.*

**Denial-of-Service (DoS) Attack**   A targeted attack specifically designed to prevent the normal operation of a system by denying legitimate access to the system by authorized users. Hackers can cause denial-of-service attacks by exploiting, modifying, or overloading servers until any access by authorized users is prevented.

**Distributed Denial-of-Service (DDoS) Attack**   A type of attack that involves multiple Internet connected systems launching or being used in attacks against one or more target systems.

**DoS Attack**   See *Denial-of-Service Attack*.

**Dropper**   A Trojan horse whose payload is the installation of a virus. A dropper that installs a virus only in memory is sometimes called an "injector." Virus authors can use droppers to shield their viruses from anti-virus software.

**Encrypted Virus**   A virus whose code begins with a decryption algorithm and continues with scrambled or encrypted code for the remaining lifespan of the virus. Each time it infects, it automatically encodes itself differently so that its code is never the same. The virus attempts to avoid detection by anti-virus software by using this encryption method.

**Encryption**   A technique used by viruses to prevent detection. Through the use of transformation, virus code converts itself into cryptic code. However, in order to launch (execute) and spread, the virus must first decrypt itself, leaving it open to detection.

**.EXE File**   An executable file program that is typically launched by double-clicking its icon or a shortcut on the desktop, or by entering the name of the program at a command prompt. Executable files can also be executed from other programs, batch files, or various script files.

**Executable Code**   A type of code that consists of instructions that are executable by the computer. This includes `.com`, `.exe`, `.bat`, and similar file extensions. Executable code can also include the programming code found in boot sectors, batch files, and even macros used by some word processing applications.

**False Positive**   A false positive occurs when a virus-scanning program falsely identifies a file as infected when, in fact, it is not.

**FAT, or File Allocation Table**   An MS-DOS file system located in the boot sector of the disk. It stores the addresses of all files contained on a disk. Malicious code and normal wear and tear can damage the FAT. If the FAT is damaged, the operating system may be unable to locate files on the disk.

**File Allocation Table**   See *FAT*.

**File Stealth Virus**   A type of virus that attacks `.com` and `.exe` (executable) files, and also hides changes in file size from the `DIR` command in DOS. Problems arise when a user attempts to use the DOS utility command `CHKDSK/F`, which displays a difference in the reported file size and the actual file size. Under this circumstance, `CHKDSK` assumes that the discrepancy is the result of cross-linked files and attempts to repair the damage. The end result is the destruction of the infected files.

**Firewall**   A program or hardware device that filters the information coming through the Internet connection into your private network or computer system. The firewall analyzes information passing between the two and rejects any data that does not conform to preconfigured rules.

**Heuristics**   A type of "artificial intelligence" employed by anti-virus programs that uses code behavior analysis. Heuristics is used by anti-virus products to identify potential or unknown viruses. Unfortunately, heuristic scanning tends to produce a false alarm when an uncontaminated program exhibits malicious code-like behavior.

**Hoax Virus**   A false alarm that is designed to cause panic. When misguided users inform their friends and colleagues about the alleged "virus" via e-mail message, the result is slower servers and wasted time. Occasionally, hoaxes trick users into damaging their own systems by instructing them to remove "virus files" that are in fact critical, legitimate files.

**Hole**   A vulnerability that exists due to a design flaw in software or hardware that allows for the circumvention of security measures.

**Host**   A name used to describe the computer or file that is infected by a virus. Many viruses are designed to run when the computer or user tries to execute the host file.

**Integrity Checker**   A utility that compares a designated set of files and directories against information stored in a previously generated database. Any differences found (including added or deleted entries) are flagged and logged. When the integrity checker is run against system files on a regular basis, any changes in critical system files will be spotted, allowing suitable defense measures to be taken immediately.

**Internet Relay Chat**   See *IRC*.

**In the Wild**   A term that refers to malicious code when it is known to be spreading (as opposed to malicious code that is confined).

**IRC, or Internet Relay Chat**   An Internet service that makes it possible to participate in written (text-based) conversations with other users connected to the same chat channel.

**JavaScript**   A compact scripting language for developing client and server Internet applications. JavaScript can be run whenever you have a suitable script interpreter, such as a Web browser or a Web server. The type of environment used to run JavaScript greatly affects the security of the host machine.

**Joke**   A program designed to trick users into thinking that they have been infected by malicious code.

**Key Logger**   A program that monitors and logs user keystrokes. With malicious code, key loggers are designed to steal passwords and other sensitive information. Organizations sometimes use key loggers to surreptitiously monitor computer activity in their systems.

**Link Virus**   A type of virus that can be harmful and, because of the manner in which it infects files, exceptionally difficult to remove. When one is active, it usually resides in the infected computer's memory, waiting for the user to launch a new application. When this happens, the virus writes a copy of itself to the new application, thereby infecting a new file as well.

**Logic Bomb**   Programming code surreptitiously inserted into an operating system or application that causes it to perform a destructive or security-compromising activity. Like a true bomb, a logic bomb lies dormant until triggered by some event. The trigger can be a specific date, the number of times a program is executed, or even a specific event. Unlike viruses, logic bombs do not replicate.

**Macro Virus**   A type of virus, written in any one of the macro languages, that spreads via infected files. Macro viruses are computer viruses that use an application's own macro programming language to distribute themselves. Macros have the ability to cause damage to documents or to other computer software. Macro viruses can infect Word or Excel files, as well as any other application that uses a macro programming language.

**Malicious Code**   A piece of programming code designed to harm a computer system or its data. Traditionally, malicious code has been classified into three categories based upon the behavior of the code: viruses, worms, and Trojan horses.

**Malware**   A generic term used for malicious software that intentionally damages data or disrupts computer systems.

**Mapped Drive**   A network drive located on a distant user's computer that are assigned local drive letters and, as such, are locally accessible.

**Master Boot Record**   The first physical sector on PC hard disks, which is reserved for the boot loader program. When the BIOS boots the machine, it looks here for instructions and information on how to boot the disk and load the operating system.

**Memory-Resident Virus**   A type of virus that resides in computer memory rather than on the computer's hard disk.

**Multipartite Virus**   A type of virus that can infect both files and boot sectors. Multipartite viruses are usually highly contagious.

**Parameter Tampering**   The exploitation of insecure Web address parameters to retrieve otherwise unavailable information.

**Partition Table**   A permanent structure that tells the operating system or boot record how information on a hard disk drive is to be laid out and stored.

**Payload**   A term that refers to the effects produced by a virus attack. Sometimes, it refers to a virus associated with a dropper or Trojan horse.

**Platform**   A computer operating system or application on which a virus can run and perform an infection. Generally, a particular operating system is required for executable viruses and a specific application is required for macro viruses.

**Polymorphic Virus**   A virus is said to be polymorphic when its code appears to be different every time it replicates. Polymorphic viruses change their code in an attempt to avoid detection by anti-virus scanners. Polymorphic viruses encrypt themselves differently each time they infect. As a result, specific anti-virus signatures must be developed to detect each variant.

**Proof-of-Concept Virus**   A virus or Trojan that indicates that something is new or that it has never been seen before. For example, VBS_Bubbleboy was a proof-of-concept worm, as it was the first e-mail worm to automatically execute without requiring a user to double-click on an attachment. Most proof-of-concept viruses are never seen in the wild. However, virus writers often take the idea (and code) from a proof-of-concept virus and implement it in future viruses.

**Script Virus**   A virus that is written in the VBScript and JavaScript programming languages. Script viruses use the Windows Scripting Host to go into action and infect other files.

**Signature**   A unique string of bits or the binary pattern of a virus. Viral signatures are made up of self-replicating codes that are expected to be found in every instance of a particular virus. For the most part, different viruses have different signatures. Since ordinary computer programs do not automatically replicate, anti-virus scanners use signatures to locate specific viruses.

**Social Engineering**   Hacking techniques that rely on weaknesses in people rather than software; the aim is to trick people into revealing passwords or other types of information that compromise a target system's security.

**Spam**   The mass mailing of information in the form of unwanted e-mail, generally of a bulk or commercial nature. Listserv mailing lists are a common method of disseminating spam. Examples may include solicitations for IT products, donations, political statements, or jokes.

**Stealth Virus**   A type of virus that attempts to hide while remaining active. When an anti-virus program tries to access files or boot sectors in an attempt to find the virus, a stealth virus "feeds" the anti-virus program an uncontaminated image of the file or boot sector.

**Terminate and Stay Resident (TSR) Virus**   A program that remains active in a computer's memory after it has been executed. After being loaded (by launching an infected program, for example), the TSR virus fixes itself inside the computer's random access memory (RAM) and takes control of the machine to infect other files when *they* access the RAM.

**Trojan Horse**   A program that carries out an unauthorized function while hiding or masquerading as an authorized program. Unlike viruses, Trojan horses do not replicate. However, they can be equally destructive.

**TSR Virus**   See *Terminate and Stay Resident Virus.*

**Tunneling**   A technique that viruses use to redirect all hard drive calls between their location in RAM and the operating system. This technique allows them to bypass any anti-viral products that are present in memory at that time.

**Universal Plug and Play, or UPnP**   A set of communications protocol standards that allow networked TCP/IP devices to announce their presence to all other devices on the network and to then interoperate in a flexible and predefined fashion.

**UPnP**   See *Universal Plug and Play.*

**USAPA**   Uniting and Strengthening America by Providing Appropriate Tools Required to Intercept and Obstruct Terrorist Act of 2001. Also known as the USA Patriot Act.

**Variant**   A modified version of an existing virus that is purposely created by the original virus author or another person. The more successful a virus, the more variants it will have. Even the slightest code change will alter the original virus signature enough so that it can avoid detection by anti-virus software.

**VBS**   A programming language from Microsoft that is graphically-oriented and easy to learn. Visual Basic can be used to create everything from simple database applications to complex commercial software. VBS can invoke any system function without the user's knowledge. VBS programs are sometimes embedded in HTML files in order to provide a more "rich" Internet experience.

**Virus**   An independent program that can reproduce itself. Viruses can attach to any executable code, including boot sectors, partition sectors, and program files. They can damage, corrupt, or destroy data and degrade the computer system's performance.

**Virus Simulator**   A program used to create files that "appear" as if they are authentic viruses.

**Visual Basic Script**   See *VBS.*

**Vulnerability**   A flaw in a computer or network that leaves it susceptible to potential exploitation, such as unauthorized use or access. Vulnerabilities include, but are not limited to, weaknesses in security procedures, administrative or internal controls, or physical configuration; or features or bugs that enable an attacker to bypass security measures.

**Worm**   A self-replicating and self-sustaining program that is able to spread functional copies of itself or its segments to other computer systems. Worm proliferation usually takes place via network connections or e-mail message attachments.

**Zoo Viruses**   Viruses that were not successful in spreading in the wild and, as a result, rarely threaten users. Zoo viruses are kept guarded in the databases of anti-virus developers (like animals in a zoo).

# Index

## Symbols & Numerics

## A

*continued*

*continued*